THE GEORGE BERKELI
By
George Berkeley

An Essay Towards a New Theory of Vision

A New Theory Of Vision.

I. My Design is to shew the Manner, wherein we perceive by Sight the Distance, Magnitude, and Situation of Objects. Also to consider the Difference there is betwixt the Ideas of Sight and Touch, and whether there be any Idea common to both Senses.

II. It is, I think, agreed by all, that Distance, of it self and immediately, cannot be seen. For Distance being a Line directed end-wise to the Eye, it projects only one Point in the Fund of the Eye, which Point remains invariably the same, whether the Distance be longer or shorter.

III. I find it also acknowledged, that the Estimate we make of the Distance of Objects considerably remote, is rather an Act of Judgment grounded on Experience, than of Sense. For Example, when I perceive a great Number of intermediate Objects, such as Houses, Fields, Rivers, and the like, which I have experienced to take up a considerable Space, I thence form a Judgment or Conclusion, that the Object I see beyond them is at a great Distance. Again, when an Object appears faint and small, which at a near Distance I have experienced to make a vigorous and large Appearance, I instantly conclude it to be far off: And this, 'tis evident is the result of Experience; without which, from the Faintness and Littleness I should not have inferred any thing concerning the Distance of Objects.

IV. But when an Object is placed at so near a Distance, as that the Interval between the Eyes bears any sensible Proportion to it, the Opinion of speculative Men is, that the two Optic Axes (the Fancy that we see only with one Eye at once being exploded) concurring at the Object do there make an Angle, by means of which, according as it is greater or lesser, the Object is perceived to be nearer or farther off. [NOTE: See what Descartes and others have written on this Subject.]

V. Betwixt which, and the foregoing Manner of estimating Distance, there is this remarkable Difference: That, whereas there was no apparent, necessary Connexion between small Distance and a large and strong Appearance, or between great Distance and a little and faint Appearance, there appears a very necessary Connexion between an obtuse Angle and near Distance, and an acute Angle and farther Distance. It does not in the least depend upon Experience, but may be evidently known by any one before he had experienced it, that the nearer the Concurrence of the Optic Axes, the greater the Angle, and the remoter their Concurrence is, the lesser will be the Angle comprehended by them.

VI. There is another way mentioned by Optic Writers, whereby they will have us judge of those Distances, in respect of which the Breadth of the Pupil hath any sensible Bigness: And that is the greater or lesser Divergency of the Rays, which issuing from the visible Point, do fall on the Pupil: That Point being judged nearest, which is seen by most diverging Rays: and that remoter which is seen by less diverging Rays: And so on, the apparent Distance still increasing, as the Divergency of the Rays decreases, till at length it becomes infinite, when the Rays that fall on the Pupil are to Sense Parallel. And after this manner it is said we perceive Distance when we look only with one Eye.

VII. In this Case also, it is plain we are not beholding to Experience: It being a certain, necessary Truth, that the nearer the direct Rays falling on the Eye approach to a Parallelism, the farther off is the Point of their Intersection, or the visible Point from whence they flow.

VIII. Now though the Accounts here given of perceiving near Distance by Sight are received for true, and accordingly made use of in determining the apparent Places of Objects, they do nevertheless seem very unsatisfactory: And that for these following Reasons.

IX. It is evident that when the Mind perceives any Idea, not immediately and of it self, it must be by the means of some other Idea: Thus, for Instance, the Passions which are in the Mind of another, are of themselves to me invisible. I may nevertheless perceive them by Sight, though not immediately, yet by means of the Colours they produce in the Countenance. We often see

Shame or Fear in the Looks of a Man, by perceiving the Changes of his Countenance to Red or Pale.

X. Moreover it is evident that no Idea, which is not it self perceived, can be the means of perceiving any other Idea. If I do not perceive the Redness or Paleness of a Man's Face themselves, it is impossible I should perceive by them the Passions which are in his Mind.

XI. Now from Sect. II. it is plain that Distance is in its own Nature imperceptible, and yet it is perceived by Sight. It remains, therefore, that it be brought into View by means of some other Idea, that is it self immediately perceived in the Act of Vision.

XII. But those Lines and Angles, by means whereof some Men pretend to explain the Perception of Distance, are themselves not at all perceived, nor are they in truth ever thought of by those unskilful in Optics. I appeal to any ones Experience, whether upon Sight of an Object, he computes its Distance by the Bigness of the Angle, made by the meeting of the two Optic Axes? Or whether he ever thinks of the greater or lesser Divergency of the Rays, which arrive from any Point to his Pupil? Every one is himself the best Judge of what he perceives, and what not. In vain shall any Man tell me, that I perceive certain Lines and Angles which introduce into my Mind the various Ideas of Distance, so long as I my self am conscious of no such thing.

XIII. Since therefore those Angles and Lines are not themselves perceived by Sight, it follows from Sect. X. that the Mind doth not by them judge of the Distance of Objects.

XIV. The Truth of this Assertion will be, yet, farther evident to any one that considers those Lines and Angles have no real Existence in Nature, being only an Hypothesis framed by the Mathematicians, and by them introduced into Optics, that they might treat of that Science in a Geometrical way.

XV. The last Reason I shall give for rejecting that Doctrine, is, that though we should grant the real Existence of those Optic Angles, &c. and that it was possible for the Mind to perceive them; yet these Principles would not be found sufficient to explain the Phænomena of Distance, as shall be shewn hereafter.

XVI. Now, it being already shewn that Distance is suggested to the Mind, by the Mediation of some other Idea which is it self perceived in the Act of Seeing; it remains that we inquire what Ideas, or Sensations there be that attend Vision, unto which we may suppose the Ideas of Distance are connected, and by which they are introduced into the Mind. And First, It is certain by Experience, that when we look at a near Object with both Eyes, according as it approaches, or recedes from us, we alter the Disposition of our Eyes, by lessening or widening the Interval between the Pupils. This Disposition or Turn of the Eyes is attended with a Sensation, which seems to me to be that which in this Case brings the Idea of greater or lesser Distance into the Mind.

XVII. Not that there is any natural or necessary Connexion between the Sensation we perceive by the Turn of the Eyes, and greater or lesser Distance: but because the Mind has by constant Experience found the different Sensations corresponding to the different Dispositions of the Eyes, to be attended each with a different Degree of Distance in the Object; There has grown an Habitual or Customary Connexion between those two sorts of Ideas, so that the Mind no sooner perceives the Sensation arising from the different Turn it gives the Eyes, in order to bring the Pupils nearer, or farther asunder, but it withal perceives the different Idea of Distance which was wont to be connected with that Sensation: Just as upon hearing a certain Sound, the Idea is immediately suggested to the Understanding, which Custom had united with it.

XVIII. Nor do I see, how I can easily be mistaken in this Matter. I know evidently that Distance is not perceived of it self. That by Consequence, it must be perceived by means of some other Idea which is immediately perceived, and varies with the different Degrees of Distance. I know also that the Sensation arising from the Turn of the Eyes is of it self immediately perceived, and various Degrees thereof are connected with different Distances, which never fail to accompany them into my Mind, when I view an Object distinctly with both Eyes, whose Distance is so small that in respect of it the Interval between the Eyes has any considerable Magnitude.

XIX. I know it is a received Opinion, that by altering the Disposition of the Eyes, the Mind perceives whether the Angle of the Optic Axes, or the lateral Angles comprehended between the Interval of the Eyes and the Optic Axes, are made greater or lesser; and that accordingly by a kind of Natural Geometry, it judges the Point of their Intersection to be nearer, or farther off. But that this is not true, I am convinced by my own Experience, since I am not conscious, that I make any such use of the Perception I have by the Turn of my Eyes. And for me to make those Judgments, and draw those Conclusions from it, without knowing that I do so, seems altogether incomprehensible.

XX. From all which it follows, that the Judgment we make of the Distance of an Object, viewed with both Eyes, is entirely the Result of Experience. If we had not constantly found certain Sensations arising from the various Disposition of the Eyes, attended with certain Degrees of Distance, we should never make those sudden Judgments from them, concerning the Distance of Objects: no more than we would pretend to judge of a Man's Thoughts by his pronouncing Words we had never heard before.

XXI. Secondly, An Object placed at a certain Distance from the Eye, to which the Breadth of the Pupil bears a considerable Proportion, being made to approach, is seen more confusedly: And the nearer it is brought, the more confused Appearance it makes. And this being found constantly to be so, there ariseth in the Mind an Habitual Connexion between the several Degrees of Confusion and Distance; the greater Confusion still implying the lesser Distance, and the lesser Confusion, the greater Distance of the Object.

XXII. This confused Appearance of the Object doth therefore seem to be the Medium, whereby the Mind judgeth of Distance in those Cases, wherein the most approved Writers of Optics will have it judge by the different Divergency, with which the Rays flowing from the Radiating Point fall on the Pupil. No Man, I believe, will pretend to see or feel those imaginary Angles, that the Rays are supposed to form according to their various Inclinations on his Eye. But he cannot choose Seeing whether the Object appear more or less confused. It is therefore a manifest Consequence from what hath been demonstrated, that instead of the greater, or lesser Divergency of the Rays, the Mind makes use of the greater or lesser Confusedness of the Appearance, thereby to determine the apparent Place of an Object.

XXIII. Nor doth it avail to say, there is not any necessary Connexion between confused Vision and Distance, great or small. For I ask any Man, what necessary Connexion he sees between the Redness of a Blush and Shame? And yet no sooner shall he behold that Colour to arise in the Face of another, but it brings into his Mind the Idea of that Passion which hath been observed to accompany it.

XXIV. What seems to have misled the Writers of Optics in this Matter is, that they imagine Men judge of Distance, as they do of a Conclusion in Mathematics; betwixt which and the Premises it is indeed absolutely requisite there be an apparent, necessary Connexion: But it is far otherwise, in the sudden Judgments Men make of Distance. We are not to think, that Brutes and Children, or even grown reasonable Men, whenever they perceive an Object to approach, or depart from them, do it by virtue of Geometry and Demonstration.

XXV. That one Idea may suggest another to the Mind, it will suffice that they have been observed to go together, without any Demonstration of the Necessity of their Coexistence, or without so much as knowing what it is that makes them so to coexist. Of this there are innumerable Instances, of which no one can be ignorant.

XXVI. Thus, greater Confusion having been constantly attended with nearer Distance, no sooner is the former Idea perceived, but it suggests the latter to our Thoughts. And if it had been the ordinary Course of Nature, that the farther off an Object were placed, the more confused it should appear, it is certain, the very same Perception, that now makes us think an Object approaches, would then have made us to imagine it went farther off. That Perception, abstracting from Custom and Experience, being equally fitted to produce the Idea of great Distance, or small Distance, or no Distance at all.

XXVII. Thirdly, An Object being placed at the Distance above specified, and brought nearer to the Eye, we may nevertheless prevent, at least for some time, the Appearances growing more confused, by straining the Eye. In which Case, that Sensation supplies the place of confused Vision, in aiding the Mind to judge of the Distance of the Object; it being esteemed so much the nearer, by how much the Effort or Straining of the Eye in order to distinct Vision is greater.

XXVIII. I have here set down those Sensations or Ideas, that seem to be the constant and general Occasions of introducing into the Mind the different Ideas of near Distance. It is true in most Cases, that divers other Circumstances contribute to frame our Idea of Distance, to wit, the particular Number, Size, Kind, &c. of the things seen. Concerning which, as well as all other the forementioned Occasions which suggest Distance, I shall only observe, they have none of them, in their own Nature, any Relation or Connexion with it: Nor is it possible, they should ever signify the various Degrees thereof, otherwise than as by Experience they have been found to be connected with them.

XXIX. I shall proceed upon these Principles to account for a Phænomenon, which has hitherto strangely puzzled the Writers of Optics, and is so far from being accounted for by any of their Theories of Vision, that it is, by their own Confession, plainly repugnant to them: And of Consequence, if nothing else could be objected, were alone sufficient to bring their Credit in Question. The whole Difficulty I shall lay before you in the Words of the learned Dr. Barrow, with which he concludes his Optic Lectures.

Hæc sunt, quæ circa partem Opticæ præcipue Mathematicam dicenda mihi suggessit meditatio. Circa reliquas, (quæ φυσικώτεραι sunt, adeoque sæpiuscule pro certis principiis plausibiles conjecturas venditare necessum habent) nihil fere quicquam admodum verisimile succurrit, a pervulgatis (ab iis, inquam, quæ Keplerus, Scheinerus, Cartesius, & post illos alii tradiderunt) alienum aut diversum. Atqui tacere malo, quam toties oblatam crambem reponere. Proinde receptui cano; nec ita tamen ut prorsùs discedam anteaquam improbam quandam difficultatem (pro sinceritate quam & vobis & veritati debeo minime dissumulandam) in medium protulero, quæ doctrinæ nostræ, hactenus inculcatæ, se objicit adversam, ab ea saltem nullam admittit solutionem. Illa, breviter, talis est: Lenti vel Speculo cavo E B F exponatur punctum visibile A, ita Distans ut Radii ex Amanantes ex inflexione versus axem A B cogantur. Sitque radiationis Limes (seu puncti A imago, qualem supra passim statuimus) punctum Z. Inter hoc autem & inflectentis verticem B uspiam positus concipiatur Oculus. Quæri jam potest ubi loci debeat punctum A apparere? Retrorsum ad punctum Z videri non fert Natura (cum omnis impressio sensum afficiens proveniat a partibus A) ac experientia reclamat. Nostris autem e placitis consequi videtur, ipsum ad partes anticas apparens ab intervallo longissime dissito, (quod & maximum sensibile quodvis Intervallum quodammodo exsuperet) apparere. Cum enim quo Radiis minus divergentibus attingitur Objectum, eo (seclusis utique prænotionibus & præjudiciis) longius abesse sentiatur; et quod Parallelos ad Oculum Radios projicit, remotissime positum æstimetur. Exigere Ratio videtur, ut quod convergentibus radiis apprehenditur, adhuc magis, si fieri posset, quoad apparentiam elongetur. Quin & circa Casum hunc generatim inquiri possit, quidnam omnino sit, quod apparentem puncti A locum determinet, faciatque quod constanti ratione nunc propius, nunc remotius appareat? Cui itidem dubio, nihil quicquam ex hactenus dictorum Analogia, responderi posse videtur, nisi debere punctum A perpetuo longissime semotum videri. Verum experientia secus attestatur, illud pro diversa Oculi inter puncta B, Z, positione varie distans; nunquam fere (si unquam) longinquius ipso A libere spectato, subinde vero multo propinquius adparere; quinimo, quo oculum appellentes radii magis convergunt eo speciem Objecti propius accedere. Nempe, si puncto B admoveatur Oculus, suo (ad lentem) fere nativo in loco conspicitur punctum A (vel æque distans, ad Speculum;) ad O reductus oculus ejusce speciem appropinquantem cernit; ad P adhuc vicinius ipsum existimat; ac ita sensim, donec alicubi tandem, velut ad Q, constituto oculo objectum summe propinquum apparens, in meram confusionem incipiat evanescere. Quæ sane cuncta rationibus atque decretis nostris repugnare videntur, aut cum iis saltem parum amice conspirant. Neque nostram tantum sententiam pulsat hoc experimentum; at ex æquo cæteras quas norim omnes, veterem imprimis ac vulgatam nostræ præ reliquis affinem ita convellere videtur, ut ejus vi coactus doctissimus A. Tacquetus isti principio (cui pene soli totam inædificaverat Catoptricam suam) ceu infido ac inconstanti renunciarit, adeoque suam ipse doctrinam labefactarit; id tamen, opinor, minime facturus, si rem totam inspexisset penitius, atque difficultatis fundum attigisset. Apud me vero non ita pollet hæc, nec eousque præpollebit ulla difficultas, ut ab iis, quæ manifeste rationi consentanea video, discedam; præsertim quum ut hic accidit, ejusmodi difficultas in singularis cujuspiam casûs disparitate fundetur. Nimirum in præsente casu peculiare quiddam, naturæ subtilitati involutum, delitescit, ægre fortassis, nisi perfectius explorato videndi modo, detegendum. Circa quod nil, fateor, hactenus excogitare potui, quod adblandiretur animo meo, nedum plane satisfaceret. Vobis itaque nodum hunc, utinam feliciore conatu, resolvendum committo.

In English as follows.
'I have here delivered what my Thoughts have suggested to me, concerning that part of Optics which is more properly Mathematical. As for the other Parts of that Science (which being rather Physical, do consequently abound with plausible Conjectures instead of certain Principles) there has in them scarce any thing occur'd to my Observation, different from what has been already said by Kepler, Scheinerus, Descartes, and others. And methinks, I had better say nothing at all, than repeat that which has been so often said by others. I think it therefore high time to take my leave of this Subject: But before I quit it for good and all, the fair and ingenuous Dealing that I owe both to You and to Truth, obliges me to acquaint you with a certain untoward Difficulty, which seems directly opposite to the Doctrine I have been hitherto inculcating, at least, admits of no Solution from it. In short it is this. Before the double Convex Glass or Concave Speculum E B F, let the Point A be placed, at such a Distance that the Rays proceeding from A, after Refraction or Reflexion, be brought to Unite somewhere in the Ax A B. And suppose the Point of Union (i.e. the Image of the Point A, as hath been already set forth) to be Z; between which and B, the Vertex of the Glass or Speculum, conceive the Eye to be any where placed. The Question now is, where the Point A ought to appear? Experience shews that it doth not appear behind at the Point Z, and it were contrary to Nature that it should; since all the Impression which affects the Sense comes from towards A. But from our Tenets it should seem to follow that it would appear before the Eye at a vast Distance off, so great as should in some Sort surpass all sensible Distance. For since if we exclude all Anticipations and Prejudices, every Object appears by so much the farther off, by how much the Rays it sends to the Eye are less diverging. And that Object is thought to be most remote, from which Parallel Rays proceed unto the Eye. Reason would make one think, that Object should appear, at yet a greater Distance, which is seen by converging Rays. Moreover it may in general be asked concerning this Case, what it is that determines the apparent Place of the Point A, and maketh it to appear after a constant manner, sometimes nearer, at other times farther off? To which Doubt, I see nothing that can be answered agreeable to the Principles we have laid down except only that the Point A ought always to appear extremely remote. But on the contrary, we are assured by Experience that the Point A appears variously distant, according to the different Situations of the Eye between the Points B and Z. And that it doth almost never (if at all) seem farther off, than it would if it were beheld by the naked Eye, but on the contrary, it doth sometimes appear much nearer. Nay, it is even certain, that by how much the Rays falling on the Eye do more converge, by so much the nearer doth the Object seem to approach. For the Eye being placed close to the Point B, the Object A appears nearly in its own natural Place, if the Point B is taken in the Glass, or at the same Distance, if in the Speculum. The Eye being brought back to O, the Object seems to draw near: and being come

to P it beholds it still nearer. And so on by little and little, till at length the Eye being placed somewhere, suppose at Q, the Object appearing extremely near, begins to vanish into mere Confusion. All which doth seem repugnant to our Principles, at least, not rightly to agree with them. Nor is our Tenet alone struck at by this Experiment, but likewise all others that ever came to my Knowledge are, every whit as much, endangered by it. The ancient one especially (which is most commonly received, and comes nearest to mine) seems to be so effectually overthrown thereby, that the most learned Tacquet has been forced to reject that Principle, as false and uncertain, on which alone he had built almost his whole Catoptrics; and consequently by taking away the Foundation, hath himself pulled down the Superstructure he had raised on it. Which, nevertheless, I do not believe he would have done, had he but considered the whole Matter more thoroughly, and examined the Difficulty to the Bottom. But as for me, neither this, nor any other Difficulty shall have so great an Influence on me, as to make me renounce that which I know to be manifestly agreeable to Reason: Especially when, as it here falls out, the Difficulty is founded in the peculiar Nature of a certain odd and particular Case. For in the present Case something peculiar lies hid, which being involved in the Subtilty of Nature will, perhaps, hardly be discovered till such time, as the Manner of Vision is more perfectly made known. Concerning which, I must own, I have hitherto been able to find out nothing that has the least shew of Probability, not to mention Certainty. I shall, therefore, leave this Knot to be untied by you, wishing you may have better Success in it than I have had.'

XXX. The ancient and received Principle, which Dr. Barrow here mentions as the main Foundation of Tacquet's Catoptrics, is that every visible Point seen by Reflexion from a Speculum, shall appear placed at the Intersection of the reflected Ray, and the Perpendicular of Incidence. Which Intersection in the present Case, happening to be behind the Eye, it greatly shakes the Authority of that Principle, whereon the aforementioned Author proceeds throughout his whole Catoptrics, in determining the apparent Place of Objects seen by Reflexion from any kind of Speculum.

XXXI. Let us now see how this Phænomenon agrees with our Tenets. The Eye the nearer it is placed to the Point B in the foregoing Figures, the more distinct is the Appearance of the Object; but as it recedes to O, the Appearance grows more confused; and at P it sees the Object yet more confused; and so on till the Eye being brought back to Z, sees the Object in the greatest Confusion of all. Wherefore by Sect. XXI. the Object should seem to approach the Eye gradually, as it recedes from the Point B, that is at O it should (in Consequence of the Principle I have laid down in the aforesaid Section) seem nearer than it did at B, and at P nearer than at O, and at Q nearer than at P; and so on, till it quite vanishes at Z. Which is the very matter of Fact, as any one that pleases may easily satisfy himself by Experiment.

XXXII. This Case is much the same, as if we should suppose an Englishman to meet a Foreigner, who used the same Words with the English, but in a direct contrary Signification. The Englishman would not fail to make a wrong Judgment, of the Ideas annexed to those Sounds, in the Mind of him that used them. Just so, in the present Case the Object speaks (if I may so say) with Words that the Eye is well acquainted with, that is, Confusions of Appearance; but whereas heretofore the greater Confusions were always wont to signify nearer Distances, they have in this Case a direct, contrary Signification, being connected with the greater Distances. Whence it follows, that the Eye must unavoidably be mistaken, since it will take the Confusions in the Sense it has been used to, which is directly opposed to the True.

XXXIII. This Phænomenon as it entirely subverts the Opinion of those, who will have us judge of Distance by Lines and Angles, on which Supposition it is altogether inexplicable, so it seems to me no small Confirmation, of the Truth of that Principle whereby it is explained. But in order to a more full Explication of this Point, and to shew how far the Hypothesis of the Mind's judging by the various Divergency of Rays, may be of use in determining the apparent Place of an Object, it will be necessary to premise some few things, which are already well known to those who have any Skill in Dioptrics.

XXXIV. First, Any radiating Point is then distinctly seen when the Rays proceeding from it are, by the Refractive Power of the Crystalline, accurately reunited in the Retina or Fund of the Eye: But if they are reunited, either before they arrive at the Retina, or after they have past it, then there is confused Vision.

XXXV. Secondly, Suppose in the adjacent Figures N P represent an Eye duly framed, and retaining its natural Figure. In Fig. 1. the Rays falling nearly Parallel on the Eye, are by the Crystalline A B refracted, so as their Focus or Point of Union F falls exactly on the Retina: But if the Rays fall sensibly diverging on the Eye, as in Fig. 2. then their Focus falls beyond the Retina: Or if the Rays are made to converge by the Lens Q S, before they come at the Eye, as in Fig. 3. their Focus F will fall before the Retina. In which two last Cases, it is evident from the foregoing Section, that the Appearance of the Point Z is confused. And by how much the greater is the Convergency, or Divergency of the Rays falling on the Pupil, by so much the farther will the Point of their Reunion be from the Retina, either before or behind it, and consequently the Point Z will appear, by so much the more confused. And this, by the bye, may shew us the Difference between confused, and faint Vision. Confused Vision is, when the Rays proceeding from each distinct Point of the Object are not accurately recollected in one corresponding Point on the Retina, but take up some Space thereon: So that Rays from different Points become mixed, and confused together. This is opposed to a distinct Vision, and attends near Objects. Faint Vision is, when by reason of the Distance of the Object or Grossness of the interjacent Medium few Rays arrive from the Object to the Eye. This is opposed to vigorous or clear Vision, and attends remote Objects. But to return.

XXXVI. The Eye, or (to speak truly) the Mind perceiving only the Confusion it self, without ever considering the Cause from which it proceeds, doth constantly annex the same Degree of Distance to the same Degree of Confusion. Whether that Confusion be occasioned by converging, or by diverging Rays, it matters not. Whence it follows, that the Eye viewing the Object Z through the Glass Q S (which by Refraction causeth the Rays Z Q, Z S, &c. to converge) should judge it to be at such a Nearness, at which if it were placed, it would radiate on the Eye with Rays diverging to that Degree, as would produce the same Confusion, which is now produced by converging Rays, i. e. would cover a Portion of the Retina equal to D C. vid. Fig. 3. supra. But then this must be understood (to use Dr. Barrow's Phrase) seclusis prænotionibus & præjudiciis, in case we abstract from all other Circumstances of Vision, such as the Figure, Size, Faintness, &c. of the visible Objects; all which do ordinarily concur to form our Idea of Distance, the Mind having by frequent Experience observed their several Sorts or Degrees, to be connected with various Distances.

XXXVII. It plainly follows from what hath been said, that a Person perfectly Purblind (i.e. that could not see an Object distinctly, but when placed close to his Eye) would not make the same wrong Judgment that others do, in the forementioned Case. For, to him, greater Confusions constantly suggesting greater Distances, he must, as he recedes from the Glass, and the Object grows more Confused, judge it to be at a farther Distance, contrary to what they do, who have had the Perception of the Objects growing more confused, connected with the Idea of Approach.

XXXVIII. Hence also it doth appear, there may be good use of Computation by Lines and Angles in Optics; not that the Mind judgeth of Distance immediately by them, but because it judgeth by somewhat which is connected with them, and to the Determination whereof they may be subservient. Thus the Mind judging of the Distance of an Object, by the Confusedness of its Appearance, and this Confusedness being greater or lesser to the naked Eye, according as the Object is seen by Rays more or less diverging, it follows, that a Man may make use of the Divergency of the Rays in computing the apparent Distance, though not for its own sake, yet on account of the Confusion with which it is connected. But, so it is, the Confusion it self is entirely neglected by Mathematicians, as having no necessary Relation with Distance, such as the greater or lesser Angles of Divergency are conceived to have. And these (especially for

that they fall under Mathematical Computation) are alone regarded, in determining the apparent Places of Objects, as though they were the sole and immediate Cause of the Judgments the Mind makes of Distance. Whereas, in Truth, they should not at all be regarded in themselves, or any otherwise, than as they are supposed to be the Cause of confused Vision.
XXXIX. The not considering of this has been a fundamental and perplexing Oversight. For Proof whereof, we need go no farther than the Case before us. It having been observed, that the most diverging Rays brought into the Mind the Idea of nearest Distance, and that still, as the Divergency decreased, the Distance increased: and it being thought, the Connexion between the various Degrees of Divergency and Distance, was immediate; this naturally leads one to conclude, from an ill grounded Analogy, that converging Rays shall make an Object appear at an immense Distance: And that, as the Convergency increases, the Distance (if it were possible) should do so likewise. That this was the Cause of Dr. Barrow's Mistake, is evident from his own Words which we have quoted. Whereas had the learned Doctor observed, that diverging and converging Rays, how opposite soever they may seem, do nevertheless agree in producing the same Effect, to wit, Confusedness of Vision, greater Degrees whereof are produced indifferently, either as the Divergency or Convergency of the Rays increaseth. And that it is by this Effect, which is the same in both, that either the Divergency or Convergency is perceived by the Eye; I say, had he but consider'd this, it is certain he would have made a quite contrary Judgment, and rightly concluded, that those Rays which fall on the Eye with greater Degrees of Convergency should make the Object from whence they proceed, appear by so much the nearer. But it is plain, it was impossible for any Man to attain to a right Notion of this Matter, so long as he had regard only to Lines and Angles, and did not apprehend the true Nature of Vision, and how far it was of Mathematical Consideration.
XL. Before we dismiss this Subject, it is fit we take notice of a Query relating thereto, proposed by the ingenious Mr. Molyneux, in his Treatise of Dioptrics, [NOTE: Par. I. Prop. 31. Sect. 9.] where speaking of this Difficulty, he has these Words: 'And so he (i. e. Dr. Barrow) leaves this Difficulty to the Solution of others, which I (after so great an Example) shall do likewise; but with the Resolution of the same admirable Author of not quitting the evident Doctrine which we have before laid down, for determining the Locus Objecti, on account of being press'd by one Difficulty, which seems inexplicable till a more intimate Knowledge of the Visive Faculty be obtained by Mortals. In the mean time, I propose it to the Consideration of the Ingenious, Whether the Locus Apparens of an Object placed as in this 9th Section, be not as much before the Eye, as the distinct Base is behind the Eye?' To which Query we may venture to answer in the Negative. For in the present Case, the Rule for determining the Distance of the distinct Base, or respective Focus from the Glass is this: As the Difference between the Distance of the Object and Focus is to the Focus or Focal Length, so the Distance of the Object from the Glass is to the Distance of the respective Focus or distinct Base from the Glass. [NOTE: Molyneux Dioptr. Par. I. Prop. 5.] Let us now suppose the Object to be placed at the Distance of the Focal Length, and one half of the Focal Length from the Glass, and the Eye close to the Glass, hence it will follow by the Rule, that the Distance of the distinct Base behind the Eye is double the true Distance of the Object before the Eye. If therefore Mr. Molyneux's Conjecture held good, it wou'd follow that the Eye should see the Object, twice as far off as it really is; and in other Cases at three or four times its due Distance, or more. But this manifestly contradicts Experience, the Object never appearing, at farthest, beyond its due Distance. Whatever therefore is built on this Supposition vid. Corol. 1. Prop. 57. ibid.) comes to the Ground along with it.
XLI. From what hath been premis'd, it is a manifest Consequence, that a Man born blind, being made to see, would, at first, have no Idea of Distance by Sight; The Sun and Stars, the remotest Objects as well as the nearer would all seem to be in his Eye, or rather in his Mind. The Objects intromitted by Sight, would seem to him (as in truth they are) no other than a new Set of Thoughts or Sensations, each whereof is as near to him, as the Perceptions of Pain or

Pleasure, or the most inward Passions of his Soul. For our judging Objects perceiv'd by Sight to be at any Distance, or without the Mind, is (vid. Sect. XXVIII.) intirely the Effect of Experience, which one in those Circumstances could not yet have attained to.

XLII. It is indeed otherwise upon the common Supposition, that Men judge of Distance by the Angle of the Optic Axes, just as one in the Dark, or a Blind-man by the Angle comprehended by two Sticks, one whereof he held in each Hand. For if this were true, it would follow that one blind from his Birth being made to see, should stand in need of no new Experience, in order to perceive Distance by Sight. But that this is false, has, I think, been sufficiently demonstrated.

XLIII. And perhaps upon a strict Inquiry, we shall not find that even those, who from their Birth have grown up in a continu'd Habit of Seeing, are irrecoverably prejudiced on the other side, to wit, in thinking what they see to be at a Distance from them. For at this time it seems agreed on all hands, by those who have had any Thoughts of that Matter, that Colours, which are the proper and immediate Object of Sight, are not without the Mind. But then it will be said, by Sight we have also the Ideas of Extension, and Figure, and Motion; all which may well be thought without, and at some Distance from the Mind, though Colour should not. In answer to this, I appeal to any Man's Experience, whether the visible Extension of any Object doth not appear as near to him, as the Colour of that Object; Nay, whether they do not both seem to be in the very same Place. Is not the Extension we see coloured, and is it possible for us, so much as in Thought, to separate and abstract Colour from Extension? Now, where the Extension is, there surely is the Figure, and there the Motion too. I speak of those which are perceived by Sight.

XLIV. But for a fuller Explication of this Point, and to shew that the immediate Objects of Sight are not so much as the Ideas or Resemblances of things placed at a Distance, it is requisite that we look nearer into the Matter, and carefully observe what is meant in common Discourse, when one says, that which he sees is at a Distance from him. Suppose, for Example, that looking at the Moon I should say it were fifty or sixty Semidiameters of the Earth distant from me. Let us see what Moon this is spoken of: It is plain it cannot be the visible Moon, or any thing like the visible Moon, or that which I see, which is only a round, luminous Plain, of about thirty visible Points in Diameter. For in case I am carried from the Place where I stand directly towards the Moon, it is manifest the Object varies, still as I go on; and by the time that I am advanced fifty or sixty Semidiameters of the Earth, I shall be so far from being near a small, round, luminous Flat, that I shall perceive nothing like it; this Object having long since disappeared, and if I would recover it, it must be by going back to the Earth from whence I set out. Again, suppose I perceive by Sight the faint and obscure Idea of something, which I doubt whether it be a Man, or a Tree, or a Tower, but judge it to be at the Distance of about a Mile. It is plain I cannot mean, that what I see is a Mile off, or that it is the Image or Likeness of any thing which is a Mile off, since that every Step I take towards it, the Appearance alters, and from being obscure, small, and faint, grows clear, large, and vigorous. And when I come to the Mile's end, that which I saw first is quite lost, neither do I find any thing in the likeness of it.

XLV. In these and the like Instances, the Truth of the Matter stands thus: Having of a long time experienced certain Ideas, perceivable by Touch, as Distance, tangible Figure, and Solidity, to have been connected with certain Ideas of Sight, I do upon perceiving these Ideas of Sight, forthwith conclude what Tangible Ideas are, by the wonted ordinary course of Nature, like to follow. Looking at an Object I perceive a certain visible Figure and Colour, with some degree of Faintness and other Circumstances, which from what I have formerly observed, determine me to think, that if I advance forward so many Paces or Miles, I shall be affected with such and such Ideas of Touch: So that in truth and strictness of Speech, I neither see Distance it self, nor any thing that I take to be at a Distance. I say, neither Distance, nor things placed at a Distance are themselves, or their Ideas, truly perceived by Sight. This I am persuaded of, as to what concerns my self: and I believe whoever will look narrowly into his own Thoughts, and examine what he means by saying, he sees this or that thing at a Distance, will agree with me, that what he sees only suggests to his Understanding, that after having passed a certain Distance, to be measured by the Motion of his Body, which is perceivable by Touch, he shall come to perceive such and such tangible Ideas which have been usually connected with such and such visible Ideas. But that one might be deceived by these Suggestions of Sense, and that there is no necessary Connexion between visible and tangible Ideas suggested by them, we need go no farther than the next Looking-glass or Picture to be convinced. Note, that when I speak of Tangible Ideas, I take the word Idea for any the immediate Object of Sense, or Understanding, in which large Signification it is commonly used by the Moderns.

XLVI. From what we have shewn it is a manifest Consequence, that the Ideas of Space, Outness, and Things placed at a Distance, are not, strictly speaking, the Object of Sight; they are not otherwise perceived by the Eye than by the Ear. Sitting in my Study I hear a Coach drive along the Street; I look through the Casement and see it; I walk out and enter into it; thus, common Speech would incline one to think, I heard, saw, and touch'd the same thing, to wit, the Coach. It is nevertheless certain, the Ideas intromitted by each Sense are widely different, and distinct from each other; but having been observed constantly to go together, they are spoken of as one and the same thing. By the Variation of the Noise I perceive the different Distances of the Coach, and know that it approaches before I look out. Thus by the Ear I perceive Distance, just after the same manner as I do by the Eye.

XLVII. I do not nevertheless say, I hear Distance in like manner as I say that I see it, the Ideas perceived by Hearing not being so apt to be confounded with the Ideas of Touch, as those of Sight are. So likewise a Man is easily convinced that Bodies and external Things are not properly the Object of Hearing; but only Sounds, by the Mediation whereof the Idea of this or that Body, or Distance is suggested to his Thoughts. But then one is with more Difficulty brought to discern the Difference there is betwixt the Ideas of Sight and Touch: Though it be certain, a Man no more sees and feels the same thing, than he hears and feels the same thing.

XLVIII. One Reason of which seems to be this. It is thought a great Absurdity to imagine, that one and the same thing should have any more than one Extension, and one Figure. But the Extension and Figure of a Body, being let into the Mind two ways, and that indifferently, either by Sight or Touch, it seems to follow that we see the same Extension and the same Figure which we feel.

XLIX. But if we take a close and accurate View of Things, it must be acknowledged that we never see and feel one and the same Object. That which is seen is one thing, and that which is felt is another. If the visible Figure and Extension be not the same with the tangible Figure and Extension, we are not to infer that one and the same thing has divers Extensions. The true Consequence is, that the Objects of Sight and Touch are two distinct things. It may perhaps require some Thought rightly to conceive this Distinction. And the Difficulty seems not a little increased, because the Combination of Visible Ideas hath constantly the same Name, as the Combination of Tangible Ideas wherewith it is connected: Which doth of Necessity arise from the use and end of Language.

L. In order therefore to treat accurately and unconfusedly of Vision, we must bear in mind, that there are two Sorts of Objects apprehended by the Eye, the one primarily and immediately, the other secondarily and by Intervention of the former. Those of the first sort neither are, nor appear to be without the Mind, or at any Distance off: they may indeed grow greater, or smaller, more confused, or more clear, or more faint, but they do not, cannot approach or recede from us. Whenever we say an Object is at a Distance, whenever we say it draws near, or goes farther off, we must always mean it of the latter sort, which properly belong to the Touch, and are not so truly perceived, as suggested by the Eye in like manner as Thoughts by the Ear.

LI. No sooner do we hear the Words of a familiar Language pronounced in our Ears, but the Ideas corresponding thereto present themselves to our Minds: in the very same Instant the

Sound and the Meaning enter the Understanding: So closely are they united, that it is not in our Power to keep out the one, except we exclude the other also. We even act in all respects as if we heard the very Thoughts themselves. So likewise the secondary Objects, or those which are only suggested by Sight, do often more strongly affect us, and are more regarded than the proper Objects of that Sense; along with which they enter into the Mind, and with which they have a far more strict Connexion, than Ideas have with Words. Hence it is, we find it so difficult to discriminate between the immediate and mediate Objects of Sight, and are so prone to attribute to the former, what belongs only to the latter. They are, as it were, most closely twisted, blended, and incorporated together. And the Prejudice is confirmed and riveted in our Thoughts by a long Tract of Time, by the use of Language, and want of Reflexion. However, I believe any one that shall attentively consider what we have already said, and shall say upon this Subject before we have done, (especially if he pursue it in his own Thoughts) may be able to deliver himself from that Prejudice. Sure I am it is worth some Attention, to whoever would understand the true Nature of Vision.

LII. I have now done with Distance, and proceed to shew how it is, that we perceive by Sight the Magnitude of Objects. It is the Opinion of some that we do it by Angles, or by Angles in conjunction with Distance: but neither Angles, nor Distance being perceivable by Sight, and the things we see being in truth at no Distance from us, it follows that as we have shewn Lines and Angles not to be the Medium, the Mind makes use of in apprehending the apparent Place, so neither are they the Medium whereby it apprehends the apparent Magnitude of Objects.

LIII. It is well known that the same Extension at a near Distance shall subtend a greater Angle, and at a farther Distance, a lesser Angle. And by this Principle (we are told) the Mind estimates the Magnitude of an Object comparing the Angle under which it is seen with its Distance, and thence inferring the Magnitude thereof. What inclines Men to this Mistake (beside the Humour of making one see by Geometry) is, that the same Perceptions or Ideas which suggest Distance, do also suggest Magnitude. But if we examine it, we shall find they suggest the latter, as immediately as the former. I say, they do not first suggest Distance, and then leave it to the Judgment to use that as a Medium, whereby to collect the Magnitude; but they have as close, and immediate a Connexion with the Magnitude, as with the Distance; and suggest Magnitude as independently of Distance, as they do Distance independently of Magnitude. All which will be evident to whoever considers what hath been already said, and what follows.

LIV. It hath been shewn, there are two sorts of Objects apprehended by Sight; each whereof hath its distinct Magnitude, or Extension. The one, properly Tangible, i. e. to be perceived and measured by Touch, and not immediately falling under the Sense of Seeing: The other, properly and immediately visible, by Mediation of which the former is brought in view. Each of these Magnitudes are greater or lesser, according as they contain in them more or fewer Points, they being made up of Points or Minimums. For, whatever may be said of Extension in Abstract, it is certain sensible Extension is not infinitely Divisible. There is a Minimum Tangibile, and a Minimum Visibile, beyond which Sense cannot perceive. This every ones Experience will inform him.

LV. The Magnitude of the Object which exists without the Mind, and is at a Distance, continues always invariably the same: But the visible Object still changing as you approach to, or recede from the Tangible Object, it hath no fixed and determinate Greatness. Whenever therefore, we speak of the Magnitude of any thing, for Instance a Tree or a House, we must mean the Tangible Magnitude, otherwise there can be nothing steady and free from Ambiguity spoken of it. But though the Tangible and Visible Magnitude in truth belong to two distinct Objects: I shall nevertheless (especially since those Objects are called by the same Name, and are observed to coexist) to avoid Tediousness and Singularity of Speech, sometimes speak of them, as belonging to one and the same thing.

LVI. Now in order to discover by what means, the Magnitude of Tangible Objects is perceived by Sight; I need only reflect on what passes in my own Mind, and observe what those things be, which introduce the Ideas of greater or lesser into my Thoughts, when I look on any Object. And these I find to be, First, the Magnitude or Extension of the Visible Object, which being immediately perceived by Sight, is connected with that other which is Tangible, and placed at a Distance. Secondly, The Confusion or Distinctness. And Thirdly, The Vigorousness or Faintness of the aforesaid visible Appearance. Cæteris paribus, by how much the greater or lesser, the Visible Object is, by so much the greater or lesser, do I conclude the Tangible Object to be. But, be the Idea immediately perceived by Sight never so large, yet if it be withal confused, I judge the Magnitude of the thing to be but small. If it be distinct and clear, I judge it greater. And if it be faint, I apprehend it to be yet greater. What is here meant, by Confusion and Faintness, hath been explained in Sect. XXXV.

LVII. Moreover the Judgments we make of Greatness do, in like manner as those of Distance, depend on the Disposition of the Eye, also on the Figure, Number, and Situation of Objects and other Circumstances that have been observed to attend great or small Tangible Magnitudes. Thus, for Instance, the very same Quantity of Visible Extension, which in the Figure of a Tower, doth suggest the Idea of great Magnitude, shall, in the Figure of a Man suggest the Idea of much smaller Magnitude. That this is owing to the Experience we have had of the usual Bigness of a Tower and a Man, no one, I suppose, need be told.

LVIII. It is also evident, that Confusion or Faintness, have no more a necessary Connexion with little or great Magnitude, than they have with little or great Distance. As they suggest the latter, so they suggest the former to our Minds. And by Consequence, if it were not for Experience, we should no more judge a faint or confused Appearance to be connected with great or little Magnitude, than we should that it was connected with great or little Distance.

LIX. Nor will it be found, that great or small visible Magnitude hath any necessary Relation to great or small Tangible Magnitude: So that the one may certainly be infer'd from the other. But, before we come to the Proof of this, it is fit we consider the Difference there is betwixt the Extension and Figure which is the proper Object of Touch, and that other which is termed Visible; and how the former is principally, though not immediately taken notice of, when we look at any Object. This has been before mentioned, but we shall here inquire into the Cause thereof. We regard the Objects that environ us, in proportion as they are adapted to benefit or injure our own Bodies, and thereby produce in our Minds the Sensations of Pleasure or Pain. Now Bodies operating on our Organs, by an immediate Application, and the Hurt or Advantage arising there-from, depending altogether on the Tangible, and not at all on the Visible, Qualities of any Object: This is a plain Reason, why those should be regarded by us as much more than these: and for this End, the Visive Sense seems to have been bestowed on Animals, to wit, that by the Perception of Visible Ideas (which in themselves are not capable of affecting, or in any wise altering the Frame of their Bodies) they may be able to foresee (from the Experience they have had, what Tangible Ideas are connected with such, and such Visible Ideas) the Damage or Benefit which is like to ensue, upon the Application of their own Bodies to this or that Body which is at a Distance. Which Foresight, how necessary it is to the Preservation of an Animal, every ones Experience can inform him. Hence it is that, when we look at an Object, the Tangible Figure and Extension thereof are principally attended to; whilst there is small heed taken of the Visible Figure and Magnitude, which, though more immediately perceived, do less concern us, and are not fitted to produce any Alteration in our Bodies.

LX. That the Matter of Fact is true, will be evident to any one, who considers that a Man placed at ten Foot Distance, is thought as great, as if he were placed at the Distance only of five Foot: which is true, not with relation to the Visible, but Tangible Greatness of the Object: The Visible Magnitude being far greater, at one Station, than it is at the other.

LXI. Inches, Feet, &c. are settled, stated Lengths, whereby we measure Objects, and estimate their Magnitude: we say, for Example, an Object appears to be six Inches or six Foot long. Now, that this cannot be meant of visible Inches, &c. is evident, because a visible Inch is it self no constant, determinate Magnitude, and cannot therefore serve to mark out, and determine the Magnitude of any other thing. Take an Inch mark'd upon a Ruler: view it, successively, at the distance of Half a Foot, a Foot, a Foot and a Half, &c. from the Eye: at each of which, and at all the intermediate Distances, the Inch shall have a different visible Extension, i. e. there shall be more or fewer Points discerned in it. Now I ask which of all these various Extensions, is that stated, determinate one, that is agreed on, for a common Measure of other Magnitudes? No Reason can be assigned, why we should pitch on one, more than another: And except there be some invariable, determinate Extension fixed on to be marked by the Word Inch, it is plain, it can be used to little purpose: and to say, a Thing contains this or that Number of Inches, shall imply no more than that it is extended, without bringing any particular Idea of that Extension into the Mind. Farther, an Inch and a Foot, from different Distances, shall both exhibit the same visible Magnitude, and yet at the same time, you shall say, that one seems several times greater than the other. From all which it is manifest, that the Judgments we make of the Magnitude of Objects by Sight, are altogether in reference to their Tangible Extension. Whenever we say an Object is great, or small, of this or that determinate Measure, I say, it must be meant of the Tangible, and not the Visible Extension, which, though immediately perceived, is nevertheless little taken notice of.

LXII. Now, that there is no necessary Connexion, between these two distinct Extensions is evident from hence: Because our Eyes might have been framed in such a manner, as to be able to see nothing but what were less than the Minimum Tangibile. In which Case, it is not impossible we might have perceived all the immediate Objects of Sight, the very same that we do now: But unto those visible Appearances, there would not be connected those different Tangible Magnitudes, that are now. Which shews, the Judgments we make of the Magnitude of Things placed at a distance, from the various Greatness of the immediate Objects of Sight, do not arise from any essential or necessary, but only a customary Tye, which has been observed between them.

LXIII. Moreover, it is not only certain, that any Idea of Sight might not have been connected with this or that Idea of Touch, we now observe to accompany it: But also, that the greater visible Magnitudes might have been connected with, and introduced into our Minds lesser Tangible Magnitudes, and the lesser Visible Magnitudes greater Tangible Magnitudes. Nay, that it actually is so, we have daily Experience; that Object which makes a strong and large Appearance, not seeming near so great as another, the Visible Magnitude whereof is much less, but more faint, and the Appearance upper, or which is the same thing painted lower on the Retina, which Faintness and Situation suggest both greater Magnitude and greater Distance.

LXIV. From which, and from Sect. LVII, and LVIII. it is manifest, that as we do not perceive the Magnitudes of Objects immediately by Sight, so neither do we perceive them, by the Mediation of any thing which has a necessary Connexion with them. Those Ideas that now suggest unto us the various Magnitudes of external Objects, before we touch them, might possibly have suggested no such thing: Or they might have signified them, in a direct contrary manner: so that the very same Ideas, on the Perception whereof we judge an Object to be small, might as well have served to make us conclude it great. Those Ideas being in their own Nature equally fitted to bring into our Minds the Idea of Small or Great, or no Size at all of outward Objects; just as the Words of any Language are in their own Nature indifferent to signify this or that thing, or nothing at all.

LXV. As we see Distance, so we see Magnitude. And we see both, in the same way that we see Shame or Anger in the Looks of a Man. Those Passions are themselves invisible, they are nevertheless let in by the Eye along with Colours and Alterations of Countenance, which are the immediate Object of Vision: And which signify them for no other Reason, than barely because they have been observed to accompany them. Without which Experience, we should no more have taken Blushing for a Sign of Shame, than of Gladness.

LXVI. We are nevertheless exceeding prone to imagine those things, which are perceived only by the Mediation of others, to be themselves the immediate Objects of Sight; or, at least, to have in their own Nature a Fitness to be suggested by them, before ever they had been experienced to coexist with them. From which Prejudice every one, perhaps, will not find it easy to emancipate himself, by any the clearest Convictions of Reason. And there are some Grounds to think, that if there was one only invariable and universal Language in the World, and that Men were born with the Faculty of speaking it, it would be the Opinion of many, that the Ideas of other Mens Minds were properly perceived by the Ear, or had at least a necessary and inseparable Tye with the Sounds that were affixed to them. All which seems to arise from a want of a due Application of our discerning Faculty, thereby to discriminate between the Ideas that are in our Understandings, and consider them apart from each other; which would preserve us from confounding those that are different, and make us see what Ideas do, and what do not include or imply this or that other Idea.

LXVII. There is a celebrated Phænomenon, the Solution whereof I shall attempt to give, by the Principles that have been laid down, in reference to the manner wherein we apprehend by Sight the Magnitude of Objects. The apparent Magnitude of the Moon when placed in the Horizon, is much greater than when it is in the Meridian. Though the Angle under which the Diameter of the Moon is seen, be not observed greater in the former Case, than in the latter: And the horizontal Moon doth not constantly appear of the same Bigness, but at some times seemeth far greater than at others.

LXVIII. Now in order to explain the Reason of the Moon's appearing greater than ordinary in the Horizon, it must be observed, that the Particles which compose our Atmosphere intercept the Rays of Light proceeding from any Object to the Eye; and by how much the greater is the Portion of Atmosphere, interjacent between the Object and the Eye, by so much the more are the Rays intercepted; and by consequence, the Appearance of the Object rendered more faint, every Object appearing more vigorous or more faint, in Proportion as it sendeth more or fewer Rays into the Eye. Now, between the Eye and the Moon, when situated in the Horizon, there lies a far greater Quantity of Atmosphere, than there does when the Moon is in the Meridian. Whence it comes to pass, that the Appearance of the Horizontal Moon is fainter, and therefore by Sect. LVI. it should be thought bigger in that Situation, than in the Meridian, or in any other Elevation above the Horizon.

LXIX. Farther, the Air being variously impregnated, sometimes more and sometimes less, with Vapours and Exhalations fitted to retund and intercept the Rays of Light, it follows, that the Appearance of the Horizontal Moon hath not always an equal Faintness, and by Consequence, that Luminary, though in the very same Situation, is at one time judged greater than at another.

LXX. That we have here given the true Account of the Phænomena of the Horizontal Moon, will, I suppose, be farther evident to any one from the following Considerations. First, It is plain, that which in this Case suggests the Idea of greater Magnitude, must be something which is it self perceived; for, that which is unperceived cannot suggest to our Perception any other thing. Secondly, It must be something that does not constantly remain the same, but is subject to some Change or Variation, since the Appearance of the Horizontal Moon varies, being at one time greater than at another. And yet, Thirdly, It cannot be the visible Figure or Magnitude, since that remains the same, or is rather lesser, by how much the Moon is nearer to the Horizon. It remains therefore, that the true Cause is that Affection or Alteration of the Visible Appearance, which proceeds from the greater Paucity of Rays arriving at the Eye, and which I term Faintness: Since this answers all the forementioned Conditions, and I am not conscious of any other Perception that doth.

LXXI. Add to this, that in misty Weather it is a common Observation, that the Appearance of the Horizontal Moon is far larger than usual, which greatly conspires with, and strengthens our Opinion. Neither would it prove in the least, irreconcileable with what we have said, if the Horizontal Moon should chance sometimes to seem enlarged beyond its usual Extent, even in more serene Weather. For we must not only have regard to the Mist, which happens to be in the place where we stand; we ought also to take into our Thoughts, the whole Sum of Vapours and Exhalations, which lie betwixt the Eye and the Moon: All which cooperating to render the Appearance of the Moon more faint, and thereby increase its Magnitude, it may chance to appear greater than it usually does, even in the Horizontal Position, at a time when, though there be no extraordinary Fog or Haziness, just in the place where we stand; yet, the Air between the Eye and the Moon, taken all together, may be loaded with a greater quantity of interspersed Vapours and Exhalations, than at other times.

LXXII. It may be objected, that in Consequence of our Principles, the Interposition of a Body in some degree Opaque, which may intercept a great Part of the Rays of Light, should render the Appearance of the Moon in the Meridian as large, as when it is viewed in the Horizon. To which I answer, it is not Faintness any how applied, that suggests greater Magnitude, there being no necessary, but only an experimental Connexion between those two things: It follows, that the Faintness, which enlarges the Appearance, must be applied in such Sort, and with such Circumstances, as have been observed to attend the Vision of great Magnitudes. When from a Distance we behold great Objects, the Particles of the intermediate Air and Vapours, which are themselves unperceivable, do interrupt the Rays of Light, and thereby render the Appearance less strong and vivid: now, Faintness of Appearance caused in this Sort, hath been experienced to coexist with great Magnitude. But when it is caused by the Interposition of an opaque sensible Body, this Circumstance alters the Case, so that a faint Appearance this way caused, doth not suggest greater Magnitude, because it hath not been experienced to coexist with it.

LXXIII. Faintness, as well as all other Ideas or Perceptions which suggest Magnitude or Distance, doth it in the same way that Words suggest the Notions to which they are annexed. Now, it is known, a Word pronounced with certain Circumstances, or in a certain Context with other Words, hath not always the same Import and Signification, that it hath when pronounced in some other Circumstances, or different Context of Words. The very same Visible Appearance as to Faintness and all other Respects, if placed on high, shall not suggest the same Magnitude that it would if it were seen at an equal Distance, on a level with the Eye. The Reason whereof is, that we are rarely accustomed to view Objects at a great Height; our Concerns lie among things situated rather before than above us; and accordingly our Eyes are not placed on the top of our Heads, but in such a Position, as is most convenient for us to see distant Objects standing in our way. And this Situation of them being a Circumstance, which usually attends the Vision of distant Objects, we may from hence account for (what is commonly observed) an Object's appearing of different Magnitude, even with respect to its Horizontal Extension, on the top of a Steeple, for example, an hundred Feet high to one standing below, from what it would if placed at an hundred Feet distance on a level with his Eye. For it hath been shewn, that the Judgment we make on the Magnitude of a thing, depends not on the visible Appearance alone, but also on divers other Circumstances, any one of which being omitted or varied may suffice to make some Alteration in our Judgment. Hence, the Circumstance of viewing a distant Object in such a Situation as is usual, and suits with the ordinary Posture of the Head and Eyes being omitted, and instead thereof a different Situation of the Object, which requires a different Posture of the Head taking place, it is not to be wondered at, if the Magnitude be judged different: but it will be demanded, why an high Object should constantly appear less than an equidistant low Object of the same Dimensions, for so it is observed to be: it may indeed be granted that the Variation of some Circumstances may vary the Judgment, made on the Magnitude of high Objects, which we are less used to look at: But it does not hence appear, why they should be judged less rather than greater? I answer, that in case the Magnitude of distant Objects was suggested by the Extent of their visible Appearance alone, and thought proportional thereto, it is certain they would then be judged much less than now they seem to be, Vide Sect. LXXIX. But, several Circumstances concurring to form the Judgment we make on the Magnitude of distant Objects, by means of which they appear far larger than others, whose visible Appearance hath an equal or even greater Extension; it follows, that upon the Change or Omission of any of those Circumstances, which are wont to attend the Vision of distant Objects, and so come to influence the Judgments made on their Magnitude, they shall proportionably appear less than otherwise they would. For any of those things that caused an Object to be thought greater, than in proportion to its visible Extension, being either omitted or applied without the usual Circumstances, the Judgment depends more intirely on the visible Extension, and consequently the Object must be judged less. Thus in the present Case, the Situation of the thing seen being different from what it usually is in those Objects we have occasion to view, and whose Magnitude we observe, it follows, that the very same Object, being an hundred Feet high, should seem less than if it was an hundred Feet off on (or nearly on) a level with the Eye. What has been here set forth, seems to me to have no small share in contributing to magnify the Appearance of the horizontal Moon, and deserves not to be passed over in the Explication of it.

LXXIV. If we attentively consider the Phænomenon before us, we shall find the not discerning between the mediate and immediate Objects of Sight, to be the chief Cause of the Difficulty that occurs in the Explication of it. The Magnitude of the visible Moon, or that which is the proper and immediate Object of Vision, is no greater when the Moon is in the Horizon, than when it is in the Meridian. How comes it therefore, to seem greater in one Situation than the other? What is it can put this Cheat on the Understanding? It has no other Perception of the Moon, than what it gets by Sight: And that which is seen, is of the same Extent, I say, the visible Appearance hath the same, or rather a less Magnitude when the Moon is viewed in the Horizontal, than when in the Meridional Position: And yet it is esteemed greater in the former than in the latter. Herein consists the difficulty, which doth vanish and admit of a most easy Solution, if we consider that as the visible Moon is not greater in the Horizon than in the Meridian, so neither is it thought to be so. It hath been already shewn, that in any act of Vision, the visible Object absolutely, or in it self, is little taken notice of, the Mind still carrying its View from that to some tangible Ideas, which have been observed to be connected with it, and by that means come to be suggested by it. So that when a thing is said to appear great or small, or whatever Estimate be made of the Magnitude of any thing, this is meant not of the visible, but of the tangible Object. This duly considered, it will be no hard matter to reconcile the seeming Contradiction there is, that the Moon should appear of a different Bigness, the visible Magnitude thereof remaining still the same. For by Sect. LVI. the very same visible Extension, with a different Faintness, shall suggest a different tangible Extension. When therefore the horizontal Moon is said to appear greater than the meridional Moon, this must be understood not of a greater visible Extension, but of a greater tangible or real Extension, which by reason of the more than ordinary Faintness of the visible Appearance, is suggested to the Mind along with it.

LXXV. Many Attempts have been made by Learned Men, to account for this Appearance. Gassendus, Descartes, Hobbes, and several others, have employed their Thoughts on that Subject; but how fruitless and unsatisfactory their Endeavours have been, is sufficiently shewn in The Philosophical Transactions, [NOTE: Phil. Trans. Num. 187. p. 314.] where you may see their several Opinions at large set forth and confuted, not without some Surprize at the gross Blunders that ingenious Men have been forced into, by endeavouring to reconcile this Appearance with the ordinary Principles of Optics. Since the Writing of which, there hath been published in the Transactions [NOTE: Numb. 187. p. 323.] another Paper relating to the same Affair by the celebrated Dr. Wallis, wherein he attempts to account for that Phænomenon, which, though it seems not to contain any thing new, or different from what had been said before by others, I shall nevertheless consider in this place.

LXXVI. His Opinion, in short, is this; We judge not of the Magnitude of an Object by the visual Angle alone, but by the visual Angle in conjunction with the Distance. Hence, though the Angle remain the same, or even become less, yet if withal the Distance seem to have been increased, the Object shall appear greater. Now, one way whereby we estimate the Distance of any thing, is by the Number and Extent of the intermediate Objects: When therefore the Moon is seen in the Horizon, the Variety of Fields, Houses, &c. together with the large Prospect of the wide extended Land or Sea, that lies between the Eye and the utmost Limb of the Horizon, suggest unto the Mind the Idea of greater Distance, and consequently magnify the Appearance. And this, according to Dr. Wallis, is the true Account of the extraordinary Largeness attributed by the Mind to the horizontal Moon, at a time when the Angle subtended by its Diameter, is not one Jot greater than it used to be.

LXXVII. With reference to this Opinion, not to repeat what hath been already said concerning Distance, I shall only observe, First, That if the Prospect of interjacent Objects be that which suggests the Idea of farther Distance, and this Idea of farther Distance be the Cause that brings into the Mind the Idea of greater Magnitude, it should hence follow, that if one looked at the horizontal Moon from behind a Wall, it would appear no bigger than ordinary. For in that Case, the Wall interposing cuts off all that Prospect of Sea and Land, &c. which might otherwise increase the apparent Distance, and thereby the apparent Magnitude of the Moon. Nor will it suffice to say, the Memory doth even then suggest all that Extent of Land, &c. which lies within the Horizon; which Suggestion occasions a sudden Judgment of Sense, that the Moon is farther off and larger than usual. For ask any Man, who from such a Station beholding the horizontal Moon, shall think her greater than usual, whether he hath at that time in his Mind any Idea of the intermediate Objects, or long Tract of Land that lies between his Eye and the extreme Edge of the Horizon? And whether it be that Idea which is the Cause of his making the aforementioned Judgment? He will, I suppose, reply in the Negative, and declare the horizontal Moon shall appear greater than the meridional, though he never thinks of all or any of those things that lie between him and it. Secondly, It seems impossible by this Hypothesis, to account for the Moon's appearing in the very same Situation, at one time greater than at another; which nevertheless has been shewn to be very agreeable to the Principles we have laid down, and receives a most easy and natural Explication from them. For the further clearing up of this Point, it is to be observed that what we immediately and properly see are only Lights and Colours in sundry Situations and Shades, and Degrees of Faintness and Clearness, Confusion and Distinctness. All which visible Objects are only in the Mind, nor do they suggest ought external, whether Distance or Magnitude, otherwise than by habitual Connexion as Words do Things. We are also to remark, that, beside the Straining of the Eyes, and beside the vivid and faint, the distinct and confused Appearances (which bearing some Proportion to Lines and Angles, have been substituted instead of them, in the foregoing Part of this Treatise) there are other means which suggest both Distance and Magnitude; particularly, the Situation of visible Points, or Objects, as upper or lower; the one suggesting a farther Distance and greater Magnitude, the other a nearer Distance and lesser Magnitude: All which is an Effect only of Custom and Experience; there being really nothing intermediate in the Line of Distance, between the uppermost and lowermost, which are both Æquidistant, or rather at no Distance from the Eye, as there is also nothing in Upper or Lower, which by necessary Connexion should suggest greater or lesser Magnitude. Now, as these customary, experimental means of suggesting Distance, do likewise suggest Magnitude, so they suggest the one as immediately as the other. I say, they do not (Vide Sect. LIII.) first suggest Distance, and then leave the Mind from thence to infer or compute Magnitude, but suggest Magnitude as immediately and directly as they suggest Distance.

LXXVIII. This Phænomenon of the horizontal Moon is a clear Instance of the insufficiency of Lines and Angles, for explaining the way wherein the Mind perceives, and estimates the Magnitude of outward Objects. There is nevertheless a Use of Computation by them, in order to determine the apparent Magnitude of things, so far as they have a Connexion with, and are proportional to those other Ideas, or Perceptions which are the true and immediate Occasions that suggest to the Mind the apparent Magnitude of Things. But this in general may, I think, be observed concerning mathematical Computation in Optics: That it can never be very precise and exact, since the Judgments we make of the Magnitude of external Things do often depend on several Circumstances, which are not proportionable to, or capable of being defined by Lines and Angles.

LXXIX. From what has been said we may safely deduce this Consequence; to wit, that a Man born blind and made to see, would, at first opening of his Eyes, make a very different Judgment of the Magnitude of Objects intromitted by them, from what others do. He would not consider the Ideas of Sight, with reference to, or as having any Connexion with the Ideas of Touch: His View of them being entirely terminated within themselves, he can no otherwise judge them great or small, than as they contain a greater or lesser Number of visible Points. Now, it being certain that any visible Point can cover or exclude from View, only one other visible Point, it follows, that whatever Object intercepts the View of another, hath an equal Number of visible Points with it; and consequently they shall both be thought by him to have the same Magnitude. Hence it is evident, one in those Circumstances would judge his Thumb, with which he might hide a Tower, or hinder its being seen, equal to that Tower, or his Hand, the Interposition whereof might conceal the Firmament from his View, equal to the Firmament: How great an Inequality soever there may, in our Apprehensions, seem to be betwixt those two things, because of the customary and close Connexion that has grown up in our Minds between the Objects of Sight and Touch; whereby the very different and distinct Ideas of those two Senses, are so blended and confounded together, as to be mistaken for one and the same thing; out of which Prejudice we cannot easily extricate our selves.

LXXX. For the better explaining the Nature of Vision, and setting the Manner wherein we perceive Magnitudes in a due Light, I shall proceed to make some Observations concerning Matters relating thereto, whereof the want of Reflexion, and duly separating between tangible and visible Ideas, is apt to create in us mistaken and confused Notions. And First, I shall observe that the Minimum Visibile is exactly equal in all Beings whatsoever, that are endowed with the visive Faculty. No exquisite Formation of the Eye, no peculiar Sharpness of Sight can make it less in one Creature than in another; for it not being distinguishable into Parts, nor in any wise consisting of them, it must necessarily be the same to all. For suppose it otherwise, and that the Minimum Visibile of a Mite, for Instance, be less than the Minimum Visibile of a Man: the latter therefore may by Detraction of some part be made equal to the former: It doth therefore consist of Parts, which is inconsistent with the Notion of a Minimum Visibile, or Point.

LXXXI. It will perhaps be objected that the Minimum Visibile of a Man doth really, and in it self contain Parts whereby it surpasses that of a Mite, though they are not perceivable by the Man. To which I answer, the Minimum Visibile having (in like manner as all other the proper and immediate Objects of Sight) been shewn not to have any Existence without the Mind of him who sees it, it follows there cannot be any Part of it that is not actually perceived, and therefore visible. Now for any Object to contain several distinct visible Parts, and at the same time to be a Minimum Visibile, is a manifest Contradiction.

LXXXII. Of these visible Points we see at all times an equal Number. It is every whit as great when our View is contracted and bounded by near Objects, as when it is extended to larger and remoter. For it being impossible that one Minimum Visibile should obscure, or keep out of Sight more than one other, it is a plain Consequence; that when my View is on all sides bounded by the Walls of my Study, I see just as many visible Points as I could, in case that by the Removal of the Study-walls, and all other Obstructions, I had a full Prospect of the circumjacent Fields, Mountains, Sea, and open Firmament: for so long as I am shut up within the Walls, by their Interposition, every Point of the external Objects is covered from my View: But each Point that is seen being able to cover or exclude from Sight, one only other corresponding Point, it follows, that whilst my Sight is confined to those narrow Walls, I see as many Points, or Minima Visibilia, as I should were those Walls away, by looking on all the external Objects, whose Prospect is intercepted by them. Whenever therefore we are said to have a greater Prospect at one time than another, this must be understood with relation, not to the proper and immediate, but the secondary and mediate Objects of Vision, which, as hath been shewn, properly belong to the Touch.

LXXXIII. The visive Faculty considered, with reference to its immediate Objects, may be found to labour of two Defects, First, In respect of the Extent or Number of visible Points that are at once perceivable by it, which is narrow and limited to a certain Degree. It can take in at one View but a certain determinate Number of Minima Visibilia, beyond which it cannot extend its Prospect. Secondly, Our Sight is defective in that its View is not only narrow, but also for the most part confused: of those things that we take in at one Prospect, we can see but a few at once clearly and unconfusedly: and the more we fix our Sight on any one Object, by so much the darker and more indistinct shall the rest appear.

LXXXIV. Corresponding to these two Defects of Sight, we may imagine as many Perfections, to wit, 1st. That of comprehending in one View a greater Number of visible Points. 2dly. Of being able to view them all equally and at once, with the utmost Clearness and Distinction. That those Perfections are not actually in some Intelligences of a different Order and Capacity from ours, it is impossible for us to know.

LXXXV. In neither of those two ways, do Microscopes contribute to the Improvement of Sight; for when we look through a Microscope, we neither see more visible Points, nor are the collateral Points more distinct than when we look with the naked Eye, at Objects placed in a due Distance. A Microscope brings us as it were into a new World: It presents us with a new Scene of visible Objects, quite different from what we behold with the naked Eye. But herein consists the most remarkable Difference, to wit, that whereas the Objects perceived by the Eye alone, have a certain Connexion with Tangible Objects, whereby we are taught to foresee what will ensue upon the Approach or Application of distant Objects to the Parts of our own Body, which much conduceth to its Preservation; there is not the like Connexion between things Tangible and those visible Objects, that are perceived by help of a fine Microscope.

LXXXVI. Hence it is evident, that were our Eyes turned into the Nature of Microscopes, we should not be much benefited by the Change; we should be deprived of the forementioned Advantage we at present receive by the visive Faculty; and have left us only the empty Amusement of Seeing, without any other Benefit arising from it. But in that Case, it will perhaps be said, our Sight would be endued with a far greater Sharpness and Penetration than it now hath. But it is certain from what we have already shewn, that the Minimum Visibile is never greater or lesser, but in all Cases constantly the same: and in the Case of microscopical Eyes, I see only this Difference, to wit, that upon the ceasing of a certain observable Connexion betwixt the divers Perceptions of Sight and Touch, which before enabled us to regulate our Actions by the Eye, it would now be rendered utterly unserviceable to that Purpose.

LXXXVII. Upon the whole, it seems that if we consider the Use and End of Sight, together with the present State and Circumstances of our Being, we shall not find any great Cause to complain of any Defect or Imperfection in it, or easily conceive how it could be mended. With such admirable Wisdom is that Faculty contrived, both for the Pleasure and Convenience of Life.

LXXXVIII. Having finished what I intended to say, concerning the Distance and Magnitude of Objects, I come now to treat of the Manner, wherein the Mind perceives by Sight their Situation. Among the Discoveries of the last Age, it is reputed none of the least, that the Manner of Vision hath been more clearly explained, than ever it had been before. There is, at this Day, no one Ignorant, that the Pictures of external Objects are painted on the Retina, or Fund of the Eye. That we can see nothing which is not so painted: And that, according as the Picture is more distinct or confused, so also is the Perception we have of the Object: But then in this Explication of Vision, there occurs one mighty Difficulty. The Objects are painted in an inverted Order on the Bottom of the Eye: The upper part of any Object being painted on the lower part of the Eye, and the lower part of the Object on the upper part of the Eye: And so also as to Right and Left. Since therefore the Pictures are thus inverted, it is demanded how it comes to pass, that we see the Objects erect and in their natural Posture?

LXXXIX. In answer to this Difficulty, we are told, that the Mind perceiving an Impulse of a

Ray of Light, on the upper part of the Eye, considers this Ray as coming in a direct Line, from the lower part of the Object; and in like manner tracing the Ray that strikes on the lower part of the Eye, it is directed to the upper part of the Object. Thus in the adjacent Figure C the lower Point of the Object A B C is projected on c the upper part of the Eye. So likewise, the highest Point A is projected on a the lowest part of the Eye, which makes the Representation c b a inverted: But the Mind considering the Stroke that is made on c as coming in the straight Line C c from the lower end of the Object; and the Stroke or Impulse on a, as coming in the Line A a from the upper end of the Object, is directed to make a right Judgment of the Situation of the Object A B C, notwithstanding the Picture of it is inverted. This is illustrated by conceiving a blind Man, who holding in his Hands two Sticks that cross each other, doth with them touch the Extremities of an Object, placed in a perpendicular Situation. It is certain, this Man will judge that to be the upper Part of the Object, which he touches with the Stick held in the undermost Hand, and that to be the lower Part of the Object, which he touches with the Stick in his uppermost Hand. This is the common Explication of the erect Appearance of Objects, which is generally received and acquiesced in, being (as Mr. Molyneux tells us [NOTE: Diopt. par. 2. c. 7. p. 289.]) allowed by all Men as Satisfactory.

XC. But this Account to me does not seem in any Degree true. Did I perceive those Impulses, Decussations, and Directions of the Rays of Light, in like manner as hath been set forth, then, indeed, it would not be altogether void of Probability. And there might be some Pretence for the Comparison of the Blind-Man and his cross Sticks. But the Case is far otherwise. I know very well that I perceive no such thing. And of Consequence, I cannot thereby make an Estimate of the Situation of Objects. I appeal to any one's Experience, whether he be conscious to himself, that he thinks on the Intersection made by the radious Pencils, or pursues the Impulses they give in right Lines, whenever he perceives by Sight the Position of any Object? To me it seems evident, that crossing and tracing of the Rays, is never thought on by Children, Idiots, or in truth by any other, save only those who have applied themselves to the Study of Optics. And for the Mind to judge of the Situation of Objects by those things, without perceiving them, or to perceive them without knowing it, is equally beyond my Comprehension. Add to this, that the explaining the manner of Vision by the Example of cross Sticks, and hunting for the Object along the Axes of the Radious Pencils, doth suppose the proper Objects of Sight to be perceived at a Distance from us, contrary to what hath been demonstrated.

XCI. It remains, therefore, that we look for some other Explication of this Difficulty: And I believe it not impossible to find one, provided we examine it to the Bottom, and carefully distinguish between the Ideas of Sight and Touch; which cannot be too oft inculcated in treating of Vision: But more especially throughout the Consideration of this Affair, we ought to carry that Distinction in our Thoughts: For that from want of a right Understanding thereof, the Difficulty of explaining erect Vision seems chiefly to arise.

XCII. In order to disentangle our Minds, from whatever Prejudices we may entertain with relation to the Subject in hand, nothing seems more apposite, than the taking into our Thoughts the Case of one born blind, and afterwards, when grown up, made to see. And though perhaps, it may not be an easy Task to divest our selves intirely of the Experience received from Sight, so as to be able to put our Thoughts exactly in the Posture of such a one's; we must, nevertheless, as far as possible, endeavour to frame true Conceptions, of what might reasonably be supposed to pass in his Mind.

XCIII. It is certain, that a Man actually blind, and who had continued so from his Birth, would by the Sense of Feeling attain to have Ideas of Upper and Lower. By the Motion of his Hand he might discern the Situation of any tangible Object placed within his Reach. That Part on which he felt himself supported, or towards which he perceived his Body to gravitate, he would term lower, and the contrary to this upper; and accordingly denominate whatsoever Objects he touched.

XCIV. But then, whatever Judgments he makes concerning the Situation of Objects, are confined to those only that are perceivable by Touch. All those things that are intangible, and of a spiritual Nature, his Thoughts and Desires, his Passions, and in general all the Modifications of the Soul, to these he would never apply the Terms Upper and Lower, except only in a metaphorical Sense. He may, perhaps, by way of Allusion, speak of high or low Thoughts: But those Terms in their proper Signification, would never be applied to any thing, that was not conceived to exist without the Mind. For a Man born blind, and remaining in the same State, could mean nothing else by the Words Higher and Lower, than a greater or lesser Distance from the Earth: Which Distance he would measure by the Motion or Application of his Hand, or some other part of his Body. It is, therefore, evident, that all those things which, in respect of each other, would by him be thought higher or lower, must be such as were conceived to exist without his Mind, in the ambient Space.

XCV. Whence it plainly follows, that such a one, if we suppose him made to see, would not at first Sight think, that any thing he saw was high or low, erect or inverted; for it hath been already demonstrated in Sect. XLI. that he would not think the Things he perceived by Sight to be at any Distance from him, or without his Mind. The Objects to which he had hitherto been used to apply the Terms Up and Down, High and Low, were such only as affected, or were some way perceived by his Touch: But the proper Objects of Vision make a new Set of Ideas, perfectly distinct and different from the former, and which can in no sort make themselves perceived by Touch. There is, therefore, nothing at all that could induce him to think those Terms applicable to them: Nor would he ever think it, till such time as he had observed their Connexion with tangible Objects, and the same Prejudice began to insinuate it self into his Understanding, which from their Infancy had grown up in the Understandings of other Men.

XCVI. To set this Matter in a clearer Light, I shall make use of an Example. Suppose the above-mentioned blind Person, by his Touch, perceives a Man to stand Erect. Let us inquire into the manner of this. By the Application of his Hand to the several Parts of a humane Body, he had perceived different tangible Ideas, which being collected into sundry complex ones have distinct Names annexed to them. Thus one Combination of a certain tangible Figure, Bulk, and Consistency of Parts is called the Head, another the Hand, a third the Foot, and so of the rest: All which complex Ideas could, in his Understanding, be made up only of Ideas perceivable by Touch. He had also by his Touch obtained an Idea of Earth or Ground, towards which he perceives the Parts of his Body to have a natural Tendency. Now, by Erect nothing more being meant, than that perpendicular Position of a Man, wherein his Feet are nearest to the Earth: If the blind Person by moving his Hand, over the Parts of the Man who stands before him, perceives the tangible Ideas that compose the Head, to be farthest from, and those that compose the Feet to be nearest to, that other Combination of tangible Ideas which he calls Earth: He will denominate that Man Erect. But if we suppose him on a sudden to receive his Sight, and that he behold a Man standing before him, it is evident in that Case, he would neither judge the Man he sees to be Erect nor Inverted; for he never having known those Terms applied to any other, save tangible Things, or which existed in the Space without him, and what he sees neither being Tangible, nor perceived as existing without, he could not know that in Propriety of Language they were applicable to it.

XCVII. Afterwards, when upon turning his Head or Eyes up and down to the right and left, he shall observe the visible Objects to change, and shall also attain to know, that they are called by the same Names, and connected with the Objects perceived by Touch; then, indeed, he will come to speak of them and their Situation, in the same Terms that he has been used to apply to tangible Things: And those that he perceives by turning up his Eyes, he will call Upper, and those that by turning down his Eyes, he will call Lower.

XCVIII. And this seems to me the true Reason, why he should think those Objects uppermost that are painted on the lower part of his Eye: For, by turning the Eye up they shall be distinctly seen; as likewise those that are painted on the highest part of the Eye shall be distinctly seen, by turning the Eye down, and are for that Reason esteemed lowest: For we have shewn that to the immediate Objects of Sight, considered in themselves, he would not attribute the Terms

High and Low. It must therefore be on account of some Circumstances, which are observed to attend them: And these, it is plain, are the Actions of turning the Eye up and down, which suggest a very obvious Reason, why the Mind should denominate the Objects of Sight accordingly High or Low. And without this Motion of the Eye, this turning it up and down in order to discern different Objects, doubtless Erect, Inverse, and other the like Terms relating to the Position of tangible Objects, would never have been transferred, or in any degree apprehended to belong to the Ideas of Sight: The meer Act of Seeing including nothing in it to that Purpose; whereas the different Situations of the Eye naturally direct the Mind to make a suitable Judgment of the Situation of Objects intromitted by it.

XCIX. Farther, when he has by Experience learned the Connexion there is between the several Ideas of Sight and Touch, he will be able, by the Perception he has of the Situation of visible Things in respect of one another, to make a sudden and true Estimate of the Situation of outward, tangible Things corresponding to them. And thus it is, he shall perceive by Sight the Situation of External Objects, which do not properly fall under that Sense.

C. I know we are very prone to think, that if just made to see, we should judge of the Situation of visible Things as we do now: But, we are also as prone to think, that at first Sight, we should in the same way apprehend the Distance and Magnitude of Objects, as we do now: Which hath been shewn to be a false and groundless Persuasion. And for the like Reasons, the same Censure may be past on the positive Assurance, that most Men, before they have thought sufficiently of the Matter, might have of their being able to determine by the Eye at first view, whether Objects were erect or inverse.

CI. It will, perhaps, be objected to our Opinion, that a Man, for instance, being thought erect when his Feet are next the Earth, and inverted when his Head is next the Earth, it doth hence follow, that by the meer Act of Vision, without any Experience or altering the Situation of the Eye, we should have determined whether he were erect or inverted: For both the Earth it self, and the Limbs of the Man who stands thereon, being equally perceived by Sight, one cannot choose seeing, what part of the Man is nearest the Earth, and what part farthest from it, i. e. whether he be erect or inverted.

CII. To which I answer, the Ideas which constitute the tangible Earth and Man, are intirely different from those which constitute the visible Earth and Man. Nor was it possible, by virtue of the visive Faculty alone, without superadding any Experience of Touch, or altering the Position of the Eye, ever to have known, or so much as suspected, there had been any Relation or Connexion between them: Hence, a Man at first view would not denominate any thing he saw Earth, or Head, or Foot; and consequently, he could not tell by the meer Act of Vision, whether the Head or Feet were nearest the Earth: Nor, indeed, would we have thereby any thought of Earth or Man, erect or inverse, at all: Which will be made yet more evident, if we nicely observe, and make a particular Comparison between the Ideas of both Senses.

CIII. That which I see is only variety of Light and Colours. That which I feel is hard, or soft, hot or cold, rough or smooth. What Similitude, what Connexion have those Ideas with these? Or how is it possible, that any one should see Reason, to give one and the same Name to Combinations of Ideas so very different, before he had experienced their Coexistence? We do not find there is any necessary Connexion betwixt this or that tangible Quality, and any Colour whatsoever. And we may sometimes perceive Colours, where there is nothing to be felt. All which doth make it manifest, that no Man at first receiving of his Sight, would know there was any Agreement between this or that particular Object of his Sight, and any Object of Touch he had been already acquainted with: The Colours therefore of the Head, would to him no more suggest the Idea of Head, than they would the Idea of Foot.

CIV. Farther, we have at large shewn (vid. Sect. LXIII. and LXIV.) there is no discoverable, necessary Connexion, between any given visible Magnitude, and any one particular tangible Magnitude; but that it is intirely the result of Custom and Experience, and depends on foreign and accidental Circumstances, that we can by the Perception of visible Extension inform our selves, what may be the Extension of any tangible Object connected with it. Hence it is certain that neither the visible Magnitude of Head or Foot, would bring along with them into the Mind, at first opening of the Eyes, the respective tangible Magnitudes of those Parts.

CV. By the foregoing Section, it is plain the visible Figure of any Part of the Body hath no necessary Connexion with the tangible Figure thereof, so as at first Sight to suggest it to the Mind: For Figure is the Termination of Magnitude; whence it follows, that no visible Magnitude having in its own Nature an aptness to suggest any one particular tangible Magnitude, so neither can any visible Figure be inseparably connected with its corresponding tangible Figure: So as of it self and in a way prior to Experience, it might suggest it to the Understanding. This will be farther evident, if we consider that what seems smooth and round to the Touch, may to Sight, if viewed through a Microscope, seem quite otherwise.

CVI. From all which laid together and duly considered, we may clearly deduce this Inference. In the first Act of Vision, no Idea entering by the Eye, would have a perceivable Connexion with the Ideas to which the Names Earth, Man, Head, Foot, &c. were annexed in the Understanding of a Person blind from his Birth; so as in any sort to introduce them into his Mind, or make themselves be called by the same Names, and reputed the same Things with them, as afterwards they come to be.

CVII. There doth, nevertheless, remain one Difficulty, which perhaps may seem to press hard on our Opinion, and deserve not to be passed over: For though it be granted that neither the Colour, Size, nor Figure of the visible Feet have any necessary Connexion with the Ideas that compose the tangible Feet, so as to bring them at first sight into my Mind, or make me in danger of confounding them before I had been used to, and for some time experienced their Connexion: Yet thus much seems undeniable, namely, that the Number of the visible Feet, being the same with that of the tangible Feet, I may from hence without any Experience of Sight, reasonably conclude, that they represent or are connected with the Feet rather than the Head. I say, it seems the Idea of two visible Feet will sooner suggest to the Mind, the Idea of two tangible Feet than of one Head; so that the blind Man upon first Reception of the visive Faculty might know, which were the Feet or Two, and which the Head or One.

CVIII. In order to get clear of this seeming Difficulty, we need only observe, that Diversity of visible Objects doth not necessarily infer diversity of tangible Objects corresponding to them. A Picture painted with great variety of Colours affects the Touch in one uniform manner; it is therefore evident, that I do not by any necessary Consecution, independent of Experience, judge of the number of things tangible, from the number of things visible. I should not therefore at first opening my Eyes conclude, that because I see two I shall feel two. How, therefore can I, before Experience teaches me, know that the visible Legs, because two, are connected with the tangible Legs, or the visible Head, because one is connected with the tangible Head? The truth is, the things I see are so very different and heterogeneous from the things I feel, that the Perception of the one would never have suggested the other to my thoughts, or enabled me to pass the least Judgment thereon, until I had experienced their Connexion.

CIX. But for a fuller Illustration of this Matter, it ought to be considered that Number (however some may reckon it amongst the primary Qualities) is nothing fixed and settled, really existing in things themselves. It is intirely the Creature of the Mind, considering, either an Idea by it self, or any Combination of Ideas to which it gives one Name, and so makes it pass for an Unite. According as the Mind variously combines its Ideas, the Unite varies: and as the Unite, so the Number, which is only a Collection of Unites, doth also vary. We call a Window one, a Chimney one; and yet a House in which there are many Windows, and many Chimneys, hath an equal right to be called one, and many Houses go to the making of one City. In these and the like Instances, it is evident the Unite constantly relates to the particular Draughts the Mind makes of its Ideas, to which it affixes Names, and wherein it includes more or less, as best suits its own Ends and Purposes. Whatever therefore the Mind considers as one, that is an Unite. Every Combination of Ideas is considered as one thing by the mind, and in token thereof is marked by one Name. Now, this naming and combining together of Ideas is perfectly arbitrary, and done by the Mind in such sort, as Experience shews it to be most convenient: Without which, our Ideas had never been collected into such sundry distinct Combinations as they now are.

CX. Hence it follows, that a Man born blind, and afterwards, when grown up, made to see, would not in the first Act of Vision, parcel out the Ideas of Sight, into the same distinct Collections that others do, who have experienced which do regularly coexist and are proper to be bundled up together under one Name. He would not, for Example, make into one complex Idea, and thereby esteem an Unite all those particular Ideas, which constitute the visible Head or Foot. For there can be no Reason assigned why he should do so, barely upon his seeing a Man stand upright before him: There croud into his Mind the Ideas which compose the visible Man, in company with all the other Ideas of Sight perceiv'd at the same time: But all these Ideas offered at once to his View, he would not distribute into sundry distinct Combinations, till such time as by observing the Motion of the Parts of the Man and other Experiences, he comes to know, which are to be separated, and which to be collected together.

CXI. From what hath been premised, it is plain the Objects of Sight and Touch make, if I may so say, two Sets of Ideas, which are widely different from each other. To Objects of either kind, we indifferently attribute the Terms high and low, right and left, and such like, denoting the Position or Situation of things: But then we must well observe that the Position of any Object is determined with respect only to Objects of the same Sense. We say any Object of Touch is high or low, according as it is more or less distant from the tangible Earth: And in like manner we denominate any Object of Sight high or low, in Proportion as it is more or less distant from the visible Earth: But to define the Situation of visible Things, with relation to the Distance they bear from any tangible Thing, or vice versa, this were absurd and perfectly unintelligible. For all visible things are equally in the Mind, and take up no part of the external Space: And consequently are equidistant from any tangible thing, which exists without the Mind.

CXII. Or rather to speak truly, the proper Objects of Sight are at no Distance, neither near nor far, from any tangible Thing. For if we inquire narrowly into the Matter we shall find that those things only are compared together in respect of Distance, which exist after the same manner, or appertain unto the same Sense. For by the Distance between any two Points, nothing more is meant than the Number of intermediate Points: If the given Points are visible, the Distance between them is marked out by the Number of the interjacent visible Points: If they are tangible, the Distance between them is a Line consisting of tangible Points; but if they are one tangible, and the other visible, the Distance between them doth neither consist of Points perceivable by Sight nor by Touch, i. e. it is utterly inconceivable. This, perhaps, will not find an easy Admission into all Mens Understanding: However, I should gladly be informed whether it be not true, by any one who will be at the pains to reflect a little, and apply it home to his Thoughts.

CXIII. The not observing what has been delivered in the two last Sections, seems to have occasioned no small part of the Difficulty that occurs in the Business of erect Appearances. The Head, which is painted nearest the Earth, seems to be farthest from it: and on the other hand, the Feet, which are painted farthest from the Earth, are thought nearest to it. Herein lies the Difficulty, which vanishes if we express the thing more clearly and free from Ambiguity, thus: How comes it that, to the Eye, the visible Head which is nearest the tangible Earth, seems farthest from the Earth, and the visible Feet, which are farthest from the tangible Earth, seem nearest the Earth? The Question being thus proposed, who sees not, the Difficulty is founded on a Supposition, that the Eye, or visive Faculty, or rather the Soul by means thereof, should judge of the Situation of visible Objects, with reference to their Distance from the tangible Earth? Whereas it is evident the tangible Earth is not perceived by Sight: And it hath been shewn in the two last preceding Sections, that the Location of visible Objects is determined only by the Distance they bear from one another; and that it is Nonsense to talk of Distance, far or near, between a visible and tangible Thing.

CXIV. If we confine our Thoughts to the proper Objects of Sight, the whole is plain and easy. The Head is painted farthest from, and the Feet nearest to the visible Earth; and so they appear to be. What is there strange or unaccountable in this? Let us suppose the Pictures in the Fund of the Eye, to be the immediate Objects of the Sight. The Consequence is, that things should appear in the same Posture they are painted in; and is it not so? The Head which is seen, seems farthest from the Earth which is seen; and the Feet, which are seen, seem nearest to the Earth which is seen; and just so they are painted.

CXV. But, say you, the Picture of the Man is inverted, and yet the Appearance is erect: I ask, what mean you by the Picture of the Man, or, which is the same thing, the visible Man's being inverted? You tell me it is inverted, because the Heels are uppermost, and the Head undermost? Explain me this. You say, that by the Head's being undermost, you mean that it is nearest to the Earth; and by the Heels being uppermost, that they are farthest from the Earth. I ask again, what Earth you mean? You cannot mean the Earth that is painted on the Eye, or the visible Earth: For the Picture of the Head is farthest from the Picture of the Earth, and the Picture of the Feet nearest to the Picture of the Earth; and accordingly the visible Head is farthest from the visible Earth, and the visible Feet nearest to it. It remains, therefore, that you mean the tangible Earth, and so determine the Situation of visible things with respect to tangible things; contrary to what hath been demonstrated in Sect. CXI. and CXII. The two distinct Provinces of Sight and Touch should be considered apart, and as if their Objects had no Intercourse, no manner of Relation one to another, in point of Distance or Position.

CXVI. Farther, what greatly contributes to make us mistake in this Matter is, that when we think of the Pictures in the Fund of the Eye, we imagine our selves looking on the Fund of another's Eye, or another looking on the Fund of our own Eye, and beholding the Pictures painted thereon. Suppose two Eyes A and B: A from some distance looking on the Pictures in B sees them inverted, and for that Reason concludes they are inverted in B: But this is wrong. There are projected in little on the Bottom of A, the Images of the Pictures of, suppose Man, Earth, &c. which are painted on B. And besides these, the Eye B it self, and the Objects which environ it, together with another Earth, are projected in a larger Size on A. Now, by the Eye A, these larger Images are deemed the true Objects, and the lesser only Pictures in miniature. And it is with respect to those greater Images, that it determines the Situation of the smaller Images: So that comparing the little Man with the great Earth, A judges him inverted, or that the Feet are farthest from, and the Head nearest to the great Earth. Whereas, if A compare the little Man with the little Earth, then he will appear erect, i. e. his Head shall seem farthest from, and his Feet nearest to the little Earth. But we must consider that B does not see two Earths as A does: It sees only what is represented by the little Pictures in A, and consequently shall judge the Man erect: For, in truth, the Man in B is not inverted, for there the Feet are next the Earth; but it is the Representation of it in A which is inverted, for there the Head of the Representation of the Picture of the Man in B is next the Earth, and the Feet farthest from the Earth, meaning the Earth which is without the Representation of the Pictures in B. For if you take the little Images of the Pictures in B, and consider them by themselves, and with respect only to one another, they are all Erect and in their natural Posture.

CXVII. Farther, there lies a Mistake in our imagining that the Pictures of external Objects are painted on the Bottom of the Eye. It hath been shewn, there is no Resemblance between the Ideas of Sight and things Tangible. It hath likewise been demonstrated, that the proper Objects of Sight do not exist without the Mind. Whence it clearly follows, that the Pictures painted on the Bottom of the Eye, are not the Pictures of external Objects. Let any one consult his own Thoughts, and then say what Affinity, what Likeness there is between that certain Variety and Disposition of Colours, which constitute the visible Man, or Picture of a Man, and that other Combination of far different Ideas, sensible by Touch, which compose the tangible Man. But if this be the Case, how come they to be accounted Pictures or Images, since that supposes them to copy or represent some Originals or other?

CXVIII. To which I answer: In the forementioned Instance, the Eye A takes the little Images, included within the Representation of the other Eye B, to be Pictures or Copies, whereof the Archetypes are not things existing without, but the larger Pictures projected on its own Fund: and which by A are not thought Pictures, but the Originals, or true Things themselves. Though if we suppose a third Eye C, from a due Distance to behold the Fund of A, then indeed the Things projected thereon, shall, to C, seem Pictures or Images, in the same Sense that those projected on B do to A.

CXIX. Rightly to conceive this Point, we must carefully distinguish between the Ideas of Sight and Touch, between the visible and tangible Eye; for certainly on the tangible Eye, nothing either is or seems to be painted. Again, the visible Eye, as well as all other visible Objects, hath been shewn to exist only in the Mind, which perceiving its own Ideas, and comparing them together, calls some Pictures in respect of others. What hath been said, being rightly comprehended and laid together, doth, I think, afford a full and genuine Explication of the erect Appearance of Objects; which Phænomenon, I must confess, I do not see how it can be explained by any Theories of Vision hitherto made publick.

CXX. In treating of these things, the use of Language is apt to occasion some Obscurity and Confusion, and create in us wrong Ideas: For Language being accommodated to the common Notions and Prejudices of Men, it is scarce possible to deliver the naked and precise Truth, without great Circumlocution, Impropriety, and (to an unwary Reader) seeming Contradictions; I do, therefore, once for all desire whoever shall think it worth his while to understand what I have written concerning Vision, that he would not stick in this or that Phrase, or Manner of Expression, but candidly collect my Meaning from the whole Sum and Tenor of my Discourse, and laying aside the Words as much as possible, consider the bare Notions themselves, and then judge whether they are agreeable to Truth and his own Experience, or no.

CXXI. We have shewn the way wherein the Mind by mediation of visible Ideas doth perceive or apprehend the Distance, Magnitude, and Situation of tangible Objects. We come now to inquire more particularly concerning the Difference between the Ideas of Sight and Touch, which are called by the same Names, and see whether there be any Idea common to both Senses. From what we have at large set forth and demonstrated in the foregoing Parts of this Treatise, it is plain there is no one self same numerical Extension, perceived both by Sight and Touch; but that the particular Figures and Extensions perceived by Sight, however they may be called by the same Names, and reputed the same Things, with those perceived by Touch, are nevertheless different, and have an Existence distinct and separate from them: So that the Question is not now concerning the same numerical Ideas, but whether there be any one and the same sort or Species of Ideas equally perceivable to both Senses; Or, in other Words, whether Extension, Figure, and Motion perceived by Sight, are not specifically distinct from Extension, Figure, and Motion perceived by Touch.

CXXII. But before I come more particularly to discuss this Matter, I find it proper to consider Extension in Abstract: For of this there is much Talk, and I am apt to think, that when Men speak of Extension, as being an Idea common to two Senses, it is with a secret Supposition, that we can single out Extension from all other tangible and visible Qualities, and form thereof an abstract Idea, which Idea they will have common both to Sight and Touch. We are therefore to understand by Extension in abstract, an Idea of Extension, for Instance, a Line or Surface, intirely stript of all other sensible Qualities and Circumstances that might determine it to any particular Existence; it is neither black nor white, nor red, nor hath it any Colour at all, or any tangible Quality whatsoever, and consequently it is of no finite determinate Magnitude: For that which bounds or distinguishes one Extension from another, is some Quality or Circumstance wherein they disagree.

CXXIII. Now I do not find that I can perceive, imagine, or any wise frame in my Mind such an abstract Idea, as is here spoken of. A Line or Surface, which is neither black, nor white, nor blue, nor yellow, &c. nor long, nor short, nor rough, nor smooth, nor square, nor round, &c. is perfectly incomprehensible. This I am sure of as to my self: how far the Faculties of other Men may reach, they best can tell.

CXXIV. It is commonly said, that the Object of Geometry is abstract Extension: but Geometry contemplates Figures: Now, Figure is the Termination of Magnitude: but we have shewn that Extension in Abstract hath no finite determinate Magnitude. Whence it clearly follows that it can have no Figure, and consequently is not the Object of Geometry. It is indeed a Tenet as well of the modern as of the ancient Philosophers, that all general Truths are concerning universal abstract Ideas; without which, we are told, there could be no Science, no Demonstration of any general Proposition in Geometry. But it were no hard matter, did I think it necessary to my present Purpose, to shew that Propositions and Demonstrations in Geometry might be universal, though they who make them, never think of abstract general Ideas of Triangles or Circles.

CXXV. After reiterated Endeavours to apprehend the general Idea of a Triangle, I have found it altogether incomprehensible. And surely if any one were able to introduce that Idea into my Mind, it must be the Author of the Essay concerning Humane Understanding; He, who has so far distinguished himself from the generality of Writers, by the Clearness and Significancy of what he says. Let us therefore see how this celebrated Author describes the general, or abstract Idea of a Triangle. 'It must be' (says he) 'neither Oblique, nor Rectangular, neither Equilateral, Equicrural, nor Scalenum; but all and none of these at once. In effect it is somewhat imperfect that cannot exist; an Idea, wherein some Parts of several different and inconsistent Ideas are put together.' Essay on Hum. Understand. B. iv. C. 7. S. 9. This is the Idea, which he thinks needful, for the Enlargement of Knowledge, which is the Subject of Mathematical Demonstration, and without which we could never come to know any general Proposition concerning Triangles. That Author acknowledges it doth 'require some Pains and Skill to form this general Idea of a Triangle.' Ibid. But had he called to mind what he says in another Place, to wit, 'That Ideas of mixed Modes wherein any inconsistent Ideas are put together, cannot so much as exist in the Mind, i. e. be conceived.' Vid. B. iii. C. 10. S. 33. Ibid. I say, had this occurred to his Thoughts, it is not improbable he would have owned it above all the Pains and Skill he was master of, to form the above-mentioned Idea of a Triangle, which is made up of manifest, staring Contradictions. That a Man who laid so great a Stress on clear and determinate Ideas, should nevertheless talk at this rate, seems very surprising. But the Wonder will lessen if it be considered, that the Source whence this Opinion flows, is the prolific Womb which has brought forth innumerable Errors and Difficulties, in all parts of Philosophy, and in all the Sciences: But this Matter, taken in its full Extent, were a Subject too comprehensive to be insisted on in this place. And so much for Extension in Abstract.

CXXVI. Some, perhaps, may think pure Space, Vacuum, or Trine Dimension to be equally the Object of Sight and Touch: But though we have a very great Propension, to think the Ideas of Outness and Space to be the immediate Object of Sight; yet, if I mistake not, in the foregoing Parts of this Essay, that hath been clearly demonstrated to be a mere Delusion, arising from the quick and sudden suggestion of Fancy, which so closely connects the Idea of Distance with those of Sight, that we are apt to think it is it self a proper and immediate Object of that Sense, till Reason corrects the Mistake.

CXXVII. It having been shewn, that there are no abstract Ideas of Figure, and that it is impossible for us, by any Precision of Thought, to frame an Idea of Extension separate from all other visible and tangible Qualities, which shall be common both to Sight and Touch: The Question now remaining is, whether the particular Extensions, Figures, and Motions perceived by Sight be of the same kind, with the particular Extensions, Figures, and Motions perceived by Touch? In answer to which, I shall venture to lay down the following Proposition, The Extension, Figures, and Motions, perceived by Sight are specifically distinct from the Ideas of Touch, called by the same Names, nor is there any such thing as one Idea, or kind of Idea common to both Senses. This Proposition may, without much Difficulty, be collected from what hath been said in several Places of this Essay. But, because it seems so remote from, and contrary to, the received Notions and settled Opinion of Mankind, I shall attempt to demonstrate it more particularly, and at large, by the following Arguments.

CXXVIII. When upon Perception of an Idea, I range it under this or that sort; it is because it is perceived after the same manner, or because it has a Likeness or Conformity with, or affects me in the same way as the Ideas of the sort I rank it under. In short, it must not be intirely new, but have something in it old, and already perceived by me: It must, I say, have so much, at least, in common with the Ideas I have before known and named, as to make me give it the same Name with them. But it has been, if I mistake not, clearly made out, that a Man born blind would not at first Reception of his Sight, think the Things he saw were of the same Nature with the Objects of Touch, or had any thing in common with them; but that they were a new Set of Ideas, perceived in a new Manner, and intirely different from all he had ever perceived before: So that he would not call them by the same Name, nor repute them to be of the same Sort, with any thing he had hitherto known.

CXXIX. Secondly, Light and Colours are allowed by all to constitute a sort or Species intirely different from the Ideas of Touch: Nor will any Man, I presume, say they can make themselves perceived by that Sense: But there is no other immediate Object of Sight, besides Light and Colours. It is therefore a direct Consequence, that there is no Idea common to both Senses.

CXXX. It is a prevailing Opinion, even amongst those who have thought and writ most accurately concerning our Ideas, and the ways whereby they enter into the Understanding, that something more is perceived by Sight, than barely Light and Colours with their Variations. Mr. Locke termeth Sight, 'The most comprehensive of all our Senses, conveying to our Minds the Ideas of Light and Colours, which are peculiar only to that Sense; and also the far different Ideas of Space, Figure, and Motion.' Essay on Humane Understand. B. ii. C. 9. S. 9. Space or Distance, we have shewn is not otherwise the Object of Sight than of Hearing. Vid. Sect. XLVI. And as for Figure and Extension, I leave it to any one, that shall calmly attend to his own clear and distinct Ideas, to decide whether he has any Idea intromitted immediately and properly by Sight, save only Light and Colours: Or whether it be possible for him, to frame in his Mind a distinct Abstract Idea of Visible Extension, or Figure, exclusive of all Colour: and on the other hand, whether he can conceive Colour without visible Extension? For my own part, I must confess, I am not able to attain so great a nicety of Abstraction: in a strict Sense, I see nothing but Light and Colours, with their several Shades and Variations. He who beside these doth also perceive by Sight Ideas far different and distinct from them, hath that Faculty in a Degree more perfect and comprehensive than I can pretend to. It must be owned, that by the Mediation of Light and Colours, other far different Ideas are suggested to my Mind: but so they are by Hearing, which beside Sounds which are peculiar to that Sense, doth by their Mediation suggest not only Space, Figure, and Motion, but also all other Ideas whatsoever that can be signified by Words.

CXXXI. Thirdly, It is, I think, an Axiom universally received, that Quantities of the same kind may be added together, and make one intire Sum. Mathematicians add Lines together: but they do not add a Line to a Solid, or conceive it as making one Sum with a Surface: These three kinds of Quantity being thought incapable of any such mutual Addition, and consequently of being compared together, in the several ways of Proportion, are by them esteemed intirely Disparate and Heterogeneous. Now let any one try in his Thoughts to add a visible Line or Surface to a tangible Line or Surface, so as to conceive them making one continued Sum or Whole. He that can do this, may think them Homogeneous: but he that cannot must, by the foregoing Axiom, think them Heterogeneous: A Blue, and a Red Line I can conceive added together into one Sum, and making one continued Line: but to make, in my Thoughts, one continued Line of a visible and tangible Line added together is, I find, a Task far more difficult, and even insurmountable: and I leave it to the Reflexion and Experience of every particular Person to determine for himself.

CXXXII. A farther Confirmation of our Tenet may be drawn from the Solution of Mr.

Molyneux's Problem, published by Mr. Locke in his Essay: Which I shall set down as it there lies, together with Mr. Locke's Opinion of it, 'Suppose a Man born Blind, and now Adult, and taught by his Touch to distinguish between a Cube, and a Sphere of the same Metal, and nighly of the same Bigness, so as to tell, when he felt one and t'other, which is the Cube, and which the Sphere. Suppose then the Cube and Sphere placed on a Table, and the blind Man to be made to See: Quære, Whether by his Sight, before he touched them, he could now distinguish, and tell, which is the Globe, which the Cube? To which the acute and judicious Proposer answers: Not. For though he has obtained the Experience of, how a Globe, how a Cube affects his Touch; yet he has not yet attained the Experience, that what affects his Touch so or so, must affect his Sight so or so: Or that a protuberant Angle in the Cube, that pressed his Hand unequally, shall appear to his Eye, as it doth in the Cube. I agree with this thinking Gentleman, whom I am proud to call my Friend, in his Answer to this his Problem; and am of opinion, that the blind Man, at first Sight would not be able with certainty to say, which was the Globe, which the Cube, whilst he only saw them.' Essay on Humane Understanding, B. ii. C. 9. S. 8.

CXXXIII. Now, if a square Surface perceived by Touch be of the same sort with a square Surface perceived by Sight; it is certain the blind Man here mentioned might know a square Surface, as soon as he saw it: It is no more but introducing into his Mind, by a new Inlet, an Idea he has been already well acquainted with. Since therefore he is supposed to have known by his Touch, that a Cube is a Body terminated by square Surfaces; and that a Sphere is not terminated by square Surfaces: upon the supposition that a visible and tangible Square differ only in numero, it follows, that he might know, by the unerring Mark of the square Surfaces, which was the Cube, and which not, while he only saw them. We must therefore allow, either that visible Extension and Figures are specifically distinct from tangible Extension and Figures, or else, that the Solution of this Problem, given by those two thoughtful and ingenious Men, is wrong.

CXXXIV. Much more might be laid together in Proof of the Proposition I have advanced: but what has been said is, if I mistake not, sufficient to convince any one that shall yield a reasonable Attention: And, as for those that will not be at the pains of a little Thought, no Multiplication of Words will ever suffice to make them understand the Truth, or rightly conceive my Meaning.

CXXXV. I cannot let go the above-mentioned Problem, without some Reflexion on it. It hath been made evident, that a Man blind from his Birth would not, at first Sight, denominate any thing he saw, by the Names he had been used to appropriate to Ideas of Touch, vid. Sect. CVI. Cube, Square, Table, are Words he has known applied to Things perceivable by Touch, but to Things perfectly intangible he never knew them applied. Those Words in their wonted Application, always marked out to his Mind Bodies, or solid Things which were perceived by the Resistance they gave: But there is no Solidity, no Resistance or Protrusion perceived by Sight. In short, the Ideas of Sight are all new Perceptions, to which there be no Names annexed in his Mind: he cannot, therefore understand what is said to him concerning them: And to ask of the two Bodies he saw placed on the Table, which was the Sphere, which the Cube? were, to him, a Question downright bantering and unintelligible; nothing he sees being able to suggest to his Thoughts, the Idea of a Body, Distance, or in general, of any thing he had already known.

CXXXVI. It is a Mistake, to think the same thing affects both Sight and Touch. If the same Angle or Square, which is the Object of Touch, be also the Object of Vision, what should hinder the blind Man, at first Sight, from knowing it? For though the Manner wherein it affects the Sight, be different from that wherein it affected his Touch; yet, there being, beside this Manner or Circumstance, which is new and unknown, the Angle or Figure, which is old and known, he cannot choose but discern it.

CXXXVII. Visible Figure and Extension having been demonstrated to be of a nature, intirely different and heterogeneous from tangible Figure and Extension, it remains that we inquire concerning Motion. Now that visible Motion is not of the same sort with tangible Motion, seems to need no farther Proof, it being an evident Corollary from what we have shewn concerning the Difference there is between visible and tangible Extension: But for a more full and express Proof hereof, we need only observe, that one who had not yet experienced Vision, would not at first sight know Motion. Whence it clearly follows, that Motion perceivable by Sight is of a sort distinct from Motion perceivable by Touch. The Antecedent I prove thus: By Touch he could not perceive any Motion, but what was up or down, to the right or left, nearer or farther from him; besides these, and their several Varieties or Complications, it is impossible he should have any Idea of Motion. He would not therefore think any thing to be Motion, or give the name Motion to any Idea, which he could not range under some or other of those particular kinds thereof. But from Sect. XCV. it is plain that by the meer act of Vision, he could not know Motion upwards or downwards, to the right or left, or in any other possible Direction. From which I conclude, he would not know Motion at all at first sight. As for the Idea of Motion in Abstract, I shall not waste Paper about it, but leave it to my Reader, to make the best he can of it. To me it is perfectly unintelligible.

CXXXVIII. The Consideration of Motion may furnish a new Field for Inquiry: But since the Manner wherein the Mind apprehends by Sight, the Motion of tangible Objects, with the various Degrees thereof, may be easily collected, from what hath been said concerning the Manner, wherein that Sense doth suggest their various Distances, Magnitudes and Situations; I shall not enlarge any farther on this Subject, but proceed to consider what may be alledged with greatest appearance of Reason, against the Proposition we have shewn to be true: For where there is so much Prejudice to be encountered, a bare and naked Demonstration of the Truth will scarce suffice. We must also satisfy the Scruples that Men may raise in favour of their preconceived Notions, shew whence the Mistake arises, how it came to spread, and carefully disclose and root out those false Persuasions, that an early Prejudice might have implanted in the Mind.

CXXXIX. First, Therefore, it will be demanded, how visible Extension and Figures come to be called by the same Name, with tangible Extension and Figures, if they are not of the same kind with them? It must be something more than Humour or Accident, that could occasion a Custom so constant and universal as this, which has obtained in all Ages and Nations of the World, and amongst all Ranks of Men, the Learned as well as the Illiterate.

CXL. To which I answer, we can no more argue a visible and tangible Square to be of the same Species, from their being called by the same Name, than we can, that a tangible Square and the Monosyllable consisting of six Letters, whereby it is marked, are of the same Species because they are both called by the same Name. It is customary to call written Words, and the Things they signify, by the same Name: For Words not being regarded in their own Nature, or otherwise than as they are Marks of Things, it had been superfluous, and beside the design of Language, to have given them Names distinct from those of the Things marked by them. The same Reason holds here also. Visible Figures are the Marks of tangible Figures, and from Sect. LIX. it is plain, that in themselves they are little regarded, or upon any other Score than for their Connexion with tangible Figures, which by Nature they are ordained to signify. And because this Language of Nature doth not vary in different Ages or Nations, hence it is, that in all Times and Places, visible Figures are called by the same Names, as the respective tangible Figures suggested by them, and not because they are alike, or of the same sort with them.

CXLI. But, say you, surely a tangible Square is liker to a visible Square, than to a visible Circle: It has four Angles, and as many Sides: so also has the visible Square: but the visible Circle has no such thing, being bounded by one uniform Curve, without right Lines or Angles, which makes it unfit to represent the tangible Square, but very fit to represent the tangible Circle. Whence it clearly follows, that visible Figures are Patterns of, or of the same Species with the respective tangible Figures represented by them: that they are like unto them, and of their own Nature fitted to represent them, as being of the same sort: and that they are in no respect arbitrary Signs, as Words.

CXLII. I answer, it must be acknowledged, the visible Square is fitter than the visible Circle, to represent the tangible Square, but then it is not because it is liker, or more of a Species with it; but because the visible Square contains in it several distinct Parts, whereby to mark the several distinct, corresponding Parts of a tangible Square, whereas the visible Circle doth not. The Square perceived by Touch, hath four distinct, equal Sides, so also hath it four distinct, equal Angles. It is therefore necessary, that the visible Figure which shall be most proper to mark it, contain four distinct equal Parts corresponding to the four Sides of the tangible Square; as likewise four other distinct and equal Parts, whereby to denote the four equal Angles of the tangible Square. And accordingly we see the visible Figures contain in them distinct visible Parts, answering to the distinct tangible Parts of the Figures signified, or suggested by them.

CXLIII. But it will not hence follow, that any visible Figure is like unto, or of the same Species with its corresponding tangible Figure, unless it be also shewn, that not only the Number, but also the Kind of the Parts be the same in both. To illustrate this, I observe that visible Figures represent tangible Figures, much after the same manner that written Words do Sounds. Now, in this respect, Words are not arbitrary, it not being indifferent, what written Word stands for any Sound: But it is requisite, that each Word contain in it so many distinct Characters, as there are Variations in the Sound it stands for. Thus the single Letter a is proper to mark one simple uniform Sound; and the word Adultery is accommodated to represent the Sound annexed to it, in the Formation whereof, there being eight different Collisions, or Modifications of the Air by the Organs of Speech, each of which produces a difference of Sound, it was fit the Word representing it should consist of as many distinct Characters, thereby to mark each particular Difference or Part of the whole Sound: And yet no Body, I presume, will say, the single Letter a, or the Word Adultery are like unto, or of the same Species with the respective Sounds by them represented. It is indeed arbitrary that, in general, Letters of any Language represent Sounds at all: but when that is once agreed, it is not arbitrary what Combination of Letters shall represent this or that particular Sound. I leave this with the Reader to pursue, and apply it in his own Thoughts.

CXLIV. It must be confessed that we are not so apt to confound other Signs with the Things signified, or to think them of the same Species, as we are visible and tangible Ideas. But a little Consideration will shew us how this may be, without our supposing them of a like Nature. These Signs are constant and universal, their Connexion with tangible Ideas has been learnt at our first Entrance into the World; and ever since, almost every Moment of our Lives, it has been occurring to our Thoughts, and fastening and striking deeper on our Minds. When we observe that Signs are variable, and of Humane Institution; when we remember, there was a time they were not connected in our Minds, with those things they now so readily suggest; but that their Signification was learned by the slow Steps of Experience: This preserves us from confounding them. But when we find the same Signs suggest the same Things all over the World; when we know they are not of Humane Institution, and cannot remember that we ever learned their Signification, but think that at first Sight they would have suggested to us the same Things they do now: All this persuades us they are of the same Species as the Things respectively represented by them, and that it is by a natural Resemblance they suggest them to our Minds.

CXLV. Add to this, that whenever we make a nice Survey of any Object, successively directing the Optic Axis to each Point thereof; there are certain Lines and Figures described by the Motion of the Head or Eye, which being in truth perceived by feeling, do nevertheless so mix themselves as it were, with the Ideas of Sight, that we can scarce think but they appertain to that Sense. Again, the Ideas of Sight enter into the Mind, several at once more distinct and unmingled, than is usual in the other Senses beside the Touch. Sounds, for example, perceived at the same Instant, are apt to coalesce, if I may so say, into one Sound: But we can perceive at the same time great variety of visible Objects, very separate and distinct from each other. Now tangible Extension being made up of several distinct coexistent parts, we may hence gather another Reason, that may dispose us to imagine a Likeness or Analogy between the immediate Objects of Sight and Touch. But nothing, certainly, doth more contribute to blend and confound them together, than the strict and close Connexion they have with each other. We cannot open our Eyes, but the Ideas of Distance, Bodies, and tangible Figures are suggested by them. So swift and sudden, and unperceived is the Transition from visible to tangible Ideas, that we can scarce forbear thinking them equally the immediate Object of Vision.

CXLVI. The Prejudice, which is grounded on these, and whatever other Causes may be assigned thereof, sticks so fast, that it is impossible without obstinate Striving, and Labour of the Mind, to get intirely clear of it. But then the Reluctancy we find, in rejecting any Opinion, can be no Argument of its Truth, to whoever considers what has been already shewn, with regard to the Prejudices we entertain concerning the Distance, Magnitude, and Situation of Objects; Prejudices so familiar to our Minds, so confirmed and inveterate, as they will hardly give way to the clearest Demonstration.

CXLVII. Upon the whole, I think we may fairly conclude, that the proper Objects of Vision constitute an universal Language of the Author of Nature, whereby we are instructed how to regulate our Actions, in order to attain those things, that are necessary to the Preservation and Well-being of our Bodies, as also to avoid whatever may be hurtful and destructive of them. It is by their Information that we are principally guided in all the Transactions and Concerns of Life. And the manner wherein they signify, and mark unto us the Objects which are at a Distance, is the same with that of Languages and Signs of Humane Appointment; which do not suggest the things signified, by any Likeness or Identity of Nature, but only by an habitual Connexion, that Experience has made us to observe between them.

CXLVIII. Suppose one who had always continued Blind, be told by his Guide, that after he has advanced so many Steps, he shall come to the Brink of a Precipice, or be stopt by a Wall; must not this to him seem very admirable and surprizing? He cannot conceive how it is possible for Mortals to frame such Predictions as these, which to him would seem as strange and unaccountable, as Prophecy doth to others. Even they who are blessed with the visive Faculty, may (though Familiarity make it less observed) find therein sufficient Cause of Admiration. The wonderful Art and Contrivance wherewith it is adjusted to those Ends and Purposes for which it was apparently designed, the vast Extent, Number, and Variety of Objects that are at once with so much Ease, and Quickness, and Pleasure suggested by it: All these afford Subject for much and pleasing Speculation; and may, if any thing, give us some Glimmering, analogous Prænotion of Things, which are placed beyond the certain Discovery and Comprehension of our present State.

CXLIX. I do not design to trouble my self with drawing Corollaries, from the Doctrine I have hitherto laid down. If it bears the Test, others may, so far as they shall think convenient, employ their Thoughts in extending it farther, and applying it to whatever Purposes it may be subservient to: Only, I cannot forbear making some Inquiry concerning the Object of Geometry, which the Subject we have been upon doth naturally lead one to. We have shewn there is no such Idea as that of Extension in Abstract, and that there are two kinds of sensible Extension and Figures, which are intirely distinct and heterogeneous from each other. Now, it is natural to inquire which of these is the Object of Geometry.

CL. Some things there are, which at first sight incline one to think Geometry conversant about visible Extension. The constant Use of the Eyes, both in the practical and speculative Parts of that Science doth very much induce us thereto. It would, without doubt, seem odd to a Mathematician to go about to convince him, the Diagrams he saw upon Paper were not the Figures, or even the Likeness of the Figures, which make the Subject of the Demonstration. The contrary being held an unquestionable Truth, not only by Mathematicians, but also by those who apply themselves more particularly to the Study of Logick; I mean, who consider the Nature of Science, Certainty, and Demonstration: It being by them assigned as one Reason, of the extraordinary Clearness and Evidence of Geometry, that in this Science the Reasonings are free from those Inconveniences, which attend the Use of arbitrary Signs, the very Ideas themselves being copied out, and exposed to View upon Paper. But, by the bye, how well this agrees with what they likewise assert of abstract Ideas, being the Object of Geometrical Demonstration, I leave to be considered.

CLI. To come to a Resolution in this Point, we need only observe what hath been said in Sect. LIX. LX. LXI. where it is shewn that visible Extensions in themselves are little regarded, and have no settled determinate Greatness, and that Men measure altogether, by the Application of tangible Extension to tangible Extension. All which makes it evident, that visible Extension and Figures are not the Object of Geometry.

CLII. It is therefore plain that visible Figures are of the same Use in Geometry, that Words are: and the one may as well be accounted the Object of that Science, as the other; neither of them being otherwise concerned therein, than as they represent or suggest to the Mind the particular tangible Figures connected with them. There is indeed this Difference between the Signification of tangible Figures by visible Figures, and of Ideas by Words: That whereas the latter is variable and uncertain, depending altogether on the arbitrary Appointment of Men, the former is fixed, and immutably the same in all Times and Places. A visible Square, for Instance, suggests to the Mind the same tangible Figure in Europe, that it doth in America. Hence it is that the Voice of the Author of Nature, which speaks to our Eyes, is not liable to that Misinterpretation and Ambiguity, that Languages of Humane Contrivance are unavoidably subject to.

CLIII. Though what has been said may suffice to shew what ought to be determined, with relation to the Object of Geometry; I shall nevertheless, for the fuller Illustration thereof, consider the Case of an Intelligence, or unbodied Spirit, which is supposed to see perfectly well, i. e. to have a clear Perception of the proper and immediate Objects of Sight, but to have no Sense of Touch. Whether there be any such Being in Nature or no, is beside my purpose to inquire. It sufficeth, that the Supposition contains no Contradiction in it. Let us now examine, what Proficiency such a one may be able to make in Geometry. Which Speculation will lead us more clearly to see, whether the Ideas of Sight can possibly be the Object of that Science.

CLIV. First, then it is certain, the aforesaid Intelligence could have no Idea of a Solid, or Quantity of three Dimensions, which followeth from its not having any Idea of Distance. We indeed are prone to think, that we have by Sight the Ideas of Space and Solids, which ariseth from our imagining that we do, strictly speaking, see Distance, and some Parts of an Object at a greater Distance than others; which has been demonstrated to be the Effect of the Experience we have had, what Ideas of Touch are connected with such and such Ideas attending Vision: But the Intelligence here spoken of is supposed to have no Experience of Touch. He would not, therefore, judge as we do, nor have any Idea of Distance, Outness, or Profundity, nor consequently of Space or Body, either immediately or by Suggestion. Whence it is plain he can have no Notion of those Parts of Geometry, which relate to the Mensuration of Solids, and their convex or concave Surfaces, and contemplate the Properties of Lines generated by the Section of a Solid. The conceiving of any Part whereof, is beyond the Reach of his Faculties.

CLV. Farther, he cannot comprehend the Manner wherein Geometers describe a right Line or Circle; the Rule and Compass with their Use, being things of which it is impossible he should have any Notion: Nor is it an easier matter for him to conceive the placing of one Plain or Angle on another, in order to prove their Equality: Since that supposeth some Idea of Distance, or external Space. All which makes it evident, our pure Intelligence could never attain to know so much as the first Elements of plain Geometry. And perhaps, upon a nice Inquiry, it will be found, he cannot even have an Idea of plain Figures any more than he can of Solids; since some Idea of Distance is necessary, to form the Idea of a Geometrical Plain, as will appear to whoever shall reflect a little on it.

CLVI. All that is properly perceived by the visive Faculty, amounts to no more than Colours with their Variations, and different Proportions of Light and Shade: But, the perpetual Mutability, and Fleetingness of those immediate Objects of Sight, render them incapable of being managed after the manner of Geometrical Figures; nor is it in any Degree useful that they should. It is true, there are divers of them perceived at once; and more of some, and less of others: But accurately to compute their Magnitude, and assign precise determinate Proportions, between things so variable and inconstant, if we suppose it possible to be done, must yet be a very trifling and insignificant Labour.

CLVII. I must confess, Men are tempted to think that flat or plain Figures are immediate Objects of Sight, though they acknowledge Solids are not. And this Opinion is grounded on what is observed in painting, wherein (it seems) the Ideas immediately imprinted on the Mind, are only of Plains variously coloured, which by a sudden Act of the Judgment are changed into Solids: But, with a little Attention we shall find the Plains here mentioned, as the immediate Objects of Sight, are not visible but tangible Plains. For when we say that Pictures are Plains: we mean thereby, that they appear to the Touch smooth and uniform. But then this Smoothness and Uniformity, or, in other Words, this Plainness of the Picture, is not perceived immediately by Vision: For it appeareth to the Eye various and multiform.

CLVIII. From all which we may conclude, that Plains are no more the immediate Object of Sight than Solids. What we strictly see are not Solids, nor yet Plains variously coloured: they are only diversity of Colours. And some of these suggest to the Mind Solids, and others plain Figures; just as they have been experienced to be connected with the one, or the other: So that we see Plains, in the same way that we see Solids; both being equally suggested by the immediate Objects of Sight, which accordingly are themselves denominated Plains and Solids: But though they are called by the same Names, with the things marked by them, they are nevertheless of a Nature intirely different, as hath been demonstrated.

CLIX. What hath been said is, if I mistake not, sufficient to decide the Question we proposed to examine, concerning the Ability of a pure Spirit, such as we have described, to know Geometry: It is, indeed, no easy Matter for us to enter precisely into the Thoughts of such an Intelligence; because we cannot, without great Pains, cleverly separate and disentangle in our Thoughts the proper Objects of Sight from those of Touch which are connected with them. This, indeed, in a compleat Degree, seems scarce possible to be performed: Which will not seem strange to us, if we consider how hard it is, for any one to hear the Words of his Native Language pronounced in his Ears without understanding them. Though he endeavour to disunite the Meaning from the Sound, it will nevertheless intrude into his Thoughts, and he shall find it extreme difficult, if not impossible, to put himself exactly in the Posture of a Foreigner, that never learned the Language, so as to be affected barely with the Sounds themselves, and not perceive the Signification annexed to them. By this time, I suppose, it is clear that neither Abstract, nor visible Extension makes the Object of Geometry; the not discerning of which may perhaps, have created some Difficulty and useless Labour in Mathematics.

A Treatise Concerning the Principles of Human Knowledge

Dedication

To the Right Honourable Thomas, Earl of Pembroke, &c., Knight of the Most Noble Order of the Garter and one of the Lords of Her Majesty's Most Honourable Privy Council

My Lord,
You will perhaps wonder that an obscure person, who has not the honour to be known to your lordship, should presume to address you in this manner. But that a man who has written something with a design to promote Useful Knowledge and Religion in the world should make choice of your lordship for his patron, will not be thought strange by any one that is not altogether unacquainted with the present state of the church and learning, and consequently ignorant how great an ornament and support you are to both. Yet, nothing could have induced me to make you this present of my poor endeavours, were I not encouraged by that candour and native goodness which is so bright a part in your lordship's character. I might add, my lord, that the extraordinary favour and bounty you have been pleased to show towards our Society gave me hopes you would not be unwilling to countenance the studies of one of its members. These considerations determined me to lay this treatise at your lordship's feet, and the rather because I was ambitious to have it known that I am with the truest and most profound respect, on account of that learning and virtue which the world so justly admires in your lordship,
My Lord,
Your lordship's most humble
and most devoted servant,
George Berkeley

Preface

WHAT I here make public has, after a long and scrupulous inquiry, seemed to me evidently true and not unuseful to be known- particularly to those who are tainted with Scepticism, or want a demonstration of the existence and immateriality of God, or the natural immortality of the soul. Whether it be so or no I am content the reader should impartially examine; since I do not think myself any farther concerned for the success of what I have written than as it is agreeable to truth. But, to the end this may not suffer, I make it my request that the reader suspend his judgment till he has once at least read the whole through with that degree of attention and thought which the subject-matter shall seem to deserve. For, as there are some passages that, taken by themselves, are very liable (nor could it be remedied) to gross misinterpretation, and to be charged with most absurd consequences, which, nevertheless, upon an entire perusal will appear not to follow from them; so likewise, though the whole should be read over, yet, if this be done transiently, it is very probable my sense may be mistaken; but to a thinking reader, I flatter myself it will be throughout clear and obvious. As for the characters of novelty and singularity which some of the following notions may seem to bear, it is, I hope, needless to make any apology on that account. He must surely be either very weak, or very little acquainted with the sciences, who shall reject a truth that is capable of demonstration, for no other reason but because it is newly known, and contrary to the prejudices of mankind. Thus much I thought fit to premise, in order to prevent, if possible, the hasty censures of a sort of men who are too apt to condemn an opinion before they rightly comprehend it.

Introduction

1. Philosophy being nothing else but the study of wisdom and truth, it may with reason be expected that those who have spent most time and pains in it should enjoy a greater calm and serenity of mind, a greater clearness and evidence of knowledge, and be less disturbed with doubts and difficulties than other men. Yet so it is, we see the illiterate bulk of mankind that walk the high-road of plain common sense, and are governed by the dictates of nature, for the most part easy and undisturbed. To them nothing that is familiar appears unaccountable or difficult to comprehend. They complain not of any want of evidence in their senses, and are out of all danger of becoming Sceptics. But no sooner do we depart from sense and instinct to follow the light of a superior principle, to reason, meditate, and reflect on the nature of things, but a thousand scruples spring up in our minds concerning those things which before we seemed fully to comprehend. Prejudices and errors of sense do from all parts discover themselves to our view; and, endeavouring to correct these by reason, we are insensibly drawn into uncouth paradoxes, difficulties, and inconsistencies, which multiply and grow upon us as we advance in speculation, till at length, having wandered through many intricate mazes, we find ourselves just where we were, or, which is worse, sit down in a forlorn Scepticism.

2. The cause of this is thought to be the obscurity of things, or the natural weakness and imperfection of our understandings. It is said, the faculties we have are few, and those designed by nature for the support and comfort of life, and not to penetrate into the inward essence and constitution of things. Besides, the mind of man being finite, when it treats of things which partake of infinity, it is not to be wondered at if it run into absurdities and contradictions, out of which it is impossible it should ever extricate itself, it being of the nature of infinite not to be comprehended by that which is finite.

3. But, perhaps, we may be too partial to ourselves in placing the fault originally in our faculties, and not rather in the wrong use we make of them. It is a hard thing to suppose that right deductions from true principles should ever end in consequences which cannot be maintained or made consistent. We should believe that God has dealt more bountifully with the sons of men than to give them a strong desire for that knowledge which he had placed quite out of their reach. This were not agreeable to the wonted indulgent methods of Providence, which, whatever appetites it may have implanted in the creatures, doth usually furnish them with such means as, if rightly made use of, will not fail to satisfy them. Upon the whole, I am inclined to think that the far greater part, if not all, of those difficulties which have hitherto amused philosophers, and blocked up the way to knowledge, are entirely owing to ourselves- that we have first raised a dust and then complain we cannot see.

4. My purpose therefore is, to try if I can discover what those Principles are which have introduced all that doubtfulness and uncertainty, those absurdities and contradictions, into the several sects of philosophy; insomuch that the wisest men have thought our ignorance incurable, conceiving it to arise from the natural dulness and limitation of our faculties. And surely it is a work well deserving our pains to make a strict inquiry concerning the First Principles of Human Knowledge, to sift and examine them on all sides, especially since there may be some grounds to suspect that those lets and difficulties, which stay and embarrass the mind in its search after truth, do not spring from any darkness and intricacy in the objects, or natural defect in the understanding, so much as from false Principles which have been insisted on, and might have been avoided.

5. How difficult and discouraging soever this attempt may seem, when I consider how many great and extraordinary men have gone before me in the like designs, yet I am not without some hopes- upon the consideration that the largest views are not always the clearest, and that he who is short-sighted will be obliged to draw the object nearer, and may, perhaps, by a close and narrow survey, discern that which had escaped far better eyes.

6. In order to prepare the mind of the reader for the easier conceiving what follows, it is proper

to premise somewhat, by way of Introduction, concerning the nature and abuse of Language. But the unravelling this matter leads me in some measure to anticipate my design, by taking notice of what seems to have had a chief part in rendering speculation intricate and perplexed, and to have occasioned innumerable errors and difficulties in almost all parts of knowledge. And that is the opinion that the mind hath a power of framing abstract ideas or notions of things. He who is not a perfect stranger to the writings and disputes of philosophers must needs acknowledge that no small part of them are spent about abstract ideas. These are in a more especial manner thought to be the object of those sciences which go by the name of Logic and Metaphysics, and of all that which passes under the notion of the most abstracted and sublime learning, in all which one shall scarce find any question handled in such a manner as does not suppose their existence in the mind, and that it is well acquainted with them.

7. It is agreed on all hands that the qualities or modes of things do never really exist each of them apart by itself, and separated from all others, but are mixed, as it were, and blended together, several in the same object. But, we are told, the mind being able to consider each quality singly, or abstracted from those other qualities with which it is united, does by that means frame to itself abstract ideas. For example, there is perceived by sight an object extended, coloured, and moved: this mixed or compound idea the mind resolving into its simple, constituent parts, and viewing each by itself, exclusive of the rest, does frame the abstract ideas of extension, colour, and motion. Not that it is possible for colour or motion to exist without extension; but only that the mind can frame to itself by abstraction the idea of colour exclusive of extension, and of motion exclusive of both colour and extension.

8. Again, the mind having observed that in the particular extensions perceived by sense there is something common and alike in all, and some other things peculiar, as this or that figure or magnitude, which distinguish them one from another; it considers apart or singles out by itself that which is common, making thereof a most abstract idea of extension, which is neither line, surface, nor solid, nor has any figure or magnitude, but is an idea entirely prescinded from all these. So likewise the mind, by leaving out of the particular colours perceived by sense that which distinguishes them one from another, and retaining that only which is common to all, makes an idea of colour in abstract which is neither red, nor blue, nor white, nor any other determinate colour. And, in like manner, by considering motion abstractedly not only from the body moved, but likewise from the figure it describes, and all particular directions and velocities, the abstract idea of motion is framed; which equally corresponds to all particular motions whatsoever that may be perceived by sense.

9. And as the mind frames to itself abstract ideas of qualities or modes, so does it, by the same precision or mental separation, attain abstract ideas of the more compounded beings which include several coexistent qualities. For example, the mind having observed that Peter, James, and John resemble each other in certain common agreements of shape and other qualities, leaves out of the complex or compounded idea it has of Peter, James, and any other particular man, that which is peculiar to each, retaining only what is common to all, and so makes an abstract idea wherein all the particulars equally partake- abstracting entirely from and cutting off all those circumstances and differences which might determine it to any particular existence. And after this manner it is said we come by the abstract idea of man, or, if you please, humanity, or human nature; wherein it is true there is included colour, because there is no man but has some colour, but then it can be neither white, nor black, nor any particular colour, because there is no one particular colour wherein all men partake. So likewise there is included stature, but then it is neither tall stature, nor low stature, nor yet middle stature, but something abstracted from all these. And so of the rest. Moreover, their being a great variety of other creatures that partake in some parts, but not all, of the complex idea of man, the mind, leaving out those parts which are peculiar to men, and retaining those only which are common to all the living creatures, frames the idea of animal, which abstracts not only from all particular men, but also all birds, beasts, fishes, and insects. The constituent parts of the abstract idea of animal are body, life, sense, and spontaneous motion. By body is meant body

without any particular shape or figure, there being no one shape or figure common to all animals, without covering, either of hair, or feathers, or scales, &c., nor yet naked: hair, feathers, scales, and nakedness being the distinguishing properties of particular animals, and for that reason left out of the abstract idea. Upon the same account the spontaneous motion must be neither walking, nor flying, nor creeping; it is nevertheless a motion, but what that motion is it is not easy to conceive.

10. Whether others have this wonderful faculty of abstracting their ideas, they best can tell: for myself, I find indeed I have a faculty of imagining, or representing to myself, the ideas of those particular things I have perceived, and of variously compounding and dividing them. I can imagine a man with two heads, or the upper parts of a man joined to the body of a horse. I can consider the hand, the eye, the nose, each by itself abstracted or separated from the rest of the body. But then whatever hand or eye I imagine, it must have some particular shape and colour. Likewise the idea of man that I frame to myself must be either of a white, or a black, or a tawny, a straight, or a crooked, a tall, or a low, or a middle-sized man. I cannot by any effort of thought conceive the abstract idea above described. And it is equally impossible for me to form the abstract idea of motion distinct from the body moving, and which is neither swift nor slow, curvilinear nor rectilinear; and the like may be said of all other abstract general ideas whatsoever. To be plain, I own myself able to abstract in one sense, as when I consider some particular parts or qualities separated from others, with which, though they are united in some object, yet it is possible they may really exist without them. But I deny that I can abstract from one another, or conceive separately, those qualities which it is impossible should exist so separated; or that I can frame a general notion, by abstracting from particulars in the manner aforesaid- which last are the two proper acceptations of abstraction. And there are grounds to think most men will acknowledge themselves to be in my case. The generality of men which are simple and illiterate never pretend to abstract notions. It is said they are difficult and not to be attained without pains and study; we may therefore reasonably conclude that, if such there be, they are confined only to the learned.

11. I proceed to examine what can be alleged in defence of the doctrine of abstraction, and try if I can discover what it is that inclines the men of speculation to embrace an opinion so remote from common sense as that seems to be. There has been a late deservedly esteemed philosopher who, no doubt, has given it very much countenance, by seeming to think the having abstract general ideas is what puts the widest difference in point of understanding betwixt man and beast. "The having of general ideas," saith he, "is that which puts a perfect distinction betwixt man and brutes, and is an excellency which the faculties of brutes do by no means attain unto. For, it is evident we observe no foot-steps in them of making use of general signs for universal ideas; from which we have reason to imagine that they have not the faculty of abstracting, or making general ideas, since they have no use of words or any other general signs." And a little after: "Therefore, I think, we may suppose that it is in this that the species of brutes are discriminated from men, and it is that proper difference wherein they are wholly separated, and which at last widens to so wide a distance. For, if they have any ideas at all, and are not bare machines (as some would have them), we cannot deny them to have some reason. It seems as evident to me that they do, some of them, in certain instances reason as that they have sense; but it is only in particular ideas, just as they receive them from their senses. They are the best of them tied up within those narrow bounds, and have not (as I think) the faculty to enlarge them by any kind of abstraction."- Essay on Human Understanding, II. xi. 10 and 11. I readily agree with this learned author, that the faculties of brutes can by no means attain to abstraction. But then if this be made the distinguishing property of that sort of animals, I fear a great many of those that pass for men must be reckoned into their number. The reason that is here assigned why we have no grounds to think brutes have abstract general ideas is, that we observe in them no use of words or any other general signs; which is built on this supposition- that the making use of words implies the having general ideas. From which it follows that men who use language are able to abstract or generalize their ideas. That this is

the sense and arguing of the author will further appear by his answering the question he in another place puts: "Since all things that exist are only particulars, how come we by general terms?" His answer is: "Words become general by being made the signs of general ideas."- Essay on Human Understanding, IV. iii. 6. But it seems that a word becomes general by being made the sign, not of an abstract general idea, but of several particular ideas, any one of which it indifferently suggests to the mind. For example, when it is said "the change of motion is proportional to the impressed force," or that "whatever has extension is divisible," these propositions are to be understood of motion and extension in general; and nevertheless it will not follow that they suggest to my thoughts an idea of motion without a body moved, or any determinate direction and velocity, or that I must conceive an abstract general idea of extension, which is neither line, surface, nor solid, neither great nor small, black, white, nor red, nor of any other determinate colour. It is only implied that whatever particular motion I consider, whether it be swift or slow, perpendicular, horizontal, or oblique, or in whatever object, the axiom concerning it holds equally true. As does the other of every particular extension, it matters not whether line, surface, or solid, whether of this or that magnitude or figure.

12. By observing how ideas become general we may the better judge how words are made so. And here it is to be noted that I do not deny absolutely there are general ideas, but only that there are any abstract general ideas; for, in the passages we have quoted wherein there is mention of general ideas, it is always supposed that they are formed by abstraction, after the manner set forth in sections 8 and 9. Now, if we will annex a meaning to our words, and speak only of what we can conceive, I believe we shall acknowledge that an idea which, considered in itself, is particular, becomes general by being made to represent or stand for all other particular ideas of the same sort. To make this plain by an example, suppose a geometrician is demonstrating the method of cutting a line in two equal parts. He draws, for instance, a black line of an inch in length: this, which in itself is a particular line, is nevertheless with regard to its signification general, since, as it is there used, it represents all particular lines whatsoever; so that what is demonstrated of it is demonstrated of all lines, or, in other words, of a line in general. And, as that particular line becomes general by being made a sign, so the name "line," which taken absolutely is particular, by being a sign is made general. And as the former owes its generality not to its being the sign of an abstract or general line, but of all particular right lines that may possibly exist, so the latter must be thought to derive its generality from the same cause, namely, the various particular lines which it indifferently denotes.

13. To give the reader a yet clearer view of the nature of abstract ideas, and the uses they are thought necessary to, I shall add one more passage out of the Essay on Human Understanding, (IV. vii. 9) which is as follows: "Abstract ideas are not so obvious or easy to children or the yet unexercised mind as particular ones. If they seem so to grown men it is only because by constant and familiar use they are made so. For, when we nicely reflect upon them, we shall find that general ideas are fictions and contrivances of the mind, that carry difficulty with them, and do not so easily offer themselves as we are apt to imagine. For example, does it not require some pains and skill to form the general idea of a triangle (which is yet none of the most abstract, comprehensive, and difficult); for it must be neither oblique nor rectangle, neither equilateral, equicrural, nor scalenon, but all and none of these at once? In effect, it is something imperfect that cannot exist, an idea wherein some parts of several different and inconsistent ideas are put together. It is true the mind in this imperfect state has need of such ideas, and makes all the haste to them it can, for the conveniency of communication and enlargement of knowledge, to both which it is naturally very much inclined. But yet one has reason to suspect such ideas are marks of our imperfection. At least this is enough to show that the most abstract and general ideas are not those that the mind is first and most easily acquainted with, nor such as its earliest knowledge is conversant about."- If any man has the faculty of framing in his mind such an idea of a triangle as is here described, it is in vain to pretend to dispute him out of it, nor would I go about it. All I desire is that the reader would

fully and certainly inform himself whether he has such an idea or no. And this, methinks, can be no hard task for anyone to perform. What more easy than for anyone to look a little into his own thoughts, and there try whether he has, or can attain to have, an idea that shall correspond with the description that is here given of the general idea of a triangle, which is "neither oblique nor rectangle, equilateral, equicrural nor scalenon, but all and none of these at once?"

14. Much is here said of the difficulty that abstract ideas carry with them, and the pains and skill requisite to the forming them. And it is on all hands agreed that there is need of great toil and labour of the mind, to emancipate our thoughts from particular objects, and raise them to those sublime speculations that are conversant about abstract ideas. From all which the natural consequence should seem to be, that so difficult a thing as the forming abstract ideas was not necessary for communication, which is so easy and familiar to all sorts of men. But, we are told, if they seem obvious and easy to grown men, it is only because by constant and familiar use they are made so. Now, I would fain know at what time it is men are employed in surmounting that difficulty, and furnishing themselves with those necessary helps for discourse. It cannot be when they are grown up, for then it seems they are not conscious of any such painstaking; it remains therefore to be the business of their childhood. And surely the great and multiplied labour of framing abstract notions will be found a hard task for that tender age. Is it not a hard thing to imagine that a couple of children cannot prate together of their sugar-plums and rattles and the rest of their little trinkets, till they have first tacked together numberless inconsistencies, and so framed in their minds abstract general ideas, and annexed them to every common name they make use of?

15. Nor do I think them a whit more needful for the enlargement of knowledge than for communication. It is, I know, a point much insisted on, that all knowledge and demonstration are about universal notions, to which I fully agree: but then it doth not appear to me that those notions are formed by abstraction in the manner premiseduniversality, so far as I can comprehend, not consisting in the absolute, positive nature or conception of anything, but in the relation it bears to the particulars signified or represented by it; by virtue whereof it is that things, names, or notions, being in their own nature particular, are rendered universal. Thus, when I demonstrate any proposition concerning triangles, it is to be supposed that I have in view the universal idea of a triangle; which ought not to be understood as if I could frame an idea of a triangle which was neither equilateral, nor scalenon, nor equicrural; but only that the particular triangle I consider, whether of this or that sort it matters not, doth equally stand for and represent all rectilinear triangles whatsoever, and is in that sense universal. All which seems very plain and not to include any difficulty in it.

16. But here it will be demanded, how we can know any proposition to be true of all particular triangles, except we have first seen it demonstrated of the abstract idea of a triangle which equally agrees to all? For, because a property may be demonstrated to agree to some one particular triangle, it will not thence follow that it equally belongs to any other triangle, which in all respects is not the same with it. For example, having demonstrated that the three angles of an isosceles rectangular triangle are equal to two right ones, I cannot therefore conclude this affection agrees to all other triangles which have neither a right angle nor two equal sides. It seems therefore that, to be certain this proposition is universally true, we must either make a particular demonstration for every particular triangle, which is impossible, or once for all demonstrate it of the abstract idea of a triangle, in which all the particulars do indifferently partake and by which they are all equally represented. To which I answer, that, though the idea I have in view whilst I make the demonstration be, for instance, that of an isosceles rectangular triangle whose sides are of a determinate length, I may nevertheless be certain it extends to all other rectilinear triangles, of what sort or bigness soever. And that because neither the right angle, nor the equality, nor determinate length of the sides are at all concerned in the demonstration. It is true the diagram I have in view includes all these particulars, but then there is not the least mention made of them in the proof of the proposition. It is not said the three angles are equal to two right ones, because one of them is a right angle, or because

the sides comprehending it are of the same length. Which sufficiently shows that the right angle might have been oblique, and the sides unequal, and for all that the demonstration have held good. And for this reason it is that I conclude that to be true of any obliquangular or scalenon which I had demonstrated of a particular right-angled equicrural triangle, and not because I demonstrated the proposition of the abstract idea of a triangle And here it must be acknowledged that a man may consider a figure merely as triangular, without attending to the particular qualities of the angles, or relations of the sides. So far he may abstract; but this will never prove that he can frame an abstract, general, inconsistent idea of a triangle. In like manner we may consider Peter so far forth as man, or so far forth as animal without framing the fore-mentioned abstract idea, either of man or of animal, inasmuch as all that is perceived is not considered.

17. It were an endless as well as an useless thing to trace the Schoolmen, those great masters of abstraction, through all the manifold inextricable labyrinths of error and dispute which their doctrine of abstract natures and notions seems to have led them into. What bickerings and controversies, and what a learned dust have been raised about those matters, and what mighty advantage has been from thence derived to mankind, are things at this day too clearly known to need being insisted on. And it had been well if the ill effects of that doctrine were confined to those only who make the most avowed profession of it. When men consider the great pains, industry, and parts that have for so many ages been laid out on the cultivation and advancement of the sciences, and that notwithstanding all this the far greater part of them remains full of darkness and uncertainty, and disputes that are like never to have an end, and even those that are thought to be supported by the most clear and cogent demonstrations contain in them paradoxes which are perfectly irreconcilable to the understandings of men, and that, taking all together, a very small portion of them does supply any real benefit to mankind, otherwise than by being an innocent diversion and amusement- I say the consideration of all this is apt to throw them into a despondency and perfect contempt of all study. But this may perhaps cease upon a view of the false principles that have obtained in the world, amongst all which there is none, methinks, hath a more wide and extended sway over the thoughts of speculative men than this of abstract general ideas.

18. I come now to consider the source of this prevailing notion, and that seems to me to be language. And surely nothing of less extent than reason itself could have been the source of an opinion so universally received. The truth of this appears as from other reasons so also from the plain confession of the ablest patrons of abstract ideas, who acknowledge that they are made in order to naming; from which it is a clear consequence that if there had been no such things as speech or universal signs there never had been any thought of abstraction. See III. vi. 39, and elsewhere of the Essay on Human Understanding. Let us examine the manner wherein words have contributed to the origin of that mistake.- First then, it is thought that every name has, or ought to have, one only precise and settled signification, which inclines men to think there are certain abstract, determinate ideas that constitute the true and only immediate signification of each general name; and that it is by the mediation of these abstract ideas that a general name comes to signify any particular thing. Whereas, in truth, there is no such thing as one precise and definite signification annexed to any general name, they all signifying indifferently a great number of particular ideas. All which doth evidently follow from what has been already said, and will clearly appear to anyone by a little reflexion. To this it will be objected that every name that has a definition is thereby restrained to one certain signification. For example, a triangle is defined to be "a plain surface comprehended by three right lines," by which that name is limited to denote one certain idea and no other. To which I answer, that in the definition it is not said whether the surface be great or small, black or white, nor whether the sides are long or short, equal or unequal, nor with what angles they are inclined to each other; in all which there may be great variety, and consequently there is no one settled idea which limits the signification of the word triangle. It is one thing for to keep a name constantly to the same definition, and another to make it stand everywhere for the same idea; the one is

necessary, the other useless and impracticable.

19. But, to give a farther account how words came to produce the doctrine of abstract ideas, it must be observed that it is a received opinion that language has no other end but the communicating our ideas, and that every significant name stands for an idea. This being so, and it being withal certain that names which yet are not thought altogether insignificant do not always mark out particular conceivable ideas, it is straightway concluded that they stand for abstract notions. That there are many names in use amongst speculative men which do not always suggest to others determinate, particular ideas, or in truth anything at all, is what nobody will deny. And a little attention will discover that it is not necessary (even in the strictest reasonings) significant names which stand for ideas should, every time they are used, excite in the understanding the ideas they are made to stand for- in reading and discoursing, names being for the most part used as letters are in Algebra, in which, though a particular quantity be marked by each letter, yet to proceed right it is not requisite that in every step each letter suggest to your thoughts that particular quantity it was appointed to stand for.

20. Besides, the communicating of ideas marked by words is not the chief and only end of language, as is commonly supposed. There are other ends, as the raising of some passion, the exciting to or deterring from an action, the putting the mind in some particular disposition- to which the former is in many cases barely subservient, and sometimes entirely omitted, when these can be obtained without it, as I think does not unfrequently happen in the familiar use of language. I entreat the reader to reflect with himself, and see if it doth not often happen, either in hearing or reading a discourse, that the passions of fear, love, hatred, admiration, disdain, and the like, arise immediately in his mind upon the perception of certain words, without any ideas coming between. At first, indeed, the words might have occasioned ideas that were fitting to produce those emotions; but, if I mistake not, it will be found that, when language is once grown familiar, the hearing of the sounds or sight of the characters is oft immediately attended with those passions which at first were wont to be produced by the intervention of ideas that are now quite omitted. May we not, for example, be affected with the promise of a good thing, though we have not an idea of what it is? Or is not the being threatened with danger sufficient to excite a dread, though we think not of any particular evil likely to befal us, nor yet frame to ourselves an idea of danger in abstract? If any one shall join ever so little reflexion of his own to what has been said, I believe that it will evidently appear to him that general names are often used in the propriety of language without the speaker's designing them for marks of ideas in his own, which he would have them raise in the mind of the hearer. Even proper names themselves do not seem always spoken with a design to bring into our view the ideas of those individuals that are supposed to be marked by them. For example, when a schoolman tells me "Aristotle hath said it," all I conceive he means by it is to dispose me to embrace his opinion with the deference and submission which custom has annexed to that name. And this effect is often so instantly produced in the minds of those who are accustomed to resign their judgment to authority of that philosopher, as it is impossible any idea either of his person, writings, or reputation should go before. Innumerable examples of this kind may be given, but why should I insist on those things which every one's experience will, I doubt not, plentifully suggest unto him?

21. We have, I think, shewn the impossibility of Abstract Ideas. We have considered what has been said for them by their ablest patrons; and endeavored to show they are of no use for those ends to which they are thought necessary. And lastly, we have traced them to the source from whence they flow, which appears evidently to be language.- It cannot be denied that words are of excellent use, in that by their means all that stock of knowledge which has been purchased by the joint labours of inquisitive men in all ages and nations may be drawn into the view and made the possession of one single person. But at the same time it must be owned that most parts of knowledge have been strangely perplexed and darkened by the abuse of words, and general ways of speech wherein they are delivered. Since therefore words are so apt to impose on the understanding, whatever ideas I consider, I shall endeavour to take them bare and naked

into my view, keeping out of my thoughts so far as I am able, those names which long and constant use hath so strictly united with them; from which I may expect to derive the following advantages:

22. First, I shall be sure to get clear of all controversies purely verbal- the springing up of which weeds in almost all the sciences has been a main hindrance to the growth of true and sound knowledge. Secondly, this seems to be a sure way to extricate myself out of that fine and subtle net of abstract ideas which has so miserably perplexed and entangled the minds of men; and that with this peculiar circumstance, that by how much the finer and more curious was the wit of any man, by so much the deeper was he likely to be ensnared and faster held therein. Thirdly, so long as I confine my thoughts to my own ideas divested of words, I do not see how I can easily be mistaken. The objects I consider, I clearly and adequately know. I cannot be deceived in thinking I have an idea which I have not. It is not possible for me to imagine that any of my own ideas are alike or unlike that are not truly so. To discern the agreements or disagreements there are between my ideas, to see what ideas are included in any compound idea and what not, there is nothing more requisite than an attentive perception of what passes in my own understanding.

23. But the attainment of all these advantages doth presuppose an entire deliverance from the deception of words, which I dare hardly promise myself; so difficult a thing it is to dissolve an union so early begun, and confirmed by so long a habit as that betwixt words and ideas. Which difficulty seems to have been very much increased by the doctrine of abstraction. For, so long as men thought abstract ideas were annexed to their words, it doth not seem strange that they should use words for ideas- it being found an impracticable thing to lay aside the word, and retain the abstract idea in the mind, which in itself was perfectly inconceivable. This seems to me the principal cause why those men who have so emphatically recommended to others the laying aside all use of words in their meditations, and contemplating their bare ideas, have yet failed to perform it themselves. Of late many have been very sensible of the absurd opinions and insignificant disputes which grow out of the abuse of words. And, in order to remedy these evils, they advise well, that we attend to the ideas signified, and draw off our attention from the words which signify them. But, how good soever this advice may be they have given others, it is plain they could not have a due regard to it themselves, so long as they thought the only immediate use of words was to signify ideas, and that the immediate signification of every general name was a determinate abstract idea.

24. But, these being known to be mistakes, a man may with greater ease prevent his being imposed on by words. He that knows he has no other than particular ideas, will not puzzle himself in vain to find out and conceive the abstract idea annexed to any name. And he that knows names do not always stand for ideas will spare himself the labour of looking for ideas where there are none to be had. It were, therefore, to be wished that everyone would use his utmost endeavours to obtain a clear view of the ideas he would consider, separating from them all that dress and incumbrance of words which so much contribute to blind the judgment and divide the attention. In vain do we extend our view into the heavens and pry into the entrails of the earth, in vain do we consult the writings of learned men and trace the dark footsteps of antiquity- we need only draw the curtain of words, to hold the fairest tree of knowledge, whose fruit is excellent, and within the reach of our hand.

25. Unless we take care to clear the First Principles of Knowledge from the embarras and delusion of words, we may make infinite reasonings upon them to no purpose; we may draw consequences from consequences, and be never the wiser. The farther we go, we shall only lose ourselves the more irrecoverably, and be the deeper entangled in difficulties and mistakes. Whoever therefore designs to read the following sheets, I entreat him to make my words the occasion of his own thinking, and endeavour to attain the same train of thoughts in reading that I had in writing them. By this means it will be easy for him to discover the truth or falsity of what I say. He will be out of all danger of being deceived by my words, and I do not see how he can be led into an error by considering his own naked, undisguised ideas.

1. It is evident to any one who takes a survey of the objects of human knowledge, that they are either ideas actually imprinted on the senses; or else such as are perceived by attending to the passions and operations of the mind; or lastly, ideas formed by help of memory and imagination- either compounding, dividing, or barely representing those originally perceived in the aforesaid ways. By sight I have the ideas of light and colours, with their several degrees and variations. By touch I perceive hard and soft, heat and cold, motion and resistance, and of all these more and less either as to quantity or degree. Smelling furnishes me with odours; the palate with tastes; and hearing conveys sounds to the mind in all their variety of tone and composition. And as several of these are observed to accompany each other, they come to be marked by one name, and so to be reputed as one thing. Thus, for example a certain colour, taste, smell, figure and consistence having been observed to go together, are accounted one distinct thing, signified by the name apple; other collections of ideas constitute a stone, a tree, a book, and the like sensible things- which as they are pleasing or disagreeable excite the passions of love, hatred, joy, grief, and so forth.

2. But, besides all that endless variety of ideas or objects of knowledge, there is likewise something which knows or perceives them, and exercises divers operations, as willing, imagining, remembering, about them. This perceiving, active being is what I call mind, spirit, soul, or myself. By which words I do not denote any one of my ideas, but a thing entirely distinct from them, wherein, they exist, or, which is the same thing, whereby they are perceivedfor the existence of an idea consists in being perceived.

3. That neither our thoughts, nor passions, nor ideas formed by the imagination, exist without the mind, is what everybody will allow. And it seems no less evident that the various sensations or ideas imprinted on the sense, however blended or combined together (that is, whatever objects they compose), cannot exist otherwise than in a mind perceiving them.- I think an intuitive knowledge may be obtained of this by any one that shall attend to what is meant by the term exists, when applied to sensible things. The table I write on I say exists, that is, I see and feel it; and if I were out of my study I should say it existed- meaning thereby that if I was in my study I might perceive it, or that some other spirit actually does perceive it. There was an odour, that is, it was smelt; there was a sound, that is, it was heard; a colour or figure, and it was perceived by sight or touch. This is all that I can understand by these and the like expressions. For as to what is said of the absolute existence of unthinking things without any relation to their being perceived, that seems perfectly unintelligible. Their esse is percepi, nor is it possible they should have any existence out of the minds or thinking things which perceive them.

4. It is indeed an opinion strangely prevailing amongst men, that houses, mountains, rivers, and in a word all sensible objects, have an existence, natural or real, distinct from their being perceived by the understanding. But, with how great an assurance and acquiescence soever this principle may be entertained in the world, yet whoever shall find in his heart to call it in question may, if I mistake not, perceive it to involve a manifest contradiction. For, what are the fore-mentioned objects but the things we perceive by sense? and what do we perceive besides our own ideas or sensations? and is it not plainly repugnant that any one of these, or any combination of them, should exist unperceived?

5. If we thoroughly examine this tenet it will, perhaps, be found at bottom to depend on the doctrine of abstract ideas. For can there be a nicer strain of abstraction than to distinguish the existence of sensible objects from their being perceived, so as to conceive them existing unperceived? Light and colours, heat and cold, extension and figures- in a word the things we see and feel- what are they but so many sensations, notions, ideas, or impressions on the sense? and is it possible to separate, even in thought, any of these from perception? For my part, I might as easily divide a thing from itself. I may, indeed, divide in my thoughts, or conceive apart from each other, those things which, perhaps I never perceived by sense so divided. Thus, I imagine the trunk of a human body without the limbs, or conceive the smell of a rose without thinking on the rose itself. So far, I will not deny, I can abstract- if that may

properly be called abstraction which extends only to the conceiving separately such objects as it is possible may really exist or be actually perceived asunder. But my conceiving or imagining power does not extend beyond the possibility of real existence or perception. Hence, as it is impossible for me to see or feel anything without an actual sensation of that thing, so is it impossible for me to conceive in my thoughts any sensible thing or object distinct from the sensation or perception of it.

6. Some truths there are so near and obvious to the mind that a man need only open his eyes to see them. Such I take this important one to be, viz., that all the choir of heaven and furniture of the earth, in a word all those bodies which compose the mighty frame of the world, have not any subsistence without a mind, that their being is to be perceived or known; that consequently so long as they are not actually perceived by me, or do not exist in my mind or that of any other created spirit, they must either have no existence at all, or else subsist in the mind of some Eternal Spirit- it being perfectly unintelligible, and involving all the absurdity of abstraction, to attribute to any single part of them an existence independent of a spirit. To be convinced of which, the reader need only reflect, and try to separate in his own thoughts the being of a sensible thing from its being perceived.

7. From what has been said it follows there is not any other Substance than Spirit, or that which perceives. But, for the fuller proof of this point, let it be considered the sensible qualities are colour, figure, motion, smell, taste, etc., i.e. the ideas perceived by sense. Now, for an idea to exist in an unperceiving thing is a manifest contradiction, for to have an idea is all one as to perceive; that therefore wherein colour, figure, and the like qualities exist must perceive them; hence it is clear there can be no unthinking substance or substratum of those ideas.

8. But, say you, though the ideas themselves do not exist without the mind, yet there may be things like them, whereof they are copies or resemblances, which things exist without the mind in an unthinking substance. I answer, an idea can be like nothing but an idea; a colour or figure can be like nothing but another colour or figure. If we look but never so little into our thoughts, we shall find it impossible for us to conceive a likeness except only between our ideas. Again, I ask whether those supposed originals or external things, of which our ideas are the pictures or representations, be themselves perceivable or no? If they are, then they are ideas and we have gained our point; but if you say they are not, I appeal to any one whether it be sense to assert a colour is something which is invisible; hard or soft, like something which is intangible; and so of the rest.

9. Some there are who make a distinction betwixt primary and secondary qualities. By the former they mean extension, figure, motion, rest, solidity or impenetrability, and number; by the latter they denote all other sensible qualities, as colours, sounds, tastes, and so forth. The ideas we have of these they acknowledge not to be the resemblances of anything existing without the mind, or unperceived, but they will have our ideas of the primary qualities to be patterns or images of things which exist without the mind, in an unthinking substance which they call Matter. By Matter, therefore, we are to understand an inert, senseless substance, in which extension, figure, and motion do actually subsist. But it is evident from what we have already shown, that extension, figure, and motion are only ideas existing in the mind, and that an idea can be like nothing but another idea, and that consequently neither they nor their archetypes can exist in an unperceiving substance. Hence, it is plain that that the very notion of what is called Matter or corporeal substance, involves a contradiction in it.

10. They who assert that figure, motion, and the rest of the primary or original qualities do exist without the mind in unthinking substances, do at the same time acknowledge that colours, sounds, heat cold, and suchlike secondary qualities, do not- which they tell us are sensations existing in the mind alone, that depend on and are occasioned by the different size, texture, and motion of the minute particles of matter. This they take for an undoubted truth, which they can demonstrate beyond all exception. Now, if it be certain that those original qualities are inseparably united with the other sensible qualities, and not, even in thought,

capable of being abstracted from them, it plainly follows that they exist only in the mind. But I desire any one to reflect and try whether he can, by any abstraction of thought, conceive the extension and motion of a body without all other sensible qualities. For my own part, I see evidently that it is not in my power to frame an idea of a body extended and moving, but I must withal give it some colour or other sensible quality which is acknowledged to exist only in the mind. In short, extension, figure, and motion, abstracted from all other qualities, are inconceivable. Where therefore the other sensible qualities are, there must these be also, to wit, in the mind and nowhere else.

11. Again, great and small, swift and slow, are allowed to exist nowhere without the mind, being entirely relative, and changing as the frame or position of the organs of sense varies. The extension therefore which exists without the mind is neither great nor small, the motion neither swift nor slow, that is, they are nothing at all. But, say you, they are extension in general, and motion in general: thus we see how much the tenet of extended movable substances existing without the mind depends on the strange doctrine of abstract ideas. And here I cannot but remark how nearly the vague and indeterminate description of Matter or corporeal substance, which the modern philosophers are run into by their own principles, resembles that antiquated and so much ridiculed notion of materia prima, to be met with in Aristotle and his followers. Without extension solidity cannot be conceived; since therefore it has been shewn that extension exists not in an unthinking substance, the same must also be true of solidity.

12. That number is entirely the creature of the mind, even though the other qualities be allowed to exist without, will be evident to whoever considers that the same thing bears a different denomination of number as the mind views it with different respects. Thus, the same extension is one, or three, or thirty-six, according as the mind considers it with reference to a yard, a foot, or an inch. Number is so visibly relative, and dependent on men's understanding, that it is strange to think how any one should give it an absolute existence without the mind. We say one book, one page, one line, etc.; all these are equally units, though some contain several of the others. And in each instance, it is plain, the unit relates to some particular combination of ideas arbitrarily put together by the mind.

13. Unity I know some will have to be a simple or uncompounded idea, accompanying all other ideas into the mind. That I have any such idea answering the word unity I do not find; and if I had, methinks I could not miss finding it: on the contrary, it should be the most familiar to my understanding, since it is said to accompany all other ideas, and to be perceived by all the ways of sensation and reflexion. To say no more, it is an abstract idea.

14. I shall farther add, that, after the same manner as modern philosophers prove certain sensible qualities to have no existence in Matter, or without the mind, the same thing may be likewise proved of all other sensible qualities whatsoever. Thus, for instance, it is said that heat and cold are affections only of the mind, and not at all patterns of real beings, existing in the corporeal substances which excite them, for that the same body which appears cold to one hand seems warm to another. Now, why may we not as well argue that figure and extension are not patterns or resemblances of qualities existing in Matter, because to the same eye at different stations, or eyes of a different texture at the same station, they appear various, and cannot therefore be the images of anything settled and determinate without the mind? Again, it is proved that sweetness is not really in the sapid thing, because the thing remaining unaltered the sweetness is changed into bitter, as in case of a fever or otherwise vitiated palate. Is it not as reasonable to say that motion is not without the mind, since if the succession of ideas in the mind become swifter, the motion, it is acknowledged, shall appear slower without any alteration in any external object?

15. In short, let any one consider those arguments which are thought manifestly to prove that colours and taste exist only in the mind, and he shall find they may with equal force be brought to prove the same thing of extension, figure, and motion. Though it must be confessed this method of arguing does not so much prove that there is no extension or colour in an outward object, as that we do not know by sense which is the true extension or colour of the

object. But the arguments foregoing plainly shew it to be impossible that any colour or extension at all, or other sensible quality whatsoever, should exist in an unthinking subject without the mind, or in truth, that there should be any such thing as an outward object.

16. But let us examine a little the received opinion.- It is said extension is a mode or accident of Matter, and that Matter is the substratum that supports it. Now I desire that you would explain to me what is meant by Matter's supporting extension. Say you, I have no idea of Matter and therefore cannot explain it. I answer, though you have no positive, yet, if you have any meaning at all, you must at least have a relative idea of Matter; though you know not what it is, yet you must be supposed to know what relation it bears to accidents, and what is meant by its supporting them. It is evident "support" cannot here be taken in its usual or literal sense- as when we say that pillars support a building; in what sense therefore must it be taken?

17. If we inquire into what the most accurate philosophers declare themselves to mean by material substance, we shall find them acknowledge they have no other meaning annexed to those sounds but the idea of Being in general, together with the relative notion of its supporting accidents. The general idea of Being appeareth to me the most abstract and incomprehensible of all other; and as for its supporting accidents, this, as we have just now observed, cannot be understood in the common sense of those words; it must therefore be taken in some other sense, but what that is they do not explain. So that when I consider the two parts or branches which make the signification of the words material substance, I am convinced there is no distinct meaning annexed to them. But why should we trouble ourselves any farther, in discussing this material substratum or support of figure and motion, and other sensible qualities? Does it not suppose they have an existence without the mind? And is not this a direct repugnancy, and altogether inconceivable?

18. But, though it were possible that solid, figured, movable substances may exist without the mind, corresponding to the ideas we have of bodies, yet how is it possible for us to know this? Either we must know it by sense or by reason. As for our senses, by them we have the knowledge only of our sensations, ideas, or those things that are immediately perceived by sense, call them what you will: but they do not inform us that things exist without the mind, or unperceived, like to those which are perceived. This the materialists themselves acknowledge. It remains therefore that if we have any knowledge at all of external things, it must be by reason, inferring their existence from what is immediately perceived by sense. But what reason can induce us to believe the existence of bodies without the mind, from what we perceive, since the very patrons of Matter themselves do not pretend there is any necessary connexion betwixt them and our ideas? I say it is granted on all hands (and what happens in dreams, phrensies, and the like, puts it beyond dispute) that it is possible we might be affected with all the ideas we have now, though there were no bodies existing without resembling them. Hence, it is evident the supposition of external bodies is not necessary for the producing our ideas; since it is granted they are produced sometimes, and might possibly be produced always in the same order, we see them in at present, without their concurrence.

19. But, though we might possibly have all our sensations without them, yet perhaps it may be thought easier to conceive and explain the manner of their production, by supposing external bodies in their likeness rather than otherwise; and so it might be at least probable there are such things as bodies that excite their ideas in our minds. But neither can this be said; for, though we give the materialists their external bodies, they by their own confession are never the nearer knowing how our ideas are produced; since they own themselves unable to comprehend in what manner body can act upon spirit, or how it is possible it should imprint any idea in the mind. Hence it is evident the production of ideas or sensations in our minds can be no reason why we should suppose Matter or corporeal substances, since that is acknowledged to remain equally inexplicable with or without this supposition. If therefore it were possible for bodies to exist without the mind, yet to hold they do so, must needs be a very precarious opinion; since it is to suppose, without any reason at all, that God has created innumerable beings that are entirely useless, and serve to no manner of purpose.

20. In short, if there were external bodies, it is impossible we should ever come to know it; and if there were not, we might have the very same reasons to think there were that we have now. Suppose what no one can deny possible- an intelligence without the help of external bodies, to be affected with the same train of sensations or ideas that you are, imprinted in the same order and with like vividness in his mind. I ask whether that intelligence hath not all the reason to believe the existence of corporeal substances, represented by his ideas, and exciting them in his mind, that you can possibly have for believing the same thing? Of this there can be no question- which one consideration were enough to make any reasonable person suspect the strength of whatever arguments he may think himself to have, for the existence of bodies without the mind.

21. Were it necessary to add any farther proof against the existence of Matter after what has been said, I could instance several of those errors and difficulties (not to mention impieties) which have sprung from that tenet. It has occasioned numberless controversies and disputes in philosophy, and not a few of far greater moment in religion. But I shall not enter into the detail of them in this place, as well because I think arguments a posteriori are unnecessary for confirming what has been, if I mistake not, sufficiently demonstrated a priori, as because I shall hereafter find occasion to speak somewhat of them.

22. I am afraid I have given cause to think I am needlessly prolix in handling this subject. For, to what purpose is it to dilate on that which may be demonstrated with the utmost evidence in a line or two, to any one that is capable of the least reflexion? It is but looking into your own thoughts, and so trying whether you can conceive it possible for a sound, or figure, or motion, or colour to exist without the mind or unperceived. This easy trial may perhaps make you see that what you contend for is a downright contradiction. Insomuch that I am content to put the whole upon this issue:- If you can but conceive it possible for one extended movable substance, or, in general, for any one idea, or anything like an idea, to exist otherwise than in a mind perceiving it, I shall readily give up the cause. And, as for all that compages of external bodies you contend for, I shall grant you its existence, though you cannot either give me any reason why you believe it exists, or assign any use to it when it is supposed to exist. I say, the bare possibility of your opinions being true shall pass for an argument that it is so.

23. But, say you, surely there is nothing easier than for me to imagine trees, for instance, in a park, or books existing in a closet, and nobody by to perceive them. I answer, you may so, there is no difficulty in it; but what is all this, I beseech you, more than framing in your mind certain ideas which you call books and trees, and the same time omitting to frame the idea of any one that may perceive them? But do not you yourself perceive or think of them all the while? This therefore is nothing to the purpose; it only shews you have the power of imagining or forming ideas in your mind: but it does not shew that you can conceive it possible the objects of your thought may exist without the mind. To make out this, it is necessary that you conceive them existing unconceived or unthought of, which is a manifest repugnancy. When we do our utmost to conceive the existence of external bodies, we are all the while only contemplating our own ideas. But the mind taking no notice of itself, is deluded to think it can and does conceive bodies existing unthought of or without the mind, though at the same time they are apprehended by or exist in itself. A little attention will discover to any one the truth and evidence of what is here said, and make it unnecessary to insist on any other proofs against the existence of material substance.

24. It is very obvious, upon the least inquiry into our thoughts, to know whether it is possible for us to understand what is meant by the absolute existence of sensible objects in themselves, or without the mind. To me it is evident those words mark out either a direct contradiction, or else nothing at all. And to convince others of this, I know no readier or fairer way than to entreat they would calmly attend to their own thoughts; and if by this attention the emptiness or repugnancy of those expressions does appear, surely nothing more is requisite for the conviction. It is on this therefore that I insist, to wit, that the absolute existence of unthinking things are words without a meaning, or which include a contradiction. This is what I repeat

and inculcate, and earnestly recommend to the attentive thoughts of the reader.

25. All our ideas, sensations, notions, or the things which we perceive, by whatsoever names they may be distinguished, are visibly inactive- there is nothing of power or agency included in them. So that one idea or object of thought cannot produce or make any alteration in another. To be satisfied of the truth of this, there is nothing else requisite but a bare observation of our ideas. For, since they and every part of them exist only in the mind, it follows that there is nothing in them but what is perceived: but whoever shall attend to his ideas, whether of sense or reflexion, will not perceive in them any power or activity; there is, therefore, no such thing contained in them. A little attention will discover to us that the very being of an idea implies passiveness and inertness in it, insomuch that it is impossible for an idea to do anything, or, strictly speaking, to be the cause of anything: neither can it be the resemblance or pattern of any active being, as is evident from sect. 8. Whence it plainly follows that extension, figure, and motion cannot be the cause of our sensations. To say, therefore, that these are the effects of powers resulting from the configuration, number, motion, and size of corpuscles, must certainly be false.

26. We perceive a continual succession of ideas, some are anew excited, others are changed or totally disappear. There is therefore some cause of these ideas, whereon they depend, and which produces and changes them. That this cause cannot be any quality or idea or combination of ideas, is clear from the preceding section. I must therefore be a substance; but it has been shewn that there is no corporeal or material substance: it remains therefore that the cause of ideas is an incorporeal active substance or Spirit.

27. A spirit is one simple, undivided, active being- as it perceives ideas it is called the understanding, and as it produces or otherwise operates about them it is called the will. Hence there can be no idea formed of a soul or spirit; for all ideas whatever, being passive and inert (vide sect. 25), they cannot represent unto us, by way of image or likeness, that which acts. A little attention will make it plain to any one, that to have an idea which shall be like that active principle of motion and change of ideas is absolutely impossible. Such is the nature of spirit, or that which acts, that it cannot be of itself perceived, but only by the effects which it produceth. If any man shall doubt of the truth of what is here delivered, let him but reflect and try if he can frame the idea of any power or active being, and whether he has ideas of two principal powers, marked by the names will and understanding, distinct from each other as well as from a third idea of Substance or Being in general, with a relative notion of its supporting or being the subject of the aforesaid powers- which is signified by the name soul or spirit. This is what some hold; but, so far as I can see, the words will, soul, spirit, do not stand for different ideas, or, in truth, for any idea at all, but for something which is very different from ideas, and which, being an agent, cannot be like unto, or represented by, any idea whatsoever. Though it must be owned at the same time that we have some notion of soul, spirit, and the operations of the mind: such as willing, loving, hating- inasmuch as we know or understand the meaning of these words.

28. I find I can excite ideas in my mind at pleasure, and vary and shift the scene as oft as I think fit. It is no more than willing, and straightway this or that idea arises in my fancy; and by the same power it is obliterated and makes way for another. This making and unmaking of ideas doth very properly denominate the mind active. Thus much is certain and grounded on experience; but when we think of unthinking agents or of exciting ideas exclusive of volition, we only amuse ourselves with words.

29. But, whatever power I may have over my own thoughts, I find the ideas actually perceived by Sense have not a like dependence on my will. When in broad daylight I open my eyes, it is not in my power to choose whether I shall see or no, or to determine what particular objects shall present themselves to my view; and so likewise as to the hearing and other senses; the ideas imprinted on them are not creatures of my will. There is therefore some other Will or Spirit that produces them.

30. The ideas of Sense are more strong, lively, and distinct than those of the imagination; they

have likewise a steadiness, order, and coherence, and are not excited at random, as those which are the effects of human wills often are, but in a regular train or series, the admirable connexion whereof sufficiently testifies the wisdom and benevolence of its Author. Now the set rules or established methods wherein the Mind we depend on excites in us the ideas of sense, are called the laws of nature; and these we learn by experience, which teaches us that such and such ideas are attended with such and such other ideas, in the ordinary course of things.

31. This gives us a sort of foresight which enables us to regulate our actions for the benefit of life. And without this we should be eternally at a loss; we could not know how to act anything that might procure us the least pleasure, or remove the least pain of sense. That food nourishes, sleep refreshes, and fire warms us; that to sow in the seed-time is the way to reap in the harvest; and in general that to obtain such or such ends, such or such means are conducive- all this we know, not by discovering any necessary connexion between our ideas, but only by the observation of the settled laws of nature, without which we should be all in uncertainty and confusion, and a grown man no more know how to manage himself in the affairs of life than an infant just born.

32. And yet this consistent uniform working, which so evidently displays the goodness and wisdom of that Governing Spirit whose Will constitutes the laws of nature, is so far from leading our thoughts to Him, that it rather sends them wandering after second causes. For, when we perceive certain ideas of Sense constantly followed by other ideas and we know this is not of our own doing, we forthwith attribute power and agency to the ideas themselves, and make one the cause of another, than which nothing can be more absurd and unintelligible. Thus, for example, having observed that when we perceive by sight a certain round luminous figure we at the same time perceive by touch the idea or sensation called heat, we do from thence conclude the sun to be the cause of heat. And in like manner perceiving the motion and collision of bodies to be attended with sound, we are inclined to think the latter the effect of the former.

33. The ideas imprinted on the Senses by the Author of nature are called real things; and those excited in the imagination being less regular, vivid, and constant, are more properly termed ideas, or images of things, which they copy and represent. But then our sensations, be they never so vivid and distinct, are nevertheless ideas, that is, they exist in the mind, or are perceived by it, as truly as the ideas of its own framing. The ideas of Sense are allowed to have more reality in them, that is, to be more strong, orderly, and coherent than the creatures of the mind; but this is no argument that they exist without the mind. They are also less dependent on the spirit, or thinking substance which perceives them, in that they are excited by the will of another and more powerful spirit; yet still they are ideas, and certainly no idea, whether faint or strong, can exist otherwise than in a mind perceiving it.

34. Before we proceed any farther it is necessary we spend some time in answering objections which may probably be made against the principles we have hitherto laid down. In doing of which, if I seem too prolix to those of quick apprehensions, I hope it may be pardoned, since all men do not equally apprehend things of this nature, and I am willing to be understood by every one.

First, then, it will be objected that by the foregoing principles all that is real and substantial in nature is banished out of the world, and instead thereof a chimerical scheme of ideas takes place. All things that exist, exist only in the mind, that is, they are purely notional. What therefore becomes of the sun, moon and stars? What must we think of houses, rivers, mountains, trees, stones; nay, even of our own bodies? Are all these but so many chimeras and illusions on the fancy? To all which, and whatever else of the same sort may be objected, I answer, that by the principles premised we are not deprived of any one thing in nature. Whatever we see, feel, hear, or anywise conceive or understand remains as secure as ever, and is as real as ever. There is a rerum natura, and the distinction between realities and chimeras retains its full force. This is evident from sect. 29, 30, and 33, where we have shewn what is meant by real things in opposition to chimeras or ideas of our own framing; but then they both equally exist in the mind, and in that sense they are alike ideas.

35. I do not argue against the existence of any one thing that we can apprehend either by sense or reflexion. That the things I see with my eyes and touch with my hands do exist, really exist, I make not the least question. The only thing whose existence we deny is that which philosophers call Matter or corporeal substance. And in doing of this there is no damage done to the rest of mankind, who, I dare say, will never miss it. The Atheist indeed will want the colour of an empty name to support his impiety; and the Philosophers may possibly find they have lost a great handle for trifling and disputation.

36. If any man thinks this detracts from the existence or reality of things, he is very far from understanding what hath been premised in the plainest terms I could think of. Take here an abstract of what has been said:- There are spiritual substances, minds, or human souls, which will or excite ideas in themselves at pleasure; but these are faint, weak, and unsteady in respect of others they perceive by sensewhich, being impressed upon them according to certain rules or laws of nature, speak themselves the effects of a mind more powerful and wise than human spirits. These latter are said to have more reality in them than the former:- by which is meant that they are more affecting, orderly, and distinct, and that they are not fictions of the mind perceiving them. And in this sense the sun that I see by day is the real sun, and that which I imagine by night is the idea of the former. In the sense here given of reality it is evident that every vegetable, star, mineral, and in general each part of the mundane system, is as much a real being by our principles as by any other. Whether others mean anything by the term reality different from what I do, I entreat them to look into their own thoughts and see.

37. I will be urged that thus much at least is true, to wit, that we take away all corporeal substances. To this my answer is, that if the word substance be taken in the vulgar sense- for a combination of sensible qualities, such as extension, solidity, weight, and the like- this we cannot be accused of taking away: but if it be taken in a philosophic sense- for the support of accidents or qualities without the mind- then indeed I acknowledge that we take it away, if one may be said to take away that which never had any existence, not even in the imagination.

38. But after all, say you, it sounds very harsh to say we eat and drink ideas, and are clothed with ideas. I acknowledge it does so- the word idea not being used in common discourse to signify the several combinations of sensible qualities which are called things; and it is certain that any expression which varies from the familiar use of language will seem harsh and ridiculous. But this doth not concern the truth of the proposition, which in other words is no more than to say, we are fed and clothed with those things which we perceive immediately by our senses. The hardness or softness, the colour, taste, warmth, figure, or suchlike qualities, which combined together constitute the several sorts of victuals and apparel, have been shewn to exist only in the mind that perceives them; and this is all that is meant by calling them ideas; which word if it was as ordinarily used as thing, would sound no harsher nor more ridiculous than it. I am not for disputing about the propriety, but the truth of the expression. If therefore you agree with me that we eat and drink and are clad with the immediate objects of sense, which cannot exist unperceived or without the mind, I shall readily grant it is more proper or conformable to custom that they should be called things rather than ideas.

39. If it be demanded why I make use of the word idea, and do not rather in compliance with custom call them things; I answer, I do it for two reasons:- first, because the term thing in contra-distinction to idea, is generally supposed to denote somewhat existing without the mind; secondly, because thing hath a more comprehensive signification than idea, including spirit or thinking things as well as ideas. Since therefore the objects of sense exist only in the mind, and are withal thoughtless and inactive, I chose to mark them by the word idea, which implies those properties.

40. But, say what we can, some one perhaps may be apt to reply, he will still believe his senses, and never suffer any arguments, how plausible soever, to prevail over the certainty of them. Be it so; assert the evidence of sense as high as you please, we are willing to do the

same. That what I see, hear, and feel doth exist, that is to say, is perceived by me, I no more doubt than I do of my own being. But I do not see how the testimony of sense can be alleged as a proof for the existence of anything which is not perceived by sense. We are not for having any man turn sceptic and disbelieve his senses; on the contrary, we give them all the stress and assurance imaginable; nor are there any principles more opposite to Scepticism than those we have laid down, as shall be hereafter clearly shewn.

41. Secondly, it will be objected that there is a great difference betwixt real fire for instance, and the idea of fire, betwixt dreaming or imagining oneself burnt, and actually being so: if you suspect it to be only the idea of fire which you see, do but put your hand into it and you will be convinced with a witness. This and the like may be urged in opposition to our tenets. To all which the answer is evident from what hath been already said; and I shall only add in this place, that if real fire be very different from the idea of fire, so also is the real pain that it occasions very different from the idea of the same pain, and yet nobody will pretend that real pain either is, or can possibly be, in an unperceiving thing, or without the mind, any more than its idea.

42. Thirdly, it will be objected that we see things actually without or at distance from us, and which consequently do not exist in the mind; it being absurd that those things which are seen at the distance of several miles should be as near to us as our own thoughts. In answer to this, I desire it may be considered that in a dream we do oft perceive things as existing at a great distance off, and yet for all that, those things are acknowledged to have their existence only in the mind.

43. But, for the fuller clearing of this point, it may be worth while to consider how it is that we perceive distance and things placed at a distance by sight. For, that we should in truth see external space, and bodies actually existing in it, some nearer, others farther off, seems to carry with it some opposition to what hath been said of their existing nowhere without the mind. The consideration of this difficulty it was that gave birth to my "Essay towards a New Theory of Vision," which was published not long since, wherein it is shewn that distance or outness is neither immediately of itself perceived by sight, nor yet apprehended or judged of by lines and angles, or anything that hath a necessary connexion with it; but that it is only suggested to our thoughts by certain visible ideas and sensations attending vision, which in their own nature have no manner of similitude or relation either with distance or things placed at a distance; but, by a connexion taught us by experience, they come to signify and suggest them to us, after the same manner that words of any language suggest the ideas they are made to stand for; insomuch that a man born blind and afterwards made to see, would not, at first sight, think the things he saw to be without his mind, or at any distance from him. See sect. 41 of the fore-mentioned treatise.

44. The ideas of sight and touch make two species entirely distinct and heterogeneous. The former are marks and prognostics of the latter. That the proper objects of sight neither exist without mind, nor are the images of external things, was shewn even in that treatise. Though throughout the same the contrary be supposed true of tangible objects- not that to suppose that vulgar error was necessary for establishing the notion therein laid down, but because it was beside my purpose to examine and refute it in a discourse concerning Vision. So that in strict truth the ideas of sight, when we apprehend by them distance and things placed at a distance, do not suggest or mark out to us things actually existing at a distance, but only admonish us what ideas of touch will be imprinted in our minds at such and such distances of time, and in consequence of such or such actions. It is, I say, evident from what has been said in the foregoing parts of this Treatise, and in sect. 147 and elsewhere of the Essay concerning Vision, that visible ideas are the Language whereby the Governing Spirit on whom we depend informs us what tangible ideas he is about to imprint upon us, in case we excite this or that motion in our own bodies. But for a fuller information in this point I refer to the Essay itself.

45. Fourthly, it will be objected that from the foregoing principles it follows things are every moment annihilated and created anew. The objects of sense exist only when they are

perceived; the trees therefore are in the garden, or the chairs in the parlour, no longer than while there is somebody by to perceive them. Upon shutting my eyes all the furniture in the room is reduced to nothing, and barely upon opening them it is again created. In answer to all which, I refer the reader to what has been said in sect. 3, 4, &c., and desire he will consider whether he means anything by the actual existence of an idea distinct from its being perceived. For my part, after the nicest inquiry I could make, I am not able to discover that anything else is meant by those words; and I once more entreat the reader to sound his own thoughts, and not suffer himself to be imposed on by words. If he can conceive it possible either for his ideas or their archetypes to exist without being perceived, then I give up the cause; but if he cannot, he will acknowledge it is unreasonable for him to stand up in defence of he knows not what, and pretend to charge on me as an absurdity the not assenting to those propositions which at bottom have no meaning in them.

46. It will not be amiss to observe how far the received principles of philosophy are themselves chargeable with those pretended absurdities. It is thought strangely absurd that upon closing my eyelids all the visible objects around me should be reduced to nothing; and yet is not this what philosophers commonly acknowledge, when they agree on all hands that light and colours, which alone are the proper and immediate objects of sight, are mere sensations that exist no longer than they are perceived? Again, it may to some perhaps seem very incredible that things should be every moment creating, yet this very notion is commonly taught in the schools. For the Schoolmen, though they acknowledge the existence of Matter, and that the whole mundane fabric is framed out of it, are nevertheless of opinion that it cannot subsist without the divine conservation, which by them is expounded to be a continual creation.

47. Farther, a little thought will discover to us that though we allow the existence of Matter or corporeal substance, yet it will unavoidably follow, from the principles which are now generally admitted, that the particular bodies, of what kind soever, do none of them exist whilst they are not perceived. For, it is evident from sect. II and the following sections, that the Matter philosophers contend for is an incomprehensible somewhat, which hath none of those particular qualities whereby the bodies falling under our senses are distinguished one from another. But, to make this more plain, it must be remarked that the infinite divisibility of Matter is now universally allowed, at least by the most approved and considerable philosophers, who on the received principles demonstrate it beyond all exception. Hence, it follows there is an infinite number of parts in each particle of Matter which are not perceived by sense. The reason therefore that any particular body seems to be of a finite magnitude, or exhibits only a finite number of parts to sense, is, not because it contains no more, since in itself it contains an infinite number of parts, but because the sense is not acute enough to discern them. In proportion therefore as the sense is rendered more acute, it perceives a greater number of parts in the object, that is, the object appears greater, and its figure varies, those parts in its extremities which were before unperceivable appearing now to bound it in very different lines and angles from those perceived by an obtuser sense. And at length, after various changes of size and shape, when the sense becomes infinitely acute the body shall seem infinite. During all which there is no alteration in the body, but only in the sense. Each body therefore, considered in itself, is infinitely extended, and consequently void of all shape or figure. From which it follows that, though we should grant the existence of Matter to be never so certain, yet it is withal as certain, the materialists themselves are by their own principles forced to acknowledge, that neither the particular bodies perceived by sense, nor anything like them, exists without the mind. Matter, I say, and each particle thereof, is according to them infinite and shapeless, and it is the mind that frames all that variety of bodies which compose the visible world, any one whereof does not exist longer than it is perceived.

48. If we consider it, the objection proposed in sect. 45 will not be found reasonably charged on the principles we have premised, so as in truth to make any objection at all against our

notions. For, though we hold indeed the objects of sense to be nothing else but ideas which cannot exist unperceived; yet we may not hence conclude they have no existence except only while they are perceived by us, since there may be some other spirit that perceives them though we do not. Wherever bodies are said to have no existence without the mind, I would not be understood to mean this or that particular mind, but all minds whatsoever. It does not therefore follow from the foregoing principles that bodies are annihilated and created every moment, or exist not at all during the intervals between our perception of them.

49. Fifthly, it may perhaps be objected that if extension and figure exist only in the mind, it follows that the mind is extended and figured; since extension is a mode or attribute which (to speak with the schools) is predicated of the subject in which it exists. I answer, those qualities are in the mind only as they are perceived by it- that is, not by way of mode or attribute, but only by way of idea; and it no more follows the soul or mind is extended, because extension exists in it alone, than it does that it is red or blue, because those colours are on all hands acknowledged to exist in it, and nowhere else. As to what philosophers say of subject and mode, that seems very groundless and unintelligible. For instance, in this proposition "a die is hard, extended, and square," they will have it that the word die denotes a subject or substance, distinct from the hardness, extension, and figure which are predicated of it, and in which they exist. This I cannot comprehend: to me a die seems to be nothing distinct from those things which are termed its modes or accidents. And, to say a die is hard, extended, and square is not to attribute those qualities to a subject distinct from and supporting them, but only an explication of the meaning of the word die.

50. Sixthly, you will say there have been a great many things explained by matter and motion; take away these and you destroy the whole corpuscular philosophy, and undermine those mechanical principles which have been applied with so much success to account for the phenomena. In short, whatever advances have been made, either by ancient or modern philosophers, in the study of nature do all proceed on the supposition that corporeal substance or Matter doth really exist. To this I answer that there is not any one phenomenon explained on that supposition which may not as well be explained without it, as might easily be made appear by an induction of particulars. To explain the phenomena, is all one as to shew why, upon such and such occasions, we are affected with such and such ideas. But how Matter should operate on a Spirit, or produce any idea in it, is what no philosopher will pretend to explain; it is therefore evident there can be no use of Matter in natural philosophy. Besides, they who attempt to account for things do it not by corporeal substance, but by figure, motion, and other qualities, which are in truth no more than mere ideas, and, therefore, cannot be the cause of anything, as hath been already shewn. See sect. 25.

51. Seventhly, it will upon this be demanded whether it does not seem absurd to take away natural causes, and ascribe everything to the immediate operation of Spirits? We must no longer say upon these principles that fire heats, or water cools, but that a Spirit heats, and so forth. Would not a man be deservedly laughed at, who should talk after this manner? I answer, he would so; in such things we ought to "think with the learned, and speak with the vulgar." They who to demonstration are convinced of the truth of the Copernican system do nevertheless say "the sun rises," "the sun sets," or "comes to the meridian"; and if they affected a contrary style in common talk it would without doubt appear very ridiculous. A little reflexion on what is here said will make it manifest that the common use of language would receive no manner of alteration or disturbance from the admission of our tenets.

52. In the ordinary affairs of life, any phrases may be retained, so long as they excite in us proper sentiments, or dispositions to act in such a manner as is necessary for our well-being, how false soever they may be if taken in a strict and speculative sense. Nay, this is unavoidable, since, propriety being regulated by custom, language is suited to the received opinions, which are not always the truest. Hence it is impossible, even in the most rigid, philosophic reasonings, so far to alter the bent and genius of the tongue we speak, as never to give a handle for cavillers to pretend difficulties and inconsistencies. But, a fair and ingenuous

reader will collect the sense from the scope and tenor and connexion of a discourse, making allowances for those inaccurate modes of speech which use has made inevitable.

53. As to the opinion that there are no Corporeal Causes, this has been heretofore maintained by some of the Schoolmen, as it is of late by others among the modern philosophers, who though they allow Matter to exist, yet will have God alone to be the immediate efficient cause of all things. These men saw that amongst all the objects of sense there was none which had any power or activity included in it; and that by consequence this was likewise true of whatever bodies they supposed to exist without the mind, like unto the immediate objects of sense. But then, that they should suppose an innumerable multitude of created beings, which they acknowledge are not capable of producing any one effect in nature, and which therefore are made to no manner of purpose, since God might have done everything as well without them: this I say, though we should allow it possible, must yet be a very unaccountable and extravagant supposition.

54. In the eighth place, the universal concurrent assent of mankind may be thought by some an invincible argument in behalf of Matter, or the existence of external things. Must we suppose the whole world to be mistaken? And if so, what cause can be assigned of so widespread and predominant an error? I answer, first, that, upon a narrow inquiry, it will not perhaps be found so many as is imagined do really believe the existence of Matter or things without the mind. Strictly speaking, to believe that which involves a contradiction, or has no meaning in it, is impossible; and whether the foregoing expressions are not of that sort, I refer it to the impartial examination of the reader. In one sense, indeed, men may be said to believe that Matter exists, that is, they act as if the immediate cause of their sensations, which affects them every moment, and is so nearly present to them, were some senseless unthinking being. But, that they should clearly apprehend any meaning marked by those words, and form thereof a settled speculative opinion, is what I am not able to conceive. This is not the only instance wherein men impose upon themselves, by imagining they believe those propositions which they have often heard, though at bottom they have no meaning in them.

55. But secondly, though we should grant a notion to be never so universally and steadfastly adhered to, yet this is weak argument of its truth to whoever considers what a vast number of prejudices and false opinions are everywhere embraced with the utmost tenaciousness, by the unreflecting (which are the far greater) part of mankind. There was a time when the antipodes and motion of the earth were looked upon as monstrous absurdities even by men of learning: and if it be considered what a small proportion they bear to the rest of mankind, we shall find that at this day those notions have gained but a very inconsiderable footing in the world.

56. But it is demanded that we assign a cause of this prejudice, and account for its obtaining in the world. To this I answer, that men knowing they perceived several ideas, whereof they themselves were not the authors- as not being excited from within nor depending on the operation of their wills- this made them maintain those ideas, or objects of perception had an existence independent of and without the mind, without ever dreaming that a contradiction was involved in those words. But, philosophers having plainly seen that the immediate objects of perception do not exist without the mind, they in some degree corrected the mistake of the vulgar; but at the same time run into another which seems no less absurd, to wit, that there are certain objects really existing without the mind, or having a subsistence distinct from being perceived, of which our ideas are only images or resemblances, imprinted by those objects on the mind. And this notion of the philosophers owes its origin to the same cause with the former, namely, their being conscious that they were not the authors of their own sensations, which they evidently knew were imprinted from without, and which therefore must have some cause distinct from the minds on which they are imprinted.

57. But why they should suppose the ideas of sense to be excited in us by things in their likeness, and not rather have recourse to Spirit which alone can act, may be accounted for, first, because they were not aware of the repugnancy there is, as well in supposing things like unto our ideas existing without, as in attributing to them power or activity. Secondly, because

the Supreme Spirit which excites those ideas in our minds, is not marked out and limited to our view by any particular finite collection of sensible ideas, as human agents are by their size, complexion, limbs, and motions. And thirdly, because His operations are regular and uniform. Whenever the course of nature is interrupted by a miracle, men are ready to own the presence of a superior agent. But, when we see things go on in the ordinary course they do not excite in us any reflexion; their order and concatenation, though it be an argument of the greatest wisdom, power, and goodness in their creator, is yet so constant and familiar to us that we do not think them the immediate effects of a Free Spirit; especially since inconsistency and mutability in acting, though it be an imperfection, is looked on as a mark of freedom.

58. Tenthly, it will be objected that the notions we advance are inconsistent with several sound truths in philosophy and mathematics. For example, the motion of the earth is now universally admitted by astronomers as a truth grounded on the clearest and most convincing reasons. But, on the foregoing principles, there can be no such thing. For, motion being only an idea, it follows that if it be not perceived it exists not; but the motion of the earth is not perceived by sense. I answer, that tenet, if rightly understood, will be found to agree with the principles we have premised; for, the question whether the earth moves or no amounts in reality to no more than this, to wit, whether we have reason to conclude, from what has been observed by astronomers, that if we were placed in such and such circumstances, and such or such a position and distance both from the earth and sun, we should perceive the former to move among the choir of the planets, and appearing in all respects like one of them; and this, by the established rules of nature which we have no reason to mistrust, is reasonably collected from the phenomena.

59. We may, from the experience we have had of the train and succession of ideas in our minds, often make, I will not say uncertain conjectures, but sure and well-grounded predictions concerning the ideas we shall be affected with pursuant to a great train of actions, and be enabled to pass a right judgment of what would have appeared to us, in case we were placed in circumstances very different from those we are in at present. Herein consists the knowledge of nature, which may preserve its use and certainty very consistently with what hath been said. It will be easy to apply this to whatever objections of the like sort may be drawn from the magnitude of the stars, or any other discoveries in astronomy or nature.

60. In the eleventh place, it will be demanded to what purpose serves that curious organization of plants, and the animal mechanism in the parts of animals; might not vegetables grow, and shoot forth leaves of blossoms, and animals perform all their motions as well without as with all that variety of internal parts so elegantly contrived and put together; which, being ideas, have nothing powerful or operative in them, nor have any necessary connexion with the effects ascribed to them? If it be a Spirit that immediately produces every effect by a fiat or act of his will, we must think all that is fine and artificial in the works, whether of man or nature, to be made in vain. By this doctrine, though an artist hath made the spring and wheels, and every movement of a watch, and adjusted them in such a manner as he knew would produce the motions he designed, yet he must think all this done to no purpose, and that it is an Intelligence which directs the index, and points to the hour of the day. If so, why may not the Intelligence do it, without his being at the pains of making the movements and putting them together? Why does not an empty case serve as well as another? And how comes it to pass that whenever there is any fault in the going of a watch, there is some corresponding disorder to be found in the movements, which being mended by a skilful hand all is right again? The like may be said of all the clockwork of nature, great part whereof is so wonderfully fine and subtle as scarce to be discerned by the best microscope. In short, it will be asked, how, upon our principles, any tolerable account can be given, or any final cause assigned of an innumerable multitude of bodies and machines, framed with the most exquisite art, which in the common philosophy have very apposite uses assigned them, and serve to explain abundance of phenomena?

61. To all which I answer, first, that though there were some difficulties relating to the

administration of Providence, and the uses by it assigned to the several parts of nature, which I could not solve by the foregoing principles, yet this objection could be of small weight against the truth and certainty of those things which may be proved a priori, with the utmost evidence and rigor of demonstration. Secondly, but neither are the received principles free from the like difficulties; for, it may still be demanded to what end God should take those roundabout methods of effecting things by instruments and machines, which no one can deny might have been effected by the mere command of His will without all that apparatus; nay, if we narrowly consider it, we shall find the objection may be retorted with greater force on those who hold the existence of those machines without of mind; for it has been made evident that solidity, bulk, figure, motion, and the like have no activity or efficacy in them, so as to be capable of producing any one effect in nature. See sect. 25. Whoever therefore supposes them to exist (allowing the supposition possible) when they are not perceived does it manifestly to no purpose; since the only use that is assigned to them, as they exist unperceived, is that they produce those perceivable effects which in truth cannot be ascribed to anything but Spirit.

62. But, to come nigher the difficulty, it must be observed that though the fabrication of all those parts and organs be not absolutely necessary to the producing any effect, yet it is necessary to the producing of things in a constant regular way according to the laws of nature. There are certain general laws that run through the whole chain of natural effects; these are learned by the observation and study of nature, and are by men applied as well to the framing artificial things for the use and ornament of life as to the explaining various phenomena- which explication consists only in shewing the conformity any particular phenomenon hath to the general laws of nature, or, which is the same thing, in discovering the uniformity there is in the production of natural effects; as will be evident to whoever shall attend to the several instances wherein philosophers pretend to account for appearances. That there is a great and conspicuous use in these regular constant methods of working observed by the Supreme Agent hath been shewn in sect. 31. And it is no less visible that a particular size, figure, motion, and disposition of parts are necessary, though not absolutely to the producing any effect, yet to the producing it according to the standing mechanical laws of nature. Thus, for instance, it cannot be denied that God, or the Intelligence that sustains and rules the ordinary course of things, might if He were minded to produce a miracle, cause all the motions on the dial-plate of a watch, though nobody had ever made the movements and put them in it: but yet, if He will act agreeably to the rules of mechanism, by Him for wise ends established and maintained in the creation, it is necessary that those actions of the watchmaker, whereby he makes the movements and rightly adjusts them, precede the production of the aforesaid motions; as also that any disorder in them be attended with the perception of some corresponding disorder in the movements, which being once corrected all is right again.

63. It may indeed on some occasions be necessary that the Author of nature display His overruling power in producing some appearance out of the ordinary series of things. Such exceptions from the general rules of nature are proper to surprise and awe men into an acknowledgement of the Divine Being; but then they are to be used but seldom, otherwise there is a plain reason why they should fail of that effect. Besides, God seems to choose the convincing our reason of His attributes by the works of nature, which discover so much harmony and contrivance in their make, and are such plain indications of wisdom and beneficence in their Author, rather than to astonish us into a belief of His Being by anomalous and surprising events.

64. To set this matter in a yet clearer light, I shall observe that what has been objected in sect. 60 amounts in reality to no more than this:- ideas are not anyhow and at random produced, there being a certain order and connexion between them, like to that of cause and effect; there are also several combinations of them made in a very regular and artificial manner, which seem like so many instruments in the hand of nature that, being hid as it were behind the scenes, have a secret operation in producing those appearances which are seen on the theatre of the world, being themselves discernible only to the curious eye of the philosopher. But,

since one idea cannot be the cause of another, to what purpose is that connexion? And, since those instruments, being barely inefficacious perceptions in the mind, are not subservient to the production of natural effects, it is demanded why they are made; or, in other words, what reason can be assigned why God should make us, upon a close inspection into His works, behold so great variety of ideas so artfully laid together, and so much according to rule; it not being credible that He would be at the expense (if one may so speak) of all that art and regularity to no purpose.

65. To all which my answer is, first, that the connexion of ideas does not imply the relation of cause and effect, but only of a mark or sign with the thing signified. The fire which I see is not the cause of the pain I suffer upon my approaching it, but the mark that forewarns me of it. In like manner the noise that I hear is not the effect of this or that motion or collision of the ambient bodies, but the sign thereof. Secondly, the reason why ideas are formed into machines, that is, artificial and regular combinations, is the same with that for combining letters into words. That a few original ideas may be made to signify a great number of effects and actions, it is necessary they be variously combined together. And, to the end their use be permanent and universal, these combinations must be made by rule, and with wise contrivance. By this means abundance of information is conveyed unto us, concerning what we are to expect from such and such actions and what methods are proper to be taken for the exciting such and such ideas; which in effect is all that I conceive to be distinctly meant when it is said that, by discerning a figure, texture, and mechanism of the inward parts of bodies, whether natural or artificial, we may attain to know the several uses and properties depending thereon, or the nature of the thing.

66. Hence, it is evident that those things which, under the notion of a cause co-operating or concurring to the production of effects, are altogether inexplicable, and run us into great absurdities, may be very naturally explained, and have a proper and obvious use assigned to them, when they are considered only as marks or signs for our information. And it is the searching after and endeavouring to understand those signs instituted by the Author of Nature, that ought to be the employment of the natural philosopher; and not the pretending to explain things by corporeal causes, which doctrine seems to have too much estranged the minds of men from that active principle, that supreme and wise Spirit "in whom we live, move, and have our being."

67. In the twelfth place, it may perhaps be objected that- though it be clear from what has been said that there can be no such thing as an inert, senseless, extended, solid, figured, movable substance existing without the mind, such as philosophers describe Matter- yet, if any man shall leave out of his idea of matter the positive ideas of extension, figure, solidity and motion, and say that he means only by that word an inert, senseless substance, that exists without the mind or unperceived, which is the occasion of our ideas, or at the presence whereof God is pleased to excite ideas in us: it doth not appear but that Matter taken in this sense may possibly exist. In answer to which I say, first, that it seems no less absurd to suppose a substance without accidents, than it is to suppose accidents without a substance. But secondly, though we should grant this unknown substance may possibly exist, yet where can it be supposed to be? That it exists not in the mind is agreed; and that it exists not in place is no less certain- since all place or extension exists only in the mind, as hath been already proved. It remains therefore that it exists nowhere at all.

68. Let us examine a little the description that is here given us of matter. It neither acts, nor perceives, nor is perceived; for this is all that is meant by saying it is an inert, senseless, unknown substance; which is a definition entirely made up of negatives, excepting only the relative notion of its standing under or supporting. But then it must be observed that it supports nothing at all, and how nearly this comes to the description of a nonentity I desire may be considered. But, say you, it is the unknown occasion, at the presence of which ideas are excited in us by the will of God. Now, I would fain know how anything can be present to us, which is neither perceivable by sense nor reflexion, nor capable of producing any idea in our

minds, nor is at all extended, nor hath any form, nor exists in any place. The words "to be present," when thus applied, must needs be taken in some abstract and strange meaning, and which I am not able to comprehend.

69. Again, let us examine what is meant by occasion. So far as I can gather from the common use of language, that word signifies either the agent which produces any effect, or else something that is observed to accompany or go before it in the ordinary course of things. But when it is applied to Matter as above described, it can be taken in neither of those senses; for Matter is said to be passive and inert, and so cannot be an agent or efficient cause. It is also unperceivable, as being devoid of all sensible qualities, and so cannot be the occasion of our perceptions in the latter sense: as when the burning my finger is said to be the occasion of the pain that attends it. What therefore can be meant by calling matter an occasion? The term is either used in no sense at all, or else in some very distant from its received signification.

70. You will Perhaps say that Matter, though it be not perceived by us, is nevertheless perceived by God, to whom it is the occasion of exciting ideas in our minds. For, say you, since we observe our sensations to be imprinted in an orderly and constant manner, it is but reasonable to suppose there are certain constant and regular occasions of their being produced. That is to say, that there are certain permanent and distinct parcels of Matter, corresponding to our ideas, which, though they do not excite them in our minds, or anywise immediately affect us, as being altogether passive and unperceivable to us, they are nevertheless to God, by whom they art perceived, as it were so many occasions to remind Him when and what ideas to imprint on our minds; that so things may go on in a constant uniform manner.

71. In answer to this, I observe that, as the notion of Matter is here stated, the question is no longer concerning the existence of a thing distinct from Spirit and idea, from perceiving and being perceived; but whether there are not certain ideas of I know not what sort, in the mind of God which are so many marks or notes that direct Him how to produce sensations in our minds in a constant and regular method- much after the same manner as a musician is directed by the notes of music to produce that harmonious train and composition of sound which is called a tune, though they who hear the music do not perceive the notes, and may be entirely ignorant of them. But, this notion of Matter seems too extravagant to deserve a confutation. Besides, it is in effect no objection against what we have advanced, viz. that there is no senseless unperceived substance.

72. If we follow the light of reason, we shall, from the constant uniform method of our sensations, collect the goodness and wisdom of the Spirit who excites them in our minds; but this is all that I can see reasonably concluded from thence. To me, I say, it is evident that the being of a spirit infinitely wise, good, and powerful is abundantly sufficient to explain all the appearances of nature. But, as for inert, senseless Matter, nothing that I perceive has any the least connexion with it, or leads to the thoughts of it. And I would fain see any one explain any the meanest phenomenon in nature by it, or shew any manner of reason, though in the lowest rank of probability, that he can have for its existence, or even make any tolerable sense or meaning of that supposition. For, as to its being an occasion, we have, I think, evidently shewn that with regard to us it is no occasion. It remains therefore that it must be, if at all, the occasion to God of exciting ideas in us; and what this amounts to we have just now seen.

73. It is worth while to reflect a little on the motives which induced men to suppose the existence of material substance; that so having observed the gradual ceasing and expiration of those motives or reasons, we may proportionably withdraw the assent that was grounded on them. First, therefore, it was thought that colour, figure, motion, and the rest of the sensible qualities or accidents, did really exist without the mind; and for this reason it seemed needful to suppose some unthinking substratum or substance wherein they did exist, since they could not be conceived to exist by themselves. Afterwards, in process of time, men being convinced that colours, sounds, and the rest of the sensible, secondary qualities had no existence without the mind, they stripped this substratum or material substance of those qualities, leaving only the primary ones, figure, motion, and suchlike, which they still conceived to exist without the

mind, and consequently to stand in need of a material support. But, it having been shewn that none even of these can possibly exist otherwise than in a Spirit or Mind which perceives them it follows that we have no longer any reason to suppose the being of Matter; nay, that it is utterly impossible there should be any such thing, so long as that word is taken to denote an unthinking substratum of qualities or accidents wherein they exist without the mind.

74. But though it be allowed by the materialists themselves that Matter was thought of only for the sake of supporting accidents, and, the reason entirely ceasing, one might expect the mind should naturally, and without any reluctance at all, quit the belief of what was solely grounded thereon; yet the prejudice is riveted so deeply in our thoughts, that we can scarce tell how to part with it, and are therefore inclined, since the thing itself is indefensible, at least to retain the name, which we apply to I know not what abstracted and indefinite notions of being, or occasion, though without any show of reason, at least so far as I can see. For, what is there on our part, or what do we perceive, amongst all the ideas, sensations, notions which are imprinted on our minds, either by sense or reflexion, from whence may be inferred the existence of an inert, thoughtless, unperceived occasion? and, on the other hand, on the part of an All-sufficient Spirit, what can there be that should make us believe or even suspect He is directed by an inert occasion to excite ideas in our minds?

75. It is a very extraordinary instance of the force of prejudice, and much to be lamented, that the mind of man retains so great a fondness, against all the evidence of reason, for a stupid thoughtless somewhat, by the interposition whereof it would as it were screen itself from the Providence of God, and remove it farther off from the affairs of the world. But, though we do the utmost we can to secure the belief of Matter, though, when reason forsakes us, we endeavour to support our opinion on the bare possibility of the thing, and though we indulge ourselves in the full scope of an imagination not regulated by reason to make out that poor possibility, yet the upshot of all is, that there are certain unknown Ideas in the mind of God; for this, if anything, is all that I conceive to be meant by occasion with regard to God. And this at the bottom is no longer contending for the thing, but for the name.

76. Whether therefore there are such Ideas in the mind of God, and whether they may be called by the name Matter, I shall not dispute. But, if you stick to the notion of an unthinking substance or support of extension, motion, and other sensible qualities, then to me it is most evidently impossible there should be any such thing, since it is a plain repugnancy that those qualities should exist in or be supported by an unperceiving substance.

77. But, say you, though it be granted that there is no thoughtless support of extension and the other qualities or accidents which we perceive, yet there may perhaps be some inert, unperceiving substance or substratum of some other qualities, as incomprehensible to us as colours are to a man born blind, because we have not a sense adapted to them. But, if we had a new sense, we should possibly no more doubt of their existence than a blind man made to see does of the existence of light and colours. I answer, first, if what you mean by the word Matter be only the unknown support of unknown qualities, it is no matter whether there is such a thing or no, since it no way concerns us; and I do not see the advantage there is in disputing about what we know not what, and we know not why.

78. But, secondly, if we had a new sense it could only furnish us with new ideas or sensations; and then we should have the same reason against their existing in an unperceiving substance that has been already offered with relation to figure, motion, colour and the like. Qualities, as hath been shewn, are nothing else but sensations or ideas, which exist only in a mind perceiving them; and this is true not only of the ideas we are acquainted with at present, but likewise of all possible ideas whatsoever.

79. But, you will insist, what if I have no reason to believe the existence of Matter? what if I cannot assign any use to it or explain anything by it, or even conceive what is meant by that word? yet still it is no contradiction to say that Matter exists, and that this Matter is in general a substance, or occasion of ideas; though indeed to go about to unfold the meaning or adhere to any particular explication of those words may be attended with great difficulties. I answer,

when words are used without a meaning, you may put them together as you please without danger of running into a contradiction. You may say, for example, that twice two is equal to seven, so long as you declare you do not take the words of that proposition in their usual acceptation but for marks of you know not what. And, by the same reason, you may say there is an inert thoughtless substance without accidents which is the occasion of our ideas. And we shall understand just as much by one proposition as the other.

80. In the last place, you will say, what if we give up the cause of material Substance, and stand to it that Matter is an unknown somewhat- neither substance nor accident, spirit nor idea, inert, thoughtless, indivisible, immovable, unextended, existing in no place. For, say you, whatever may be urged against substance or occasion, or any other positive or relative notion of Matter, hath no place at all, so long as this negative definition of Matter is adhered to. I answer, you may, if so it shall seem good, use the word "Matter" in the same sense as other men use "nothing," and so make those terms convertible in your style. For, after all, this is what appears to me to be the result of that definition, the parts whereof when I consider with attention, either collectively or separate from each other, I do not find that there is any kind of effect or impression made on my mind different from what is excited by the term nothing.

81. You will reply, perhaps, that in the fore-said definition is included what doth sufficiently distinguish it from nothing- the positive abstract idea of quiddity, entity, or existence. I own, indeed, that those who pretend to the faculty of framing abstract general ideas do talk as if they had such an idea, which is, say they, the most abstract and general notion of all; that is, to me, the most incomprehensible of all others. That there are a great variety of spirits of different orders and capacities, whose faculties both in number and extent are far exceeding those the Author of my being has bestowed on me, I see no reason to deny. And for me to pretend to determine by my own few, stinted narrow inlets of perception, what ideas the inexhaustible power of the Supreme Spirit may imprint upon them were certainly the utmost folly and presumption- since there may be, for aught that I know, innumerable sorts of ideas or sensations, as different from one another, and from all that I have perceived, as colours are from sounds. But, how ready soever I may be to acknowledge the scantiness of my comprehension with regard to the endless variety of spirits and ideas that may possibly exist, yet for any one to pretend to a notion of Entity or Existence, abstracted from spirit and idea, from perceived and being perceived, is, I suspect, a downright repugnancy and trifling with words.- It remains that we consider the objections which may possibly be made on the part of Religion.

82. Some there are who think that, though the arguments for the real existence of bodies which are drawn from Reason be allowed not to amount to demonstration, yet the Holy Scriptures are so clear in the point as will sufficiently convince every good Christian that bodies do really exist, and are something more than mere ideas; there being in Holy Writ innumerable facts related which evidently suppose the reality of timber and stone, mountains and rivers, and cities, and human bodies. To which I answer that no sort of writings whatever, sacred or profane, which use those and the like words in the vulgar acceptation, or so as to have a meaning in them, are in danger of having their truth called in question by our doctrine. That all those things do really exist, that there are bodies, even corporeal substances, when taken in the vulgar sense, has been shewn to be agreeable to our principles; and the difference betwixt things and ideas, realities and chimeras, has been distinctly explained. See sect. 29, 30, 33, 36, &c. And I do not think that either what philosophers call Matter, or the existence of objects without the mind, is anywhere mentioned in Scripture.

83. Again, whether there can be or be not external things, it is agreed on all hands that the proper use of words is the marking our conceptions, or things only as they are known and perceived by us; whence it plainly follows that in the tenets we have laid down there is nothing inconsistent with the right use and significancy of language, and that discourse, of what kind soever, so far as it is intelligible, remains undisturbed. But all this seems so manifest, from what has been largely set forth in the premises, that it is needless to insist any farther on it.

84. But, it will be urged that miracles do, at least, lose much of their stress and import by our principles. What must we think of Moses' rod? was it not really turned into a serpent; or was there only a change of ideas in the minds of the spectators? And, can it be supposed that our Saviour did no more at the marriage-feast in Cana than impose on the sight, and smell, and taste of the guests, so as to create in them the appearance or idea only of wine? The same may be said of all other miracles; which, in consequence of the foregoing principles, must be looked upon only as so many cheats, or illusions of fancy. To this I reply, that the rod was changed into a real serpent, and the water into real wine. That this does not in the least contradict what I have elsewhere said will be evident from sect. 34 and 35. But this business of real and imaginary has been already so plainly and fully explained, and so often referred to, and the difficulties about it are so easily answered from what has gone before, that it were an affront to the reader's understanding to resume the explication of it in its place. I shall only observe that if at table all who were present should see, and smell, and taste, and drink wine, and find the effects of it, with me there could be no doubt of its reality; so that at bottom the scruple concerning real miracles has no place at all on ours, but only on the received principles, and consequently makes rather for than against what has been said.

85. Having done with the Objections, which I endeavoured to propose in the clearest light, and gave them all the force and weight I could, we proceed in the next place to take a view of our tenets in their Consequences. Some of these appear at first sight as that several difficult and obscure questions, on which abundance of speculation has been thrown away, are entirely banished from philosophy. "Whether corporeal substance can think," "whether Matter be infinitely divisible," and "how it operates on spirit"- these and like inquiries have given infinite amusement to philosophers in all ages; but depending on the existence of Matter, they have no longer any place on our principles. Many other advantages there are, as well with regard to religion as the sciences, which it is easy for any one to deduce from what has been premised; but this will appear more plainly in the sequel.

86. From the principles we have laid down it follows human knowledge may naturally be reduced to two heads- that of ideas and that of spirits. Of each of these I shall treat in order. And first as to ideas or unthinking things. Our knowledge of these hath been very much obscured and confounded, and we have been led into very dangerous errors, by supposing a twofold existence of the objects of sense- the one intelligible or in the mind, the other real and without the mind; whereby unthinking things are thought to have a natural subsistence of their own distinct from being perceived by spirits. This, which, if I mistake not, hath been shewn to be a most groundless and absurd notion, is the very root of Scepticism; for, so long as men thought that real things subsisted without the mind, and that their knowledge was only so far forth real as it was conformable to real things, it follows they could not be certain they had any real knowledge at all. For how can it be known that the things which are perceived are conformable to those which are not perceived, or exist without the mind?

87. Colour, figure, motion, extension, and the like, considered only as so many sensations in the mind, are perfectly known, there being nothing in them which is not perceived. But, if they are looked on as notes or images, referred to things or archetypes existing without the mind, then are we involved all in scepticism. We see only the appearances, and not the real qualities of things. What may be the extension, figure, or motion of anything really and absolutely, or in itself, it is impossible for us to know, but only the proportion or relation they bear to our senses. Things remaining the same, our ideas vary, and which of them, or even whether any of them at all, represent the true quality really existing in the thing, it is out of our reach to determine. So that, for aught we know, all we see, hear, and feel may be only phantom and vain chimera, and not at all agree with the real things existing in rerum natura. All this scepticism follows from our supposing a difference between things and ideas, and that the former have a subsistence without the mind or unperceived. It were easy to dilate on this subject, and show how the arguments urged by sceptics in all ages depend on the supposition of external objects.

88. So long as we attribute a real existence to unthinking things, distinct from their being perceived, it is not only impossible for us to know with evidence the nature of any real unthinking being, but even that it exists. Hence it is that we see philosophers distrust their senses, and doubt of the existence of heaven and earth, of everything they see or feel, even of their own bodies. And, after all their labour and struggle of thought, they are forced to own we cannot attain to any self-evident or demonstrative knowledge of the existence of sensible things. But, all this doubtfulness, which so bewilders and confounds the mind and makes philosophy ridiculous in the eyes of the world, vanishes if we annex a meaning to our words. and not amuse ourselves with the terms "absolute," "external," "exist, "and such-like, signifying we know not what. I can as well doubt of my own being as of the being of those things which I actually perceive by sense; it being a manifest contradiction that any sensible object should be immediately perceived by sight or touch, and at the same time have no existence in nature, since the very existence of an unthinking being consists in being perceived.

89. Nothing seems of more importance towards erecting a firm system of sound and real knowledge, which may be proof against the assaults of Scepticism, than to lay the beginning in a distinct explication of what is meant by thing, reality, existence; for in vain shall we dispute concerning the real existence of things, or pretend to any knowledge thereof, so long as we have not fixed the meaning of those words. Thing or Being is the most general name of all; it comprehends under it two kinds entirely distinct and heterogeneous, and which have nothing common but the name. viz. spirits and ideas. The former are active, indivisible substances: the latter are inert, fleeting, dependent beings, which subsist not by themselves, but are supported by, or exist in minds or spiritual substances. We comprehend our own existence by inward feeling or reflexion, and that of other spirits by reason. We may be said to have some knowledge or notion of our own minds, of spirits and active beings, whereof in a strict sense we have not ideas. In like manner, we know and have a notion of relations between things or ideas- which relations are distinct from the ideas or things related, inasmuch as the latter may be perceived by us without our perceiving the former. To me it seems that ideas, spirits, and relations are all in their respective kinds the object of human knowledge and subject of discourse; and that the term idea would be improperly extended to signify everything we know or have any notion of.

90. Ideas imprinted on the senses are real things, or do really exist; this we do not deny, but we deny they can subsist without the minds which perceive them, or that they are resemblances of any archetypes existing without the mind; since the very being of a sensation or idea consists in being perceived, and an idea can be like nothing but an idea. Again, the things perceived by sense may be termed external, with regard to their origin- in that they are not generated from within by the mind itself, but imprinted by a Spirit distinct from that which perceives them. Sensible objects may likewise be said to be "without the mind" in another sense, namely when they exist in some other mind; thus, when I shut my eyes, the things I saw may still exist, but it must be in another mind.

91. It were a mistake to think that what is here said derogates in the least from the reality of things. It is acknowledged, on the received principles, that extension, motion, and in a word all sensible qualities have need of a support, as not being able to subsist by themselves. But the objects perceived by sense are allowed to be nothing but combinations of those qualities, and consequently cannot subsist by themselves. Thus far it is agreed on all hand. So that in denying the things perceived by sense an existence independent of a substance of support wherein they may exist, we detract nothing from the received opinion of their reality, and are guilty of no innovation in that respect. All the difference is that, according to us, the unthinking beings perceived by sense have no existence distinct from being perceived, and cannot therefore exist in any other substance than those unextended indivisible substances or spirits which act and think and perceive them; whereas philosophers vulgarly hold that the sensible qualities do exist in an inert, extended, unperceiving substance which they call

Matter, to which they attribute a natural subsistence, exterior to all thinking beings, or distinct from being perceived by any mind whatsoever, even the eternal mind of the Creator, wherein they suppose only ideas of the corporeal substances created by him; if indeed they allow them to be at all created.

92. For, as we have shewn the doctrine of Matter or corporeal substance to have been the main pillar and support of Scepticism, so likewise upon the same foundation have been raised all the impious schemes of Atheism and Irreligion. Nay, so great a difficulty has it been thought to conceive Matter produced out of nothing, that the most celebrated among the ancient philosophers, even of those who maintained the being of a God, have thought Matter to be uncreated and co-eternal with Him. How great a friend material substance has been to Atheists in all ages were needless to relate. All their monstrous systems have so visible and necessary a dependence on it that, when this corner-stone is once removed, the whole fabric cannot choose but fall to the ground, insomuch that it is no longer worth while to bestow a particular consideration on the absurdities of every wretched sect of Atheists.

93. That impious and profane persons should readily fall in with those systems which favour their inclinations, by deriding immaterial substance, and supposing the soul to be divisible and subject to corruption as the body; which exclude all freedom, intelligence, and design from the formation of things, and instead thereof make a self-existent, stupid, unthinking substance the root and origin of all beings; that they should hearken to those who deny a Providence, or inspection of a Superior Mind over the affairs of the world, attributing the whole series of events either to blind chance or fatal necessity arising from the impulse of one body or anotherall this is very natural. And, on the other hand, when men of better principles observe the enemies of religion lay so great a stress on unthinking Matter, and all of them use so much industry and artifice to reduce everything to it, methinks they should rejoice to see them deprived of their grand support, and driven from that only fortress, without which your Epicureans, Hobbists, and the like, have not even the shadow of a pretence, but become the most cheap and easy triumph in the world.

94. The existence of Matter, or bodies unperceived, has not only been the main support of Atheists and Fatalists, but on the same principle doth Idolatry likewise in all its various forms depend. Did men but consider that the sun, moon, and stars, and every other object of the senses are only so many sensations in their minds, which have no other existence but barely being perceived, doubtless they would never fall down and worship their own ideas, but rather address their homage to that ETERNAL INVISIBLE MIND which produces and sustains all things.

95. The same absurd principle, by mingling itself with the articles of our faith, has occasioned no small difficulties to Christians. For example, about the Resurrection, how many scruples and objections have been raised by Socinians and others? But do not the most plausible of them depend on the supposition that a body is denominated the same, with regard not to the form or that which is perceived by sense, but the material substance, which remains the same under several forms? Take away this material substance, about the identity whereof all the dispute is, and mean by body what every plain ordinary person means by that word, to wit, that which is immediately seen and felt, which is only a combination of sensible qualities or ideas, and then their most unanswerable objections come to nothing.

96. Matter being once expelled out of nature drags with it so many sceptical and impious notions, such an incredible number of disputes and puzzling questions, which have been thorns in the sides of divines as well as philosophers, and made so much fruitless work for mankind, that if the arguments we have produced against it are not found equal to demonstration (as to me they evidently seem), yet I am sure all friends to knowledge, peace, and religion have reason to wish they were.

97. Beside the external existence of the objects of perception, another great source of errors and difficulties with regard to ideal knowledge is the doctrine of abstract ideas, such as it hath been set forth in the Introduction. The plainest things in the world, those we are most

intimately acquainted with and perfectly know, when they are considered in an abstract way, appear strangely difficult and incomprehensible. Time, place, and motion, taken in particular or concrete, are what everybody knows, but, having passed through the hands of a metaphysician, they become too abstract and fine to be apprehended by men of ordinary sense. Bid your servant meet you at such a time in such a place, and he shall never stay to deliberate on the meaning of those words; in conceiving that particular time and place, or the motion by which he is to get thither, he finds not the least difficulty. But if time be taken exclusive of all those particular actions and ideas that diversify the day, merely for the continuation of existence or duration in abstract, then it will perhaps gravel even a philosopher to comprehend it.

98. For my own part, whenever I attempt to frame a simple idea of time, abstracted from the succession of ideas in my mind, which flows uniformly and is participated by all beings, I am lost and embrangled in inextricable difficulties. I have no notion of it at all, only I hear others say it is infinitely divisible, and speak of it in such a manner as leads me to entertain odd thoughts of my existence; since that doctrine lays one under an absolute necessity of thinking, either that he passes away innumerable ages without a thought, or else that he is annihilated every moment of his life, both which seem equally absurd. Time therefore being nothing, abstracted from the sucession of ideas in our minds, it follows that the duration of any finite spirit must be estimated by the number of ideas or actions succeeding each other in that same spirit or mind. Hence, it is a plain consequence that the soul always thinks; and in truth whoever shall go about to divide in his thoughts, or abstract the existence of a spirit from its cogitation, will, I believe, find it no easy task.

99. So likewise when we attempt to abstract extension and motion from all other qualities, and consider them by themselves, we presently lose sight of them, and run into great extravagances. All which depend on a twofold abstraction; first, it is supposed that extension, for example, may be abstracted from all other sensible qualities; and secondly, that the entity of extension may be abstracted from its being perceived. But, whoever shall reflect, and take care to understand what he says, will, if I mistake not, acknowledge that all sensible qualities are alike sensations and alike real; that where the extension is, there is the colour, too, i.e., in his mind, and that their archetypes can exist only in some other mind; and that the objects of sense are nothing but those sensations combined, blended, or (if one may so speak) concreted together; none of all which can be supposed to exist unperceived.

100. What it is for a man to be happy, or an object good, every one may think he knows. But to frame an abstract idea of happiness, prescinded from all particular pleasure, or of goodness from everything that is good, this is what few can pretend to. So likewise a man may be just and virtuous without having precise ideas of justice and virtue. The opinion that those and the like words stand for general notions, abstracted from all particular persons and actions, seems to have rendered morality very difficult, and the study thereof of small use to mankind. And in effect the doctrine of abstraction has not a little contributed towards spoiling the most useful parts of knowledge.

101. The two great provinces of speculative science conversant about ideas received from sense, are Natural Philosophy and Mathematics; with regard to each of these I shall make some observations. And first I shall say somewhat of Natural Philosophy. On this subject it is that the sceptics triumph. All that stock of arguments they produce to depreciate our faculties and make mankind appear ignorant and low, are drawn principally from this head, namely, that we are under an invincible blindness as to the true and real nature of things. This they exaggerate, and love to enlarge on. We are miserably bantered, say they, by our senses, and amused only with the outside and show of things. The real essence, the internal qualities and constitution of every the meanest object, is hid from our view; something there is in every drop of water, every grain of sand, which is beyond the power of human understanding to fathom or comprehend. But, it is evident from what has been shewn that all this complaint is groundless, and that we are influenced by false principles to that degree as to mistrust our

senses, and think we know nothing of those things which we perfectly comprehend.

102. One great inducement to our pronouncing ourselves ignorant of the nature of things is the current opinion that everything includes within itself the cause of its properties; or that there is in each object an inward essence which is the source whence its discernible qualities flow, and whereon they depend. Some have pretended to account for appearances by occult qualities, but of late they are mostly resolved into mechanical causes, to wit. the figure, motion, weight, and suchlike qualities, of insensible particles; whereas, in truth, there is no other agent or efficient cause than spirit, it being evident that motion, as well as all other ideas, is perfectly inert. See sect. 25. Hence, to endeavour to explain the production of colours or sounds, by figure, motion, magnitude, and the like, must needs be labour in vain. And accordingly we see the attempts of that kind are not at all satisfactory. Which may be said in general of those instances wherein one idea or quality is assigned for the cause of another. I need not say how many hypotheses and speculations are left out, and how much the study of nature is abridged by this doctrine.

103. The great mechanical principle now in vogue is attraction. That a stone falls to the earth, or the sea swells towards the moon, may to some appear sufficiently explained thereby. But how are we enlightened by being told this is done by attraction? Is it that that word signifies the manner of the tendency, and that it is by the mutual drawing of bodies instead of their being impelled or protruded towards each other? But, nothing is determined of the manner or action, and it may as truly (for aught we know) be termed "impulse," or "protrusion," as "attraction." Again, the parts of steel we see cohere firmly together, and this also is accounted for by attraction; but, in this as in the other instances, I do not perceive that anything is signified besides the effect itself; for as to the manner of the action whereby it is produced, or the cause which produces it, these are not so much as aimed at.

104. Indeed, if we take a view of the several phenomena, and compare them together, we may observe some likeness and conformity between them. For example, in the falling of a stone to the ground, in the rising of the sea towards the moon, in cohesion, crystallization, etc, there is something alike, namely, an union or mutual approach of bodies. So that any one of these or the like phenomena may not seem strange or surprising to a man who has nicely observed and compared the effects of nature. For that only is thought so which is uncommon, or a thing by itself, and out of the ordinary course of our observation. That bodies should tend towards the centre of the earth is not thought strange, because it is what we perceive every moment of our lives. But, that they should have a like gravitation towards the centre of the moon may seem odd and unaccountable to most men, because it is discerned only in the tides. But a philosopher, whose thoughts take in a larger compass of nature, having observed a certain similitude of appearances, as well in the heavens as the earth, that argue innumerable bodies to have a mutual tendency towards each other, which he denotes by the general name "attraction," whatever can be reduced to that he thinks justly accounted for. Thus he explains the tides by the attraction of the terraqueous globe towards the moon, which to him does not appear odd or anomalous, but only a particular example of a general rule or law of nature.

105. If therefore we consider the difference there is betwixt natural philosophers and other men, with regard to their knowledge of the phenomena, we shall find it consists not in an exacter knowledge of the efficient cause that produces them- for that can be no other than the will of a spirit- but only in a greater largeness of comprehension, whereby analogies, harmonies, and agreements are discovered in the works of nature, and the particular effects explained, that is, reduced to general rules, see sect. 62, which rules, grounded on the analogy and uniformness observed in the production of natural effects, are most agreeable and sought after by the mind; for that they extend our prospect beyond what is present and near to us, and enable us to make very probable conjectures touching things that may have happened at very great distances of time and place, as well as to predict things to come; which sort of endeavour towards omniscience is much affected by the mind.

106. But we should proceed warily in such things, for we are apt to lay too great stress on

analogies, and, to the prejudice of truth, humour that eagerness of the mind whereby it is carried to extend its knowledge into general theorems. For example, in the business of gravitation or mutual attraction, because it appears in many instances, some are straightway for pronouncing it universal; and that to attract and be attracted by every other body is an essential quality inherent in all bodies whatsoever. Whereas it is evident the fixed stars have no such tendency towards each other; and, so far is that gravitation from being essential to bodies that in some instances a quite contrary principle seems to shew itself; as in the perpendicular growth of plants, and the elasticity of the air. There is nothing necessary or essential in the case, but it depends entirely on the will of the Governing Spirit, who causes certain bodies to cleave together or tend towards each other according to various laws, whilst He keeps others at a fixed distance; and to some He gives a quite contrary tendency to fly asunder just as He sees convenient.

107. After what has been premised, I think we may lay down the following conclusions. First, it is plain philosophers amuse themselves in vain, when they inquire for any natural efficient cause, distinct from a mind or spirit. Secondly, considering the whole creation is the workmanship of a wise and good Agent, it should seem to become philosophers to employ their thoughts (contrary to what some hold) about the final causes of things; and I confess I see no reason why pointing out the various ends to which natural things are adapted, and for which they were originally with unspeakable wisdom contrived, should not be thought one good way of accounting for them, and altogether worthy a philosopher. Thirdly, from what has been premised no reason can be drawn why the history of nature should not still be studied, and observations and experiments made, which, that they are of use to mankind, and enable us to draw any general conclusions, is not the result of any immutable habitudes or relations between things themselves, but only of God's goodness and kindness to men in the administration of the world. See sect. 30 and 31 Fourthly, by a diligent observation of the phenomena within our view, we may discover the general laws of nature, and from them deduce the other phenomena; I do not say demonstrate, for all deductions of that kind depend on a supposition that the Author of nature always operates uniformly, and in a constant observance of those rules we take for principles: which we cannot evidently know.

108. Those men who frame general rules from the phenomena and afterwards derive the phenomena from those rules, seem to consider signs rather than causes. A man may well understand natural signs without knowing their analogy, or being able to say by what rule a thing is so or so. And, as it is very possible to write improperly, through too strict an observance of general grammar rules; so, in arguing from general laws of nature, it is not impossible we may extend the analogy too far, and by that means run into mistakes.

109. As in reading other books a wise man will choose to fix his thoughts on the sense and apply it to use, rather than lay them out in grammatical remarks on the language; so, in perusing the volume of nature, it seems beneath the dignity of the mind to affect an exactness in reducing each particular phenomenon to general rules, or shewing how it follows from them. We should propose to ourselves nobler views, namely, to recreate and exalt the mind with a prospect of the beauty, order. extent, and variety of natural things: hence, by proper inferences, to enlarge our notions of the grandeur, wisdom, and beneficence of the Creator; and lastly, to make the several parts of the creation, so far as in us lies, subservient to the ends they were designed for, God's glory, and the sustentation and comfort of ourselves and fellow-creatures.

110. The best key for the aforesaid analogy or natural Science will be easily acknowledged to be a certain celebrated Treatise of Mechanics. In the entrance of which justly admired treatise, Time, Space, and Motion are distinguished into absolute and relative, true and apparent, mathematical and vulgar; which distinction, as it is at large explained by the author, does suppose these quantities to have an existence without the mind; and that they are ordinarily conceived with relation to sensible things, to which nevertheless in their own nature they bear no relation at all.

111. As for Time, as it is there taken in an absolute or abstracted sense, for the duration or perseverance of the existence of things, I have nothing more to add concerning it after what has been already said on that subject. Sect. 97 and 98. For the rest, this celebrated author holds there is an absolute Space, which, being unperceivable to sense, remains in itself similar and immovable; and relative space to be the measure thereof, which, being movable and defined by its situation in respect of sensible bodies, is vulgarly taken for immovable space. Place he defines to be that part of space which is occupied by any body; and according as the space is absolute or relative so also is the place. Absolute Motion is said to be the translation of a body from absolute place to absolute place, as relative motion is from one relative place to another. And, because the parts of absolute space do not fall under our senses, instead of them we are obliged to use their sensible measures, and so define both place and motion with respect to bodies which we regard as immovable. But, it is said in philosophical matters we must abstract from our senses, since it may be that none of those bodies which seem to be quiescent are truly so, and the same thing which is moved relatively may be really at rest; as likewise one and the same body may be in relative rest and motion, or even moved with contrary relative motions at the same time, according as its place is variously defined. All which ambiguity is to be found in the apparent motions, but not at all in the true or absolute, which should therefore be alone regarded in philosophy. And the true as we are told are distinguished from apparent or relative motions by the following properties.- First, in true or absolute motion all parts which preserve the same position with respect of the whole, partake of the motions of the whole. Secondly, the place being moved, that which is placed therein is also moved; so that a body moving in a place which is in motion doth participate the motion of its place. Thirdly, true motion is never generated or changed otherwise than by force impressed on the body itself. Fourthly, true motion is always changed by force impressed on the body moved. Fifthly, in circular motion barely relative there is no centrifugal force, which, nevertheless, in that which is true or absolute, is proportional to the quantity of motion.

112. But, notwithstanding what has been said, I must confess it does not appear to me that there can be any motion other than relative; so that to conceive motion there must be at least conceived two bodies, whereof the distance or position in regard to each other is varied. Hence, if there was one only body in being it could not possibly be moved. This seems evident, in that the idea I have of motion doth necessarily include relation.

113. But, though in every motion it be necessary to conceive more bodies than one, yet it may be that one only is moved, namely, that on which the force causing the change in the distance or situation of the bodies, is impressed. For, however some may define relative motion, so as to term that body moved which changes its distance from some other body, whether the force or action causing that change were impressed on it or no, yet as relative motion is that which is perceived by sense, and regarded in the ordinary affairs of life, it should seem that every man of common sense knows what it is as well as the best philosopher. Now, I ask any one whether, in his sense of motion as he walks along the streets, the stones he passes over may be said to move, because they change distance with his feet? To me it appears that though motion includes a relation of one thing to another, yet it is not necessary that each term of the relation be denominated from it. As a man may think of somewhat which does not think, so a body may be moved to or from another body which is not therefore itself in motion.

114. As the place happens to be variously defined, the motion which is related to it varies. A man in a ship may be said to be quiescent with relation to the sides of the vessel, and yet move with relation to the land. Or he may move eastward in respect of the one, and westward in respect of the other. In the common affairs of life men never go beyond the earth to define the place of any body; and what is quiescent in respect of that is accounted absolutely to be so. But philosophers, who have a greater extent of thought, and juster notions of the system of things, discover even the earth itself to be moved. In order therefore to fix their notions they seem to conceive the corporeal world as finite, and the utmost unmoved walls or shell thereof to be the place whereby they estimate true motions. If we sound our own conceptions, I

believe we may find all the absolute motion we can frame an idea of to be at bottom no other than relative motion thus defined. For, as hath been already observed, absolute motion, exclusive of all external relation, is incomprehensible; and to this kind of relative motion all the above-mentioned properties, causes, and effects ascribed to absolute motion will, if I mistake not, be found to agree. As to what is said of the centrifugal force, that it does not at all belong to circular relative motion, I do not see how this follows from the experiment which is brought to prove it. See Philosophiae Naturalis Principia Mathematica, in Schol. Def. VIII. For the water in the vessel at that time wherein it is said to have the greatest relative circular motion, hath, I think, no motion at all; as is plain from the foregoing section.

115. For, to denominate a body moved it is requisite, first, that it change its distance or situation with regard to some other body; and secondly, that the force occasioning that change be applied to it. If either of these be wanting, I do not think that, agreeably to the sense of mankind, or the propriety of language, a body can be said to be in motion. I grant indeed that it is possible for us to think a body which we see change its distance from some other to be moved, though it have no force applied to it (in which sense there may be apparent motion), but then it is because the force causing the change of distance is imagined by us to be applied or impressed on that body thought to move; which indeed shews we are capable of mistaking a thing to be in motion which is not, and that is all.

116. From what has been said it follows that the philosophic consideration of motion does not imply the being of an absolute Space, distinct from that which is perceived by sense and related bodies; which that it cannot exist without the mind is clear upon the same principles that demonstrate the like of all other objects of sense. And perhaps, if we inquire narrowly, we shall find we cannot even frame an idea of pure Space exclusive of all body. This I must confess seems impossible, as being a most abstract idea. When I excite a motion in some part of my body, if it be free or without resistance, I say there is Space; but if I find a resistance, then I say there is Body; and in proportion as the resistance to motion is lesser or greater, I say the space is more or less pure. So that when I speak of pure or empty space, it is not to be supposed that the word "space" stands for an idea distinct from or conceivable without body and motion- though indeed we are apt to think every noun substantive stands for a distinct idea that may be separated from all others; which has occasioned infinite mistakes. When, therefore, supposing all the world to be annihilated besides my own body, I say there still remains pure Space, thereby nothing else is meant but only that I conceive it possible for the limbs of my body to be moved on all sides without the least resistance, but if that, too, were annihilated then there could be no motion, and consequently no Space. Some, perhaps, may think the sense of seeing doth furnish them with the idea of pure space; but it is plain from what we have elsewhere shewn, that the ideas of space and distance are not obtained by that sense. See the Essay concerning Vision.

117. What is here laid down seems to put an end to all those disputes and difficulties that have sprung up amongst the learned concerning the nature of pure Space. But the chief advantage arising from it is that we are freed from that dangerous dilemma, to which several who have employed their thoughts on that subject imagine themselves reduced, to wit, of thinking either that Real Space is God, or else that there is something beside God which is eternal, uncreated, infinite, indivisible, immutable. Both which may justly be thought pernicious and absurd notions. It is certain that not a few divines, as well as philosophers of great note, have, from the difficulty they found in conceiving either limits or annihilation of space, concluded it must be divine. And some of late have set themselves particularly to shew the incommunicable attributes of God agree to it. Which doctrine, how unworthy soever it may seem of the Divine Nature, yet I do not see how we can get clear of it, so long as we adhere to the received opinions.

118. Hitherto of Natural Philosophy: we come now to make some inquiry concerning that other great branch of speculative knowledge, to wit, Mathematics. These, how celebrated soever they may be for their clearness and certainty of demonstration, which is hardly

anywhere else to be found, cannot nevertheless be supposed altogether free from mistakes, if in their principles there lurks some secret error which is common to the professors of those sciences with the rest of mankind. Mathematicians, though they deduce their theorems from a great height of evidence, yet their first principles are limited by the consideration of quantity: and they do not ascend into any inquiry concerning those transcendental maxims which influence all the particular sciences, each part whereof, Mathematics not excepted, does consequently participate of the errors involved in them. That the principles laid down by mathematicians are true, and their way of deduction from those principles clear and incontestible, we do not deny; but, we hold there may be certain erroneous maxims of greater extent than the object of Mathematics, and for that reason not expressly mentioned, though tacitly supposed throughout the whole progress of that science; and that the ill effects of those secret unexamined errors are diffused through all the branches thereof. To be plain, we suspect the mathematicians are as well as other men concerned in the errors arising from the doctrine of abstract general ideas, and the existence of objects without the mind.

119. Arithmetic has been thought to have for its object abstract ideas of Number; of which to understand the properties and mutual habitudes, is supposed no mean part of speculative knowledge. The opinion of the pure and intellectual nature of numbers in abstract has made them in esteem with those philosophers who seem to have affected an uncommon fineness and elevation of thought. It hath set a price on the most trifling numerical speculations which in practice are of no use, but serve only for amusement; and hath therefore so far infected the minds of some, that they have dreamed of mighty mysteries involved in numbers, and attempted the explication of natural things by them. But, if we inquire into our own thoughts, and consider what has been premised, we may perhaps entertain a low opinion of those high flights and abstractions, and look on all inquiries, about numbers only as so many difficiles nugae, so far as they are not subservient to practice, and promote the benefit of life.

120. Unity in abstract we have before considered in sect. 13, from which and what has been said in the Introduction, it plainly follows there is not any such idea. But, number being defined a "collection of units," we may conclude that, if there be no such thing as unity or unit in abstract, there are no ideas of number in abstract denoted by the numeral names and figures. The theories therefore in Arithmetic. if they are abstracted from the names and figures, as likewise from all use and practice, as well as from the particular things numbered, can be supposed to have nothing at all for their object; hence we may see how entirely the science of numbers is subordinate to practice, and how jejune and trifling it becomes when considered as a matter of mere speculation.

121. However, since there may be some who, deluded by the specious show of discovering abstracted verities, waste their time in arithmetical theorems and problems which have not any use, it will not be amiss if we more fully consider and expose the vanity of that pretence; and this will plainly appear by taking a view of Arithmetic in its infancy, and observing what it was that originally put men on the study of that science, and to what scope they directed it. It is natural to think that at first, men, for ease of memory and help of computation, made use of counters, or in writing of single strokes, points, or the like, each whereof was made to signify an unit, i.e., some one thing of whatever kind they had occasion to reckon. Afterwards they found out the more compendious ways of making one character stand in place of several strokes or points. And, lastly, the notation of the Arabians or Indians came into use, wherein, by the repetition of a few characters or figures, and varying the signification of each figure according to the place it obtains, all numbers may be most aptly expressed; which seems to have been done in imitation of language, so that an exact analogy is observed betwixt the notation by figures and names, the nine simple figures answering the nine first numeral names and places in the former, corresponding to denominations in the latter. And agreeably to those conditions of the simple and local value of figures, were contrived methods of finding, from the given figures or marks of the parts, what figures and how placed are proper to denote the whole, or vice versa. And having found the sought figures, the same rule or analogy being

observed throughout, it is easy to read them into words; and so the number becomes perfectly known. For then the number of any particular things is said to be known, when we know the name of figures (with their due arrangement) that according to the standing analogy belong to them. For, these signs being known, we can by the operations of arithmetic know the signs of any part of the particular sums signified by them; and, thus computing in signs (because of the connexion established betwixt them and the distinct multitudes of things whereof one is taken for an unit), we may be able rightly to sum up, divide, and proportion the things themselves that we intend to number.

122. In Arithmetic, therefore, we regard not the things, but the signs, which nevertheless are not regarded for their own sake, but because they direct us how to act with relation to things, and dispose rightly of them. Now, agreeably to what we have before observed of words in general (sect. 19, Introd.) it happens here likewise that abstract ideas are thought to be signified by numeral names or characters, while they do not suggest ideas of particular things to our minds. I shall not at present enter into a more particular dissertation on this subject, but only observe that it is evident from what has been said, those things which pass for abstract truths and theorems concerning numbers, are in reality conversant about no object distinct from particular numeral things, except only names and characters, which originally came to be considered on no other account but their being signs, or capable to represent aptly whatever particular things men had need to compute. Whence it follows that to study them for their own sake would be just as wise, and to as good purpose as if a man, neglecting the true use or original intention and subserviency of language, should spend his time in impertinent criticisms upon words, or reasonings and controversies purely verbal.

123. From numbers we proceed to speak of Extension, which, considered as relative, is the object of Geometry. The infinite divisibility of finite extension, though it is not expressly laid down either as an axiom or theorem in the elements of that science, yet is throughout the same everywhere supposed and thought to have so inseparable and essential a connexion with the principles and demonstrations in Geometry, that mathematicians never admit it into doubt, or make the least question of it. And, as this notion is the source from whence do spring all those amusing geometrical paradoxes which have such a direct repugnancy to the plain common sense of mankind, and are admitted with so much reluctance into a mind not yet debauched by learning; so it is the principal occasion of all that nice and extreme subtilty which renders the study of Mathematics so difficult and tedious. Hence, if we can make it appear that no finite extension contains innumerable parts, or is infinitely divisible, it follows that we shall at once clear the science of Geometry from a great number of difficulties and contradictions which have ever been esteemed a reproach to human reason, and withal make the attainment thereof a business of much less time and pains than it hitherto has been.

124. Every particular finite extension which may possibly be the object of our thought is an idea existing only in the mind, and consequently each part thereof must be perceived. If, therefore, I cannot perceive innumerable parts in any finite extension that I consider, it is certain they are not contained in it; but, it is evident that I cannot distinguish innumerable parts in any particular line, surface, or solid, which I either perceive by sense, or figure to myself in my mind: wherefore I conclude they are not contained in it. Nothing can be plainer to me than that the extensions I have in view are no other than my own ideas; and it is no less plain that I cannot resolve any one of my ideas into an infinite number of other ideas, that is, that they are not infinitely divisible. If by finite extension be meant something distinct from a finite idea, I declare I do not know what that is, and so cannot affirm or deny anything of it. But if the terms "extension," "parts," &c., are taken in any sense conceivable, that is, for ideas, then to say a finite quantity or extension consists of parts infinite in number is so manifest a contradiction, that every one at first sight acknowledges it to be so; and it is impossible it should ever gain the assent of any reasonable creature who is not brought to it by gentle and slow degrees, as a converted Gentile to the belief of transubstantiation. Ancient and rooted prejudices do often pass into principles; and those propositions which once obtain the force and credit of a

principle, are not only themselves, but likewise whatever is deducible from them, thought privileged from all examination. And there is no absurdity so gross, which, by this means, the mind of man may not be prepared to swallow.

125. He whose understanding is possessed with the doctrine of abstract general ideas may be persuaded that (whatever be thought of the ideas of sense) extension in abstract is infinitely divisible. And one who thinks the objects of sense exist without the mind will perhaps in virtue thereof be brought to admit that a line but an inch long may contain innumerable parts- really existing, though too small to be discerned. These errors are grafted as well in the minds of geometricians as of other men, and have a like influence on their reasonings; and it were no difficult thing to shew how the arguments from Geometry made use of to support the infinite divisibility of extension are bottomed on them. At present we shall only observe in general whence it is the mathematicians are all so fond and tenacious of that doctrine.

126. It hath been observed in another place that the theorems and demonstrations in Geometry are conversant about universal ideas (sect. 15, Introd.); where it is explained in what sense this ought to be understood, to wit, the particular lines and figures included in the diagram are supposed to stand for innumerable others of different sizes; or, in other words, the geometer considers them abstracting from their magnitude- which does not imply that he forms an abstract idea, but only that he cares not what the particular magnitude is, whether great or small, but looks on that as a thing different to the demonstration. Hence it follows that a line in the scheme but an inch long must be spoken of as though it contained ten thousand parts, since it is regarded not in itself, but as it is universal; and it is universal only in its signification, whereby it represents innumerable lines greater than itself, in which may be distinguished ten thousand parts or more, though there may not be above an inch in it. After this manner, the properties of the lines signified are (by a very usual figure) transferred to the sign, and thence, through mistake, though to appertain to it considered in its own nature.

127. Because there is no number of parts so great but it is possible there may be a line containing more, the inch-line is said to contain parts more than any assignable number; which is true, not of the inch taken absolutely, but only for the things signified by it. But men, not retaining that distinction in their thoughts, slide into a belief that the small particular line described on paper contains in itself parts innumerable. There is no such thing as the ten-thousandth part of an inch; but there is of a mile or diameter of the earth, which may be signified by that inch. When therefore I delineate a triangle on paper, and take one side not above an inch, for example, in length to be the radius, this I consider as divided into 10,000 or 100,000 parts or more; for, though the ten-thousandth part of that line considered in itself is nothing at all, and consequently may be neglected without an error or inconveniency, yet these described lines, being only marks standing for greater quantities, whereof it may be the ten-thousandth part is very considerable, it follows that, to prevent notable errors in practice, the radius must be taken of 10,000 parts or more.

128. From what has been said the reason is plain why, to the end any theorem become universal in its use, it is necessary we speak of the lines described on paper as though they contained parts which really they do not. In doing of which, if we examine the matter thoroughly, we shall perhaps discover that we cannot conceive an inch itself as consisting of, or being divisible into, a thousand parts, but only some other line which is far greater than an inch, and represented by it; and that when we say a line is infinitely divisible, we must mean a line which is infinitely great. What we have here observed seems to be the chief cause why, to suppose the infinite divisibility of finite extension has been thought necessary in geometry.

129. The several absurdities and contradictions which flowed from this false principle might, one would think, have been esteemed so many demonstrations against it. But, by I know not what logic, it is held that proofs a posteriori are not to be admitted against propositions relating to infinity, as though it were not impossible even for an infinite mind to reconcile contradictions; or as if anything absurd and repugnant could have a necessary connexion with truth or flow from it. But, whoever considers the weakness of this pretence will think it was

contrived on purpose to humour the laziness of the mind which had rather acquiesce in an indolent scepticism than be at the pains to go through with a severe examination of those principles it has ever embraced for true.

130. Of late the speculations about Infinities have run so high, and grown to such strange notions, as have occasioned no small scruples and disputes among the geometers of the present age. Some there are of great note who, not content with holding that finite lines may be divided into an infinite number of parts, do yet farther maintain that each of those infinitesimals is itself subdivisible into an infinity of other parts or infinitesimals of a second order, and so on ad infinitum. These, I say, assert there are infinitesimals of infinitesimals of infinitesimals, &c., without ever coming to an end; so that according to them an inch does not barely contain an infinite number of parts, but an infinity of an infinity of an infinity ad infinitum of parts. Others there be who hold all orders of infinitesimals below the first to be nothing at all; thinking it with good reason absurd to imagine there is any positive quantity or part of extension which, though multiplied infinitely, can never equal the smallest given extension. And yet on the other hand it seems no less absurd to think the square, cube or other power of a positive real root, should itself be nothing at all; which they who hold infinitesimals of the first order, denying all of the subsequent orders, are obliged to maintain.

131. Have we not therefore reason to conclude they are both in the wrong, and that there is in effect no such thing as parts infinitely small, or an infinite number of parts contained in any finite quantity? But you will say that if this doctrine obtains it will follow the very foundations of Geometry are destroyed, and those great men who have raised that science to so astonishing a height, have been all the while building a castle in the air. To this it may be replied that whatever is useful in geometry, and promotes the benefit of human life, does still remain firm and unshaken on our principles; that science considered as practical will rather receive advantage than any prejudice from what has been said. But to set this in a due light may be the proper business of another place. For the rest, though it should follow that some of the more intricate and subtle parts of Speculative Mathematics may be pared off without any prejudice to truth, yet I do not see what damage will be thence derived to mankind. On the contrary, I think it were highly to be wished that men of great abilities and obstinate application would draw off their thoughts from those amusements, and employ them in the study of such things as lie nearer the concerns of life, or have a more direct influence on the manners.

132. It be said that several theorems undoubtedly true are discovered by methods in which infinitesimals are made use of, which could never have been if their existence included a contradiction in it; I answer that upon a thorough examination it will not be found that in any instance it is necessary to make use of or conceive infinitesimal parts of finite lines, or even quantities less than the minimum sensible; nay, it will be evident this is never done, it being impossible.

133. By what we have premised, it is plain that very numerous and important errors have taken their rise from those false Principles which were impugned in the foregoing parts of this treatise; and the opposites of those erroneous tenets at the same time appear to be most fruitful Principles, from whence do flow innumerable consequences highly advantageous to true philosophy. as well as to religion. Particularly Matter, or the absolute existence of corporeal objects, hath been shewn to be that wherein the most avowed and pernicious enemies of all knowledge, whether human or divine, have ever placed their chief strength and confidence. And surely, if by distinguishing the real existence of unthinking things from their being perceived, and allowing them a subsistance of their own out of the minds of spirits, no one thing is explained in nature, but on the contrary a great many inexplicable difficulties arise; if the supposition of Matter is barely precarious, as not being grounded on so much as one single reason; if its consequences cannot endure the light of examination and free inquiry, but screen themselves under the dark and general pretence of "infinites being incomprehensible"; if withal the removal of this Matter be not attended with the least evil consequence; if it be not even missed in the world, but everything as well, nay much easier conceived without it; if,

lastly, both Sceptics and Atheists are for ever silenced upon supposing only spirits and ideas, and this scheme of things is perfectly agreeable both to Reason and Religion: methinks we may expect it should be admitted and firmly embraced, though it were proposed only as an hypothesis, and the existence of Matter had been allowed possible, which yet I think we have evidently demonstrated that it is not.

134. True it is that, in consequence of the foregoing principles, several disputes and speculations which are esteemed no mean parts of learning, are rejected as useless. But, how great a prejudice soever against our notions this may give to those who have already been deeply engaged, and make large advances in studies of that nature, yet by others we hope it will not be thought any just ground of dislike to the principles and tenets herein laid down, that they abridge the labour of study, and make human sciences far more clear, compendious and attainable than they were before.

135. Having despatched what we intended to say concerning the knowledge of IDEAS, the method we proposed leads us in the next place to treat of SPIRITS- with regard to which, perhaps, human knowledge is not so deficient as is vulgarly imagined. The great reason that is assigned for our being thought ignorant of the nature of spirits is our not having an idea of it. But, surely it ought not to be looked on as a defect in a human understanding that it does not perceive the idea of spirit, if it is manifestly impossible there should be any such idea. And this if I mistake not has been demonstrated in section 27; to which I shall here add that a spirit has been shewn to be the only substance or support wherein unthinking beings or ideas can exist; but that this substance which supports or perceives ideas should itself be an idea or like an idea is evidently absurd.

136. It will perhaps be said that we want a sense (as some have imagined) proper to know substances withal, which, if we had, we might know our own soul as we do a triangle. To this I answer, that, in case we had a new sense bestowed upon us, we could only receive thereby some new sensations or ideas of sense. But I believe nobody will say that what he means by the terms soul and substance is only some particular sort of idea or sensation. We may therefore infer that, all things duly considered, it is not more reasonable to think our faculties defective, in that they do not furnish us with an idea of spirit or active thinking substance, than it would be if we should blame them for not being able to comprehend a round square.

137. From the opinion that spirits are to be known after the manner of an idea or sensation have risen many absurd and heterodox tenets, and much scepticism about the nature of the soul. It is even probable that this opinion may have produced a doubt in some whether they had any soul at all distinct from their body since upon inquiry they could not find they had an idea of it. That an idea which is inactive, and the existence whereof consists in being perceived, should be the image or likeness of an agent subsisting by itself, seems to need no other refutation than barely attending to what is meant by those words. But, perhaps you will say that though an idea cannot resemble a spirit in its thinking, acting, or subsisting by itself, yet it may in some other respects; and it is not necessary that an idea or image be in all respects like the original.

138. I answer, if it does not in those mentioned, it is impossible it should represent it in any other thing. Do but leave out the power of willing, thinking, and perceiving ideas, and there remains nothing else wherein the idea can be like a spirit. For, by the word spirit we mean only that which thinks, wills, and perceives; this, and this alone, constitutes the signification of the term. If therefore it is impossible that any degree of those powers should be represented in an idea, it is evident there can be no idea of a spirit.

139. But it will be objected that, if there is no idea signified by the terms soul, spirit, and substance, they are wholly insignificant, or have no meaning in them. I answer, those words do mean or signify a real thing, which is neither an idea nor like an idea, but that which perceives ideas, and wills, and reasons about them. What I am myself, that which I denote by the term I, is the same with what is meant by soul or spiritual substance. If it be said that this is only quarrelling at a word, and that, since the immediately significations of other names are by

common consent called ideas, no reason can be assigned why that which is signified by the name spirit or soul may not partake in the same appellation. I answer, all the unthinking objects of the mind agree in that they are entirely passive, and their existence consists only in being perceived; whereas a soul or spirit is an active being, whose existence consists, not in being perceived, but in perceiving ideas and thinking. It is therefore necessary, in order to prevent equivocation and confounding natures perfectly disagreeing and unlike, that we distinguish between spirit and idea. See sect. 27.

140. In a large sense, indeed, we may be said to have an idea or rather a notion of spirit; that is, we understand the meaning of the word, otherwise we could not affirm or deny anything of it. Moreover, as we conceive the ideas that are in the minds of other spirits by means of our own, which we suppose to be resemblances of them; so we know other spirits by means of our own soul- which in that sense is the image or idea of them; it having a like respect to other spirits that blueness or heat by me perceived has to those ideas perceived by another.

141. It must not be supposed that they who assert the natural immortality of the soul are of opinion that it is absolutely incapable of annihilation even by the infinite power of the Creator who first gave it being, but only that it is not liable to be broken or dissolved by the ordinary laws of nature or motion. They indeed who hold the soul of man to be only a thin vital flame, or system of animal spirits, make it perishing and corruptible as the body; since there is nothing more easily dissipated than such a being, which it is naturally impossible should survive the ruin of the tabernacle wherein it is enclosed. And this notion has been greedily embraced and cherished by the worst part of mankind, as the most effectual antidote against all impressions of virtue and religion. But it has been made evident that bodies, of what frame or texture soever, are barely passive ideas in the mind, which is more distant and heterogeneous from them than light is from darkness. We have shewn that the soul is indivisible, incorporeal, unextended, and it is consequently incorruptible. Nothing can be plainer than that the motions, changes, decays, and dissolutions which we hourly see befall natural bodies (and which is what we mean by the course of nature) cannot possibly affect an active, simple, uncompounded substance; such a being therefore is indissoluble by the force of nature; that is to say, "the soul of man is naturally immortal."

142. After what has been said, it is, I suppose, plain that our souls are not to be known in the same manner as senseless, inactive objects, or by way of idea. Spirits and ideas are things so wholly different, that when we say "they exist," "they are known," or the like, these words must not be thought to signify anything common to both natures. There is nothing alike or common in them: and to expect that by any multiplication or enlargement of our faculties we may be enabled to know a spirit as we do a triangle, seems as absurd as if we should hope to see a sound. This is inculcated because I imagine it may be of moment towards clearing several important questions, and preventing some very dangerous errors concerning the nature of the soul. We may not, I think, strictly be said to have an idea of an active being, or of an action, although we may be said to have a notion of them. I have some knowledge or notion of my mind, and its acts about ideas, inasmuch as I know or understand what is meant by these words. What I know, that I have some notion of. I will not say that the terms idea and notion may not be used convertibly, if the world will have it so; but yet it conduceth to clearness and propriety that we distinguish things very different by different names. It is also to be remarked that, all relations including an act of the mind, we cannot so properly be said to have an idea, but rather a notion of the relations and habitudes between things. But if, in the modern way, the word idea is extended to spirits, and relations, and acts, this is, after all, an affair of verbal concern.

143. It will not be amiss to add, that the doctrine of abstract ideas has had no small share in rendering those sciences intricate and obscure which are particularly conversant about spiritual things. Men have imagined they could frame abstract notions of the powers and acts of the mind, and consider them prescinded as well from the mind or spirit itself, as from their respective objects and effects. Hence a great number of dark and ambiguous terms, presumed

to stand for abstract notions, have been introduced into metaphysics and morality, and from these have grown infinite distractions and disputes amongst the learned.

144. But, nothing seems more to have contributed towards engaging men in controversies and mistakes with regard to the nature and operations of the mind, than the being used to speak of those things in terms borrowed from sensible ideas. For example, the will is termed the motion of the soul; this infuses a belief that the mind of man is as a ball in motion, impelled and determined by the objects of sense, as necessarily as that is by the stroke of a racket. Hence arise endless scruples and errors of dangerous consequence in morality. All which, I doubt not, may be cleared, and truth appear plain, uniform, and consistent, could but philosophers be prevailed on to retire into themselves, and attentively consider their own meaning.

145. From what has been said, it is plain that we cannot know the existence of other spirits otherwise than by their operations, or the ideas by them excited in us. I perceive several motions, changes, and combinations of ideas, that inform me there are certain particular agents, like myself, which accompany them and concur in their production. Hence, the knowledge I have of other spirits is not immediate, as is the knowledge of my ideas; but depending on the intervention of ideas, by me referred to agents or spirits distinct from myself, as effects or concomitant signs.

146. But, though there be some things which convince us human agents are concerned in producing them; yet it is evident to every one that those things which are called the Works of Nature, that is, the far greater part of the ideas or sensations perceived by us, are not produced by, or dependent on, the wills of men. There is therefore some other Spirit that causes them; since it is repugnant that they should subsist by themselves. See sect. 29. But, if we attentively consider the constant regularity, order, and concatenation of natural things, the surprising magnificence, beauty, and perfection of the larger, and the exquisite contrivance of the smaller parts of creation, together with the exact harmony and correspondence of the whole, but above all the never-enough-admired laws of pain and pleasure, and the instincts or natural inclinations, appetites, and passions of animals; I say if we consider all these things, and at the same time attend to the meaning and import of the attributes One, Eternal, Infinitely Wise, Good, and Perfect, we shall clearly perceive that they belong to the aforesaid Spirit, "who works all in all," and "by whom all things consist."

147. Hence, it is evident that God is known as certainly and immediately as any other mind or spirit whatsoever distinct from ourselves. We may even assert that the existence of God is far more evidently perceived than the existence of men; because the effects of nature are infinitely more numerous and considerable than those ascribed to human agents. There is not any one mark that denotes a man, or effect produced by him, which does not more strongly evince the being of that Spirit who is the Author of Nature. For, it is evident that in affecting other persons the will of man has no other object than barely the motion of the limbs of his body; but that such a motion should be attended by, or excite any idea in the mind of another, depends wholly on the will of the Creator. He alone it is who, "upholding all things by the word of His power," maintains that intercourse between spirits whereby they are able to perceive the existence of each other. And yet this pure and clear light which enlightens every one is itself invisible.

148. It seems to be a general pretence of the unthinking herd that they cannot see God. Could we but see Him, say they, as we see a man, we should believe that He is, and believing obey His commands. But alas, we need only open our eyes to see the Sovereign Lord of all things, with a more full and clear view than we do any one of our fellow-creatures. Not that I imagine we see God (as some will have it) by a direct and immediate view; or see corporeal things, not by themselves, but by seeing that which represents them in the essence of God, which doctrine is, I must confess, to me incomprehensible. But I shall explain my meaning;- A human spirit or person is not perceived by sense, as not being an idea; when therefore we see the colour, size, figure, and motions of a man, we perceive only certain sensations or ideas excited in our own minds; and these being exhibited to our view in sundry distinct collections, serve to mark

out unto us the existence of finite and created spirits like ourselves. Hence it is plain we do not see a man- if by man is meant that which lives, moves, perceives, and thinks as we do- but only such a certain collection of ideas as directs us to think there is a distinct principle of thought and motion, like to ourselves, accompanying and represented by it. And after the same manner we see God; all the difference is that, whereas some one finite and narrow assemblage of ideas denotes a particular human mind, whithersoever we direct our view, we do at all times and in all places perceive manifest tokens of the Divinity: everything we see, hear, feel, or anywise perceive by sense, being a sign or effect of the power of God; as is our perception of those very motions which are produced by men.

149. It is therefore plain that nothing can be more evident to any one that is capable of the least reflexion than the existence of God, or a Spirit who is intimately present to our minds, producing in them all that variety of ideas or sensations which continually affect us, on whom we have an absolute and entire dependence, in short "in whom we live, and move, and have our being." That the discovery of this great truth, which lies so near and obvious to the mind, should be attained to by the reason of so very few, is a sad instance of the stupidity and inattention of men, who, though they are surrounded with such clear manifestations of the Deity, are yet so little affected by them that they seem, as it were, blinded with excess of light.

150. But you will say, Hath Nature no share in the production of natural things, and must they be all ascribed to the immediate and sole operation of God? I answer, if by Nature is meant only the visible series of effects or sensations imprinted on our minds, according to certain fixed and general laws, then it is plain that Nature, taken in this sense, cannot produce anything at all. But, if by Nature is meant some being distinct from God, as well as from the laws of nature, and things perceived by sense, I must confess that word is to me an empty sound without any intelligible meaning annexed to it. Nature, in this acceptation, is a vain chimera, introduced by those heathens who had not just notions of the omnipresence and infinite perfection of God. But, it is more unaccountable that it should be received among Christians, professing belief in the Holy Scriptures, which constantly ascribe those effects to the immediate hand of God that heathen philosophers are wont to impute to Nature. "The Lord He causeth the vapours to ascend; He maketh lightnings with rain; He bringeth forth the wind out of his treasures." Jerem. 10. 13. "He turneth the shadow of death into the morning, and maketh the day dark with night." Amos, 5. 8. "He visiteth the earth, and maketh it soft with showers: He blesseth the springing thereof, and crowneth the year with His goodness; so that the pastures are clothed with flocks, and the valleys are covered over with corn." See Psalm 65. But, notwithstanding that this is the constant language of Scripture, yet we have I know not what aversion from believing that God concerns Himself so nearly in our affairs. Fain would we suppose Him at a great distance off, and substitute some blind unthinking deputy in His stead, though (if we may believe Saint Paul) "He be not far from every one of us."

151. It will, I doubt not, be objected that the slow and gradual methods observed in the production of natural things do not seem to have for their cause the immediate hand of an Almighty Agent. Besides, monsters, untimely births, fruits blasted in the blossom, rains falling in desert places, miseries incident to human life, and the like, are so many arguments that the whole frame of nature is not immediately actuated and superintended by a Spirit of infinite wisdom and goodness. But the answer to this objection is in a good measure plain from sect. 62; it being visible that the aforesaid methods of nature are absolutely necessary, in order to working by the most simple and general rules, and after a steady and consistent manner; which argues both the wisdom and goodness of God. Such is the artificial contrivance of this mighty machine of nature that, whilst its motions and various phenomena strike on our senses, the hand which actuates the whole is itself unperceivable to men of flesh and blood. "Verily" (saith the prophet) "thou art a God that hidest thyself." Isaiah, 45. 15. But, though the Lord conceal Himself from the eyes of the sensual and lazy, who will not be at the least expense of thought, yet to an unbiased and attentive mind nothing can be more plainly legible than the intimate presence of an All-wise Spirit, who fashions, regulates and sustains the whole system

of beings. It is clear, from what we have elsewhere observed, that the operating according to general and stated laws is so necessary for our guidance in the affairs of life, and letting us into the secret of nature, that without it all reach and compass of thought, all human sagacity and design, could serve to no manner of purpose; it were even impossible there should be any such faculties or powers in the mind. See sect. 31. Which one consideration abundantly outbalances whatever particular inconveniences may thence arise.

152. We should further consider that the very blemishes and defects of nature are not without their use, in that they make an agreeable sort of variety, and augment the beauty of the rest of the creation, as shades in a picture serve to set off the brighter and more enlightened parts. We would likewise do well to examine whether our taxing the waste of seeds and embryos, and accidental destruction of plants and animals, before they come to full maturity, as an imprudence in the Author of nature, be not the effect of prejudice contracted by our familiarity with impotent and saving mortals. In man indeed a thrifty management of those things which he cannot procure without much pains and industry may be esteemed wisdom. But, we must not imagine that the inexplicably fine machine of an animal or vegetable costs the great Creator any more pains or trouble in its production than a pebble does; nothing being more evident than that an Omnipotent Spirit can indifferently produce everything by a mere fiat or act of His will. Hence, it is plain that the splendid profusion of natural things should not be interpreted weakness or prodigality in the agent who produces them, but rather be looked on as an argument of the riches of His power.

153. As for the mixture of pain or uneasiness which is in the world, pursuant to the general laws of nature, and the actions of finite, imperfect spirits, this, in the state we are in at present, is indispensably necessary to our well-being. But our prospects are too narrow. We take, for instance, the idea of some one particular pain into our thoughts, and account it evil; whereas, if we enlarge our view, so as to comprehend the various ends, connexions, and dependencies of things, on what occasions and in what proportions we are affected with pain and pleasure, the nature of human freedom, and the design with which we are put into the world; we shall be forced to acknowledge that those particular things which, considered in themselves, appear to be evil, have the nature of good, when considered as linked with the whole system of beings.

154. From what has been said, it will be manifest to any considering person, that it is merely for want of attention and comprehensiveness of mind that there are any favourers of Atheism or the Manichean Heresy to be found. Little and unreflecting souls may indeed burlesque the works of Providence, the beauty and order whereof they have not capacity, or will not be at the pains, to comprehend; but those who are masters of any justness and extent of thought, and are withal used to reflect, can never sufficiently admire the divine traces of Wisdom and Goodness that shine throughout the Economy of Nature. But what truth is there which shineth so strongly on the mind that by an aversion of thought, a wilful shutting of the eyes, we may not escape seeing it? Is it therefore to be wondered at, if the generality of men, who are ever intent on business or pleasure, and little used to fix or open the eye of their mind, should not have all that conviction and evidence of the Being of God which might be expected in reasonable creatures?

155. We should rather wonder that men can be found so stupid as to neglect, than that neglecting they should be unconvinced of such an evident and momentous truth. And yet it is to be feared that too many of parts and leisure, who live in Christian countries, are, merely through a supine and dreadful negligence, sunk into Atheism. Since it is downright impossible that a soul pierced and enlightened with a thorough sense of the omnipresence, holiness, and justice of that Almighty Spirit should persist in a remorseless violation of His laws. We ought, therefore, earnestly to meditate and dwell on those important points; that so we may attain conviction without all scruple "that the eyes of the Lord are in every place beholding the evil and the good; that He is with us and keepeth us in all places whither we go, and giveth us bread to eat and raiment to put on"; that He is present and conscious to our innermost thoughts; and that we have a most absolute and immediate dependence on Him. A clear view

of which great truths cannot choose but fill our hearts with an awful circumspection and holy fear, which is the strongest incentive to Virtue, and the best guard against Vice.

156. For, after all, what deserves the first place in our studies is the consideration of GOD and our DUTY; which to promote, as it was the main drift and design of my labours, so shall I esteem them altogether useless and ineffectual if, by what I have said, I cannot inspire my readers with a pious sense of the Presence of God; and, having shewn the falseness or vanity of those barren speculations which make the chief employment of learned men, the better dispose them to reverence and embrace the salutary truths of the Gospel, which to know and to practice is the highest perfection of human nature.

Three Dialogues between Hylas and Philonous

In Opposition to Sceptics and Atheists

The First Dialogue

Philonous. Good morrow, Hylas: I did not expect to find you abroad so early.

Hylas. It is indeed something unusual; but my thoughts were so taken up with a subject I was discoursing of last night, that finding I could not sleep, I resolved to rise and take a turn in the garden.

Phil. It happened well, to let you see what innocent and agreeable pleasures you lose every morning. Can there be a pleasanter time of the day, or a more delightful season of the year? That purple sky, those wild but sweet notes of birds, the fragrant bloom upon the trees and flowers, the gentle influence of the rising sun, these and a thousand nameless beauties of nature inspire the soul with secret transports; its faculties too being at this time fresh and lively, are fit for those meditations, which the solitude of a garden and tranquillity of the morning naturally dispose us to. But I am afraid I interrupt your thoughts: for you seemed very intent on something.

Hyl. It is true, I was, and shall be obliged to you if you will permit me to go on in the same vein; not that I would by any means deprive myself of your company, for my thoughts always flow more easily in conversation with a friend, than when I am alone: but my request is, that you would suffer me to impart my reflexions to you.

Phil. With all my heart, it is what I should have requested myself if you had not prevented me.

Hyl. I was considering the odd fate of those men who have in all ages, through an affectation of being distinguished from the vulgar, or some unaccountable turn of thought, pretended either to believe nothing at all, or to believe the most extravagant things in the world. This however might be borne, if their paradoxes and scepticism did not draw after them some consequences of general disadvantage to mankind. But the mischief lieth here; that when men of less leisure see them who are supposed to have spent their whole time in the pursuits of knowledge professing an entire ignorance of all things, or advancing such notions as are repugnant to plain and commonly received principles, they will be tempted to entertain suspicions concerning the most important truths, which they had hitherto held sacred and unquestionable.

Phil. I entirely agree with you, as to the ill tendency of the affected doubts of some philosophers, and fantastical conceits of others. I am even so far gone of late in this way of thinking, that I have quitted several of the sublime notions I had got in their schools for vulgar opinions. And I give it you on my word; since this revolt from metaphysical notions to the plain dictates of nature and common sense, I find my understanding strangely enlightened, so that I can now easily comprehend a great many things which before were all mystery and riddle.

Hyl. I am glad to find there was nothing in the accounts I heard of you.

Phil. Pray, what were those?

Hyl. You were represented, in last night's conversation, as one who maintained the most extravagant opinion that ever entered into the mind of man, to wit, that there is no such thing as MATERIAL SUBSTANCE in the world.

Phil. That there is no such thing as what PHILOSOPHERS CALL MATERIAL SUBSTANCE, I am seriously persuaded: but, if I were made to see anything absurd or sceptical in this, I should then have the same reason to renounce this that I imagine I have now to reject the contrary opinion.

Hyl. What I can anything be more fantastical, more repugnant to Common Sense, or a more manifest piece of Scepticism, than to believe there is no such thing as MATTER?

Phil. Softly, good Hylas. What if it should prove that you, who hold there is, are, by virtue of that opinion, a greater sceptic, and maintain more paradoxes and repugnances to Common Sense, than I who believe no such thing?

Hyl. You may as soon persuade me, the part is greater than the whole, as that, in order to avoid absurdity and Scepticism, I should ever be obliged to give up my opinion in this point.

Phil. Well then, are you content to admit that opinion for true, which upon examination shall appear most agreeable to Common Sense, and remote from Scepticism?

Hyl. With all my heart. Since you are for raising disputes about the plainest things in nature, I am content for once to hear what you have to say.

Phil. Pray, Hylas, what do you mean by a SCEPTIC?

Hyl. I mean what all men mean — one that doubts of everything.

Phil. He then who entertains no doubts concerning some particular point, with regard to that point cannot be thought a sceptic.

Hyl. I agree with you.

Phil. Whether doth doubting consist in embracing the affirmative or negative side of a question?

Hyl. In neither; for whoever understands English cannot but know that DOUBTING signifies a suspense between both.

Phil. He then that denies any point, can no more be said to doubt of it, than he who affirmeth it with the same degree of assurance.

Hyl. True.

Phil. And, consequently, for such his denial is no more to be esteemed a sceptic than the other.

Hyl. I acknowledge it.

Phil. How cometh it to pass then, Hylas, that you pronounce me A SCEPTIC, because I deny what you affirm, to wit, the existence of Matter? Since, for aught you can tell, I am as peremptory in my denial, as you in your affirmation.

Hyl. Hold, Philonous, I have been a little out in my definition; but every false step a man makes in discourse is not to be insisted on. I said indeed that a SCEPTIC was one who doubted of everything; but I should have added, or who denies the reality and truth of things.

Phil. What things? Do you mean the principles and theorems of sciences? But these you know are universal intellectual notions, and consequently independent of Matter. The denial therefore of this doth not imply the denying them.

Hyl. I grant it. But are there no other things? What think you of distrusting the senses, of denying the real existence of sensible things, or pretending to know nothing of them. Is not this sufficient to denominate a man a SCEPTIC?

Phil. Shall we therefore examine which of us it is that denies the reality of sensible things, or professes the greatest ignorance of them; since, if I take you rightly, he is to be esteemed the greatest SCEPTIC?

Hyl. That is what I desire.

Phil. What mean you by Sensible Things?

Hyl. Those things which are perceived by the senses. Can you imagine that I mean anything else?

Phil. Pardon me, Hylas, if I am desirous clearly to apprehend your notions, since this may much shorten our inquiry. Suffer me then to ask you this farther question. Are those things only perceived by the senses which are perceived immediately? Or, may those things properly be said to be SENSIBLE which are perceived mediately, or not without the intervention of others?

Hyl. I do not sufficiently understand you.

Phil. In reading a book, what I immediately perceive are the letters; but mediately, or by means of these, are suggested to my mind the notions of God, virtue, truth, &c. Now, that the letters are truly sensible things, or perceived by sense, there is no doubt: but I would know whether you take the things suggested by them to be so too.

Hyl. No, certainly: it were absurd to think GOD or VIRTUE sensible things; though they may be signified and suggested to the mind by sensible marks, with which they have an arbitrary connexion.

Phil. It seems then, that by SENSIBLE THINGS you mean those only which can be perceived IMMEDIATELY by sense?

Hyl. Right.

Phil. Doth it not follow from this, that though I see one part of the sky red, and another blue, and that my reason doth thence evidently conclude there must be some cause of that diversity of colours, yet that cause cannot be said to be a sensible thing, or perceived by the sense of seeing?

Hyl. It doth.

Phil. In like manner, though I hear variety of sounds, yet I cannot be said to hear the causes of those sounds?

Hyl. You cannot.

Phil. And when by my touch I perceive a thing to be hot and heavy, I cannot say, with any truth or propriety, that I feel the cause of its heat or weight?

Hyl. To prevent any more questions of this kind, I tell you once for all, that by SENSIBLE THINGS I mean those only which are perceived by sense; and that in truth the senses perceive nothing which they do not perceive IMMEDIATELY: for they make no inferences. The deducing therefore of causes or occasions from effects and appearances, which alone are perceived by sense, entirely relates to reason.

Phil. This point then is agreed between us — That SENSIBLE THINGS ARE THOSE ONLY WHICH ARE IMMEDIATELY PERCEIVED BY SENSE. You will farther inform me, whether we immediately perceive by sight anything beside light, and colours, and figures; or by hearing, anything but sounds; by the palate, anything beside tastes; by the smell, beside odours; or by the touch, more than tangible qualities.

Hyl. We do not.

Phil. It seems, therefore, that if you take away all sensible qualities, there remains nothing sensible?

Hyl. I grant it.

Phil. Sensible things therefore are nothing else but so many sensible qualities, or combinations of sensible qualities?

Hyl. Nothing else.

Phil. HEAT then is a sensible thing?

Hyl. Certainly.

Phil. Doth the REALITY of sensible things consist in being perceived? or, is it something distinct from their being perceived, and that bears no relation to the mind?

Hyl. To EXIST is one thing, and to be PERCEIVED is another.

Phil. I speak with regard to sensible things only. And of these I ask, whether by their real existence you mean a subsistence exterior to the mind, and distinct from their being perceived?

Hyl. I mean a real absolute being, distinct from, and without any relation to, their being perceived.

Phil. Heat therefore, if it be allowed a real being, must exist without the mind?

Hyl. It must.

Phil. Tell me, Hylas, is this real existence equally compatible to all degrees of heat, which we perceive; or is there any reason why we should attribute it to some, and deny it to others? And if there be, pray let me know that reason.

Hyl. Whatever degree of heat we perceive by sense, we may be sure the same exists in the object that occasions it.

Phil. What! the greatest as well as the least?

Hyl. I tell you, the reason is plainly the same in respect of both. They are both perceived by sense; nay, the greater degree of heat is more sensibly perceived; and consequently, if there is any difference, we are more certain of its real existence than we can be of the reality of a lesser degree.

Phil. But is not the most vehement and intense degree of heat a very great pain?

Hyl. No one can deny it.

Phil. And is any unperceiving thing capable of pain or pleasure?

Hyl. No, certainly.

Phil. Is your material substance a senseless being, or a being endowed with sense and perception?

Hyl. It is senseless without doubt.

Phil. It cannot therefore be the subject of pain?

Hyl. By no means.

Phil. Nor consequently of the greatest heat perceived by sense, since you acknowledge this to be no small pain?

Hyl. I grant it.

Phil. What shall we say then of your external object; is it a material Substance, or no?

Hyl. It is a material substance with the sensible qualities inhering in it.

Phil. How then can a great heat exist in it, since you own it cannot in a material substance? I desire you would clear this point.

Hyl. Hold, Philonous, I fear I was out in yielding intense heat to be a pain. It should seem rather, that pain is something distinct from heat, and the consequence or effect of it.

Phil. Upon putting your hand near the fire, do you perceive one simple uniform sensation, or two distinct sensations?

Hyl. But one simple sensation.

Phil. Is not the heat immediately perceived?

Hyl. It is.

Phil. And the pain?

Hyl. True.

Phil. Seeing therefore they are both immediately perceived at the same time, and the fire affects you only with one simple or uncompounded idea, it follows that this same simple idea is both the intense heat immediately perceived, and the pain; and, consequently, that the intense heat immediately perceived is nothing distinct from a particular sort of pain.

Hyl. It seems so.

Phil. Again, try in your thoughts, Hylas, if you can conceive a vehement sensation to be without pain or pleasure.

Hyl. I cannot.

Phil. Or can you frame to yourself an idea of sensible pain or pleasure in general, abstracted from every particular idea of heat, cold, tastes, smells? &c.

Hyl. I do not find that I can.

Phil. Doth it not therefore follow, that sensible pain is nothing distinct from those sensations or ideas, in an intense degree?

Hyl. It is undeniable; and, to speak the truth, I begin to suspect a very great heat cannot exist but in a mind perceiving it.

Phil. What! are you then in that sceptical state of suspense, between affirming and denying?

Hyl. I think I may be positive in the point. A very violent and painful heat cannot exist without the mind.

Phil. It hath not therefore according to you, any REAL being?

Hyl. I own it.

Phil. Is it therefore certain, that there is no body in nature really hot?

Hyl. I have not denied there is any real heat in bodies. I only say, there is no such thing as an intense real heat.

Phil. But, did you not say before that all degrees of heat were equally real; or, if there was any difference, that the greater were more undoubtedly real than the lesser?

Hyl. True: but it was because I did not then consider the ground there is for distinguishing between them, which I now plainly see. And it is this: because intense heat is nothing else but a particular kind of painful sensation; and pain cannot exist but in a perceiving being; it follows that no intense heat can really exist in an unperceiving corporeal substance. But this is no reason why we should deny heat in an inferior degree to exist in such a substance.

Phil. But how shall we be able to discern those degrees of heat which exist only in the mind from those which exist without it?

Hyl. That is no difficult matter. You know the least pain cannot exist unperceived; whatever, therefore, degree of heat is a pain exists only in the mind. But, as for all other degrees of heat, nothing obliges us to think the same of them.

Phil. I think you granted before that no unperceiving being was capable of pleasure, any more than of pain.

Hyl. I did.

Phil. And is not warmth, or a more gentle degree of heat than what causes uneasiness, a pleasure?

Hyl. What then?

Phil. Consequently, it cannot exist without the mind in an unperceiving substance, or body.

Hyl. So it seems.

Phil. Since, therefore, as well those degrees of heat that are not painful, as those that are, can exist only in a thinking substance; may we not conclude that external bodies are absolutely incapable of any degree of heat whatsoever?

Hyl. On second thoughts, I do not think it so evident that warmth is a pleasure as that a great degree of heat is a pain.

Phil. I do not pretend that warmth is as great a pleasure as heat is a pain. But, if you grant it to be even a small pleasure, it serves to make good my conclusion.

Hyl. I could rather call it an INDOLENCE. It seems to be nothing more than a privation of both pain and pleasure. And that such a quality or state as this may agree to an unthinking substance, I hope you will not deny.

Phil. If you are resolved to maintain that warmth, or a gentle degree of heat, is no pleasure, I know not how to convince you otherwise than by appealing to your own sense. But what think you of cold?

Hyl. The same that I do of heat. An intense degree of cold is a pain; for to feel a very great cold, is to perceive a great uneasiness: it cannot therefore exist without the mind; but a lesser degree of cold may, as well as a lesser degree of heat.

Phil. Those bodies, therefore, upon whose application to our own, we perceive a moderate degree of heat, must be concluded to have a moderate degree of heat or warmth in them; and those, upon whose application we feel a like degree of cold, must be thought to have cold in them.

Hyl. They must.

Phil. Can any doctrine be true that necessarily leads a man into an absurdity?

Hyl. Without doubt it cannot.

Phil. Is it not an absurdity to think that the same thing should be at the same time both cold and warm?

Hyl. It is.

Phil. Suppose now one of your hands hot, and the other cold, and that they are both at once put into the same vessel of water, in an intermediate state; will not the water seem cold to one hand, and warm to the other?

Hyl. It will.

Phil. Ought we not therefore, by your principles, to conclude it is really both cold and warm at the same time, that is, according to your own concession, to believe an absurdity?

Hyl. I confess it seems so.

Phil. Consequently, the principles themselves are false, since you have granted that no true principle leads to an absurdity.

Hyl. But, after all, can anything be more absurd than to say, THERE IS NO HEAT IN THE FIRE?

Phil. To make the point still clearer; tell me whether, in two cases exactly alike, we ought not to make the same judgment?

Hyl. We ought.

Phil. When a pin pricks your finger, doth it not rend and divide the fibres of your flesh?

Hyl. It doth.

Phil. And when a coal burns your finger, doth it any more?

Hyl. It doth not.

Phil. Since, therefore, you neither judge the sensation itself occasioned by the pin, nor anything like it to be in the pin; you should not, conformably to what you have now granted, judge the sensation occasioned by the fire, or anything like it, to be in the fire.

Hyl. Well, since it must be so, I am content to yield this point, and acknowledge that heat and cold are only sensations existing in our minds. But there still remain qualities enough to secure the reality of external things.

Phil. But what will you say, Hylas, if it shall appear that the case is the same with regard to all other sensible qualities, and that they can no more be supposed to exist without the mind, than heat and cold?

Hyl. Then indeed you will have done something to the purpose; but that is what I despair of seeing proved.

Phil. Let us examine them in order. What think you of TASTES, do they exist without the mind, or no?

Hyl. Can any man in his senses doubt whether sugar is sweet, or wormwood bitter?

Phil. Inform me, Hylas. Is a sweet taste a particular kind of pleasure or pleasant sensation, or is it not?

Hyl. It is.

Phil. And is not bitterness some kind of uneasiness or pain?

Hyl. I grant it.

Phil. If therefore sugar and wormwood are unthinking corporeal substances existing without the mind, how can sweetness and bitterness, that is, Pleasure and pain, agree to them?

Hyl. Hold, Philonous, I now see what it was delude time. You asked whether heat and cold, sweetness at were not particular sorts of pleasure and pain; to which simply, that they were. Whereas I should have thus distinguished: those qualities, as perceived by us, are pleasures or pair existing in the external objects. We must not therefore conclude absolutely, that there is no heat in the fire, or sweetness in the sugar, but only that heat or sweetness, as perceived by us, are not in the fire or sugar. What say you to this?

Phil. I say it is nothing to the purpose. Our discourse proceeded altogether concerning sensible things, which you defined to be, THE THINGS WE IMMEDIATELY PERCEIVE BY OUR SENSES. Whatever other qualities, therefore, you speak of as distinct from these, I know nothing of them, neither do they at all belong to the point in dispute. You may, indeed, pretend to have discovered certain qualities which you do not perceive, and assert those insensible qualities exist in fire and sugar. But what use can be made of this to your present purpose, I am at a loss to conceive. Tell me then once more, do you acknowledge that heat and cold, sweetness and bitterness (meaning those qualities which are perceived by the senses), do not exist without the mind?

Hyl. I see it is to no purpose to hold out, so I give up the cause as to those mentioned qualities. Though I profess it sounds oddly, to say that sugar is not sweet.

Phil. But, for your farther satisfaction, take this along with you: that which at other times seems sweet, shall, to a distempered palate, appear bitter. And, nothing can be plainer than that divers persons perceive different tastes in the same food; since that which one man delights in, another abhors. And how could this be, if the taste was something really inherent in the food?

Hyl. I acknowledge I know not how.

Phil. In the next place, ODOURS are to be considered. And, with regard to these, I would fain know whether what hath been said of tastes doth not exactly agree to them? Are they not so many pleasing or displeasing sensations?

Hyl. They are.

Phil. Can you then conceive it possible that they should exist in an unperceiving thing?

Hyl. I cannot.

Phil. Or, can you imagine that filth and ordure affect those brute animals that feed on them out of choice, with the same smells which we perceive in them?

Hyl. By no means.

Phil. May we not therefore conclude of smells, as of the other forementioned qualities, that they cannot exist in any but a perceiving substance or mind?

Hyl. I think so.

Phil. Then as to SOUNDS, what must we think of them: are they accidents really inherent in external bodies, or not?

Hyl. That they inhere not in the sonorous bodies is plain from hence: because a bell struck in the exhausted receiver of an air-pump sends forth no sound. The air, therefore, must be thought the subject of sound.

Phil. What reason is there for that, Hylas?

Hyl. Because, when any motion is raised in the air, we perceive a sound greater or lesser, according to the air's motion; but without some motion in the air, we never hear any sound at all.

Phil. And granting that we never hear a sound but when some motion is produced in the air, yet I do not see how you can infer from thence, that the sound itself is in the air.

Hyl. It is this very motion in the external air that produces in the mind the sensation of SOUND. For, striking on the drum of the ear, it causeth a vibration, which by the auditory nerves being communicated to the brain, the soul is thereupon affected with the sensation called SOUND.

Phil. What! is sound then a sensation?

Hyl. I tell you, as perceived by us, it is a particular sensation in the mind.

Phil. And can any sensation exist without the mind?

Hyl. No, certainly.

Phil. How then can sound, being a sensation, exist in the air, if by the AIR you mean a senseless substance existing without the mind?

Hyl. You must distinguish, Philonous, between sound as it is perceived by us, and as it is in itself; or (which is the same thing) between the sound we immediately perceive, and that which exists without us. The former, indeed, is a particular kind of sensation, but the latter is merely a vibrative or undulatory motion the air.

Phil. I thought I had already obviated that distinction, by answer I gave when you were applying it in a like case before. But, to say no more of that, are you sure then that sound is really nothing but motion?

Hyl. I am.

Phil. Whatever therefore agrees to real sound, may with truth be attributed to motion?

Hyl. It may.

Phil. It is then good sense to speak of MOTION as of a thing that is LOUD, SWEET, ACUTE, or GRAVE.

Hyl. I see you are resolved not to understand me. Is it not evident those accidents or modes belong only to sensible sound, or SOUND in the common acceptation of the word, but not to sound in the real and philosophic sense; which, as I just now told you, is nothing but a certain motion of the air?

Phil. It seems then there are two sorts of sound — the one vulgar, or that which is heard, the other philosophical and real?

Hyl. Even so.

Phil. And the latter consists in motion?

Hyl. I told you so before.

Phil. Tell me, Hylas, to which of the senses, think you, the idea of motion belongs? to the hearing?

Hyl. No, certainly; but to the sight and touch.

Phil. It should follow then, that, according to you, real sounds may possibly be SEEN OR FELT, but never HEARD.

Hyl. Look you, Philonous, you may, if you please, make a jest of my opinion, but that will not alter the truth of things. I own, indeed, the inferences you draw me into sound something oddly; but common language, you know, is framed by, and for the use of the vulgar: we must not therefore wonder if expressions adapted to exact philosophic notions seem uncouth and out of the way.

Phil. Is it come to that? I assure you, I imagine myself to have gained no small point, since you make so light of departing from common phrases and opinions; it being a main part of our inquiry, to examine whose notions are widest of the common road, and most repugnant to the general sense of the world. But, can you think it no more than a philosophical paradox, to say that REAL SOUNDS ARE NEVER HEARD, and that the idea of them is obtained by some other sense? And is there nothing in this contrary to nature and the truth of things?

Hyl. To deal ingenuously, I do not like it. And, after the concessions already made, I had as well grant that sounds too have no real being without the mind.

Phil. And I hope you will make no difficulty to acknowledge the same of COLOURS.

Hyl. Pardon me: the case of colours is very different. Can anything be plainer than that we see them on the objects?

Phil. The objects you speak of are, I suppose, corporeal Substances existing without the mind?

Hyl. They are.

Phil. And have true and real colours inhering in them?

Hyl. Each visible object hath that colour which we see in it.

Phil. How! is there anything visible but what we perceive by sight?

Hyl. There is not.

Phil. And, do we perceive anything by sense which we do not perceive immediately?

Hyl. How often must I be obliged to repeat the same thing? I tell you, we do not.

Phil. Have patience, good Hylas; and tell me once more, whether there is anything immediately perceived by the senses, except sensible qualities. I know you asserted there was not; but I would now be informed, whether you still persist in the same opinion.

Hyl. I do.

Phil. Pray, is your corporeal substance either a sensible quality, or made up of sensible qualities?

Hyl. What a question that is! who ever thought it was?

Phil. My reason for asking was, because in saying, EACH VISIBLE OBJECT HATH THAT COLOUR WHICH WE SEE IN IT, you make visible objects to be corporeal substances; which implies either that corporeal substances are sensible qualities, or else that there is something besides sensible qualities perceived by sight: but, as this point was formerly agreed between us, and is still maintained by you, it is a clear consequence, that your CORPOREAL SUBSTANCE is nothing distinct from SENSIBLE QUALITIES.

Hyl. You may draw as many absurd consequences as you please, and endeavour to perplex the plainest things; but you shall never persuade me out of my senses. I clearly understand my own meaning.

Phil. I wish you would make me understand it too. But, since you are unwilling to have your notion of corporeal substance examined, I shall urge that point no farther. Only be pleased to let me know, whether the same colours which we see exist in external bodies, or some other.

Hyl. The very same.

Phil. What! are then the beautiful red and purple we see on yonder clouds really in them? Or do you imagine they have in themselves any other form than that of a dark mist or vapour?

Hyl. I must own, Philonous, those colours are not really in the clouds as they seem to be at this distance. They are only apparent colours.

Phil. APPARENT call you them? how shall we distinguish these apparent colours from real?

Hyl. Very easily. Those are to be thought apparent which, appearing only at a distance, vanish upon a nearer approach.

Phil. And those, I suppose, are to be thought real which are discovered by the most near and exact survey.

Hyl. Right.

Phil. Is the nearest and exactest survey made by the help of a microscope, or by the naked eye?

Hyl. By a microscope, doubtless.

Phil. But a microscope often discovers colours in an object different from those perceived by the unassisted sight. And, in case we had microscopes magnifying to any assigned degree, it is certain that no object whatsoever, viewed through them, would appear in the same colour which it exhibits to the naked eye.

Hyl. And what will you conclude from all this? You cannot argue that there are really and naturally no colours on objects: because by artificial managements they may be altered, or made to vanish.

Phil. I think it may evidently be concluded from your own concessions, that all the colours we see with our naked eyes are only apparent as those on the clouds, since they vanish upon a more close and accurate inspection which is afforded us by a microscope. Then' as to what you say by way of prevention: I ask you whether the real and natural state of an object is better discovered by a very sharp and piercing sight, or by one which is less sharp?

Hyl. By the former without doubt.

Phil. Is it not plain from DIOPTRICS that microscopes make the sight more penetrating, and represent objects as they would appear to the eye in case it were naturally endowed with a most exquisite sharpness?

Hyl. It is.

Phil. Consequently the microscopical representation is to be thought that which best sets forth the real nature of the thing, or what it is in itself. The colours, therefore, by it perceived are more genuine and real than those perceived otherwise.

Hyl. I confess there is something in what you say.

Phil. Besides, it is not only possible but manifest, that there actually are animals whose eyes are by nature framed to perceive those things which by reason of their minuteness escape our sight. What think you of those inconceivably small animals perceived by glasses? must we suppose they are all stark blind? Or, in case they see, can it be imagined their sight hath not the same use in preserving their bodies from injuries, which appears in that of all other animals? And if it hath, is it not evident they must see particles less than their own bodies; which will present them with a far different view in each object from that which strikes our senses? Even our own eyes do not always represent objects to us after the same manner. In the jaundice every one knows that all things seem yellow. Is it not therefore highly probable those animals in whose eyes we discern a very different texture from that of ours, and whose bodies abound with different humours, do not see the same colours in every object that we do? From all which, should it not seem to follow that all colours are equally apparent, and that none of those which we perceive are really inherent in any outward object?

Hyl. It should.

Phil. The point will be past all doubt, if you consider that, in case colours were real properties or affections inherent in external bodies, they could admit of no alteration without some change wrought in the very bodies themselves: but, is it not evident from what hath been said that, upon the use of microscopes, upon a change happening in the burnouts of the eye, or a variation of distance, without any manner of real alteration in the thing itself, the colours of any object are either changed, or totally disappear? Nay, all other circumstances remaining the same, change but the situation of some objects, and they shall present different colours to the eye. The same thing happens upon viewing an object in various degrees of light. And what is more known than that the same bodies appear differently coloured by candle-light from what they do in the open day? Add to these the experiment of a prism which, separating the heterogeneous rays of light, alters the colour of any object, and will cause the whitest to appear of a deep blue or red to the naked eye. And now tell me whether you are still of opinion that every body hath its true real colour inhering in it; and, if you think it hath, I would fain know farther from you, what certain distance and position of the object, what peculiar texture and formation of the eye, what degree or kind of light is necessary for ascertaining that true colour, and distinguishing it from apparent ones.

Hyl. I own myself entirely satisfied, that they are all equally apparent, and that there is no such thing as colour really inhering in external bodies, but that it is altogether in the light. And what confirms me in this opinion is, that in proportion to the light colours are still more or less vivid; and if there be no light, then are there no colours perceived. Besides, allowing there are colours on external objects, yet, how is it possible for us to perceive them? For no external body affects the mind, unless it acts first on our organs of sense. But the only action of bodies is motion; and motion cannot be communicated otherwise than by impulse. A distant object therefore cannot act on the eye; nor consequently make itself or its properties perceivable to the soul. Whence it plainly follows that it is immediately some contiguous substance, which, operating on the eye, occasions a perception of colours: and such is light.

Phil. Howl is light then a substance?

Hyl.. I tell you, Philonous, external light is nothing but a thin fluid substance, whose minute particles being agitated with a brisk motion, and in various manners reflected from the different surfaces of outward objects to the eyes, communicate different motions to the optic nerves; which, being propagated to the brain, cause therein various impressions; and these are attended with the sensations of red, blue, yellow, &c.

Phil. It seems then the light doth no more than shake the optic nerves.

Hyl. Nothing else.

Phil. And consequent to each particular motion of the nerves, the mind is affected with a sensation, which is some particular colour.

Hyl. Right.

Phil. And these sensations have no existence without the mind.

Hyl. They have not.

Phil. How then do you affirm that colours are in the light; since by LIGHT you understand a corporeal substance external to the mind?

Hyl. Light and colours, as immediately perceived by us, I grant cannot exist without the mind. But in themselves they are only the motions and configurations of certain insensible particles of matter.

Phil. Colours then, in the vulgar sense, or taken for the immediate objects of sight, cannot agree to any but a perceiving substance.

Hyl. That is what I say.

Phil. Well then, since you give up the point as to those sensible qualities which are alone thought colours by all mankind beside, you may hold what you please with regard to those invisible ones of the philosophers. It is not my business to dispute about THEM; only I would advise you to bethink yourself, whether, considering the inquiry we are upon, it be prudent for you to affirm — THE RED AND BLUE WHICH WE SEE ARE NOT REAL COLOURS, BUT CERTAIN UNKNOWN MOTIONS AND FIGURES WHICH NO MAN EVER DID OR CAN SEE ARE TRULY SO. Are not these shocking notions, and are not they subject to as many ridiculous inferences, as those you were obliged to renounce before in the case of sounds?

Hyl. I frankly own, Philonous, that it is in vain to longer. Colours, sounds, tastes, in a word all those termed SECONDARY QUALITIES, have certainly no existence without the mind. But by this acknowledgment I must not be supposed to derogate, the reality of Matter, or external objects; seeing it is no more than several philosophers maintain, who nevertheless are the farthest imaginable from denying Matter. For the clearer understanding of this, you must know sensible qualities are by philosophers divided into PRIMARY and SECONDARY. The former are Extension, Figure, Solidity, Gravity, Motion, and Rest; and these they hold exist really in bodies. The latter are those above enumerated; or, briefly, ALL SENSIBLE QUALITIES BESIDE THE PRIMARY; which they assert are only so many sensations or ideas existing nowhere but in the mind. But all this, I doubt not, you are apprised of. For my part, I have been a long time sensible there was such an opinion current among philosophers, but was never thoroughly convinced of its truth until now.

Phil. You are still then of opinion that EXTENSION and FIGURES are inherent in external unthinking substances?

Hyl. I am.

Phil. But what if the same arguments which are brought against Secondary Qualities will hold good against these also?

Hyl. Why then I shall be obliged to think, they too exist only in the mind.

Phil. Is it your opinion the very figure and extension which you perceive by sense exist in the outward object or material substance? HYL. It is.

Phil. Have all other animals as good grounds to think the same of the figure and extension which they see and feel?

Hyl. Without doubt, if they have any thought at all.

Phil. Answer me, Hylas. Think you the senses were bestowed upon all animals for their preservation and well-being in life? or were they given to men alone for this end?

Hyl. I make no question but they have the same use in all other animals.

Phil. If so, is it not necessary they should be enabled by them to perceive their own limbs, and those bodies which are capable of harming them?

Hyl. Certainly.

Phil. A mite therefore must be supposed to see his own foot, and things equal or even less than it, as bodies of some considerable dimension; though at the same time they appear to you scarce discernible, or at best as so many visible points?

Hyl. I cannot deny it.

Phil. And to creatures less than the mite they will seem yet larger?

Hyl. They will.

Phil. Insomuch that what you can hardly discern will to another extremely minute animal appear as some huge mountain?

Hyl. All this I grant.

Phil. Can one and the same thing be at the same time in itself of different dimensions?

Hyl. That were absurd to imagine.

Phil. But, from what you have laid down it follows that both the extension by you perceived, and that perceived by the mite itself, as likewise all those perceived by lesser animals, are each of them the true extension of the mite's foot; that is to say, by your own principles you are led into an absurdity.

Hyl. There seems to be some difficulty in the point.

Phil. Again, have you not acknowledged that no real inherent property of any object can be changed without some change in the thing itself?

Hyl. I have.

Phil. But, as we approach to or recede from an object, the visible extension varies, being at one distance ten or a hundred times greater than another. Doth it not therefore follow from hence likewise that it is not really inherent in the object?

Hyl. I own I am at a loss what to think.

Phil. Your judgment will soon be determined, if you will venture to think as freely concerning this quality as you have done concerning the rest. Was it not admitted as a good argument, that neither heat nor cold was in the water, because it seemed warm to one hand and cold to the other?

Hyl. It was.

Phil. Is it not the very same reasoning to conclude, there is no extension or figure in an object, because to one eye it shall seem little, smooth, and round, when at the same time it appears to the other, great, uneven, and regular?

Hyl. The very same. But does this latter fact ever happen?

Phil. You may at any time make the experiment, by looking with one eye bare, and with the other through a microscope.

Hyl. I know not how to maintain it; and yet I am loath to give up EXTENSION, I see so many odd consequences following upon such a concession.

Phil. Odd, say you? After the concessions already made, I hope you will stick at nothing for its oddness. But, on the other hand, should it not seem very odd, if the general reasoning which includes all other sensible qualities did not also include extension? If it be allowed that no idea, nor anything like an idea, can exist in an unperceiving substance, then surely it follows that no figure, or mode of extension, which we can either perceive, or imagine, or have any idea of, can be really inherent in Matter; not to mention the peculiar difficulty there must be in conceiving a material substance, prior to and distinct from extension to be the SUBSTRATUM of extension. Be the sensible quality what it will — figure, or sound, or colour, it seems alike impossible it should subsist in that which doth not perceive it.

Hyl. I give up the point for the present, reserving still a right to retract my opinion, in case I shall hereafter discover any false step in my progress to it.

Phil. That is a right you cannot be denied. Figures and extension being despatched, we proceed next to MOTION. Can a real motion in any external body be at the same time very swift and very slow?

Hyl. It cannot.

Phil. Is not the motion of a body swift in a reciprocal proportion to the time it takes up in describing any given space? Thus a body that describes a mile in an hour moves three times faster than it would in case it described only a mile in three hours.

Hyl. I agree with you.

Phil. And is not time measured by the succession of ideas in our minds?

Hyl. It is.

Phil. And is it not possible ideas should succeed one another twice as fast in your mind as they do in mine, or in that of some spirit of another kind?

Hyl. I own it.

Phil. Consequently the same body may to another seem to perform its motion over any space in half the time that it doth to you. And the same reasoning will hold as to any other proportion: that is to say, according to your principles (since the motions perceived are both really in the object) it is possible one and the same body shall be really moved the same way at once, both very swift and very slow. How is this consistent either with common sense, or with what you just now granted?

Hyl. I have nothing to say to it.

Phil. Then as for SOLIDITY; either you do not mean any sensible quality by that word, and so it is beside our inquiry: or if you do, it must be either hardness or resistance. But both the one and the other are plainly relative to our senses: it being evident that what seems hard to one animal may appear soft to another, who hath greater force and firmness of limbs. Nor is it less plain that the resistance I feel is not in the body.

Hyl. I own the very SENSATION of resistance, which is all you immediately perceive, is not in the body; but the CAUSE of that sensation is.

Phil. But the causes of our sensations are not things immediately perceived, and therefore are not sensible. This point I thought had been already determined.

Hyl. I own it was; but you will pardon me if I seem a little embarrassed: I know not how to quit my old notions.

Phil. To help you out, do but consider that if EXTENSION be once acknowledged to have no existence without the mind, the same must necessarily be granted of motion, solidity, and gravity; since they all evidently suppose extension. It is therefore superfluous to inquire particularly concerning each of them. In denying extension, you have denied them all to have any real existence.

Hyl. I wonder, Philonous, if what you say be true, why those philosophers who deny the Secondary Qualities any real existence should yet attribute it to the Primary. If there is no difference between them, how can this be accounted for?

Phil. It is not my business to account for every opinion of the philosophers. But, among other reasons which may be assigned for this, it seems probable that pleasure and pain being rather annexed to the former than the latter may be one. Heat and cold, tastes and smells, have something more vividly pleasing or disagreeable than the ideas of extension, figure, and motion affect us with. And, it being too visibly absurd to hold that pain or pleasure can be in an unperceiving substance, men are more easily weaned from believing the external existence of the Secondary than the Primary Qualities. You will be satisfied there is something in this, if you recollect the difference you made between an intense and more moderate degree of heat; allowing the one a real existence, while you denied it to the other. But, after all, there is no rational ground for that distinction; for, surely an indifferent sensation is as truly a SENSATION as one more pleasing or painful; and consequently should not any more than they be supposed to exist in an unthinking subject.

Hyl. It is just come into my head, Philonous, that I have somewhere heard of a distinction between absolute and sensible extension. Now, though it be acknowledged that GREAT and SMALL, consisting merely in the relation which other extended beings have to the parts of our own bodies, do not really inhere in the substances themselves; yet nothing obliges us to hold the same with regard to ABSOLUTE EXTENSION, which is something abstracted from GREAT and SMALL, from this or that particular magnitude or figure. So likewise as to motion; SWIFT and SLOW are altogether relative to the succession of ideas in our own minds. But, it doth not follow, because those modifications of motion exist not without the mind, that therefore absolute motion abstracted from them doth not.

Phil. Pray what is it that distinguishes one motion, or one part of extension, from another? Is it not something sensible, as some degree of swiftness or slowness, some certain magnitude or figure peculiar to each?

Hyl. I think so.

Phil. These qualities, therefore, stripped of all sensible properties, are without all specific and numerical differences, as the schools call them.

Hyl. They are.

Phil. That is to say, they are extension in general, and motion in general.

Hyl. Let it be so.

Phil. But it is a universally received maxim that EVERYTHING WHICH EXISTS IS PARTICULAR. How then can motion in general, or extension in general, exist in any corporeal substance?

Hyl. I will take time to solve your difficulty.

Phil. But I think the point may be speedily decided. Without doubt you can tell whether you are able to frame this or that idea. Now I am content to put our dispute on this issue. If you can frame in your thoughts a distinct ABSTRACT IDEA of motion or extension, divested of all those sensible modes, as swift and slow, great and small, round and square, and the like, which are acknowledged to exist only in the mind, I will then yield the point you contend for. But if you cannot, it will be unreasonable on your side to insist any longer upon what you have no notion of.

Hyl. To confess ingenuously, I cannot.

Phil. Can you even separate the ideas of extension and motion from the ideas of all those qualities which they who make the distinction term SECONDARY?

Hyl. What! is it not an easy matter to consider extension and motion by themselves, abstracted from all other sensible qualities? Pray how do the mathematicians treat of them?

Phil. I acknowledge, Hylas, it is not difficult to form general propositions and reasonings about those qualities, without mentioning any other; and, in this sense, to consider or treat of them abstractedly. But, how doth it follow that, because I can pronounce the word MOTION by itself, I can form the idea of it in my mind exclusive of body? or, because theorems may be made of extension and figures, without any mention of GREAT or SMALL, or any other sensible mode or quality, that therefore it is possible such an abstract idea of extension, without any particular size or figure, or sensible quality, should be distinctly formed, and apprehended by the mind? Mathematicians treat of quantity, without regarding what other sensible. qualities it is attended with, as being altogether indifferent to their demonstrations. But, when laying aside the words, they contemplate the bare ideas, I believe you will find, they are not the pure abstracted ideas of extension.

Hyl. But what say you to PURE INTELLECT? May not abstracted ideas be framed by that faculty?

Phil. Since I cannot frame abstract ideas at all, it is plain I cannot frame them by the help of PURE INTELLECT; whatsoever faculty you understand by those words. Besides, not to inquire into the nature of pure intellect and its spiritual objects, as VIRTUE, REASON, GOD, or the like, thus much seems manifest — that sensible things are only to be perceived by sense, or represented by the imagination. Figures, therefore, and extension, being originally perceived by sense, do not belong to pure intellect: but, for your farther satisfaction, try if you can frame the idea of any figure, abstracted from all particularities of size, or even from other sensible qualities.

Hyl. Let me think a little — I do not find that I can.

Phil. And can you think it possible that should really exist in nature which implies a repugnancy in its conception?

Hyl. By no means.

Phil. Since therefore it is impossible even for the mind to disunite the ideas of extension and motion from all other sensible qualities, doth it not follow, that where the one exist there necessarily the other exist likewise?

Hyl. It should seem so.

Phil. Consequently, the very same arguments which you admitted as conclusive against the Secondary Qualities are, without any farther application of force, against the Primary too. Besides, if you will trust your senses, is it not plain all sensible qualities coexist, or to them appear as being in the same place? Do they ever represent a motion, or figure, as being divested of all other visible and tangible qualities?

Hyl. You need say no more on this head. I am free to own, if there be no secret error or oversight in our proceedings hitherto, that all sensible qualities are alike to be denied existence without the mind. But, my fear is that I have been too liberal in my former concessions, or overlooked some fallacy or other. In short, I did not take time to think.

Phil. For that matter, Hylas, you may take what time you please in reviewing the progress of our inquiry. You are at liberty to recover any slips you might have made, or offer whatever you have omitted which makes for your first opinion.

Hyl. One great oversight I take to be this — that I did not sufficiently distinguish the OBJECT from the SENSATION. Now, though this latter may not exist without the mind, yet it will not thence follow that the former cannot.

Phil. What object do you mean? the object of the senses?

Hyl. The same.

Phil. It is then immediately perceived?

Hyl. Right.

Phil. Make me to understand the difference between what is immediately perceived and a sensation.

Hyl. The sensation I take to be an act of the mind perceiving; besides which, there is something perceived; and this I call the OBJECT. For example, there is red and yellow on that tulip. But then the act of perceiving those colours is in me only, and not in the tulip.

Phil. What tulip do you speak of? Is it that which you see?

Hyl. The same.

Phil. And what do you see beside colour, figure, and extension?

Hyl. Nothing.

Phil. What you would say then is that the red and yellow are coexistent with the extension; is it not?

Hyl. That is not all; I would say they have a real existence without the mind, in some unthinking substance.

Phil. That the colours are really in the tulip which I see is manifest. Neither can it be denied that this tulip may exist independent of your mind or mine; but, that any immediate object of the senses — that is, any idea, or combination of ideas — should exist in an unthinking substance, or exterior to ALL minds, is in itself an evident contradiction. Nor can I imagine how this follows from what you said just now, to wit, that the red and yellow were on the tulip you SAW, since you do not pretend to SEE that unthinking substance.

Hyl. You have an artful way, Philonous, of diverting our inquiry from the subject.

Phil. I see you have no mind to be pressed that way. To return then to your distinction between SENSATION and OBJECT; if I take you right, you distinguish in every perception two things, the one an action of the mind, the other not.

Hyl. True.

Phil. And this action cannot exist in, or belong to, any unthinking thing; but, whatever beside is implied in a perception may?

Hyl. That is my meaning.

Phil. So that if there was a perception without any act of the mind, it were possible such a perception should exist in an unthinking substance?

Hyl. I grant it. But it is impossible there should be such a perception.

Phil. When is the mind said to be active?

Hyl. When it produces, puts an end to, or changes, anything.

Phil. Can the mind produce, discontinue, or change anything, but by an act of the will?

Hyl. It cannot.

Phil. The mind therefore is to be accounted ACTIVE in its perceptions so far forth as VOLITION is included in them?

Hyl. It is.

Phil. In plucking this flower I am active; because I do it by the motion of my hand, which was consequent upon my volition; so likewise in applying it to my nose. But is either of these smelling?

Hyl. NO.

Phil. I act too in drawing the air through my nose; because my breathing so rather than otherwise is the effect of my volition. But neither can this be called SMELLING: for, if it were, I should smell every time I breathed in that manner?

Hyl. True.

Phil. Smelling then is somewhat consequent to all this?

Hyl. It is.

Phil. But I do not find my will concerned any farther. Whatever more there is — as that I perceive such a particular smell, or any smell at all — this is independent of my will, and therein I am altogether passive. Do you find it otherwise with you, Hylas?

Hyl. No, the very same.

Phil. Then, as to seeing, is it not in your power to open your eyes, or keep them shut; to turn them this or that way?

Hyl. Without doubt.

Phil. But, doth it in like manner depend on YOUR will that in looking on this flower you perceive WHITE rather than any other colour? Or, directing your open eyes towards yonder part of the heaven, can you avoid seeing the sun? Or is light or darkness the effect of your volition?

Hyl. No, certainly.

Phil. You are then in these respects altogether passive? HYL. I am.

Phil. Tell me now, whether SEEING consists in perceiving light and colours, or in opening and turning the eyes?

Hyl. Without doubt, in the former.

Phil. Since therefore you are in the very perception of light and colours altogether passive, what is become of that action you were speaking of as an ingredient in every sensation? And, doth it not follow from your own concessions, that the perception of light and colours, including no action in it, may exist in an unperceiving substance? And is not this a plain contradiction?

Hyl. I know not what to think of it.

Phil. Besides, since you distinguish the ACTIVE and PASSIVE in every perception, you must do it in that of pain. But how is it possible that pain, be it as little active as you please, should exist in an unperceiving substance? In short, do but consider the point, and then confess ingenuously, whether light and colours, tastes, sounds, &c. are not all equally passions or sensations in the soul. You may indeed call them EXTERNAL OBJECTS, and give them in words what subsistence you please. But, examine your own thoughts, and then tell me whether it be not as I say?

Hyl. I acknowledge, Philonous, that, upon a fair observation of what passes in my mind, I can discover nothing else but that I am a thinking being, affected with variety of sensations; neither is it possible to conceive how a sensation should exist in an unperceiving substance. But then, on the other hand, when I look on sensible things in a different view, considering them as so many modes and qualities, I find it necessary to suppose a MATERIAL SUBSTRATUM, without which they cannot be conceived to exist.

Phil. MATERIAL SUBSTRATUM call you it? Pray, by which of your senses came you acquainted with that being?

Hyl. It is not itself sensible; its modes and qualities only being perceived by the senses.

Phil. I presume then it was by reflexion and reason you obtained the idea of it?

Hyl. I do not pretend to any proper positive IDEA of it. However, I conclude it exists, because qualities cannot be conceived to exist without a support.

Phil. It seems then you have only a relative NOTION of it, or that you conceive it not otherwise than by conceiving the relation it bears to sensible qualities?

Hyl. Right.

Phil. Be pleased therefore to let me know wherein that relation consists.

Hyl. Is it not sufficiently expressed in the term SUBSTRATUM, or SUBSTANCE?

Phil. If so, the word SUBSTRATUM should import that it is spread under the sensible qualities or accidents?

Hyl. True.

Phil. And consequently under extension?

Hyl. I own it.

Phil. It is therefore somewhat in its own nature entirely distinct from extension?

Hyl. I tell you, extension is only a mode, and Matter is something that supports modes. And is it not evident the thing supported is different from the thing supporting?

Phil. So that something distinct from, and exclusive of, extension is supposed to be the SUBSTRATUM of extension?

Hyl. Just so.

Phil. Answer me, Hylas. Can a thing be spread without extension? or is not the idea of extension necessarily included in SPREADING?

Hyl. It is.

Phil. Whatsoever therefore you suppose spread under anything must have in itself an extension distinct from the extension of that thing under which it is spread?

Hyl. It must.

Phil. Consequently, every corporeal substance, being the SUBSTRATUM of extension, must have in itself another extension, by which it is qualified to be a SUBSTRATUM: and so on to infinity. And I ask whether this be not absurd in itself, and repugnant to what you granted just now, to wit, that the SUBSTRATUM was something distinct from and exclusive of extension?

Hyl. Aye but, Philonous, you take me wrong. I do not mean that Matter is SPREAD in a gross literal sense under extension. The word SUBSTRATUM is used only to express in general the same thing with SUBSTANCE.

Phil. Well then, let us examine the relation implied in the term SUBSTANCE. Is it not that it stands under accidents?

Hyl. The very same.

Phil. But, that one thing may stand under or support another, must it not be extended?

Hyl. It must.

Phil. Is not therefore this supposition liable to the same absurdity with the former?

Hyl. You still take things in a strict literal sense. That is not fair, Philonous.

Phil. I am not for imposing any sense on your words: you are at liberty to explain them as you please. Only, I beseech you, make me understand something by them. You tell me Matter supports or stands under accidents. How! is it as your legs support your body?

Hyl. No; that is the literal sense.

Phil. Pray let me know any sense, literal or not literal, that you understand it in. — How long must I wait for an answer, Hylas?

Hyl. I declare I know not what to say. I once thought I understood well enough what was meant by Matter's supporting accidents. But now, the more I think on it the less can I comprehend it: in short I find that I know nothing of it.

Phil. It seems then you have no idea at all, neither relative nor positive, of Matter; you know neither what it is in itself, nor what relation it bears to accidents?

Hyl. I acknowledge it.

Phil. And yet you asserted that you could not conceive how qualities or accidents should really exist, without conceiving at the same time a material support of them?

Hyl. I did.

Phil. That is to say, when you conceive the real existence of qualities, you do withal conceive Something which you cannot conceive?

Hyl. It was wrong, I own. But still I fear there is some fallacy or other. Pray what think you of this? It is just come into my head that the ground of all our mistake lies in your treating of each quality by itself. Now, I grant that each quality cannot singly subsist without the mind. Colour cannot without extension, neither can figure without some other sensible quality. But, as the several qualities united or blended together form entire sensible things, nothing hinders why such things may not be supposed to exist without the mind.

Phil. Either, Hylas, you are jesting, or have a very bad memory. Though indeed we went through all the qualities by name one after another, yet my arguments or rather your concessions, nowhere tended to prove that the Secondary Qualities did not subsist each alone by itself; but, that they were not AT ALL without the mind. Indeed, in treating of figure and motion we concluded they could not exist without the mind, because it was impossible even in thought to separate them from all secondary qualities, so as to conceive them existing by themselves. But then this was not the only argument made use of upon that occasion. But (to pass by all that hath been hitherto said, and reckon it for nothing, if you will have it so) I am content to put the whole upon this issue. If you can conceive it possible for any mixture or combination of qualities, or any sensible object whatever, to exist without the mind, then I will grant it actually to be so.

Hyl. If it comes to that the point will soon be decided. What more easy than to conceive a tree or house existing by itself, independent of, and unperceived by, any mind whatsoever? I do at this present time conceive them existing after that manner.

Phil. How say you, Hylas, can you see a thing which is at the same time unseen?

Hyl. No, that were a contradiction.

Phil. Is it not as great a contradiction to talk of CONCEIVING a thing which is UNCONCEIVED?

Hyl. It is.

Phil. The, tree or house therefore which you think of is conceived by you?

Hyl. How should it be otherwise?

Phil. And what is conceived is surely in the mind?

Hyl. Without question, that which is conceived is in the mind.

Phil. How then came you to say, you conceived a house or tree existing independent and out of all minds whatsoever?

Hyl. That was I own an oversight; but stay, let me consider what led me into it. — It is a pleasant mistake enough. As I was thinking of a tree in a solitary place, where no one was present to see it, methought that was to conceive a tree as existing unperceived or unthought of; not considering that I myself conceived it all the while. But now I plainly see that all I can do is to frame ideas in my own mind. I may indeed conceive in my own thoughts the idea of a tree, or a house, or a mountain, but that is all. And this is far from proving that I can conceive them EXISTING OUT OF THE MINDS OF ALL SPIRITS.

Phil. You acknowledge then that you cannot possibly conceive how any one corporeal sensible thing should exist otherwise than in the mind?

Hyl. I do.

Phil. And yet you will earnestly contend for the truth of that which you cannot so much as conceive?

Hyl. I profess I know not what to think; but still there are some scruples remain with me. Is it not certain I SEE THINGS at a distance? Do we not perceive the stars and moon, for example, to be a great way off? Is not this, I say, manifest to the senses?

Phil. Do you not in a dream too perceive those or the like objects?

Hyl. I do.

Phil. And have they not then the same appearance of being distant?

Hyl. They have.

Phil. But you do not thence conclude the apparitions in a dream to be without the mind?

Hyl. By no means.

Phil. You ought not therefore to conclude that sensible objects are without the mind, from their appearance, or manner wherein they are perceived.

Hyl. I acknowledge it. But doth not my sense deceive me in those cases?

Phil. By no means. The idea or thing which you immediately perceive, neither sense nor reason informs you that it actually exists without the mind. By sense you only know that you are affected with such certain sensations of light and colours, &c. And these you will not say are without the mind.

Hyl. True: but, beside all that, do you not think the sight suggests something of OUTNESS OR DISTANCE?

Phil. Upon approaching a distant object, do the visible size and figure change perpetually, or do they appear the same at all distances?

Hyl. They are in a continual change.

Phil. Sight therefore doth not suggest, or any way inform you, that the visible object you immediately perceive exists at a distance, or will be perceived when you advance farther onward; there being a continued series of visible objects succeeding each other during the whole time of your approach.

Hyl. It doth not; but still I know, upon seeing an object, what object I shall perceive after having passed over a certain distance: no matter whether it be exactly the same or no: there is still something of distance suggested in the case.

Phil. Good Hylas, do but reflect a little on the point, and then tell me whether there be any more in it than this: from the ideas you actually perceive by sight, you have by experience learned to collect what other ideas you will (according to the standing order of nature) be affected with, after such a certain succession of time and motion.

Hyl. Upon the whole, I take it to be nothing else.

Phil. Now, is it not plain that if we suppose a man born blind was on a sudden made to see, he could at first have no experience of what may be SUGGESTED by sight?

Hyl. It is.

Phil. He would not then, according to you, have any notion of distance annexed to the things he saw; but would take them for a new set of sensations, existing only in his mind?

Hyl. It is undeniable.

Phil. But, to make it still more plain: is not DISTANCE a line turned endwise to the eye?

Hyl. It is.

Phil. And can a line so situated be perceived by sight?

Hyl. It cannot.

Phil. Doth it not therefore follow that distance is not properly and immediately perceived by sight?

Hyl. It should seem so.

Phil. Again, is it your opinion that colours are at a distance?

Hyl. It must be acknowledged they are only in the mind.

Phil. But do not colours appear to the eye as coexisting in the same place with extension and figures?

Hyl. They do.

Phil. How can you then conclude from sight that figures exist without, when you acknowledge colours do not; the sensible appearance being the very same with regard to both?

Hyl. I know not what to answer.

Phil. But, allowing that distance was truly and immediately perceived by the mind, yet it would not thence follow it existed out of the mind. For, whatever is immediately perceived is an idea: and can any idea exist out of the mind?

Hyl. To suppose that were absurd: but, inform me, Philonous, can we perceive or know nothing beside our ideas?

Phil. As for the rational deducing of causes from effects, that is beside our inquiry. And, by the senses you can best tell whether you perceive anything which is not immediately perceived. And I ask you, whether the things immediately perceived are other than your own sensations or ideas? You have indeed more than once, in the course of this conversation, declared yourself on those points; but you seem, by this last question, to have departed from what you then thought.

Hyl. To speak the truth, Philonous, I think there are two kinds of objects:— the one perceived immediately, which are likewise called IDEAS; the other are real things or external objects, perceived by the mediation of ideas, which are their images and representations. Now, I own ideas do not exist without the mind; but the latter sort of objects do. I am sorry I did not think of this distinction sooner; it would probably have cut short your discourse.

Phil. Are those external objects perceived by sense or by some other faculty?

Hyl. They are perceived by sense.

Phil. Howl Is there any thing perceived by sense which is not immediately perceived?

Hyl. Yes, Philonous, in some sort there is. For example, when I look on a picture or statue of Julius Caesar, I may be said after a manner to perceive him (though not immediately) by my senses.

Phil. It seems then you will have our ideas, which alone are immediately perceived, to be pictures of external things: and that these also are perceived by sense, inasmuch as they have a conformity or resemblance to our ideas?

Hyl. That is my meaning.

Phil. And, in the same way that Julius Caesar, in himself invisible, is nevertheless perceived by sight; real things, in themselves imperceptible, are perceived by sense.

Hyl. In the very same.

Phil. Tell me, Hylas, when you behold the picture of Julius Caesar, do you see with your eyes any more than some colours and figures, with a certain symmetry and composition of the whole?

Hyl. Nothing else.

Phil. And would not a man who had never known anything of Julius Caesar see as much?

Hyl. He would.

Phil. Consequently he hath his sight, and the use of it, in as perfect a degree as you?

Hyl. I agree with you.

Phil. Whence comes it then that your thoughts are directed to the Roman emperor, and his are not? This cannot proceed from the sensations or ideas of sense by you then perceived; since you acknowledge you have no advantage over him in that respect. It should seem therefore to proceed from reason and memory: should it not?

Hyl. It should.

Phil. Consequently, it will not follow from that instance that anything is perceived by sense which is not, immediately perceived. Though I grant we may, in one acceptation, be said to perceive sensible things mediately by sense: that is, when, from a frequently perceived connexion, the immediate perception of ideas by one sense SUGGESTS to the mind others, perhaps belonging to another sense, which are wont to be connected with them. For instance, when I hear a coach drive along the streets, immediately I perceive only the sound; but, from the experience I have had that such a sound is connected with a coach, I am said to hear the coach. It is nevertheless evident that, in truth and strictness, nothing can be HEARD BUT SOUND; and the coach is not then properly perceived by sense, but suggested from experience. So likewise when we are said to see a red-hot bar of iron; the solidity and heat of the iron are not the objects of sight, but suggested to the imagination by the colour and figure which are properly perceived by that sense. In short, those things alone are actually and strictly perceived by any sense, which would have been perceived in case that same sense had then been first conferred on us. As for other things, it is plain they are only suggested to the mind by experience, grounded on former perceptions. But, to return to your comparison of Caesar's picture, it is plain, if you keep to that, you must hold the real things, or archetypes of our ideas, are not perceived by sense, but by some internal faculty of the soul, as reason or memory. I would therefore fain know what arguments you can draw from reason for the existence of what you call REAL THINGS OR MATERIAL OBJECTS. Or, whether you remember to have seen them formerly as they are in themselves; or, if you have heard or read of any one that did.

Hyl. I see, Philonous, you are disposed to raillery; but that will never convince me.

Phil. My aim is only to learn from you the way to come at the knowledge of MATERIAL BEINGS. Whatever we perceive is perceived immediately or mediately: by sense, or by reason and reflexion. But, as you have excluded sense, pray shew me what reason you have to believe their existence; or what MEDIUM you can possibly make use of to prove it, either to mine or your own understanding.

Hyl. To deal ingenuously, Philonous, now I consider the point, I do not find I can give you any good reason for it. But, thus much seems pretty plain, that it is at least possible such things may really exist. And, as long as there is no absurdity in supposing them, I am resolved to believe as I did, till you bring good reasons to the contrary.

Phil. What! Is it come to this, that you only BELIEVE the existence of material objects, and that your belief is founded barely on the possibility of its being true? Then you will have me bring reasons against it: though another would think it reasonable the proof should lie on him who holds the affirmative. And, after all, this very point which you are now resolved to maintain, without any reason, is in effect what you have more than once during this discourse seen good reason to give up. But, to pass over all this; if I understand you rightly, you say our ideas do not exist without the mind, but that they are copies, images, or representations, of certain originals that do?

Hyl. You take me right.

Phil. They are then like external things?

Hyl. They are.

Phil. Have those things a stable and permanent nature, independent of our senses; or are they in a perpetual change, upon our producing any motions in our bodies — suspending, exerting, or altering, our faculties or organs of sense?

Hyl. Real things, it is plain, have a fixed and real nature, which remains the same notwithstanding any change in our senses, or in the posture and motion of our bodies; which indeed may affect the ideas in our minds, but it were absurd to think they had the same effect on things existing without the mind.

Phil. How then is it possible that things perpetually fleeting and variable as our ideas should be copies or images of anything fixed and constant? Or, in other words, since all sensible qualities, as size, figure, colour, &c., that is, our ideas, are continually changing, upon every alteration in the distance, medium, or instruments of sensation; how can any determinate material objects be properly represented or painted forth by several distinct things, each of which is so different from and unlike the rest? Or, if you say it resembles some one only of our ideas, how shall we be able to distinguish the true copy from all the false ones?

Hyl. I profess, Philonous, I am at a loss. I know not what to say to this.

Phil. But neither is this all. Which are material objects in themselves — perceptible or imperceptible?

Hyl. Properly and immediately nothing can be perceived but ideas. All material things, therefore, are in themselves insensible, and to be perceived only by our ideas.

Phil. Ideas then are sensible, and their archetypes or originals insensible?

Hyl. Right.

Phil. But how can that which is sensible be like that which is insensible? Can a real thing, in itself INVISIBLE, be like a COLOUR; or a real thing, which is not AUDIBLE, be like a SOUND? In a word, can anything be like a sensation or idea, but another sensation or idea?

Hyl. I must own, I think not.

Phil. Is it possible there should be any doubt on the point? Do you not perfectly know your own ideas?

Hyl. I know them perfectly; since what I do not perceive or know can be no part of my idea.

Phil. Consider, therefore, and examine them, and then tell me if there be anything in them which can exist without the mind: or if you can conceive anything like them existing without the mind.

Hyl. Upon inquiry, I find it is impossible for me to conceive or understand how anything but an idea can be like an idea. And it is most evident that NO IDEA CAN EXIST WITHOUT THE MIND.

Phil. You are therefore, by your principles, forced to deny the REALITY of sensible things; since you made it to consist in an absolute existence exterior to the mind. That is to say, you are a downright sceptic. So I have gained my point, which was to shew your principles led to Scepticism.

Hyl. For the present I am, if not entirely convinced, at least silenced.

Phil. I would fain know what more you would require in order to a perfect conviction. Have you not had the liberty of explaining yourself all manner of ways? Were any little slips in discourse laid hold and insisted on? Or were you not allowed to retract or reinforce anything you had offered, as best served your purpose? Hath not everything you could say been heard and examined with all the fairness imaginable? In a word have you not in every point been convinced out of your own mouth? And, if you can at present discover any flaw in any of your former concessions, or think of any remaining subterfuge, any new distinction, colour, or comment whatsoever, why do you not produce it?

Hyl. A little patience, Philonous. I am at present so amazed to see myself ensnared, and as it were imprisoned in the labyrinths you have drawn me into, that on the sudden it cannot be expected I should find my way out. You must give me time to look about me and recollect myself.

Phil. Hark; is not this the college bell?

Hyl. It rings for prayers.

Phil. We will go in then, if you please, and meet here again tomorrow morning. In the meantime, you may employ your thoughts on this morning's discourse, and try if you can find any fallacy in it, or invent any new means to extricate yourself.

Hyl. Agreed.

The Second Dialogue

Hyl. I beg your pardon, Philonous, for not meeting you sooner. All this morning my head was so filled with our late conversation that I had not leisure to think of the time of the day, or indeed of anything else.

Philonous. I am glad you were so intent upon it, in hopes if there were any mistakes in your concessions, or fallacies in my reasonings from them, you will now discover them to me.

Hyl. I assure you I have done nothing ever since I saw you but search after mistakes and fallacies, and, with that view, have minutely examined the whole series of yesterday's discourse: but all in vain, for the notions it led me into, upon review, appear still more clear and evident; and, the more I consider them, the more irresistibly do they force my assent.

Phil. And is not this, think you, a sign that they are genuine, that they proceed from nature, and are conformable to right reason? Truth and beauty are in this alike, that the strictest survey sets them both off to advantage; while the false lustre of error and disguise cannot endure being reviewed, or too nearly inspected.

Hyl. I own there is a great deal in what you say. Nor can any one be more entirely satisfied of the truth of those odd consequences, so long as I have in view the reasonings that lead to them. But, when these are out of my thoughts, there seems, on the other hand, something so satisfactory, so natural and intelligible, in the modern way of explaining things that, I profess, I know not how to reject it.

Phil. I know not what way you mean.

Hyl. I mean the way of accounting for our sensations or ideas.

Phil. How is that?

Hyl. It is supposed the soul makes her residence in some part of the brain, from which the nerves take their rise, and are thence extended to all parts of the body; and that outward objects, by the different impressions they make on the organs of sense, communicate certain vibrative motions to the nerves; and these being filled with spirits propagate them to the brain or seat of the soul, which, according to the various impressions or traces thereby made in the brain, is variously affected with ideas.

Phil. And call you this an explication of the manner whereby we are affected with ideas?

Hyl. Why not, Philonous? Have you anything to object against it?

Phil. I would first know whether I rightly understand your hypothesis. You make certain traces in the brain to be the causes or occasions of our ideas. Pray tell me whether by the BRAIN you mean any sensible thing.

Hyl. What else think you I could mean?

Phil. Sensible things are all immediately perceivable; and those things which are immediately perceivable are ideas; and these exist only in the mind. Thus much you have, if I mistake not, long since agreed to.

Hyl. I do not deny it.

Phil. The brain therefore you speak of, being a sensible thing, exists only in the mind. Now, I would fain know whether you think it reasonable to suppose that one idea or thing existing in the mind occasions all other ideas. And, if you think so, pray how do you account for the origin of that primary idea or brain itself?

Hyl. I do not explain the origin of our ideas by that brain which is perceivable to sense — this being itself only a combination of sensible ideas — but by another which I imagine.

Phil. But are not things imagined as truly IN THE MIND as things perceived?

Hyl. I must confess they are.

Phil. It comes, therefore, to the same thing; and you have been all this while accounting for ideas by certain motions or impressions of the brain; that is, by some alterations in an idea, whether sensible or imaginable it matters not.

Hyl. I begin to suspect my hypothesis.

Phil. Besides spirits, all that we know or conceive are our own ideas. When, therefore, you say all ideas are occasioned by impressions in the brain, do you conceive this brain or no? If you do, then you talk of ideas imprinted in an idea causing that same idea, which is absurd. If you do not conceive it, you talk unintelligibly, instead of forming a reasonable hypothesis.

Hyl. I now clearly see it was a mere dream. There is nothing in it.

Phil. You need not be much concerned at it; for after all, this way of explaining things, as you called it, could never have satisfied any reasonable man. What connexion is there between a motion in the nerves, and the sensations of sound or colour in the mind? Or how is it possible these should be the effect of that?

Hyl. But I could never think it had so little in it as now it seems to have.

Phil. Well then, are you at length satisfied that no sensible things have a real existence; and that you are in truth an arrant sceptic?

Hyl. It is too plain to be denied.

Phil. Look! are not the fields covered with a delightful verdure? Is there not something in the woods and groves, in the rivers and clear springs, that soothes, that delights, that transports the soul? At the prospect of the wide and deep ocean, or some huge mountain whose top is lost in the clouds, or of an old gloomy forest, are not our minds filled with a pleasing horror? Even in rocks and deserts is there not an agreeable wildness? How sincere a pleasure is it to behold the natural beauties of the earth! To preserve and renew our, relish for them, is not the veil of night alternately drawn over her face, and doth she not change her dress with the seasons? How aptly are the elements disposed! What variety and use in the meanest productions of nature! What delicacy, what beauty, what contrivance, in animal and vegetable bodies I How exquisitely are all things suited, as well to their particular ends, as to constitute opposite parts of the whole I And, while they mutually aid and support, do they not also set off and illustrate each other? Raise now your thoughts from this ball of earth to all those glorious luminaries that adorn the high arch of heaven. The motion and situation of the planets, are they not admirable for use and order? Were those (miscalled ERRATIC) globes once known to stray, in their repeated journeys through the pathless void? Do they not measure areas round the sun ever proportioned to the times? So fixed, so immutable are the laws by which the unseen Author of nature actuates the universe. How vivid and radiant is the lustre of the fixed stars! How magnificent and rich that negligent profusion with which they appear to be scattered throughout the whole azure vault! Yet, if you take the telescope, it brings into your sight a new host of stars that escape the naked eye. Here they seem contiguous and minute, but to a nearer view immense orbs of fight at various distances, far sunk in the abyss of space. Now you must call imagination to your aid. The feeble narrow sense cannot descry innumerable worlds revolving round the central fires; and in those worlds the energy of an all-perfect Mind displayed in endless forms. But, neither sense nor imagination are big enough to comprehend the boundless extent, with all its glittering furniture. Though the labouring mind exert and strain each power to its utmost reach, there still stands out ungrasped a surplusage immeasurable. Yet all the vast bodies that compose this mighty frame, how distant and remote soever, are by some secret mechanism, some Divine art and force, linked in a mutual dependence and intercourse with each other; even with this earth, which was almost slipt from my thoughts and lost in the crowd of worlds. Is not the whole system immense, beautiful, glorious beyond expression and beyond thought! What treatment, then, do those philosophers deserve, who would deprive these noble and delightful scenes of all REALITY? How should those Principles be entertained that lead us to think all the visible beauty of the creation a false imaginary glare? To be plain, can you expect this Scepticism of yours will not be thought extravagantly absurd by all men of sense?

Hyl. Other men may think as they please; but for your part you have nothing to reproach me with. My comfort is, you are as much a sceptic as I am.

Phil. There, Hylas, I must beg leave to differ from you.

Hyl. What! Have you all along agreed to the premises, and do you now deny the conclusion, and leave me to maintain those paradoxes by myself which you led me into? This surely is not fair.

Phil. I deny that I agreed with you in those notions that led to Scepticism. You indeed said the REALITY of sensible things consisted in AN ABSOLUTE EXISTENCE OUT OF THE MINDS OF SPIRITS, or distinct from their being perceived. And pursuant to this notion of reality, YOU are obliged to deny sensible things any real existence: that is, according to your own definition, you profess yourself a sceptic. But I neither said nor thought the reality of sensible things was to be defined after that manner. To me it is evident for the reasons you allow of, that sensible things cannot exist otherwise than in a mind or spirit. Whence I conclude, not that they have no real existence, but that, seeing they depend not on my thought, and have all existence distinct from being perceived by me, THERE MUST BE SOME OTHER MIND WHEREIN THEY EXIST. As sure, therefore, as the sensible world really exists, so sure is there an infinite omnipresent Spirit who contains and supports it.

Hyl. What! This is no more than I and all Christians hold; nay, and all others too who believe there is a God, and that He knows and comprehends all things.

Phil. Aye, but here lies the difference. Men commonly believe that all things are known or perceived by God, because they believe the being of a God; whereas I, on the other side, immediately and necessarily conclude the being of a God, because all sensible things must be perceived by Him.

Hyl. But, so long as we all believe the same thing, what matter is it how we come by that belief?

Phil. But neither do we agree in the same opinion. For philosophers, though they acknowledge all corporeal beings to be perceived by God, yet they attribute to them an absolute subsistence distinct from their being perceived by any mind whatever; which I do not. Besides, is there no difference between saying, THERE IS A GOD, THEREFORE HE PERCEIVES ALL THINGS; and saying, SENSIBLE THINGS DO REALLY EXIST; AND, IF THEY REALLY EXIST, THEY ARE NECESSARILY PERCEIVED BY AN INFINITE MIND: THEREFORE THERE IS AN INFINITE MIND OR GOD? This furnishes you with a direct and immediate demonstration, from a most evident principle, of the BEING OF A GOD. Divines and philosophers had proved beyond all controversy, from the beauty and usefulness of the several parts of the creation, that it was the workmanship of God. But that — setting aside all help of astronomy and natural philosophy, all contemplation of the contrivance, order, and adjustment of things — an infinite Mind should be necessarily inferred from the bare EXISTENCE OF THE SENSIBLE WORLD, is an advantage to them only who have made this easy reflexion: that the sensible world is that which we perceive by our several senses; and that nothing is perceived by the senses beside ideas; and that no idea or archetype of an idea can exist otherwise than in a mind. You may now, without any laborious search into the sciences, without any subtlety of reason, or tedious length of discourse, oppose and baffle the most strenuous advocate for Atheism. Those miserable refuges, whether in an eternal succession of unthinking causes and effects, or in a fortuitous concourse of atoms; those wild imaginations of Vanini, Hobbes, and Spinoza: in a word, the whole system of Atheism, is it not entirely overthrown, by this single reflexion on the repugnancy included in supposing the whole, or any part, even the most rude and shapeless, of the visible world, to exist without a mind? Let any one of those abettors of impiety but look into his own thoughts, and there try if he can conceive how so much as a rock, a desert, a chaos, or confused jumble of atoms; how anything at all, either sensible or imaginable, can exist independent of a Mind, and he need go no farther to be convinced of his folly. Can anything be fairer than to put a dispute on such an issue, and leave it to a man himself to see if he can conceive, even in thought, what he holds to be true in fact, and from a notional to allow it a real existence?

Hyl. It cannot be denied there is something highly serviceable to religion in what you advance. But do you not think it looks very like a notion entertained by some eminent moderns, of SEEING ALL THINGS IN GOD?

Phil. I would gladly know that opinion: pray explain it to me.

Hyl. They conceive that the soul, being immaterial, is incapable of being united with material things, so as to perceive them in themselves; but that she perceives them by her union with the substance of God, which, being spiritual, is therefore purely intelligible, or capable of being the immediate object of a spirit's thought. Besides the Divine essence contains in it perfections correspondent to each created being; and which are, for that reason, proper to exhibit or represent them to the mind.

Phil. I do not understand how our ideas, which are things altogether passive and inert, can be the essence, or any part (or like any part) of the essence or substance of God, who is an impassive, indivisible, pure, active being. Many more difficulties and objections there are which occur at first view against this hypothesis; but I shall only add that it is liable to all the absurdities of the common hypothesis, in making a created world exist otherwise than in the mind of a Spirit. Besides all which it hath this peculiar to itself; that it makes that material world serve to no purpose. And, if it pass for a good argument against other hypotheses in the sciences, that they suppose Nature, or the Divine wisdom, to make something in vain, or do that by tedious roundabout methods which might have been performed in a much more easy and compendious way, what shall we think of that hypothesis which supposes the whole world made in vain?

Hyl. But what say you? Are not you too of opinion that we see all things in God? If I mistake not, what you advance comes near it.

Phil. Few men think; yet all have opinions. Hence men's opinions are superficial and confused. It is nothing strange that tenets which in themselves are ever so different, should nevertheless be confounded with each other, by those who do not consider them attentively. I shall not therefore be surprised if some men imagine that I run into the enthusiasm of Malebranche; though in truth I am very remote from it. He builds on the most abstract general ideas, which I entirely disclaim. He asserts an absolute external world, which I deny. He maintains that we are deceived by our senses, and, know not the real natures or the true forms and figures of extended beings; of all which I hold the direct contrary. So that upon the whole there are no Principles more fundamentally opposite than his and mine. It must be owned that I entirely agree with what the holy Scripture saith, "That in God we live and move and have our being." But that we see things in His essence, after the manner above set forth, I am far from believing. Take here in brief my meaning:— It is evident that the things I perceive are my own ideas, and that no idea can exist unless it be in a mind: nor is it less plain that these ideas or things by me perceived, either themselves or their archetypes, exist independently of my mind, since I know myself not to be their author, it being out of my power to determine at pleasure what particular ideas I shall be affected with upon opening my eyes or ears: they must therefore exist in some other Mind, whose Will it is they should be exhibited to me. The things, I say, immediately perceived are ideas or sensations, call them which you will. But how can any idea or sensation exist in, or be produced by, anything but a mind or spirit? This indeed is inconceivable. And to assert that which is inconceivable is to talk nonsense: is it not?

Hyl. Without doubt.

Phil. But, on the other hand, it is very conceivable that they should exist in and be produced by a spirit; since this is no more than I daily experience in myself, inasmuch as I perceive numberless ideas; and, by an act of my will, can form a great variety of them, and raise them up in my imagination: though, it must be confessed, these creatures of the fancy are not altogether so distinct, so strong, vivid, and permanent, as those perceived by my senses — which latter are called RED THINGS. From all which I conclude, THERE IS A MIND WHICH AFFECTS ME EVERY MOMENT WITH ALL THE SENSIBLE IMPRESSIONS I PERCEIVE. AND, from the variety, order, and manner of these, I conclude THE AUTHOR OF THEM TO BE WISE, POWERFUL, AND GOOD, BEYOND COMPREHENSION. MARK it well; I do not say, I see things by perceiving that which represents them in the intelligible Substance of God. This I do not understand; but I say, the things by me perceived are known by the understanding, and produced by the will of an infinite Spirit. And is not all this most plain and evident? Is there any more in it than what a little observation in our own minds, and that which passeth in them, not only enables us to conceive, but also obliges us to acknowledge.

Hyl. I think I understand you very clearly; and own the proof you give of a Deity seems no less evident than it is surprising. But, allowing that God is the supreme and universal Cause of an things, yet, may there not be still a Third Nature besides Spirits and Ideas? May we not admit a subordinate and limited cause of our ideas? In a word, may there not for all that be

MATTER?

Phil. How often must I inculcate the same thing? You allow the things immediately perceived by sense to exist nowhere without the mind; but there is nothing perceived by sense which is not perceived immediately: therefore there is nothing sensible that exists without the mind. The Matter, therefore, which you still insist on is something intelligible, I suppose; something that may be discovered by reason, and not by sense.

Hyl. You are in the right.

Phil. Pray let me know what reasoning your belief of Matter is grounded on; and what this Matter is, in your present sense of it.

Hyl. I find myself affected with various ideas, whereof I know I am not the cause; neither are they the cause of themselves, or of one another, or capable of subsisting by themselves, as being altogether inactive, fleeting, dependent beings. They have therefore SOME cause distinct from me and them: of which I pretend to know no more than that it is THE CAUSE OF MY IDEAS. And this thing, whatever it be, I call Matter.

Phil. Tell me, Hylas, hath every one a liberty to change the current proper signification attached to a common name in any language? For example, suppose a traveller should tell you that in a certain country men pass unhurt through the fire; and, upon explaining himself, you found he meant by the word fire that which others call WATER. Or, if he should assert that there are trees that walk upon two legs, meaning men by the term TREES. Would you think this reasonable?

Hyl. No; I should think it very absurd. Common custom is the standard of propriety in language. And for any man to affect speaking improperly is to pervert the use of speech, and can never serve to a better purpose than to protract and multiply disputes, where there is no difference in opinion.

Phil. And doth not MATTER, in the common current acceptation of the word, signify an extended, solid, moveable, unthinking, inactive Substance?

Hyl. It doth.

Phil. And, hath it not been made evident that no SUCH substance can possibly exist? And, though it should be allowed to exist, yet how can that which is INACTIVE be a CAUSE; or that which is UNTHINKING be a CAUSE OF THOUGHT? You may, indeed, if you please, annex to the word MATTER a contrary meaning to what is vulgarly received; and tell me you understand by it, an unextended, thinking, active being, which is the cause of our ideas. But what else is this than to play with words, and run into that very fault you just now condemned with so much reason? I do by no means find fault with your reasoning, in that you collect a cause from the PHENOMENA: BUT I deny that THE cause deducible by reason can properly be termed Matter.

Hyl. There is indeed something in what you say. But I am afraid you do not thoroughly comprehend my meaning. I would by no means be thought to deny that God, or an infinite Spirit, is the Supreme Cause of all things. All I contend for is, that, subordinate to the Supreme Agent, there is a cause of a limited and inferior nature, which CONCURS in the production of our ideas, not by any act of will, or spiritual efficiency, but by that kind of action which belongs to Matter, viz. MOTION.

Phil. I find you are at every turn relapsing into your old exploded conceit, of a moveable, and consequently an extended, substance, existing without the mind. What! Have you already forgotten you were convinced; or are you willing I should repeat what has been said on that head? In truth this is not fair dealing in you, still to suppose the being of that which you have so often acknowledged to have no being. But, not to insist farther on what has been so largely handled, I ask whether all your ideas are not perfectly passive and inert, including nothing of action in them.

Hyl. They are.

Phil. And are sensible qualities anything else but ideas?

Hyl. How often have I acknowledged that they are not.

Phil. But is not MOTION a sensible quality?

Hyl. It is.

Phil. Consequently it is no action?

Hyl. I agree with you. And indeed it is very plain that when I stir my finger, it remains passive; but my will which produced the motion is active.

Phil. Now, I desire to know, in the first place, whether, motion being allowed to be no action, you can conceive any action besides volition: and, in the second place, whether to say something and conceive nothing be not to talk nonsense: and, lastly, whether, having considered the premises, you do not perceive that to suppose any efficient or active Cause of our ideas, other than SPIRIT, is highly absurd and unreasonable?

Hyl. I give up the point entirely. But, though Matter may not be a cause, yet what hinders its being an INSTRUMENT, subservient to the supreme Agent in the production of our ideas?

Phil. An instrument say you; pray what may be the figure, springs, wheels, and motions, of that instrument?

Hyl. Those I pretend to determine nothing of, both the substance and its qualities being entirely unknown to me.

Phil. What? You are then of opinion it is made up of unknown parts, that it hath unknown motions, and an unknown shape?

Hyl. I do not believe that it hath any figure or motion at all, being already convinced, that no sensible qualities can exist in an unperceiving substance.

Phil. But what notion is it possible to frame of an instrument void of all sensible qualities, even extension itself?

Hyl. I do not pretend to have any notion of it.

Phil. And what reason have you to think this unknown, this inconceivable Somewhat doth exist? Is it that you imagine God cannot act as well without it; or that you find by experience the use of some such thing, when you form ideas in your own mind?

Hyl. You are always teasing me for reasons of my belief. Pray what reasons have you not to believe it?

Phil. It is to me a sufficient reason not to believe the existence of anything, if I see no reason for believing it. But, not to insist on reasons for believing, you will not so much as let me know WHAT IT IS you would have me believe; since you say you have no manner of notion of it. After all, let me entreat you to consider whether it be like a philosopher, or even like a man of common sense, to pretend to believe you know not what and you know not why.

Hyl. Hold, Philonous. When I tell you Matter is an INSTRUMENT, I do not mean altogether nothing. It is true I know not the particular kind of instrument; but, however, I have some notion of INSTRUMENT IN GENERAL, which I apply to it.

Phil. But what if it should prove that there is something, even in the most general notion of INSTRUMENT, as taken in a distinct sense from CAUSE, which makes the use of it inconsistent with the Divine attributes?

Hyl. Make that appear and I shall give up the point.

Phil. What mean you by the general nature or notion of INSTRUMENT?

Hyl. That which is common to all particular instruments composeth the general notion.

Phil. Is it not common to all instruments, that they are applied to the doing those things only which cannot be performed by the mere act of our wills? Thus, for instance, I never use an instrument to move my finger, because it is done by a volition. But I should use one if I were to remove part of a rock, or tear up a tree by the roots. Are you of the same mind? Or, can you shew any example where an instrument is made use of in producing an effect IMMEDIATELY depending on the will of the agent?

Hyl. I own I cannot.

Phil. How therefore can you suppose that an All-perfect Spirit, on whose Will all things have an absolute and immediate dependence, should need an instrument in his operations, or, not needing it, make use of it? Thus it seems to me that you are obliged to own the use of a lifeless inactive instrument to be incompatible with the infinite perfection of God; that is, by your own confession, to give up the point.

Hyl. It doth not readily occur what I can answer you.

Phil. But, methinks you should be ready to own the truth, when it has been fairly proved to you. We indeed, who are beings of finite powers, are forced to make use of instruments. And the use of an instrument sheweth the agent to be limited by rules of another's prescription, and that he cannot obtain his end but in such a way, and by such conditions. Whence it seems a clear consequence, that the supreme unlimited agent useth no tool or instrument at all. The will of an Omnipotent Spirit is no sooner exerted than executed, without the application of means; which, if they are employed by inferior agents, it is not upon account of any real efficacy that is in them, or necessary aptitude to produce any effect, but merely in compliance with the laws of nature, or those conditions prescribed to them by the First Cause, who is Himself above all limitation or prescription whatsoever.

Hyl. I will no longer maintain that Matter is an instrument. However, I would not be understood to give up its existence neither; since, notwithstanding what hath been said, it may still be an OCCASION.

Phil. How many shapes is your Matter to take? Or, how often must it be proved not to exist, before you are content to part with it? But, to say no more of this (though by all the laws of disputation I may justly blame you for so frequently changing the signification of the principal term)— I would fain know what you mean by affirming that matter is an occasion, having already denied it to be a cause. And, when you have shewn in what sense you understand OCCASION, pray, in the next place, be pleased to shew me what reason induceth you to believe there is such an occasion of our ideas?

Hyl. As to the first point: by OCCASION I mean an inactive unthinking being, at the presence whereof God excites ideas in our minds.

Phil. And what may be the nature of that inactive unthinking being?

Hyl. I know nothing of its nature.

Phil. Proceed then to the second point, and assign some reason why we should allow an existence to this inactive, unthinking, unknown thing.

Hyl. When we see ideas produced in our minds, after an orderly and constant manner, it is natural to think they have some fixed and regular occasions, at the presence of which they are excited.

Phil. You acknowledge then God alone to be the cause of our ideas, and that He causes them at the presence of those occasions.

Hyl. That is my opinion.

Phil. Those things which you say are present to God, without doubt He perceives.

Hyl. Certainly; otherwise they could not be to Him an occasion of acting.

Phil. Not to insist now on your making sense of this hypothesis, or answering all the puzzling questions and difficulties it is liable to: I only ask whether the order and regularity observable in the series of our ideas, or the course of nature, be not sufficiently accounted for by the wisdom and power of God; and whether it doth not derogate from those attributes, to suppose He is influenced, directed, or put in mind, when and what He is to act, by an unthinking substance? And, lastly, whether, in case I granted all you contend for, it would make anything to your purpose; it not being easy to conceive how the external or absolute existence of an unthinking substance, distinct from its being perceived, can be inferred from my allowing that there are certain things perceived by the mind of God, which are to Him the occasion of producing ideas in us?

Hyl. I am perfectly at a loss what to think, this notion of OCCASION seeming now altogether as groundless as the rest.

Phil. Do you not at length perceive that in all these different acceptations of MATTER, you have been only supposing you know not what, for no manner of reason, and to no kind of use?

Hyl. I freely own myself less fond of my notions since they have been so accurately examined. But still, methinks, I have some confused perception that there is such a thing as MATTER.

Phil. Either you perceive the being of Matter immediately or mediately. If immediately, pray inform me by which of the senses you perceive it. If mediately, let me know by what reasoning it is inferred from those things which you perceive immediately. So much for the perception. Then for the Matter itself, I ask whether it is object, SUBSTRATUM, cause, instrument, or occasion? You have already pleaded for each of these, shifting your notions, and making Matter to appear sometimes in one shape, then in another. And what you have offered hath been disapproved and rejected by yourself. If you have anything new to advance I would gladly bear it.

Hyl. I think I have already offered all I had to say on those heads. I am at a loss what more to urge.

Phil. And yet you are loath to part with your old prejudice. But, to make you quit it more easily, I desire that, beside what has been hitherto suggested, you will farther consider whether, upon. supposition that Matter exists, you can possibly conceive how you should be affected by it. Or, supposing it did not exist, whether it be not evident you might for all that be affected with the same ideas you now are, and consequently have the very same reasons to believe its existence that you now can have.

Hyl. I acknowledge it is possible we might perceive all things just as we do now, though there was no Matter in the world; neither can I conceive, if there be Matter, how it should produce' any idea in our minds. And, I do farther grant you have entirely satisfied me that it is impossible there should be such a thing as matter in any of the foregoing acceptations. But still I cannot help supposing that there is MATTER in some sense or other. WHAT THAT IS I do not indeed pretend to determine.

Phil. I do not expect you should define exactly the nature of that unknown being. Only be pleased to tell me whether it is a Substance; and if so, whether you can suppose a Substance without accidents; or, in case you suppose it to have accidents or qualities, I desire you will let me know what those qualities are, at least what is meant by Matter's supporting them?

Hyl. We have already argued on those points. I have no more to say to them. But, to prevent any farther questions, let me tell you I at present understand by MATTER neither substance nor accident, thinking nor extended being, neither cause, instrument, nor occasion, but Something entirely unknown, distinct from all these.

Phil. It seems then you include in your present notion of Matter nothing but the general abstract idea of ENTITY.

Hyl. Nothing else; save only that I super-add to this general idea the negation of all those particular things, qualities, or ideas, that I perceive, imagine, or in anywise apprehend.

Phil. Pray where do you suppose this unknown Matter to exist?

Hyl. Oh Philonous! now you think you have entangled me; for, if I say it exists in place, then you will infer that it exists in the mind, since it is agreed that place or extension exists only in the mind. But I am not ashamed to own my ignorance. I know not where it exists; only I am sure it exists not in place. There is a negative answer for you. And you must expect no other to all the questions you put for the future about Matter.

Phil. Since you will not tell me where it exists, be pleased to inform me after what manner you suppose it to exist, or what you mean by its EXISTENCE?

Hyl. It neither thinks nor acts, neither perceives nor is perceived.

Phil. But what is there positive in your abstracted notion of its existence?

Hyl. Upon a nice observation, I do not find I have any positive notion or meaning at all. I tell you again, I am not ashamed to own my ignorance. I know not what is meant by its EXISTENCE, or how it exists.

Phil. Continue, good Hylas, to act the same ingenuous part, and tell me sincerely whether you can frame a distinct idea of Entity in general, prescinded from and exclusive of all thinking and corporeal beings, all particular things whatsoever.

Hyl. Hold, let me think a little — I profess, Philonous, I do not find that I can. At first glance, methought I had some dilute and airy notion of Pure Entity in abstract; but, upon closer attention, it hath quite vanished out of sight. The more I think on it, the more am I confirmed in my prudent resolution of giving none but negative answers, and not pretending to the least degree of any positive knowledge or conception of Matter, its WHERE, its HOW, its ENTITY, or anything belonging to it.

Phil. When, therefore, you speak of the existence of Matter, you have not any notion in your mind?

Hyl. None at all.

Phil. Pray tell me if the case stands not thus — At first, from a belief of material substance, you would have it that the immediate objects existed without the mind; then that they are archetypes; then causes; next instruments; then occasions: lastly SOMETHING IN GENERAL, which being interpreted proves NOTHING. So Matter comes to nothing. What think you, Hylas, is not this a fair summary of your whole proceeding?

Hyl. Be that as it will, yet I still insist upon it, that our not being able to conceive a thing is no argument against its existence.

Phil. That from a cause, effect, operation, sign, or other circumstance, there may reasonably be inferred the existence of a thing not immediately perceived; and that it were absurd for any man to argue against the existence of that thing, from his having no direct and positive notion of it, I freely own. But, where there is nothing of all this; where neither reason nor revelation induces us to believe the existence of a thing; where we have not even a relative notion of it; where an abstraction is made from perceiving and being perceived, from Spirit and idea: lastly, where there is not so much as the most inadequate or faint idea pretended to — I will not indeed thence conclude against the reality of any notion, or existence of anything; but my inference shall be, that you mean nothing at all; that you employ words to no manner of purpose, without any design or signification whatsoever. And I leave it to you to consider how mere jargon should be treated.

Hyl. To deal frankly with you, Philonous, your arguments seem in themselves unanswerable; but they have not so great an effect on me as to produce that entire conviction, that hearty acquiescence, which attends demonstration. I find myself relapsing into an obscure surmise of I know not what, MATTER.

Phil. But, are you not sensible, Hylas, that two things must concur to take away all scruple, and work a plenary assent in the mind? Let a visible object be set in never so clear a light, yet, if there is any imperfection in the sight, or if the eye is not directed towards it, it will not be distinctly seen. And though a demonstration be never so well grounded and fairly proposed, yet, if there is withal a stain of prejudice, or a wrong bias on the understanding, can it be expected on a sudden to perceive clearly, and adhere firmly to the truth? No; there is need of time and pains: the attention must be awakened and detained by a frequent repetition of the same thing placed oft in the same, oft in different lights. I have said it already, and find I must still repeat and inculcate, that it is an unaccountable licence you take, in pretending to maintain you know not what, for you know not what reason, to you know not what purpose. Can this be paralleled in any art or science, any sect or profession of men? Or is there anything so barefacedly groundless and unreasonable to be met with even in the lowest of common conversation? But, perhaps you will still say, Matter may exist; though at the same time you neither know WHAT IS MEANT by MATTER, or by its EXISTENCE. This indeed is surprising, and the more so because it is altogether voluntary and of your own head, you not being led to it by any one reason; for I challenge you to shew me that thing in nature which needs Matter to explain or account for it.

Hyl. THE REALITY of things cannot be maintained without supposing the existence of Matter. And is not this, think you, a good reason why I should be earnest in its defence?

Phil. The reality of things! What things? sensible or intelligible?

Hyl. Sensible things.

Phil. My glove for example?

Hyl. That, or any other thing perceived by the senses.

Phil. But to fix on some particular thing. Is it not a sufficient evidence to me of the existence of this GLOVE, that I see it, and feel it, and wear it? Or, if this will not do, how is it possible I should be assured of the reality of this thing, which I actually see in this place, by supposing that some unknown thing, which I never did or can see, exists after an unknown manner, in an unknown place, or in no place at all? How can the supposed reality of that which is intangible be a proof that anything tangible really exists? Or, of that which is invisible, that any visible thing, or, in general of anything which is imperceptible, that a perceptible exists? Do but explain this and I shall think nothing too hard for you.

Hyl. Upon the whole, I am content to own the existence of matter is highly improbable; but the direct and absolute impossibility of it does not appear to me.

Phil. But granting Matter to be possible, yet, upon that account merely, it can have no more claim to existence than a golden mountain, or a centaur.

Hyl. I acknowledge it; but still you do not deny it is possible; and that which is possible, for aught you know, may actually exist.

Phil. I deny it to be possible; and have, if I mistake not, evidently proved, from your own concessions, that it is not. In the common sense of the word MATTER, is there any more implied than an extended, solid, figured, moveable substance, existing without the mind? And have not you acknowledged, over and over, that you have seen evident reason for denying the possibility of such a substance?

Hyl. True, but that is only one sense of the term MATTER.

Phil. But is it not the only proper genuine received sense? And, if Matter, in such a sense, be proved impossible, may it not be thought with good grounds absolutely impossible? Else how could anything be proved impossible? Or, indeed, how could there be any proof at all one way or other, to a man who takes the liberty to unsettle and change the common signification of words?

Hyl. I thought philosophers might be allowed to speak more accurately than the vulgar, and were not always confined to the common acceptation of a term.

Phil. But this now mentioned is the common received sense among philosophers themselves. But, not to insist on that, have you not been allowed to take Matter in what sense you pleased? And have you not used this privilege in the utmost extent; sometimes entirely changing, at others leaving out, or putting into the definition of it whatever, for the present, best served your design, contrary to all the known rules of reason and logic? And hath not this shifting, unfair method of yours spun out our dispute to an unnecessary length; Matter having been particularly examined, and by your own confession refuted in each of those senses? And can any more be required to prove the absolute impossibility of a thing, than the proving it impossible in every particular sense that either you or any one else understands it in?

Hyl. But I am not so thoroughly satisfied that you have proved the impossibility of Matter, in the last most obscure abstracted and indefinite sense.

Phil.. When is a thing shewn to be impossible?

Hyl. When a repugnancy is demonstrated between the ideas comprehended in its definition.

Phil. But where there are no ideas, there no repugnancy can be demonstrated between ideas?

Hyl. I agree with you.

Phil. Now, in that which you call the obscure indefinite sense of the word MATTER, it is plain, by your own confession, there was included no idea at all, no sense except an unknown sense; which is the same thing as none. You are not, therefore, to expect I should prove a repugnancy between ideas, where there are no ideas; or the impossibility of Matter taken in an UNKNOWN sense, that is, no sense at all. My business was only to shew you meant NOTHING; and this you were brought to own. So that, in all your various senses, you have been shewed either to mean nothing at all, or, if anything, an absurdity. And if this be not sufficient to prove the impossibility of a thing, I desire you will let me know what is.

Hyl. I acknowledge you have proved that Matter is impossible; nor do I see what more can be said in defence of it. But, at the same time that I give up this, I suspect all my other notions. For surely none could be more seemingly evident than this once was: and yet it now seems as false and absurd as ever it did true before. But I think we have discussed the point sufficiently for the present. The remaining part of the day I would willingly spend in running over in my thoughts the several heads of this morning's conversation, and tomorrow shall be glad to meet you here again about the same time.

Phil. I will not fail to attend you.

The Third Dialogue

Philonous. Tell me, Hylas, what are the fruits of yesterday's meditation? Has it confirmed you in the same mind you were in at parting? or have you since seen cause to change your opinion?

Hylas. Truly my opinion is that all our opinions are alike vain and uncertain. What we approve today, we condemn tomorrow. We keep a stir about knowledge, and spend our lives in the pursuit of it, when, alas I we know nothing all the while: nor do I think it possible for us ever to know anything in this life. Our faculties are too narrow and too few. Nature certainly never intended us for speculation.

Phil. What! Say you we can know nothing, Hylas?

Hyl. There is not that single thing in the world whereof we can know the real nature, or what it is in itself.

Phil. Will you tell me I do not really know what fire or water is?

Hyl. You may indeed know that fire appears hot, and water fluid; but this is no more than knowing what sensations are produced in your own mind, upon the application of fire and water to your organs of sense. Their internal constitution, their true and real nature, you are utterly in the dark as to THAT.

Phil. Do I not know this to be a real stone that I stand on, and that which I see before my eyes to be a real tree?

Hyl. KNOW? No, it is impossible you or any man alive should know it. All you know is, that you have such a certain idea or appearance in your own mind. But what is this to the real tree or stone? I tell you that colour, figure, and hardness, which you perceive, are not the real natures of those things, or in the least like them. The same may be said of all other real things, or corporeal substances, which compose the world. They have none of them anything of themselves, like those sensible qualities by us perceived. We should not therefore pretend to affirm or know anything of them, as they are in their own nature.

Phil. But surely, Hylas, I can distinguish gold, for example, from iron: and how could this be, if I knew not what either truly was?

Hyl. Believe me, Philonous, you can only distinguish between your own ideas. That yellowness, that weight, and other sensible qualities, think you they are really in the gold? They are only relative to the senses, and have no absolute existence in nature. And in pretending to distinguish the species of real things, by the appearances in your mind, you may perhaps act as wisely as he that should conclude two men were of a different species, because their clothes were not of the same colour.

Phil. It seems, then, we are altogether put off with the appearances of things, and those false ones too. The very meat I eat, and the cloth I wear, have nothing in them like what I see and feel.

Hyl. Even so.

Phil. But is it not strange the whole world should be thus imposed on, and so foolish as to believe their senses? And yet I know not how it is, but men eat, and drink, and sleep, and perform all the offices of life, as comfortably and conveniently as if they really knew the things they are conversant about.

Hyl. They do so: but you know ordinary practice does not require a nicety of speculative knowledge. Hence the vulgar retain their mistakes, and for all that make a shift to bustle through the affairs of life. But philosophers know better things.

Phil. You mean, they KNOW that they KNOW NOTHING.

Hyl. That is the very top and perfection of human knowledge.

Phil. But are you all this while in earnest, Hylas; and are you seriously persuaded that you know nothing real in the world? Suppose you are going to write, would you not call for pen, ink, and paper, like another man; and do you not know what it is you call for?

Hyl. How often must I tell you, that I know not the real nature of any one thing in the universe? I may indeed upon occasion make use of pen, ink, and paper. But what any one of them is in its own true nature, I declare positively I know not. And the same is true with regard to every, other corporeal thing. And, what is more, we are not only ignorant of the true and real nature of things, but even of their existence. It cannot be denied that we perceive such certain appearances or ideas; but it cannot be concluded from thence that bodies really exist. Nay, now I think on it, I must, agreeably to my former concessions, farther declare that it is impossible any REAL corporeal thing should exist in nature.

Phil. You amaze me. Was ever anything more wild and extravagant than the notions you now maintain: and is it not evident you are led into all these extravagances by the belief of MATERIAL SUBSTANCE? This makes you dream of those unknown natures in everything. It is this occasions your distinguishing between the reality and sensible appearances of things. It is to this you are indebted for being ignorant of what everybody else knows perfectly well. Nor is this all: you are not only ignorant of the true nature of everything, but you know not whether anything really exists, or whether there are any true natures at all; forasmuch as you attribute to your material beings an absolute or external existence, wherein you suppose their reality consists. And, as you are forced in the end to acknowledge such an existence means either a direct repugnancy, or nothing at all, it follows that you are obliged to pull down your own hypothesis of material Substance, and positively to deny the real existence of any part of the universe. And so you are plunged into the deepest and most deplorable scepticism that ever man was. Tell me, Hylas, is it not as I say?

Hyl. I agree with you. MATERIAL SUBSTANCE was no more than an hypothesis; and a false and groundless one too. I will no longer spend my breath in defence of it. But whatever hypothesis you advance, or whatsoever scheme of things you introduce in its stead, I doubt not it will appear every whit as false: let me but be allowed to question you upon it. That is, suffer me to serve you in your own kind, and I warrant it shall conduct you through as many perplexities and contradictions, to the very same state of scepticism that I myself am in at present.

Phil. I assure you, Hylas, I do not pretend to frame any hypothesis at all. I am of a vulgar cast, simple enough to believe my senses, and leave things as I find them. To be plain, it is my opinion that the real things are those very things I see, and feel, and perceive by my senses. These I know; and, finding they answer all the necessities and purposes of life, have no reason to be solicitous about any other unknown beings. A piece of sensible bread, for instance, would stay my stomach better than ten thousand times as much of that insensible, unintelligible, real bread you speak of. It is likewise my opinion that colours and other sensible qualities are on the objects. I cannot for my life help thinking that snow is white, and fire hot. You indeed, who by SNOW and fire mean certain external, unperceived, unperceiving substances, are in the right to deny whiteness or heat to be affections inherent in THEM. But I, who understand by those words the things I see and feel, am obliged to think like other folks. And, as I am no sceptic with regard to the nature of things, so neither am I as to their existence. That a thing should be really perceived by my senses, and at the same time not really exist, is to me a plain contradiction; since I cannot prescind or abstract, even in thought, the existence of a sensible thing from its being perceived. Wood, stones, fire, water, flesh, iron, and the like things, which I name and discourse of, are things that I know. And I should not have known them but that I perceived them by my senses; and things perceived by the senses are immediately perceived; and things immediately perceived are ideas; and ideas cannot exist without the mind; their existence therefore consists in being perceived; when, therefore, they are actually perceived there can be no doubt of their existence. Away then with all that scepticism, all those ridiculous philosophical doubts. What a jest is it for a philosopher to question the existence of sensible things, till he hath it proved to him from the veracity of God; or to pretend our knowledge in this point falls short of intuition or demonstration! I might as well doubt of my own being, as of the being of those things I actually see and feel.

Hyl. Not so fast, Philonous: you say you cannot conceive how sensible things should exist without the mind. Do you not?

Phil. I do.

Hyl. Supposing you were annihilated, cannot you conceive it possible that things perceivable by sense may still exist?

Phil. I can; but then it must be in another mind. When I deny sensible things an existence out of the mind, I do not mean my mind in particular, but all minds. Now, it is plain they have an existence exterior to my mind; since I find them by experience to be independent of it. There is therefore some other Mind wherein they exist, during the intervals between the times of my perceiving them: as likewise they did before my birth, and would do after my supposed annihilation. And, as the same is true with regard to all other finite created spirits, it necessarily follows there is an OMNIPRESENT ETERNAL MIND, which knows and comprehends all things, and exhibits them to our view in such a manner, and according to such rules, as He Himself hath ordained, and are by us termed the LAWS OF NATURE.

Hyl. Answer me, Philonous. Are all our ideas perfectly inert beings? Or have they any agency included in them?

Phil. They are altogether passive and inert.

Hyl. And is not God an agent, a being purely active?

Phil. I acknowledge it.

Hyl. No idea therefore can be like unto, or represent the nature of God?

Phil. It cannot.

Hyl. Since therefore you have no IDEA of the mind of God, how can you conceive it possible that things should exist in His mind? Or, if you can conceive the mind of God, without having an idea of it, why may not I be allowed to conceive the existence of Matter, notwithstanding I have no idea of it?

Phil. As to your first question: I own I have properly no IDEA, either of God or any other spirit; for these being active, cannot be represented by things perfectly inert, as our ideas are. I do nevertheless know that I, who am a spirit or thinking substance, exist as certainly as I know my ideas exist. Farther, I know what I mean by the terms I AND MYSELF; and I know this immediately or intuitively, though I do not perceive it as I perceive a triangle, a colour, or a sound. The Mind, Spirit, or Soul is that indivisible unextended thing which thinks, acts, and perceives. I say INDIVISIBLE, because unextended; and UNEXTENDED, because extended, figured, moveable things are ideas; and that which perceives ideas, which thinks and wills, is plainly itself no idea, nor like an idea. Ideas are things inactive, and perceived. And Spirits a sort of beings altogether different from them. I do not therefore say my soul is an idea, or like an idea. However, taking the word IDEA in a large sense, my soul may be said to furnish me with an idea, that is, an image or likeness of God — though indeed extremely inadequate. For, all the notion I have of God is obtained by reflecting on my own soul, heightening its powers, and removing its imperfections. I have, therefore, though not an inactive idea, yet in MYSELF some sort of an active thinking image of the Deity. And, though I perceive Him not by sense, yet I have a notion of Him, or know Him by reflexion and reasoning. My own mind and my own ideas I have an immediate knowledge of; and, by the help of these, do mediately apprehend the possibility of the existence of other spirits and ideas. Farther, from my own being, and from the dependency I find in myself and my ideas, I do, by an act of reason, necessarily infer the existence of a God, and of all created things in the mind of God. So much for your first question. For the second: I suppose by this time you can answer it yourself. For you neither perceive Matter objectively, as you do an inactive being or idea; nor know it, as you do yourself, by a reflex act, neither do you mediately apprehend it by similitude of the one or the other; nor yet collect it by reasoning from that which you know immediately. All which makes the case of MATTER widely different from that of the DEITY.

Hyl. You say your own soul supplies you with some sort of an idea or image of God. But, at the same time, you acknowledge you have, properly speaking, no IDEA of your own soul. You even affirm that spirits are a sort of beings altogether different from ideas. Consequently that no idea can be like a spirit. We have therefore no idea of any spirit. You admit nevertheless that there is spiritual Substance, although you have no idea of it; while you deny there can be such a thing as material Substance, because you have no notion or idea of it. Is this fair dealing? To act consistently, you must either admit Matter or reject Spirit. What say you to this?

Phil. I say, in the first place, that I do not deny the existence of material substance, merely because I have no notion of it' but because the notion of it is inconsistent; or, in other words, because it is repugnant that there should be a notion of it. Many things, for aught I know, may exist, whereof neither I nor any other man hath or can have any idea or notion whatsoever. But then those things must be possible, that is, nothing inconsistent must be included in their definition. I say, secondly, that, although we believe things to exist which we do not perceive, yet we may not believe that any particular thing exists, without some reason for such belief: but I have no reason for believing the existence of Matter. I have no immediate intuition thereof: neither can I immediately from my sensations, ideas, notions, actions, or passions, infer an unthinking, unperceiving, inactive Substance — either by probable deduction, or necessary consequence. Whereas the being of my Self, that is, my own soul, mind, or thinking principle, I evidently know by reflexion. You will forgive me if I repeat the same things in answer to the same objections. In the very notion or definition of MATERIAL SUBSTANCE, there is included a manifest repugnance and inconsistency. But this cannot be said of the notion of Spirit. That ideas should exist in what doth not perceive, or be produced by what doth not act, is repugnant. But, it is no repugnancy to say that a perceiving thing should be the subject of ideas, or an active thing the cause of them. It is granted we have neither an immediate evidence nor a demonstrative knowledge of the existence of other finite spirits; but it will not thence follow that such spirits are on a foot with material substances: if to suppose the one be inconsistent, and it be not inconsistent to suppose the other; if the one can be inferred by no argument, and there is a probability for the other; if we see signs and effects indicating distinct finite agents like ourselves, and see no sign or symptom whatever that leads to a rational belief of Matter. I say, lastly, that I have a notion of Spirit, though I have not, strictly speaking, an idea of it. I do not perceive it as an idea, or by means of an idea, but know it by reflexion.

Hyl. Notwithstanding all you have said, to me it seems that, according to your own way of thinking, and in consequence of your own principles, it should follow that YOU are only a system of floating ideas, without any substance to support them. Words are not to be used without a meaning. And, as there is no more meaning in SPIRITUAL SUBSTANCE than in MATERIAL SUBSTANCE, the one is to be exploded as well as the other.

Phil. How often must I repeat, that I know or am conscious of my own being; and that I MYSELF am not my ideas, but somewhat else, a thinking, active principle that perceives, knows, wifls, and operates about ideas. I know that I, one and the same self, perceive both colours and sounds: that a colour cannot perceive a sound, nor a sound a colour: that I am therefore one individual principle, distinct from colour and sound; and, for the same reason, from aft other sensible things and inert ideas. But, I am not in like manner conscious either of the existence or essence of Matter. On the contrary, I know that nothing inconsistent can exist, and that the existence of Matter implies an inconsistency. Farther, I know what I mean when I affirm that there is a spiritual substance or support of ideas, that is, that a spirit knows and perceives ideas. But, I do not know what is meant when it is said that an unperceiving substance hath inherent in it and supports either ideas or the archetypes of ideas. There is therefore upon the whole no parity of case between Spirit and Matter.

Hyl. I own myself satisfied in this point. But, do you in earnest think the real existence of sensible things consists in their being actually perceived? If so; how comes it that all mankind distinguish between them? Ask the first man you meet, and he shall tell you, TO BE PERCEIVED is one thing, and TO EXIST is another.

Phil. I am content, Hylas, to appeal to the common sense of the world for the truth of my notion. Ask the gardener why he thinks yonder cherry-tree exists in the garden, and he shall tell you, because he sees and feels it; in a word, because he perceives it by his senses. Ask him why he thinks an orange-tree not to be there, and he shall tell you, because he does not perceive it. What he perceives by sense, that he terms a real, being, and saith it IS OR EXISTS; but, that which is not perceivable, the same, he saith, hath no being.

Hyl. Yes, Philonous, I grant the existence of a sensible thing consists in being perceivable, but not in being actually perceived.

Phil. And what is perceivable but an idea? And can an idea exist without being actually perceived? These are points long since agreed between us.

Hyl. But, be your opinion never so true, yet surely you will not deny it is shocking, and contrary to the common sense of men. Ask the fellow whether yonder tree hath an existence out of his mind: what answer think you he would make?

Phil. The same that I should myself, to wit, that it doth exist out of his mind. But then to a Christian it cannot surely be shocking to say, the real tree, existing without his mind, is truly known and comprehended by (that is EXISTS IN) the infinite mind of God. Probably he may not at first glance be aware of the direct and immediate proof there is of this; inasmuch as the very being of a tree, or any other sensible thing, implies a mind wherein it is. But the point itself he cannot deny. The question between the Materialists and me is not, whether things have a REAL existence out of the mind of this or that person, but whether they have an ABSOLUTE existence, distinct from being perceived by God, and exterior to all minds. This indeed some heathens and philosophers have affirmed, but whoever entertains notions of the Deity suitable to the Holy Scriptures will be of another opinion.

Hyl. But, according to your notions, what difference is there between real things, and chimeras formed by the imagination, or the visions of a dream — since they are all equally in the mind?

Phil. The ideas formed by the imagination are faint and indistinct; they have, besides, an entire dependence on the will. But the ideas perceived by sense, that is, real things, are more vivid and clear; and, being imprinted on the mind by a spirit distinct from us, have not the like dependence on our will. There is therefore no danger of confounding these with the foregoing: and there is as little of confounding them with the visions of a dream, which are dim, irregular, and confused. And, though they should happen to be never so lively and natural, yet, by their not being connected, and of a piece with the preceding and subsequent transactions of our lives, they might easily be distinguished from realities. In short, by whatever method you distinguish THINGS FROM CHIMERAS on your scheme, the same, it is evident, will hold also upon mine. For, it must be, I presume, by some perceived difference; and I am not for depriving you of any one thing that you perceive.

Hyl. But still, Philonous, you hold, there is nothing in the world but spirits and ideas. And this, you must needs acknowledge, sounds very oddly.

Phil. I own the word IDEA, not being commonly used for THING, sounds something out of the way. My reason for using it was, because a necessary relation to the mind is understood to be implied by that term; and it is now commonly used by philosophers to denote the immediate objects of the understanding. But, however oddly the proposition may sound in words, yet it includes nothing so very strange or shocking in its sense; which in effect amounts to no more than this, to wit, that there are only things perceiving, and things perceived; or that every unthinking being is necessarily, and from the very nature of its existence, perceived by some mind; if not by a finite created mind, yet certainly by the infinite mind of God, in whom "we five, and move, and have our being." Is this as strange as to say, the sensible qualities are not on the objects: or that we cannot be sure of the existence of things, or know any thing of their real natures — though we both see and feel them, and perceive them by all our senses?

Hyl. And, in consequence of this, must we not think there are no such things as physical or corporeal causes; but that a Spirit is the immediate cause of all the phenomena in nature? Can there be anything more extravagant than this?

Phil. Yes, it is infinitely more extravagant to say — a thing which is inert operates on the mind, and which is unperceiving is the cause of our perceptions, without any regard either to consistency, or the old known axiom, NOTHING CAN GIVE TO ANOTHER THAT WHICH

IT HATH NOT ITSELF. Besides, that which to you, I know not for what reason, seems so extravagant is no more than the Holy Scriptures assert in a hundred places. In them God is represented as the sole and immediate Author of all those effects which some heathens and philosophers are wont to ascribe to Nature, Matter, Fate, or the like unthinking principle. This is so much the constant language of Scripture that it were needless to confirm it by citations.

Hyl. You are not aware, Philonous, that in making God the immediate Author of all the motions in nature, you make Him the Author of murder, sacrilege, adultery, and the like heinous sins.

Phil. In answer to that, I observe, first, that the imputation of guilt is the same, whether a person commits an action with or without an instrument. In case therefore you suppose God to act by the mediation of an instrument or occasion, called MATTER, you as truly make Him the author of sin as I, who think Him the immediate agent in all those operations vulgarly ascribed to Nature. I farther observe that sin or moral turpitude doth not consist in the outward physical action or motion, but in the internal deviation of the will from the laws of reason and religion. This is plain, in that the killing an enemy in a battle, or putting a criminal legally to death, is not thought sinful; though the outward act be the very same with that in the case of murder. Since, therefore, sin doth not consist in the physical action, the making God an immediate cause of all such actions is not making Him the Author of sin. Lastly, I have nowhere said that God is the only agent who produces all the motions in bodies. It is true I have denied there are any other agents besides spirits; but this is very consistent with allowing to thinking rational beings, in the production of motions, the use of limited powers, ultimately indeed derived from God, but immediately under the direction of their own wills, which is sufficient to entitle them to all the guilt of their actions.

Hyl. But the denying Matter, Philonous, or corporeal Substance; there is the point. You can never persuade me that this is not repugnant to the universal sense of mankind. Were our dispute to be determined by most voices, I am confident you would give up the point, without gathering the votes.

Phil. I wish both our opinions were fairly stated and submitted to the judgment of men who had plain common sense, without the prejudices of a learned education. Let me be represented as one who trusts his senses, who thinks he knows the things he sees and feels, and entertains no doubts of their existence; and you fairly set forth with all your doubts, your paradoxes, and your scepticism about you, and I shall willingly acquiesce in the determination of any indifferent person. That there is no substance wherein ideas can exist beside spirit is to me evident. And that the objects immediately perceived are ideas, is on all hands agreed. And that sensible qualities are objects immediately perceived no one can deny. It is therefore evident there can be no SUBSTRATUM of those qualities but spirit; in which they exist, not by way of mode or property, but as a thing perceived in that which perceives it. I deny therefore that there is ANY UNTHINKING-SUBSTRATUM of the objects of sense, and IN THAT ACCEPTATION that there is any material substance. But if by MATERIAL SUBSTANCE is meant only SENSIBLE BODY, THAT which is seen and felt (and the unphilosophical part of the world, I dare say, mean no more)— then I am more certain of matter's existence than you or any other philosopher pretend to be. If there be anything which makes the generality of mankind averse from the notions I espouse, it is a misapprehension that I deny the reality of sensible things. But, as it is you who are guilty of that, and not I, it follows that in truth their aversion is against your notions and not mine. I do therefore assert that I am as certain as of my own being, that there are bodies or corporeal substances (meaning the things I perceive by my senses); and that, granting this, the bulk of mankind will take no thought about, nor think themselves at all concerned in the fate of those unknown natures, and philosophical quiddities, which some men are so fond of.

Hyl. What say you to this? Since, according to you, men judge of the reality of things by their senses, how can a man be mistaken in thinking the moon a plain lucid surface, about a foot in diameter; or a square tower, seen at a distance, round; or an oar, with one end in the water, crooked?

Phil. He is not mistaken with regard to the ideas he actually perceives, but in the inference he makes from his present perceptions. Thus, in the case of the oar, what he immediately perceives by sight is certainly crooked; and so far he is in the right. But if he thence conclude that upon taking the oar out of the water he shall perceive the same crookedness; or that it would affect his touch as crooked things are wont to do: in that he is mistaken. In like manner, if he shall conclude from what he perceives in one station, that, in case he advances towards the moon or tower, he should still be affected with the like ideas, he is mistaken. But his mistake lies not in what he perceives immediately, and at present, (it being a manifest contradiction to suppose he should err in respect of that) but in the wrong judgment he makes concerning the ideas he apprehends to be connected with those immediately perceived: or, concerning the ideas that, from what he perceives at present, he imagines would be perceived in other circumstances. The case is the same with regard to the Copernican system. We do not here perceive any motion of the earth: but it were erroneous thence to conclude, that, in case we were placed at as great a distance from that as we are now from the other planets, we should not then perceive its motion.

Hyl. I understand you; and must needs own you say things plausible enough. But, give me leave to put you in mind of one thing. Pray, Philonous, were you not formerly as positive that Matter existed, as you are now that it does not?

Phil. I was. But here lies the difference. Before, my positiveness was founded, without examination, upon prejudice; but now, after inquiry, upon evidence.

Hyl. After all, it seems our dispute is rather about words than things. We agree in the thing, but differ in the name. That we are affected with ideas FROM WITHOUT is evident; and it is no less evident that there must be (I will not say archetypes, but) Powers without the mind, corresponding to those ideas. And, as these Powers cannot subsist by themselves, there is some subject of them necessarily to be admitted; which I call MATTER, and you call SPIRIT. This is all the difference.

Phil. Pray, Hylas, is that powerful Being, or subject of powers, extended?

Hyl. It hath not extension; but it hath the power to raise in you the idea of extension.

Phil. It is therefore itself unextended?

Hyl. I grant it.

Phil. Is it not also active?

Hyl. Without doubt. Otherwise, how could we attribute powers to it?

Phil. Now let me ask you two questions: FIRST, Whether it be agreeable to the usage either of philosophers or others to give the name MATTER to an unextended active being? And, SECONDLY, Whether it be not ridiculously absurd to misapply names contrary to the common use of language?

Hyl. Well then, let it not be called Matter, since you will have it so, but some THIRD NATURE distinct from Matter and Spirit. For what reason is there why you should call it Spirit? Does not the notion of spirit imply that it is thinking, as well as active and unextended?

Phil. My reason is this: because I have a mind to have some notion of meaning in what I say: but I have no notion of any action distinct from volition, neither. can I conceive volition to be anywhere but in a spirit: therefore, when I speak of an active being, I am obliged to mean a Spirit. Beside, what can be plainer than that a thing which hath no ideas in itself cannot impart them to me; and, if it hath ideas, surely it must be a Spirit. To make you comprehend the point still more clearly if it be possible, I assert as well as you that, since we are affected from without, we must allow Powers to be without, in a Being distinct from ourselves. So far we are agreed. But then we differ as to the kind of this powerful Being. I will have it to be Spirit, you Matter, or I know not what (I may add too, you know not what) Third Nature. Thus, I prove it to be Spirit. From the effects I see produced, I conclude there are actions; and, because actions, volitions; and, because there are volitions, there must be a WILL. Again, the things I perceive must have an existence, they or their archetypes, out of MY mind: but, being ideas, neither they nor their archetypes can exist otherwise than in an understanding; there is therefore an UNDERSTANDING. But will and understanding constitute in the strictest sense a mind or spirit. The powerful cause, therefore, of my ideas is in strict propriety of speech a SPIRIT.

Hyl. And now I warrant you think you have made the point very clear, little suspecting that what you advance leads directly to a contradiction. Is it not an absurdity to imagine any imperfection in God?

Phil. Without a doubt.

Hyl. To suffer pain is an imperfection?

Phil. It is.

Hyl. Are we not sometimes affected with pain and uneasiness by some other Being?

Phil. We are.

Hyl. And have you not said that Being is a Spirit, and is not that Spirit God?

Phil. I grant it.

Hyl. But you have asserted that whatever ideas we perceive from without are in the mind which affects us. The ideas, therefore, of pain and uneasiness are in God; or, in other words, God suffers pain: that is to say, there is an imperfection in the Divine nature: which, you acknowledged, was absurd. So you are caught in a plain contradiction.

Phil. That God knows or understands all things, and that He knows, among other things, what pain is, even every sort of painful sensation, and what it is for His creatures to suffer pain, I make no question. But, that God, though He knows and sometimes causes painful sensations in us, can Himself suffer pain, I positively deny. We, who are limited and dependent spirits, are liable to impressions of sense, the effects of an external Agent, which, being produced against our wills, are sometimes painful and uneasy. But God, whom no external being can affect, who perceives nothing by sense as we do; whose will is absolute and independent, causing all things, and liable to be thwarted or resisted by nothing: it is evident, such a Being as this can suffer nothing, nor be affected with any painful sensation, or indeed any sensation at all. We are chained to a body: that is to say, our perceptions are connected with corporeal motions. By the law of our nature, we are affected upon every alteration in the nervous parts of our sensible body; which sensible body, rightly considered, is nothing but a complexion of such qualities or ideas as have no existence distinct from being perceived by a mind. So that this connexion of sensations with corporeal motions means no more than a correspondence in the order of nature, between two sets of ideas, or things immediately perceivable. But God is a Pure Spirit, disengaged from all such sympathy, or natural ties. No corporeal motions are attended with the sensations of pain or pleasure in His mind. To know everything knowable, is certainly a perfection; but to endure, or suffer, or feel anything by sense, is an imperfection. The former, I say, agrees to God, but not the latter. God knows, or hath ideas; but His ideas are not conveyed to Him by sense, as ours are. Your not distinguishing, where there is so manifest a difference, makes you fancy you see an absurdity where there is none.

Hyl. But, all this while you have not considered that the quantity of Matter has been demonstrated to be proportioned to the gravity of bodies. And what can withstand demonstration?

Phil. Let me see how you demonstrate that point.

Hyl. I lay it down for a principle, that the moments or quantities of motion in bodies are in a direct compounded reason of the velocities and quantities of Matter contained in them. Hence, where the velocities are equal, it follows the moments are directly as the quantity of Matter in each. But it is found by experience that all bodies (bating the small inequalities, arising from the resistance of the air) descend with an equal velocity; the motion therefore of descending bodies, and consequently their gravity, which is the cause or principle of that motion, is proportional to the quantity of Matter; which was to be demonstrated.

Phil. You lay it down as a self-evident principle that the quantity of motion in any body is proportional to the velocity and MATTER taken together; and this is made use of to prove a proposition from whence the existence of CARTER is inferred. Pray is not this arguing in a circle?

Hyl. In the premise I only mean that the motion is proportional to the velocity, jointly with the extension and solidity.

Phil. But, allowing this to be true, yet it will not thence follow that gravity is proportional to MATTER, in your philosophic sense of the word; except you take it for granted that unknown SUBSTRATUM, or whatever else you call it, is proportional to those sensible qualities; which to suppose is plainly begging the question. That there is magnitude and solidity, or resistance, perceived by sense, I readily grant; as likewise, that gravity may be proportional to those qualities I will not dispute. But that either these qualities as perceived by us, or the powers producing them, do exist in a MATERIAL SUBSTRATUM; this is what I deny, and you indeed affirm, but, notwithstanding your demonstration, have not yet proved.

Hyl. I shall insist no longer on that point. Do you think, however, you shall persuade me that the natural philosophers have been dreaming all this while? Pray what becomes of all their hypotheses and explications of the phenomena, which suppose the existence of Matter?

Phil. What mean you, Hylas, by the PHENOMENA?

Hyl. I mean the appearances which I perceive by my senses.

Phil. And the appearances perceived by sense, are they not ideas?

Hyl. I have told you so a hundred times.

Phil. Therefore, to explain the phenomena, is, to shew how we come to be affected with ideas, in that manner and order wherein they are imprinted on our senses. Is it not?

Hyl. It is.

Phil. Now, if you can prove that any philosopher has explained the production of any one idea in our minds by the help of MATTER, I shall for ever acquiesce, and look on all that hath been said against it as nothing; but, if you cannot, it is vain to urge the explication of phenomena. That a Being endowed with knowledge and will should produce or exhibit ideas is easily understood. But that a Being which is utterly destitute of these faculties should be able to produce ideas, or in any sort to affect an intelligence, this I can never understand. This I say, though we had some positive conception of Matter, though we knew its qualities, and could comprehend its existence, would yet be so far from explaining things, that it is itself the most inexplicable thing in the world. And yet, for all this, it will not follow that philosophers have been doing nothing; for, by observing and reasoning upon the connexion of ideas, they discover the laws and methods of nature, which is a part of knowledge both useful and entertaining.

Hyl. After all, can it be supposed God would deceive all mankind? Do you imagine He would have induced the whole world to believe the being of Matter, if there was no such thing?

Phil. That every epidemical opinion, arising from prejudice, or passion, or thoughtlessness, may be imputed to God, as the Author of it, I believe you will not affirm. Whatsoever opinion we father on Him, it must be either because He has discovered it to us by supernatural revelation; or because it is so evident to our natural faculties, which were framed and given us by God, that it is impossible we should withhold our assent from it. But where is the revelation? or where is the evidence that extorts the belief of Matter? Nay, how does it appear, that Matter, TAKEN FOR SOMETHING DISTINCT FROM WHAT WE PERCEIVE BY OUR SENSES, is thought to exist by all mankind; or indeed, by any except a few philosophers, who do not know what they would be at? Your question supposes these points are clear; and, when you have cleared them, I shall think myself obliged to give you another answer. In the meantime, let it suffice that I tell you, I do not suppose God has deceived mankind at all.

Hyl. But the novelty, Philonous, the novelty! There lies the danger. New notions should always be discountenanced; they unsettle men's minds, and nobody knows where they will end.

Phil. Why the rejecting a notion that has no foundation, either in sense, or in reason, or in Divine authority, should be thought to unsettle the belief of such opinions as are grounded on all or any of these, I cannot imagine. That innovations in government and religion are dangerous, and ought to be discountenanced, I freely own. But is there the like reason why they should be discouraged in philosophy? The making anything known which was unknown before is an innovation in knowledge: and, if all such innovations had been forbidden, men would have made a notable progress in the arts and sciences. But it is none of my business to plead for novelties and paradoxes. That the qualities we perceive are not on the objects: that we must not believe our senses: that we know nothing of the real nature of things, and can never be assured even of their existence: that real colours and sounds are nothing but certain unknown figures and motions: that motions are in themselves neither swift nor slow: that there are in bodies absolute extensions, without any particular magnitude or figure: that a thing stupid, thoughtless, and inactive, operates on a spirit: that the least particle of a body contains innumerable extended parts:— these are the novelties, these are the strange notions which shock the genuine uncorrupted judgment of all mankind; and being once admitted, embarrass the mind with endless doubts and difficulties. And it is against these and the like innovations I endeavour to vindicate Common Sense. It is true, in doing this, I may perhaps be obliged to use some AMBAGES, and ways of speech not common. But, if my notions are once thoroughly understood, that which is most singular in them will, in effect, be found to amount to no more than this. — that it is absolutely impossible, and a plain contradiction, to suppose any unthinking Being should exist without being perceived by a Mind. And, if this notion be singular, it is a shame it should be so, at this time of day, and in a Christian country.

Hyl. As for the difficulties other opinions may be liable to, those are out of the question. It is your business to defend your own opinion. Can anything be plainer than that you are for changing all things into ideas? You, I say, who are not ashamed to charge me WITH SCEPTICISM. This is so plain, there is no denying it.

Phil. You mistake me. I am not for changing things into ideas, but rather ideas into things; since those immediate objects of perception, which, according to you, are only appearances of things, I take to be the real things themselves.

Hyl. Things! You may pretend what you please; but it is certain you leave us nothing but the empty forms of things, the outside only which strikes the senses.

Phil. What you call the empty forms and outside of things seem to me the very things themselves. Nor are they empty or incomplete, otherwise than upon your supposition — that Matter is an essential part of all corporeal things. We both, therefore, agree in this, that we perceive only sensible forms: but herein we differ — you will have them to be empty appearances, I, real beings. In short, you do not trust your senses, I do.

Hyl. You say you believe your senses; and seem to applaud yourself that in this you agree with the vulgar. According to you, therefore, the true nature of a thing is discovered by the senses. If so, whence comes that disagreement? Why is not the same figure, and other sensible qualities, perceived all manner of ways? and why should we use a microscope the better to discover the true nature of a body, if it were discoverable to the naked eye?

Phil. Strictly speaking, Hylas, we do not see the same object that we feel; neither is the same object perceived by the microscope which was by the naked eye. But, in case every variation was thought sufficient to constitute a new kind of individual, the endless number of confusion of names would render language impracticable. Therefore, to avoid this, as well as other inconveniences which are obvious upon a little thought, men combine together several ideas, apprehended by divers senses, or by the same sense at different times, or in different circumstances, but observed, however, to have some connexion in nature, either with respect to co-existence or succession; all which they refer to one name, and consider as one thing. Hence it follows that when I examine, by my other senses, a thing I have seen, it is not in order to understand better the same object which I had perceived by sight, the object of one sense not being perceived by the other senses. And, when I look through a microscope, it is not that I may perceive more clearly what I perceived already with my bare eyes; the object perceived by the glass being quite different from the former. But, in both cases, my aim is only to know what ideas are connected together; and the more a man knows of the connexion of ideas, the more he is said to know of the nature of things. What, therefore, if our ideas are variable; what if our senses are not in all circumstances affected with the same appearances. It will not thence follow they are not to be trusted; or that they are inconsistent either with themselves or anything else: except it be with your preconceived notion of (I know not what) one single, unchanged, unperceivable, real Nature, marked by each name. Which prejudice seems to have taken its rise from not rightly understanding the common language of men, speaking of several distinct ideas as united into one thing by the mind. And, indeed, there is cause to suspect several erroneous conceits of the philosophers are owing to the same original: while they began to build their schemes not so much on notions as on words, which were framed by the vulgar, merely for conveniency and dispatch in the common actions of life, without any regard to speculation.

Hyl. Methinks I apprehend your meaning.

Phil. It is your opinion the ideas we perceive by our senses are not real things, but images or copies of them. Our knowledge, therefore, is no farther real than as our ideas are the true REPRESENTATIONS OF THOSE ORIGINALS. But, as these supposed originals are in themselves unknown, it is impossible to know how far our ideas resemble them; or whether they resemble them at all. We cannot, therefore, be sure we have any real knowledge. Farther, as our ideas are perpetually varied, without any change in the supposed real things, it necessarily follows they cannot all be true copies of them: or, if some are and others are not, it is impossible to distinguish the former from the latter. And this plunges us yet deeper in uncertainty. Again, when we consider the point, we cannot conceive how any idea, or anything like an idea, should have an absolute existence out of a mind: nor consequently, according to you, how there should be any real thing in nature. The result of all which is that we are thrown into the most hopeless and abandoned scepticism. Now, give me leave to ask you, First, Whether your referring ideas to certain absolutely existing unperceived substances, as their originals, be not the source of all this scepticism? Secondly, whether you are informed, either by sense or reason, of the existence of those unknown originals? And, in case you are not, whether it be not absurd to suppose them? Thirdly, Whether, upon inquiry, you find there is anything distinctly conceived or meant by the ABSOLUTE OR EXTERNAL EXISTENCE OF UNPERCEIVING SUBSTANCES? Lastly, Whether, the premises considered, it be not the wisest way to follow nature, trust your senses, and, laying aside all anxious thought about unknown natures or substances, admit with the vulgar those for real things which are perceived by the senses?

Hyl. For the present, I have no inclination to the answering part. I would much rather see how you can get over what follows. Pray are not the objects perceived by the SENSES of one, likewise perceivable to others present? If there were a hundred more here, they would all see the garden, the trees, and flowers, as I see them. But they are not in the same manner affected with the ideas I frame in my IMAGINATION. Does not this make a difference between the former sort of objects and the latter?

Phil. I grant it does. Nor have I ever denied a difference between the objects of sense and those of imagination. But what would you infer from thence? You cannot say that sensible objects exist unperceived, because they are perceived by many.

Hyl. I own I can make nothing of that objection: but it hath led me into another. Is it not your opinion that by our senses we perceive only the ideas existing in our minds?

Phil. It is.

Hyl. But the SAME idea which is in my mind cannot be in yours, or in any other mind. Doth it not therefore follow, from your principles, that no two can see the same thing? And is not this highly, absurd?

Phil. If the term SAME be taken in the vulgar acceptation, it is certain (and not at all repugnant to the principles I maintain) that different persons may perceive the same thing; or the same thing or idea exist in different minds. Words are of arbitrary imposition; and, since men are used to apply the word SAME where no distinction or variety is perceived, and I do not pretend to alter their perceptions, it follows that, as men have said before, SEVERAL SAW THE SAME THING, so they may, upon like occasions, still continue to use the same phrase, without any deviation either from propriety of language, or the truth of things. But, if the term SAME be used in the acceptation of philosophers, who pretend to an abstracted notion of identity, then, according to their sundry definitions of this notion (for it is not yet agreed wherein that philosophic identity consists), it may or may not be possible for divers persons to perceive the same thing. But whether philosophers shall think fit to CALL a thing the SAME or no, is, I conceive, of small importance. Let us suppose several men together, all endued with the same faculties, and consequently affected in like sort by their senses, and who had yet never known the use of language; they would, without question, agree in their perceptions. Though perhaps, when they came to the use of speech, some regarding the uniformness of what was perceived, might call it the SAME thing: others, especially regarding the diversity of persons who perceived, might choose the denomination of DIFFERENT things. But who sees not that all the dispute is about a word? to wit, whether. what is perceived by different persons may yet have the term SAME applied to it? Or, suppose a house, whose walls or outward shell remaining unaltered, the chambers are all pulled down, and new ones built in their place; and that you should call this the SAME, and I should say it was not the SAME house. — would we not, for all this, perfectly agree in our thoughts of the house, considered in itself? And would not all the difference consist in a sound? If you should say, We differed in our notions; for that you super-added to your idea of the house the simple abstracted idea of identity, whereas I did not; I would tell you, I know not what you mean by THE ABSTRACTED IDEA OF IDENTITY; and should desire you to look into your own thoughts, and be sure you understood yourself. — Why so silent, Hylas? Are you not yet satisfied men may dispute about identity and diversity, without any real difference in their thoughts and opinions, abstracted from names? Take this farther reflexion with you: that whether Matter be allowed to exist or no, the case is exactly the same as to the point in hand. For the Materialists themselves acknowledge what we immediately perceive by our senses to be our own ideas. Your difficulty, therefore, that no two see the same thing, makes equally against the Materialists and me.

Hyl. Ay, Philonous, but they suppose an external archetype, to which referring their several ideas they may truly be said to perceive the same thing.

Phil. And (not to mention your having discarded those archetypes) so may you suppose an external archetype on my principles; — EXTERNAL, I MEAN, TO YOUR OWN MIND: though indeed it must be' supposed to exist in that Mind which comprehends all things; but then, this serves all the ends of IDENTITY, as well as if it existed out of a mind. And I am sure you yourself will not say it is less intelligible.

Hyl. You have indeed clearly satisfied me — either that there is no difficulty at bottom in this point; or, if there be, that it makes equally against both opinions.

Phil. But that which makes equally against two contradictory opinions can be a proof against neither.

Hyl. I acknowledge it. But, after all, Philonous, when I consider the substance of what you advance against SCEPTICISM, it amounts to no more than this: We are sure that we really see, hear, feel; in a word, that we are affected with sensible impressions.

Phil. And how are WE concerned any farther? I see this cherry, I feel it, I taste it: and I am sure NOTHING cannot be seen, or felt, or. tasted: it is therefore red. Take away the sensations of softness, moisture, redness, tartness, and you take away the cherry, since it is not a being distinct from sensations. A cherry, I say, is nothing but a congeries of sensible impressions, or ideas perceived by various senses: which ideas are united into one thing (or have one name given them) by the mind, because they are observed to attend each other. Thus, when the palate is affected with such a particular taste, the sight is affected with a red colour, the touch with roundness, softness, &c. Hence, when I see, and feel, and taste, in such sundry certain manners, I am sure the cherry exists, or is real; its reality being in my opinion nothing abstracted from those sensations. But if by the word CHERRY you, mean an unknown nature, distinct from all those sensible qualities, and by its EXISTENCE something distinct from its being perceived; then, indeed, I own, neither you nor I, nor any one else, can be sure it exists.

Hyl. But, what would you say, Philonous, if I should bring the very same reasons against the existence of sensible things IN A MIND, which you have offered against their existing IN A MATERIAL SUBSTRATUM?

Phil. When I see your reasons, you shall hear what I have to say to them.

Hyl. Is the mind extended or unextended?

Phil. Unextended, without doubt.

Hyl. Do you say the things you perceive are in your mind?

Phil. They are.

Hyl. Again, have I not heard you speak of sensible impressions?

Phil. I believe you may.

Hyl. Explain to me now, O Philonous! how it is possible there should be room for all those trees and houses to exist in your mind. Can extended things be contained in that which is unextended? Or, are we to imagine impressions made on a thing void of all solidity? You cannot say objects are in your mind, as books in your study: or that things are imprinted on it, as the figure of a seal upon wax. In what sense, therefore, are we to understand those expressions? Explain me this if you can: and I shall then be able to answer all those queries you formerly put to me about my SUBSTRATUM.

Phil. Look you, Hylas, when I speak of objects as existing in the mind, or imprinted on the senses, I would not be understood in the gross literal sense; as when bodies are said to exist in a place, or a seal to make an impression upon wax. My meaning is only that the mind comprehends or perceives them; and that it is affected from without, or by some being distinct from itself. This is my explication of your difficulty; and how it can serve to make your tenet of an unperceiving material SUBSTRATUM intelligible, I would fain know.

Hyl. Nay, if that be all, I confess I do not see what use can be made of it. But are you not guilty of some abuse of language in this?

Phil. None at all. It is no more than common custom, which you know is the rule of language, hath authorised: nothing being more usual, than for philosophers to speak of the immediate objects of the understanding as things existing in the mind. 'Nor is there anything in this but what is conformable to the general analogy of language; most part of the mental operations being signified by words borrowed from sensible things; as is plain in the terms COMPREHEND, reflect, DISCOURSE, &C., which, being applied to the mind, must not be taken in their gross, original sense.

Hyl. You have, I own, satisfied me in this point. But there still remains one great difficulty, which I know not how you will get over. And, indeed, it is of such importance that if you could solve all others, without being able to find a solution for this, you must never expect to make me a proselyte to your principles.

Phil. Let me know this mighty difficulty.

Hyl. The Scripture account of the creation is what appears to me utterly irreconcilable with your notions. Moses tells us of a creation: a creation of what? of ideas? No, certainly, but of things, of real things, solid corporeal substances. Bring your principles to agree with this, and I shall perhaps agree with you.

Phil. Moses mentions the sun, moon, and stars, earth and sea, plants and animals. That all these do really exist, and were in the beginning created by God, I make no question. If by IDEAS you mean fictions and fancies of the mind, then these are no ideas. If by IDEAS you mean immediate objects of the understanding, or sensible things, which cannot exist unperceived, or out of a mind, then these things are ideas. But whether you do or do not call them IDEAS, IT matters little. The difference is only about a name. And, whether that name be retained or rejected, the sense, the truth, and reality of things continues the same. In common talk, the objects of our senses are not termed IDEAS, but THINGS. Call them so still: provided you do not attribute to them any absolute external existence, and I shall never quarrel with you for a word. The creation, therefore, I allow to have been a creation of things, of RED things. Neither is this in the least inconsistent with my principles, as is evident from what I have now said; and would have been evident to you without this, if you had not forgotten what had been so often said before. But as for solid corporeal substances, I desire you to show where Moses makes any mention of them; and, if they should be mentioned by him, or any other inspired writer, it would still be incumbent on you to shew those words were not taken in the vulgar acceptation, for things falling under our senses, but in the philosophic acceptation, for Matter, or AN UNKNOWN QUIDDITY, WITH AN ABSOLUTE EXISTENCE. When you have proved these points, then (and not till then) may you bring the authority of Moses into our dispute.

Hyl. It is in vain to dispute about a point so clear. I am content to refer it to your own conscience. Are you not satisfied there is some peculiar repugnancy between the Mosaic account of the creation and your notions?

Phil. If all possible sense which can be put on the first chapter of Genesis may be conceived as consistently with my principles as any other, then it has no peculiar repugnancy with them. But there is no sense you may not as well conceive, believing as I do. Since, besides spirits, all you conceive are ideas; and the existence of these I do not deny. Neither do you pretend they exist without the mind.

Hyl. Pray let me see any sense you can understand it in.

Phil. Why, I imagine that if I had been present at the creation, I should have seen things produced into being — that is become perceptible — in the order prescribed by the sacred historian. I ever before believed the Mosaic account of the creation, and now find no alteration in my manner of believing it. When things are said to begin or end their existence, we do not mean this with regard to God, but His creatures. All objects are eternally known by God, or, which is the same thing, have an eternal existence in His mind: but when things, before imperceptible to creatures, are, by a decree of God, perceptible to them, then are they said to begin a relative existence, with respect to created minds. Upon reading therefore the Mosaic account of the creation, I understand that the several parts of the world became gradually perceivable to finite spirits, endowed with proper faculties; so that, whoever such were present, they were in truth perceived by them. This is the literal obvious sense suggested to me by the words of the Holy Scripture: in which is included no mention, or no thought, either of SUBSTRATUM, INSTRUMENT, OCCASION, or ABSOLUTE EXISTENCE. And, upon inquiry, I doubt not it will be found that most plain honest men, who believe the creation, never think of those things any more than I. What metaphysical sense you may understand it in, you only can tell.

Hyl. But, Philonous, you do not seem to be aware that you allow created things, in the beginning, only a relative, and consequently hypothetical being: that is to say, upon supposition there were MEN to perceive them; without which they have no actuality of absolute existence, wherein creation might terminate. Is it not, therefore, according to you, plainly impossible the creation of any inanimate creatures should precede that of man? And is not this directly contrary to the Mosaic account?

Phil. In answer to that, I say, first, created beings might begin to exist in the mind of other created intelligences, beside men. You will not therefore be able to prove any contradiction between Moses and my notions, unless you first shew there was no other order of finite created spirits in being, before man. I say farther, in case we conceive the creation, as we should at this time, a parcel of plants or vegetables of all sorts produced, by an invisible Power, in a desert where nobody was present — that this way of explaining or conceiving it is consistent with my principles, since they deprive you of nothing, either sensible or imaginable; that it exactly suits with the common, natural, and undebauched notions of mankind; that it manifests the dependence of all things on God; and consequently hath all the good effect or influence, which it is possible that important article of our faith should have in making men humble, thankful, and resigned to their great Creator. I say, moreover, that, in this naked conception of things, divested of words, there will not be found any notion of what you call the ACTUALITY OF ABSOLUTE EXISTENCE. You may indeed raise a dust with those terms, and so lengthen our dispute to no purpose. But I entreat you calmly to look into your own thoughts, and then tell me if they are not a useless and unintelligible jargon.

Hyl. I own I have no very clear notion annexed to them. But what say you to this? Do you not make the existence of sensible things consist in their being in a mind? And were not all things eternally in the mind of God? Did they not therefore exist from all eternity, according to you? And how could that which was eternal be created in time? Can anything be clearer or better connected than this?

Phil. And are not you too of opinion, that God knew all things from eternity?

Hyl. I am.

Phil. Consequently they always had a being in the Divine intellect.

Hyl. This I acknowledge.

Phil. By your own confession, therefore, nothing is new, or begins to be, in respect of the mind of God. So we are agreed in that point.

Hyl. What shall we make then of the creation?

Phil. May we not understand it to have been entirely in respect of finite spirits; so that things, with regard to us, may properly be said to begin their existence, or be created, when God decreed they should become perceptible to intelligent creatures, in that order and manner which He then established, and we now call the laws of nature? You may call this a RELATIVE, or HYPOTHETICAL EXISTENCE if you please. But, so long as it supplies us with the most natural, obvious, and literal sense of the Mosaic history of the creation; so long as it answers all the religious ends of that great article; in a word, so long as you can assign no other sense or meaning in its stead; why should we reject this? Is it to comply with a ridiculous sceptical humour of making everything nonsense and unintelligible? I am sure you cannot say it is for the glory of God. For, allowing it to be a thing possible and conceivable that the corporeal world should have an absolute existence extrinsical to the mind of God, as well as to the minds of all created spirits; yet how could this set forth either the immensity or omniscience of the Deity, or the necessary and immediate dependence of all things on Him? Nay, would it not rather seem to derogate from those attributes?

Hyl. Well, but as to this decree of God's, for making things perceptible, what say you, Philonous? Is it not plain, God did either execute that decree from all eternity, or at some certain time began to will what He had not actually willed before, but only designed to will? If the former, then there could be no creation, or beginning of existence, in finite things. If the latter, then we must acknowledge something new to befall the Deity; which implies a sort of change: and all change argues imperfection.

Phil. Pray consider what you are doing. Is it not evident this objection concludes equally against a creation in any sense; nay, against every other act of the Deity, discoverable by the light of nature? None of which can WE conceive, otherwise than as performed in time, and having a beginning. God is a Being of transcerident and unlimited perfections: His nature, therefore, is incomprehensible to finite spirits. It is not, therefore, to be expected, that any man, whether Materialist or Immaterialist, should have exactly just notions of the Deity, His attributes, and ways of operation. If then you would infer anything against me, your difficulty must not be drawn from the inadequateness of our conceptions of the Divine nature, which is unavoidable on any scheme; but from the denial of Matter, of which there is not one word, directly or indirectly, in what you have now objected.

Hyl. I must acknowledge the difficulties you are concerned to clear are such only as arise from the non-existence of Matter, and are peculiar to that notion. So far you are in the right. But I cannot by any means bring myself to think there is no such peculiar repugnancy between the creation and your opinion; though indeed where to fix it, I do not distinctly know.

Phil. What would you have? Do I not acknowledge a twofold state of things — the one ectypal or natural, the other archetypal and eternal? The former was created in time; the latter existed from everlasting in the mind of God. Is not this agreeable to the common notions of divines? or, is any more than this necessary in order to conceive the creation? But you suspect some peculiar repugnancy, though you know not where it lies. To take away all possibility of scruple in the case, do but consider this one point. Either you are not able to conceive the Creation on any hypothesis whatsoever; and, if so, there is no ground for dislike or complaint against any particular opinion on that score: or you are able to conceive it; and, if so, why not on my Principles, since thereby nothing conceivable is taken away? You have all along been allowed the full scope of sense, imagination, and reason. Whatever, therefore, you could before apprehend, either immediately or mediately by your senses, or by ratiocination from your senses; whatever you could perceive, imagine, or understand, remains still with you. If, therefore, the notion you have of the creation by other Principles be intelligible, you have it still upon mine; if it be not intelligible, I conceive it to be no notion at all; and so there is no loss of it. And indeed it seems to me very plain that the supposition of Matter, that is a thing perfectly unknown and inconceivable, cannot serve to make us conceive anything. And, I hope it need not be proved to you that if the existence of Matter doth not make the creation conceivable, the creation's being without it inconceivable can be no objection against its non-existence.

Hyl. I confess, Philonous, you have almost satisfied me in this point of the creation.

Phil. I would fain know why you are not quite satisfied. You tell me indeed of a repugnancy between the Mosaic history and Immaterialism: but you know not where it lies. Is this reasonable, Hylas? Can you expect I should solve a difficulty without knowing what it is? But, to pass by all that, would not a man think you were assured there is no repugnancy between the received notions of Materialists and the inspired writings?

Hyl. And so I am.

Phil. Ought the historical part of Scripture to be understood in a plain obvious sense, or in a sense which is metaphysical and out of the way?

Hyl. In the plain sense, doubtless.

Phil. When Moses speaks of herbs, earth, water, &c. as having been created by God; think you not the sensible things commonly signified by those words are suggested to every unphilosophical reader?

Hyl. I cannot help thinking so.

Phil. And are not all ideas, or things perceived by sense, to be denied a real existence by the doctrine of the Materialist?

Hyl. This I have already acknowledged.

Phil. The creation, therefore, according to them, was not the creation of things sensible, which have only a relative being, but of certain unknown natures, which have an absolute being, wherein creation might terminate?

Hyl. True.

Phil. Is it not therefore evident the assertors of Matter destroy the plain obvious sense of Moses, with which their notions are utterly inconsistent; and instead of it obtrude on us I know not what; something equally unintelligible to themselves and me?

Hyl. I cannot contradict you.

Phil. Moses tells us of a creation. A creation of what? of unknown quiddities, of occasions, or SUBSTRATUM? No, certainly; but of things obvious to the senses. You must first reconcile this with your notions, if you expect I should be reconciled to them.

Hyl. I see you can assault me with my own weapons.

Phil. Then as to ABSOLUTE EXISTENCE; was there ever known a more jejune notion than that? Something it is so abstracted and unintelligible that you have frankly owned you could not conceive it, much less explain anything by it. But allowing Matter to exist, and the notion of absolute existence to be clear as light; yet, was this ever known to make the creation more credible? Nay, hath it not furnished the atheists and infidels of all ages with the most plausible arguments against a creation? That a corporeal substance, which hath an absolute existence without the minds of spirits, should be produced out of nothing, by the mere will of a Spirit, hath been looked upon as a thing so contrary to all reason, so impossible and absurd! that not only the most celebrated among the ancients, but even divers modern and Christian philosophers have thought Matter co-eternal with the Deity. Lay these things together, and then judge you whether Materialism disposes men to believe the creation of things.

Hyl. I own, Philonous, I think it does not. This of the CREATION is the last objection I can think of; and I must needs own it hath been sufficiently answered as well as the rest. Nothing now remains to be overcome but a sort of unaccountable backwardness that I find in myself towards your notions.

Phil. When a man is swayed, he knows not why, to one side of the question, can this, think you, be anything else but the effect of prejudice, which never fails to attend old and rooted notions? And indeed in this respect I cannot deny the belief of Matter to have very much the advantage over the contrary opinion, with men of a learned, education.

Hyl. I confess it seems to be as you say.

Phil. As a balance, therefore, to this weight of prejudice, let us throw into the scale the great advantages that arise from the belief of Immaterialism, both in regard to religion and human learning. The being of a God, and incorruptibility of the soul, those great articles of religion, are they not proved with the clearest and most immediate evidence? When I say the being of a God, I do not mean an obscure general Cause of things, whereof we have no conception, but God, in the strict and proper sense of the word. A Being whose spirituality, omnipresence, providence, omniscience, infinite power and goodness, are as conspicuous as the existence of sensible things, of which (notwithstanding the fallacious pretences and affected scruples of Sceptics) there is no more reason to doubt than of our own being. — Then, with relation to human sciences. In Natural Philosophy, what intricacies, what obscurities, what contradictions hath the belief of Matter led men into! To say nothing of the numberless disputes about its extent, continuity, homogeneity, gravity, divisibility, &c. — do they not pretend to explain all things by bodies operating on bodies, according to the laws of motion? and yet, are they able to comprehend how one body should move another? Nay, admitting there was no difficulty in reconciling the notion of an inert being with a cause, or in conceiving how an accident might pass from one body to another; yet, by all their strained thoughts and extravagant suppositions, have they been able to reach the MECHANICAL production of any one animal or vegetable body? Can they account, by the laws of motion, for sounds, tastes, smells, or colours; or for the regular course of things? Have they accounted, by physical principles, for the aptitude and contrivance even of the most inconsiderable parts of the universe? But, laying aside Matter and corporeal, causes, and admitting only the efficiency of an All-perfect Mind, are not all the effects of nature easy and intelligible? If the PHENOMENA are nothing else but IDEAS; God is a SPIRIT, but Matter an unintelligent, unperceiving being. If they demonstrate an unlimited power in their cause; God is active and omnipotent, but Matter an inert mass. If the order, regularity, and usefulness of them can never be sufficiently admired; God is infinitely wise and provident, but Matter destitute of all contrivance and design. These surely are great advantages in PHYSICS. Not to mention that the apprehension of a distant Deity naturally disposes men to a negligence in their moral actions; which they would be more cautious of, in case they thought Him immediately present, and acting on their minds, without the interposition of Matter, or unthinking second causes. — Then in METAPHYSICS: what difficulties concerning entity in abstract, substantial forms, hylarchic principles, plastic natures, substance and accident, principle of individuation, possibility of Matter's thinking, origin of ideas, the manner how two independent substances so widely different as SPIRIT AND MATTER, should mutually operate on each other? what difficulties, I say, and endless disquisitions, concerning these and innumerable other the like points, do we escape, by supposing only Spirits and ideas? — Even the MATHEMATICS themselves, if we take away the absolute existence of extended things, become much more clear and easy; the most shocking paradoxes and intricate speculations in those sciences depending on the. infinite divisibility of finite extension; which depends on that supposition — But what need is there to insist on the particular sciences? Is not that opposition to all science whatsoever, that frenzy of the ancient and modern Sceptics, built on the same foundation? Or can you produce so much as one argument against the reality of corporeal things, or in behalf of that avowed utter ignorance of their natures, which doth not suppose their reality to consist in an external absolute existence? Upon this supposition, indeed, the objections from the change of colours in a pigeon's neck, or the appearance of the broken oar in the water, must be allowed to have weight. But these and the like objections vanish, if we do not maintain the being of absolute external originals, but place the reality of things in ideas, fleeting indeed, and changeable; — however, not changed at random, but according to the fixed order of nature. For, herein consists that constancy and truth of things which secures all the concerns of life, and distinguishes that which is real from the IRREGULAR VISIONS of the fancy.

Hyl. I agree to all you have now said, and must own that nothing can incline me to embrace your opinion more than the advantages I see it is attended with. I am by nature lazy; and this would be a mighty abridgment in knowledge. What doubts, what hypotheses, what labyrinths of amusement, what fields of disputation, what an ocean of false learning, may be avoided by that single notion of IMMATERIALISM!

Phil. After all, is there anything farther remaining to be done? You may remember you promised to embrace that opinion which upon examination should appear most agreeable to Common Sense and remote from Scepticism. This, by your own confession, is that which denies Matter, or the ABSOLUTE existence of corporeal things. Nor is this all; the same notion has been proved several ways, viewed in different lights, pursued in its consequences, and all objections against it cleared. Can there be a greater evidence of its truth? or is it possible it should have all the marks of a true opinion and yet be false?

Hyl. I own myself entirely satisfied for the present in all respects. But, what security can I have that I shall still continue the same full assent to your opinion, and that no unthought-of objection or difficulty will occur hereafter?

Phil. Pray, Hylas, do you in other cases, when a point is once evidently proved, withhold your consent on account of objections or difficulties it may be liable to? Are the difficulties that attend the doctrine of incommensurable quantities, of the angle of contact, of the asymptotes to curves, or the like, sufficient to make you hold out against mathematical demonstration? Or will you disbelieve the Providence of God, because there may be some particular things which you know not how to reconcile with it? If there are difficulties ATTENDING IMMATERIALISM, there are at the same time direct and evident proofs of it. But for the existence of Matter there is not one proof, and far more numerous and insurmountable objections lie against it. But where are those mighty difficulties you insist on? Alas! you know not where or what they are; something which may possibly occur hereafter. If this be a sufficient pretence for withholding your full assent, you should never yield it to any proposition, how free soever from exceptions, how clearly and solidly soever demonstrated.

Hyl. You have satisfied me, Philonous.

Phil. But, to arm you against all future objections, do but consider: That which bears equally hard on two contradictory opinions can be proof against neither. Whenever, therefore, any difficulty occurs, try if you can find a solution for it on the hypothesis of the MATERIALISTS. Be not deceived by words; but sound your own thoughts. And in case you cannot conceive it easier by the help of MATERIALISM, it is plain it can be no objection against IMMATERIALISM. Had you proceeded all along by this rule, you would probably have spared yourself abundance of trouble in objecting; since of all your difficulties I challenge you to shew one that is explained by Matter: nay, which is not more unintelligible with than without that supposition; and consequently makes rather AGAINST than FOR it. You should consider, in each particular, whether the difficulty arises from the NON-EXISTENCE OF MATTER. If it doth not, you might as well argue from the infinite divisibility of extension against the Divine prescience, as from such a difficulty against IMMATERIALISM. And yet, upon recollection, I believe you will find this to have been often, if not always, the case. You should likewise take heed not to argue on a PETITIO PRINCIPII. One is apt to say — The unknown substances ought to be esteemed real things, rather than the ideas in our minds: and who can tell but the unthinking external substance may concur, as a cause or instrument, in the productions of our ideas? But is not this proceeding on a supposition that there are such external substances? And to suppose this, is it not begging the question? But, above all things, you should beware of imposing on yourself by that vulgar sophism which is called IGNORATIO ELENCHI. You talked often as if you thought I maintained the non-existence of Sensible Things. Whereas in truth no one can be more thoroughly assured of their existence than I am. And it is you who doubt; I should have said, positively deny it. Everything that is seen, felt, heard, or any way perceived by the senses, is, on the principles I embrace, a real being; but not on yours. Remember, the Matter you contend for is an Unknown Somewhat (if indeed it may be termed SOMEWHAT), which is quite stripped of all sensible qualities, and can neither be perceived by sense, nor apprehended by the mind. Remember I say, that it is not any object which is hard or soft, hot or cold, blue or white, round or square, &c. For all these things I affirm do exist. Though indeed I deny they have an existence distinct from being perceived; or that they exist out of all minds whatsoever. Think on these points; let them be attentively considered and still kept in view. Otherwise you will not comprehend the state of the question; without which your objections will always be wide of the mark, and, instead of mine, may possibly be directed (as more than once they have been) against your own notions.

Hyl. I must needs own, Philonous, nothing seems to have kept me from agreeing with you more than this same MISTAKING THE QUESTION. In denying Matter, at first glimpse I am tempted to imagine you deny the things we see and feel: but, upon reflexion, find there is no ground for it. What think you, therefore, of retaining the name MATTER, and applying it to

SENSIBLE THINGS? This may be done without any change in your sentiments: and, believe me, it would be a means of reconciling them to some persons who may be more shocked at an innovation in words than in opinion.

Phil. With all my heart: retain the word MATTER, and apply it to the objects of sense, if you please; provided you do not attribute to them any subsistence distinct from their being perceived. I shall never quarrel with you for an expression. MATTER, or MATERIAL SUBSTANCE, are terms introduced by philosophers; and, as used by them, imply a sort of independency, or a subsistence distinct from being perceived by a mind: but are never used by common people; or, if ever, it is to signify the immediate objects of sense. One would think, therefore, so long as the names of all particular things, with the TERMS SENSIBLE, SUBSTANCE, BODY, STUFF, and the like, are retained, the word MATTER should be never missed in common talk. And in philosophical discourses it seems the best way to leave it quite out: since there is not, perhaps, any one thing that hath more favoured and strengthened the depraved bent of the mind towards Atheism than the use of that general confused term.

Hyl. Well but, Philonous, since I am content to give up the notion of an unthinking substance exterior to the mind, I think you ought not to deny me the privilege of using the word MATTER as I please, and annexing it to a collection of sensible qualities subsisting only in the mind. I freely own there is no other substance, in a strict sense, than SPIRIT. But I have been so long accustomed to the term MATTER that I know not how to part with it: to say, there is no MATTER in the world, is still shocking to me. Whereas to say — There is no MATTER, if by that term be meant an unthinking substance existing without the mind; but if by MATTER is meant some sensible thing, whose existence consists in being perceived, then there is MATTER:— THIS distinction gives it quite another turn; and men will come into your notions with small difficulty, when they are proposed in that manner. For, after all, the controversy about MATTER in the strict acceptation of it, lies altogether between you and the philosophers: whose principles, I acknowledge, are not near so natural, or so agreeable to the common sense of mankind, and Holy Scripture, as yours. There is nothing we either desire or shun but as it makes, or is apprehended to make, some part of our happiness or misery. But what hath happiness or misery, joy or grief, pleasure or pain, to do with Absolute Existence; or with unknown entities, ABSTRACTED FROM ALL RELATION TO US? It is evident, things regard us only as they are pleasing or displeasing: and they can please or displease only so far forth as they are perceived. Farther, therefore, we are not concerned; and thus far you leave things as you found them. Yet still there is something new in this doctrine. It is plain, I do not now think with the Philosophers; nor yet altogether with the vulgar. I would know how the case stands in that respect; precisely, what you have added to, or altered in my former notions.

Phil. I do not pretend to be a setter-up of new notions. My endeavours tend only to unite, and place in a clearer light, that truth which was before shared between the vulgar and the philosophers:— the former being of opinion, that THOSE THINGS THEY IMMEDIATELY PERCEIVE ARE THE REAL THINGS; and the latter, that THE THINGS IMMEDIATELY PERCEIVED ARE IDEAS, WHICH EXIST ONLY IN THE MIND. Which two notions put together, do, in effect, constitute the substance of what I advance.

Hyl. I have been a long time distrusting my senses: methought I saw things by a dim light and through false glasses. Now the glasses are removed and a new light breaks in upon my understanding. I am clearly convinced that I see things in their native forms, and am no longer in pain about their UNKNOWN NATURES OR ABSOLUTE EXISTENCE. This is the state I find myself in at present; though, indeed, the course that brought me to it I do not yet thoroughly comprehend. You set out upon the same principles that Academics, Cartesians, and the like sects usually do; and for a long time it looked as if you were advancing their philosophical Scepticism: but, in the end, your conclusions are directly opposite to theirs.

Phil. You see, Hylas, the water of yonder fountain, how it is forced upwards, in a round column, to a certain height; at which it breaks, and falls back into the basin from whence it rose: its ascent, as well as descent, proceeding from the same uniform law or principle of GRAVITATION. just so, the same Principles which, at first view, lead to Scepticism, pursued to a certain point, bring men back to Common Sense.

The Querist

Containing Several Queries Proposed to the Consideration of the Public

Part I

Query 1.
Whether there ever was, is, or will be, an industrious nation poor, or an idle rich?
2. Qu. Whether a people can be called poor, where the common sort are well fed, clothed, and lodged?
3. Qu. Whether the drift and aim of every wise State should not be, to encourage industry in its members? And whether those who employ neither heads nor hands for the common benefit deserve not to be expelled like drones out of a well-governed State?
4. Qu. Whether the four elements, and man's labour therein, be not the true source of wealth?
5. Qu. Whether money be not only so far useful, as it stirreth up industry, enabling men mutually to participate the fruits of each other's labour?
6. Qu. Whether any other means, equally conducing to excite and circulate the industry of mankind, may not be as useful as money.
7. Qu. Whether the real end and aim of men be not power? And whether he who could have everything else at his wish or will would value money?
8. Qu. Whether the public aim in every well-govern'd State be not that each member, according to his just pretensions and industry, should have power?
9. Qu. Whether power be not referred to action; and whether action doth not follow appetite or will?
10. Qu. Whether fashion doth not create appetites; and whether the prevailing will of a nation is not the fashion?
11. Qu. Whether the current of industry and commerce be not determined by this prevailing will?
12. Qu. Whether it be not owing to custom that the fashions are agreeable?
13. Qu. Whether it may not concern the wisdom of the legislature to interpose in the making of fashions; and not leave an affair of so great influence to the management of women and fops, tailors and vintners?
14. Qu. Whether reasonable fashions are a greater restraint on freedom than those which are unreasonable?
15. Qu. Whether a general good taste in a people would not greatly conduce to their thriving? And whether an uneducated gentry be not the greatest of national evils?
16. Qu. Whether customs and fashions do not supply the place of reason in the vulgar of all ranks? Whether, therefore, it doth not very much import that they should be wisely framed?
17. Qu. Whether the imitating those neighbours in our fashions, to whom we bear no likeness in our circumstances, be not one cause of distress to this nation?
18. Qu. Whether frugal fashions in the upper rank, and comfortable living in the lower, be not the means to multiply inhabitants?
19. Qu. Whether the bulk of our Irish natives are not kept from thriving, by that cynical content in dirt and beggary which they possess to a degree beyond any other people in Christendom?
20. Qu. Whether the creating of wants be not the likeliest way to produce industry in a people? And whether, if our peasants were accustomed to eat beef and wear shoes, they would not be more industrious?
21. Qu. Whether other things being given, as climate, soil, etc., the wealth be not proportioned

to the industry, and this to the circulation of credit, be the credit circulated or transferred by what marks or tokens soever?

22. Qu. Whether, therefore, less money swiftly circulating, be not, in effect, equivalent to more money slowly circulating? Or, whether, if the circulation be reciprocally as the quantity of coin, the nation can be a loser?

23. Qu. Whether money is to be considered as having an intrinsic value, or as being a commodity, a standard, a measure, or a pledge, as is variously suggested by writers? And whether the true idea of money, as such, be not altogether that of a ticket or counter?

24. Qu. Whether the value or price of things be not a compounded proportion, directly as the demand, and reciprocally as the plenty?

25. Qu. Whether the terms crown, livre, pound sterling, etc., are not to be considered as exponents or denominations of such proportion? And whether gold, silver, and paper are not tickets or counters for reckoning, recording, and transferring thereof?

26. Qu. Whether the denominations being retained, although the bullion were gone, things might not nevertheless be rated, bought, and sold, industry promoted, and a circulation of commerce maintained?

27. Qu. Whether an equal raising of all sorts of gold, silver, and copper coin can have any effect in bringing money into the kingdom? And whether altering the proportions between the kingdom several sorts can have any other effect but multiplying one kind and lessening another, without any increase of the sum total?

28. Qu. Whether arbitrary changing the denomination of coin be not a public cheat?

29. Qu. Whether, nevertheless, the damage would be very considerable, if by degrees our money were brought back to the English value there to rest for ever?

30. Qu. Whether the English crown did not formerly pass with us for six shillings? And what inconvenience ensued to the public upon its reduction to the present value, and whether what hath been may not be?

31. Qu. What makes a wealthy people? Whether mines of gold and silver are capable of doing this? And whether the negroes, amidst the gold sands of Afric, are not poor and destitute?

32. Qu. Whether there be any vertue in gold or silver, other than as they set people at work, or create industry?

33. Qu. Whether it be not the opinion or will of the people, exciting them to industry, that truly enricheth a nation? And whether this doth not principally depend on the means for counting, transferring, and preserving power, that is, property of all kinds?

34. Qu. Whether if there was no silver or gold in the kingdom, our trade might not, nevertheless, supply bills of exchange, sufficient to answer the demands of absentees in England or elsewhere?

35. Qu. Whether current bank notes may not be deemed money? And whether they are not actually the greater part of the money of this kingdom?

36. Qu. Provided the wheels move, whether it is not the same thing, as to the effect of the machine, be this done by the force of wind, or water, or animals?

37. Qu. Whether power to command the industry of others be not real wealth? And whether money be not in truth tickets or tokens for conveying and recording such power, and whether it be of great consequence what materials the tickets are made of?

38. Qu. Whether trade, either foreign or domestic, be in truth any more than this commerce of industry?

39. Qu. Whether to promote, transfer, and secure this commerce, and this property in human labour, or, in other words, this power, be not the sole means of enriching a people, and how far this may be done independently of gold and silver?

40. Qu. Whether it were not wrong to suppose land itself to be wealth? And whether the industry of the people is not first to be consider'd, as that which constitutes wealth, which makes even land and silver to be wealth, neither of which would have, any value but as means and motives to industry?

41. Qu. Whether in the wastes of America a man might not possess twenty miles square of land, and yet want his dinner, or a coat to his back?
42. Qu. Whether a fertile land, and the industry of its inhabitants, would not prove inexhaustible funds of real wealth, be the counters for conveying and recording thereof what you will, paper, gold, or silver?
43. Qu. Whether a single hint be sufficient to overcome a prejudice? And whether even obvious truths will not sometimes bear repeating?
44. Qu. Whether, if human labour be the true source of wealth, it doth not follow that idleness should of all things be discouraged in a wise State?
45. Qu. Whether even gold or silver, if they should lessen the industry of its inhabitants, would not be ruinous to a country? And whether Spain be not an instance of this?
46. Qu. Whether the opinion of men, and their industry consequent thereupon, be not the true wealth of Holland and not the silver supposed to be deposited in the bank at Amsterdam?
47. Qu. Whether there is in truth any such treasure lying dead? And whether it be of great consequence to the public that it should be real rather than notional?
48. Qu. Whether in order to understand the true nature of wealth and commerce, it would not be right to consider a ship's crew cast upon a desert island, and by degrees forming themselves to business and civil life, while industry begot credit, and credit moved to industry?
49. Qu. Whether such men would not all set themselves to work? Whether they would not subsist by the mutual participation of each other's industry? Whether, when one man had in his way procured more than he could consume, he would not exchange his superfluities to supply his wants? Whether this must not produce credit? Whether, to facilitate these conveyances, to record and circulate this credit, they would not soon agree on certain tallies, tokens, tickets, or counters?
50. Qu. Whether reflection in the better sort might not soon remedy our evils? And whether our real defect be not a wrong way of thinking?
51. Qu. Whether it would not be an unhappy turn in our gentlemen, if they should take more thought to create an interest to themselves in this or that county, or borough, than to promote the real interest of their country?
52. Qu. Whether it be not a bull to call that making an interest, whereby a man spendeth much and gaineth nothing?
53. Qu. Whether if a man builds a house he doth not in the first place provide a plan which governs his work? And shall the pubic act without an end, a view, a plan?
54. Qu. Whether by how much the less particular folk think for themselves, the public be not so much the more obliged to think for them?
55. Qu. Whether cunning be not one thing and good sense another? and whether a cunning tradesman doth not stand in his own light?
56. Qu. Whether small gains be not the way to great profit? And if our tradesmen are beggars, whether they may not thank themselves for it?
57. Qu. Whether some way might not be found for making criminals useful in public works, instead of sending them either to America, or to the other world?
58. Qu. Whether we may not, as well as other nations, contrive employment for them? And whether servitude, chains, and hard labour, for a term of years, would not be a more discouraging as well as a more adequate punishment for felons than even death itself?
59. Qu. Whether there are not such things in Holland as bettering houses for bringing young gentlemen to order? And whether such an institution would be useless among us?
60. Qu. Whether it be true that the poor in Holland have no resource but their own labour, and yet there are no beggars in their streets?
61. Qu. Whether he whose luxury consumeth foreign products, and whose industry produceth nothing domestic to exchange for them, is not so far forth injurious to his country?
62. Qu. Whether, consequently, the fine gentlemen, whose employment is only to dress, drink, and play, be not a pubic nuisance?

63. Qu. Whether necessity is not to be hearkened to before convenience, and convenience before luxury?
64. Qu. Whether to provide plentifully for the poor be not feeding the root, the substance whereof will shoot upwards into the branches, and cause the top to flourish?
65. Qu. Whether there be any instance of a State wherein the people, living neatly and plentifully, did not aspire to wealth?
66. Qu. Whether nastiness and beggary do not, on the contrary, extinguish all such ambition, making men listless, hopeless, and slothful?
67. Qu. Whether a country inhabited by people well fed, clothed and lodged would not become every day more populous? And whether a numerous stock of people in such circumstances would? and how far the product of not constitute a flourishing nation; our own country may suffice for the compassing of this end?
68. Qu. Whether a people who had provided themselves with the necessaries of life in good plenty would not soon extend their industry to new arts and new branches of commerce?
69. Qu. Whether those same manufactures which England imports from other countries may not be admitted from Ireland? And, if so, whether lace, carpets, and tapestry, three considerable articles of English importation, might not find encouragement in Ireland? And whether an academy for design might not greatly conduce to the perfecting those manufactures among us?
70. Qu. Whether France and Flanders could have drawn so much money from England for figured silks, lace, and tapestry, if they had not had academies for designing?
71. Qu. Whether, when a room was once prepared, and models in plaster of Paris, the annual expense of such an academy need stand the pubic in above two hundred pounds a year?
72. Qu. Whether our linen-manufacture would not find the benefit of this institution? And whether there be anything that makes us fall short of the Dutch in damasks, diapers, and printed linen, but our ignorance in design?
73. Qu. Whether those specimens of our own manufacture, hung up in a certain public place, do not sufficiently declare such our ignorance? and whether for the honour of the nation they ought not to be removed?
74. Qu. Whether those who may slight this affair as notional have sufficiently considered the extensive use of the art of design, and its influence in most trades and manufactures, wherein the forms of things are often more regarded than the materials?
75. Qu. Whether there be any art sooner learned than that of making carpets? And whether our women, with little time and pains, may not make more beautiful carpets than those imported from Turkey? And whether this branch of the woollen manufacture be not open to us?
76. Qu. Whether human industry can produce, from such cheap materials, a manufacture of so great value by any other art as by those of sculpture and painting?
77. Qu. Whether pictures and statues are not in fact so much treasure? And whether Rome and Florence would not be poor towns without them?
78. Qu. Whether they do not bring ready money as well as jewels? Whether in Italy debts are not paid, and children portioned with them, as with gold and silver?
79. Qu. Whether it would not be more prudent, to strike out and exert ourselves in permitted branches of trade, than to fold our hands, and repine that we are not allowed the woollen?
80. Qu. Whether it be true that two millions are yearly expended by England in foreign lace and linen?
81. Qu. Whether immense sums are not drawn yearly into the Northern countries, for supplying the British navy with hempen manufactures?
82. Qu. Whether there be anything more profitable than. hemp? And whether there should not be great premiums for encouraging our hempen trade? What advantages may not Great Britain make of a country where land and labour are so cheap?
83. Qu. Whether Ireland alone might not raise hemp sufficient for the British navy? And whether it would not be vain to expect this from the British Colonies in America, where hands

are so scarce, and labour so excessively dear?

84. Qu. Whether, if our own people want will or capacity for such an attempt, it might not be worth while for some undertaking spirits in England to make settlements, and raise hemp in the counties of Clare and Limerick, than which, perhaps, there is not fitter land in the world for that purpose? And whether both nations would not find their advantage therein?

85. Qu. Whether if all the idle hands in this kingdom were employed on hemp and flax, we might not find sufficient vent for these manufactures?

86. Qu. How far it may be in our own power to better our affairs, without interfering with our neighbours?

87. Qu. Whether the prohibition of our woollen trade ought not naturally to put us on other methods which give no jealousy?

88. Qu. Whether paper be not a valuable article of commerce? And whether it be not true that one single bookseller in London yearly expended above four thousand pounds in that foreign commodity?

89. Qu. How it comes to pass that the Venetians and Genoese, who wear so much less linen, and so much worse than we do, should yet make very good paper, and in great quantity, while we make very little?

90. Qu. How long it will be before my countrymen find out that it is worth while to spend a penny in order to get a groat?

91. Qu. If all the land were tilled that is fit for tillage, and all that sowed with hemp and flax that is fit for raising them, whether we should have much sheep-walk beyond what was sufficient to supply the necessities of the kingdom?

92. Qu. Whether other countries have not flourished without the woollen trade?

93. Qu. Whether it be not a sure sign or effect of a country's inhabitants? And, thriving, to see it well cultivated and full of; if so, whether a great quantity of sheep-walk be not ruinous to a country, rendering it waste and thinly inhabited?

94. Qu. Whether the employing so much of our land under sheep be not in fact an Irish blunder?

95. Qu. Whether our hankering after our woollen trade be not the true and only reason which hath created a jealousy in England towards Ireland? And whether anything can hurt us more than such jealousy?

96. Qu. Whether it be not the true interest of both nations to become one people? And whether either be sufficiently apprised of this?

97. Qu. Whether the upper part of this people are not truly English, by blood, language, religion, manners, inclination, and interest?

98. Qu. Whether we are not as much Englishmen as the children of old Romans, born in Britain, were still Romans?

99. Qu. Whether it be not our true interest not to interfere with them; and, in every other case, whether it be not their true interest to befriend us?

100. Qu. Whether a mint in Ireland might not be of great convenience to the kingdom; and whether it could be attended with any possible inconvenience to Great Britain? And whether there were not mints in Naples and Sicily, when those kingdoms were provinces to Spain or the house of Austria?

101. Qu. Whether anything can be more ridiculous than for the north of Ireland to be jealous of a linen manufacturer in the south?

102. Qu. Whether the county of Tipperary be not much better land than the county of Armagh; and yet whether the latter is not much better improved and inhabited than the former?

103. Qu. Whether every landlord in the kingdom doth not know the cause of this? And yet how few are the better for such their knowledge?

104. Qu. Whether large farms under few hands, or small ones under many, are likely to be made most of? And whether flax and tillage do not naturally multiply hands, and divide land into small holdings, and well-improved?

105. Qu. Whether, as our exports are lessened, we ought not to lessen our imports? And whether these will not be lessened as our demands, and these as our wants, and these as our customs or fashions? Of how great consequence therefore are fashions to the public?

106. Qu. Whether it would not be more reasonable to mend our state than to complain of it; and how far this may be in our own power?

107. Qu. What the nation gains by those who live in Ireland upon the produce of foreign Countries?

108. Qu. How far the vanity of our ladies in dressing, and of our gentlemen in drinking, contributes to the general misery of the people?

109. Qu. Whether nations, as wise and opulent as ours, have not made sumptuary laws; and what hinders us from doing the same?

110. Qu. Whether those who drink foreign liquors, and deck themselves and their families with foreign ornaments, are not so far forth to be reckoned absentees?

111. Qu. Whether, as our trade is limited, we ought not to limit our expenses; and whether this be not the natural and obvious remedy?

112. Qu. Whether the dirt, and famine, and nakedness of the bulk of our people might not be remedied, even although we had no foreign trade? And whether this should not be our first care; and whether, if this were once provided for, the conveniences of the rich would not soon follow?

113. Qu. Whether comfortable living doth not produce wants, and wants industry, and industry wealth?

114. Qu. Whether there is not a great difference between Holland and Ireland? And whether foreign commerce, without which the one could not subsist, be so necessary for the other?

115. Qu. Might we not put a hand to the plough, or the spade, although we had no foreign commerce?

116. Qu. Whether the exigencies of nature are not to be answered by industry on our own soil? And how far the conveniences and comforts of life may be procured by a domestic commerce between the several parts of this kingdom?

117. Qu. Whether the women may not sew, spin, weave, embroider sufficiently for the embellishment of their persons, and even enough to raise envy in each other, without being beholden to foreign countries?

118. Qu. Suppose the bulk of our inhabitants had shoes to their feet, clothes to their backs, and beef in their bellies, might not such a state be eligible for the public, even though the squires were condemned to drink ale and cider?

119. Qu. Whether, if drunkenness be a necessary evil, men may not as well drink the growth of their own country?

120. Qu. Whether a nation within itself might not have real wealth, sufficient to give its inhabitants power and distinction, without the help of gold and silver?

121. Qu. Whether, if the arts of sculpture and painting were encouraged among us, we might not furnish our houses in a much nobler manner with our own manufactures?

122. Qu. Whether we have not, or may not have, all the necessary materials for building at home?

123. Qu. Whether tiles and plaster may not supply the place of Norway fir for flooring and wainscot?

124. Qu. Whether plaster be not warmer, as well as more secure, than deal? And whether a modern fashionable house, lined with fir, daubed over with oil and paint, be not like a fire-ship, ready to be lighted up by all accidents?

125. Qu. Whether larger houses, better built and furnished, a greater train of servants, the difference with regard to equipage and table between finer and coarser, more and less elegant, may not be sufficient to feed a reasonable share of vanity, or support all proper distinctions? And whether all these may not be procured by domestic industry out of the four elements, without ransacking the four quarters of the globe?

126. Qu. Whether anything is a nobler ornament, in the eye of the world, than an Italian palace, that is, stone and mortar skilfully put together, and adorned with sculpture and painting; and whether this may not be compassed without foreign trade?
127. Qu. Whether an expense in gardens and plantations would not be an elegant distinction for the rich, a domestic magnificence employing many hands within, and drawing nothing from abroad?
128. Qu. Whether the apology which is made for foreign luxury in England, to wit, that they could not carry on their trade without imports as well as exports, will hold in Ireland?
129. Qu. Whether one may not be allowed to conceive and suppose a society or nation of human creatures, clad in woollen cloths and stuffs, eating good bread, beef and mutton, poultry and fish, in great plenty, drinking ale, mead, and cider, inhabiting decent houses built of brick and marble, taking their pleasure in fair parks and gardens, depending on no foreign imports either for food or raiment? And whether such people ought much to be pitied?
130. Qu. Whether Ireland be not as well qualified for such a state as any nation under the sun?
131. Qu. Whether in such a state the inhabitants may not contrive to pass the twenty-four hours with tolerable ease and cheerfulness? And whether any people upon earth can do more?
132. Qu. Whether they may not eat, drink, play, dress, visit, sleep in good beds, sit by good fires, build, plant, raise a name, make estates, and spend them?
133. Qu. Whether, upon the whole, a domestic trade may not suffice in such a country as Ireland, to nourish and clothe its inhabitants, and provide them with the reasonable conveniences and even comforts of life?
134. Qu. Whether a general habit of living well would not produce numbers and industry' and whether, considering the tendency of human kind, the consequence thereof would not be foreign trade and riches, how unnecessary soever?
135. Qu. Whether, nevertheless, it be a crime to inquire how far we may do without foreign trade, and what would follow on such a supposition?
136. Qu. Whether the number and welfare of the subjects be not the true strength of the crown?
137. Qu. Whether in all public institutions there should not be an end proposed, which is to be the rule and limit of the means? Whether this end should not be the well-being of the whole? And whether, in order to this, the first step should not be to clothe and feed our people?
138. Qu. Whether there be upon earth any Christian or civilized people so beggarly, wretched, and destitute as the common Irish?
139. Qu. Whether, nevertheless, there is any other people whose wants may be more easily supplied from home?
140. Qu. Whether, if there was a wall of brass a thousand cubits high round this kingdom, our natives might not nevertheless live cleanly and comfortably, till the land, and reap the fruits of it?
141. Qu. What should hinder us from exerting ourselves, using our hands and brains, doing something or other, man, woman, and child, like the other inhabitants of God's earth?
142. Qu. Be the restraining our trade well or ill advised in our neighbours, with respect to their own interest, yet whether it be not plainly ours to accommodate ourselves to it?
143. Qu. Whether it be not vain to think of persuading other people to see their interest, while we continue blind to our own?
144. Qu. Whether there be any other nation possess'd of so much good land, and so many able hands to work it, which yet is beholden for bread to foreign countries?
145. Qu. Whether it be true that we import corn to the value of two hundred thousand pounds in some years?
146. Qu. Whether we are not undone by fashions made for other people? And whether it be not madness in a poor nation to imitate a rich one?
147. Qu. Whether a woman of fashion ought not to be declared a public enemy?
148. Qu. Whether it be not certain that from the single town of Cork were exported, in one

year, no less than one hundred and seven thousand one hundred and sixty-one barrels of beef; seven thousand three hundred and seventy-nine barrels of pork; thirteen thousand four hundred and sixty-one casks, and eighty-five thousand seven hundred and twenty-seven firkins of butter? And what hands were employed in this manufacture?

149. Qu. Whether a foreigner could imagine that one half of the people were starving, in a country which sent out such plenty of provisions?

150. Qu. Whether an Irish lady, set out with French silks and Flanders lace, may not be said to consume more beef and butter than a hundred of our labouring peasants?

151. Qu. Whether nine-tenths of our foreign trade be not carried on singly to support the article of vanity?

152. Qu. Whether it can be hoped that private persons will not indulge this folly, unless restrained by the public?

153. Qu. How vanity is maintained in other countries? Whether in Hungary, for instance, a proud nobility are not subsisted with small imports from abroad?

154. Qu. Whether there be a prouder people upon earth than the noble Venetians, although they all wear plain black clothes?

155. Qu. Whether a people are to be pitied that will not sacrifice their little particular vanities to the public. good? And yet, whether each part would not except their own foible from this public sacrifice, the squire his bottle, the lady her lace?

156. Qu. Whether claret be not often drank rather for vanity than for health, or pleasure?

157. Qu. Whether it be true that men of nice palates have been imposed on, by elder wine for French claret, and by mead for palm sack?

158. Qu. Do not Englishmen abroad purchase beer and cider at ten times the price of wine?

159. Qu. How many gentlemen are there in England of a thousand pounds per annum who never drink wine in their own houses? Whether the same may be said of any in Ireland who have even? one hundred pounds per annum.

160. Qu. What reasons have our neighbours in England for discouraging French wines which may not hold with respect to us also?

161. Qu. How much of the necessary sustenance of our people is yearly exported for brandy?

162. Qu. Whether, if people must poison themselves, they had not better do it with their own growth?

163. Qu. If we imported neither claret from France, nor fir from Norway, what the nation would save by it?

164. Qu. When the root yieldeth insufficient nourishment, whether men do not top the tree to make the lower branches thrive?

165. Qu. Whether, if our ladies drank sage or balm tea out of Irish ware, it would be an insupportable national calamity?

166. Qu. Whether it be really true that such wine is best as most encourages drinking, i.e., that must be given in the largest dose to produce its effect? And whether this holds with regard to any other medicine?

167. Qu. Whether that trade should not be accounted most pernicious wherein the balance is most against us? And whether this be not the trade with France?

168. Qu. Whether it be not even madness to encourage trade with a nation that takes nothing of our manufacture?

169. Qu. Whether Ireland can hope to thrive if the major part of her patriots shall be found in the French interest?

170. Qu. Why, if a bribe by the palate or the purse be in effect the same thing, they should not be alike infamous?

171. Qu. Whether the vanity and luxury of a few ought to stand in competition with the interest of a nation?

172. Qu. Whether national wants ought not to be the rule of trade? And whether the most pressing wants of. the majority ought not to be first consider'd?

173. Qu. Whether it is possible the country should be well improved, while our beef is exported, and our labourers live upon potatoes?
174. Qu. If it be resolved that we cannot do without foreign trade, whether, at least, it may not be worth while to consider what branches thereof deserve to be entertained, and how far we may be able to carry it on under our present limitations?
175. Qu. What foreign imports may be necessary for clothing and feeding the families of persons not worth above one hundred pounds a year? And how many wealthier there are in the kingdom, and what proportion they bear to the other inhabitants?
176. Qu. Whether trade be not then on a right foot, when foreign commodities are imported in exchange only for domestic superfluities?
177. Qu. Whether the quantities of beef, butter, wool, and leather, exported from this island, can be reckoned the superfluities of a country, where there are so many natives naked and famished?
178. Qu. Whether it would not be wise so to order our trade as to export manufactures rather than provisions, and of those such as employ most hands?
179. Qu. Whether she would not be a very vile matron, and justly thought either mad or foolish, that should give away the necessaries of life from her naked and famished children, in exchange for pearls to stick in her hair, and sweetmeats to please her own palate?
180. Qu. Whether a nation might not be consider'd as a family?
181. Qu. Whether other methods may not be found for supplying the funds, besides the custom on things imported?
182. Qu. Whether any art or manufacture be so difficult as the making of good laws?
183. Qu. Whether our peers and gentlemen are born legislators? Or, whether that faculty be acquired by study and reflection?
184. Qu. Whether to comprehend the real interest of a people, and the means to procure it, doth not imply some fund of knowledge, historical, moral, and political, with a faculty of reason improved by learning?
185. Qu. Whether every enemy to learning be not a Goth? And whether every such Goth among us be not an enemy to the country?
186. Qu. Whether, therefore, it would not be an omen of ill presage, a dreadful phenomenon in the land, if our great men should take it in their heads to deride learning and education?
187. Qu. Whether, on the contrary, it should not seem worth while to erect a mart of literature in this kingdom, under wiser regulations and better discipline than in any other part of Europe? And whether this would not be an infallible means of drawing men and money into the kingdom?
188. Qu. Whether the governed be not too numerous for the governing part of our college? And whether it might not be expedient to convert thirty natives-places into twenty fellowships?
189. Qu. Whether, if we had two colleges, there might not spring a useful emulation between them? And whether it might not be contrived so to divide the fellows, scholars, and revenues between both, as that no member should be a loser thereby?
190. Qu. Whether ten thousand pounds well laid out might not build a decent college, fit to contain two hundred persons; and whether the purchase money of the chambers would not go a good way towards defraying the expense?
191. Qu. Where this college should be situated?
192. Qu. Whether it is possible a State should not thrive, whereof the lower part were industrious, and the upper wise?
193. Qu. Whether the collected wisdom of ages and nations be not found in books, improved and applied by study?
194. Qu. Whether it was not an Irish professor who first opened the public schools at Oxford? Whether this island hath not been anciently famous for learning? And whether at this day it hath any better chance for being considerable?

195. Qu. Whether we may not with better grace sit down and complain, when we have done all that lies in our power to help ourselves?
196. Qu. Whether the gentleman of estate hath a right to be idle; and whether he ought not to be the great promoter and director of industry among his tenants and neighbours?
197. Qu. Whether the real foundation for wealth must not be laid in the numbers, the frugality, and the industry of the people? And whether all attempts to enrich a nation by other means, as raising the coin, stock-jobbing, and such arts are not vain?
198. Qu. Whether a door ought not to be shut against all other methods of growing rich, save only by industry and. merit? And whether wealth got otherwise would not be ruinous to the public?
199. Qu. Whether the abuse of banks and paper-money is a just objection against the use thereof? And whether such abuse might not easily be prevented?
200. Qu. Whether national banks are not found useful in Venice, Holland, and Hamburg? And whether it is not possible to contrive one that may be useful also in Ireland?
201. Qu. Whether any nation ever was in greater want of such an expedient than Ireland?
202. Qu. Whether the banks of Venice and Amsterdam are not in the hands of the public?
203. Qu. Whether it may not be worth while to inform ourselves in the nature of those banks? And what reason can be assigned why Ireland should not reap the benefit of such public banks as well as other countries?
204. Qu. Whether a bank of national credit, supported by public funds and secured by Parliament, be a chimera or impossible thing? And if not, what would follow from the supposal of such a bank?
205. Qu. Whether the currency of a credit so well secured would not be of great advantage to our trade and manufactures?
206. Qu. Whether the notes of such public bank would not have a more general circulation than those of private banks, as being less subject to frauds and hazards?
207. Qu. Whether it be not agreed that paper hath in many respects the advantage above coin, as being of more dispatch in payments, more easily transferred, preserved, and recovered when lost?
208. Qu. Whether, besides these advantages, there be not an evident necessity for circulating credit by paper, from the defect of coin in this kingdom?
209. Qu. Whether the public may not as well save the interest which it now pays?
210. Qu. What would happen if two of our banks should break at once? And whether it be wise to neglect providing against an event which experience hath shewn us not to be impossible?
211. Qu. Whether such an accident would not particularly affect the bankers? And therefore whether a national bank would not be a security even to private bankers?
212. Qu. Whether we may not easily avoid the inconveniencies attending the paper-money of New England, which were incurred by their issuing too great a quantity of notes, by their having no silver in bank to exchange for notes, by their not insisting upon repayment of the loans at the time prefixed, and especially by their want of manufactures to answer their imports from Europe?
213. Qu. Whether a combination of bankers might not do wonders, and whether bankers know their own strength?
214. Qu. Whether a bank in private hands might not even overturn a government? and whether this was not the case of the Bank of St. George in Genoa? [Footnote: See the Vindication and Advancement of our national Constitution and Credit. Printed in London 1710.]
215. Qu. Whether we may not easily prevent the ill effects of such a bank as Mr Law proposed for Scotland, which was faulty in not limiting the quantum of bills, and permitting all persons to take out what bills they pleased, upon the mortgage of lands, whence by a glut of paper, the prices of things must rise? Whence also the fortunes of men must increase in denomination, though not in value; whence pride, idleness, and beggary?

216. Qu. Whether such banks as those of England and Scotland might not be attended with great inconveniences, as lodging too much power in the hands of private men, and giving handle for monopolies, stock-jobbing, and destructive schemes?

217. Qu. Whether the national bank, projected by an anonymous writer in the latter end of Queen Anne's reign, might not on the other hand be attended with as great inconveniencies by lodging too much power in the Government?

218. Qu. Whether the bank projected by Murray, though it partake, in many useful particulars, with that of Amsterdam, yet, as it placeth too great power in the hands of a private society, might not be dangerous to the public?

219. Qu. Whether it be rightly remarked by some that, as banking brings no treasure into the kingdom like trade, private wealth must sink as the bank riseth? And whether whatever causeth industry to flourish and circulate may not be said to increase our treasure?

220. Qu. Whether the ruinous effects of Mississippi, South Sea, and such schemes were not owing to an abuse of paper money or credit, in making it a means for idleness and gaming, instead of a motive and help to industry?

221. Qu. Whether those effects could have happened had there been no stock-jobbing? And whether stock-jobbing could at first have been set on foot, without an imaginary foundation of some improvement to the stock by trade? Whether, therefore, when there are no such prospects, or cheats, or private schemes proposed, the same effects can be justly feared?

222. Qu. Whether by a national bank, be not properly understood a bank, not only established by public authority as the Bank of England, but a bank in the hands of the public, wherein there are no shares: whereof the public alone is proprietor, and reaps all the benefit?

223. Qu. Whether, having considered the conveniencies of banking and paper-credit in some countries, and the inconveniencies thereof in others, we may not contrive to adopt the former, and avoid the latter?

224. Qu. Whether great evils, to which other schemes are liable, may not be prevented, by excluding the managers of the bank from a share in the legislature?

225. Qu. Whether the rise of the bank of Amsterdam was not purely casual, for the security and dispatch of payments? And whether the good effects thereof, in supplying the place of coin, and promoting a ready circulation of industry and commerce may not be a lesson to us, to do that by design which others fell upon by chance?

226. Qu. Whether the bank proposed to be established in Ireland, under the notion of a national bank, by the voluntary subscription of three hundred thousand pounds, to pay off the national debt, the interest of which sum to be paid the subscribers, subject to certain terms of redemption, be not in reality a private bank, as those of England and Scotland, which are national only in name, being in the hands of particular persons, and making dividends on the money paid in by subscribers? [Footnote: See a Proposal for the Relief of Ireland, &c. Printed in Dublin A. D. 1734]

227. Qu. Whether plenty of small cash be not absolutely necessary for keeping up a circulation among the people; that is, whether copper be not more necessary than gold?

228. Qu. Whether it is not worth while to reflect on the expedients made use of by other nations, paper-money, bank-notes, public funds, and credit in all its shapes, to examine what hath been done and devised to add to our own animadversions, and upon the whole offer such hints as seem not unworthy the attention of the public?

229. Qu. Whether that, which increaseth the stock of a nation be not a means of increasing its trade? And whether that which increaseth the current credit of a nation may not be said to increase its stock?

230. Qu. Whether it may not be expedient to appoint certain funds or stock for a national bank, under direction of certain persons, one-third whereof to be named by the Government, and one-third by each House of Parliament?

231. Qu. Whether the directors should not be excluded from sitting in either House, and whether they should not be subject to the audit and visitation of a standing committee of both

Houses?

232. Qu. Whether such committee of inspectors should not be changed every two years, one-half going out, and another coming in by ballot?

233. Qu. Whether the notes ought not to be issued in lots, to be let at interest on mortgaged lands, the whole number of lots to be divided among the four provinces, rateably to the number of hearths in each?

234. Qu. Whether it may not be expedient to appoint four counting-houses, one in each province, for converting notes into specie?

235. Qu. Whether a limit should not be fixed, which no person might exceed, in taking out notes?

236. Qu. Whether, the better to answer domestic circulation, it may not be right to issue notes as low as twenty shillings?

237. Qu. Whether all the bills should be issued at once, or rather by degrees, that so men may be gradually accustomed and reconciled to the bank?

238. Qu. Whether the keeping of the cash, and the direction of the bank, ought not to be in different hands, and both under public control?

239. Qu. Whether the same rule should not alway be observed, of lending out money or notes, only to half the value of the mortgaged land? and whether this value should not alway be rated at the same number of years' purchase as at first?

240. Qu. Whether care should not be taken to prevent an undue rise of the value of land?

241. Qu. Whether the increase of industry and people will not of course raise the value of land? And whether this rise may not be sufficient?

242. Qu. Whether land may not be apt to rise on the issuing too great plenty of notes?

243. Qu. Whether this may not be prevented by the gradual and slow issuing of notes, and by frequent sales of lands?

244. Qu. Whether interest doth not measure the true value of land; for instance, where money is at five per cent, whether land is not worth twenty years' purchase?

245. Qu. Whether too small a proportion of money would not hurt the landed man, and too great a proportion the monied man? And whether the quantum of notes ought not to bear proportion to the pubic demand? And whether trial must not shew what this demand will be?

246. Qu. Whether the exceeding this measure might not produce divers bad effects, one whereof would be the loss of our silver?

247. Qu. Whether interest paid into the bank ought not to go on augmenting its stock?

248. Qu. Whether it would or would not be right to appoint that the said interest be paid in notes only?

249. Qu. Whether the notes of this national bank should not be received in all payments into the exchequer?

250. Qu. Whether on supposition that the specie should fail, the credit would not, nevertheless, still pass, being admitted in all payments of the public revenue?

251. Qu. Whether the pubic can become bankrupt so long as the notes are issued on good security?

252. Qu. Whether mismanagement, prodigal living, hazards by trade, which often affect private banks, are equally to be apprehended in a pubic one?

253. Qu. Whether as credit became current, and this raised the value of land, the security must not of course rise?

254. Qu. Whether, as our current domestic credit grew, industry would not grow likewise; and if industry, our manufactures; and if these, our foreign credit?

255. Qu. Whether by degrees, as business and people multiplied, more bills may not be issued, without augmenting the capital stock, provided still, that they are issued on good security; which further issuing of new bills, not to be without consent of Parliament?

256. Qu. Whether such bank would not be secure? Whether the profits accruing to the pubic would not be very considerable? And whether industry in private persons would not be

supplied, and a general circulation encouraged?
257. Qu. Whether such bank should, or should not, be allowed to issue notes for money deposited therein? And, if not, whether the bankers would have cause to complain?
258. Qu. Whether, if the public thrives, all particular persons must not feel the benefit thereof, even the bankers themselves?
259. Qu. Whether, beside the Bank–Company, there are not in England many private wealthy bankers, and whether they were more before the erecting of that company?
260. Qu. Whether as industry increased, our manufactures would not flourish; and as these flourished, whether better returns would not be made from estates to their landlords, both within and without the kingdom?
261. Qu. Whether we have not paper-money circulating among, whether, therefore, we might not as well have that us already which is secured by the public, and whereof the pubic reaps the benefit?
262. Qu. Whether there are not two general ways of circulating money, to wit, play and traffic? and whether stock-jobbing is not to be ranked under the former?
263. Qu. Whether there are more than two things that might draw silver out of the bank, when its credit was once well established, to wit, foreign demands and small payments at home?
264. Qu. Whether, if our trade with France were checked, the former of these causes could be supposed to operate at all? and whether the latter could operate to any great degree?
265. Qu. Whether the sure way to supply people with tools and materials, and to set them at work, be not a free circulation of money, whether silver or paper?
266. Qu. Whether in New England all trade and business is not as much at a stand, upon a scarcity of paper-money, as with us from the want of specie?
267. Qu. Whether paper-money or notes may not be issued from the national bank, on the security of hemp, of linen, or other manufactures whereby the poor might be supported in their industry?
268. Qu. Whether it be certain that the quantity of silver in the bank of Amsterdam be greater now than at first; but whether it be not certain that there is a greater circulation of industry and extent of trade, more people, ships, houses, and commodities of all sorts, more power by sea and land?
269. Qu. Whether money, lying dead in the bank of Amsterdam, would not be as useless as in the mine?
270. Qu. Whether our visible security in land could be doubted? And whether there be anything like this in the bank of Amsterdam?
271. Qu. Whether it be just to apprehend danger from trusting a national bank with power to extend its credit, to circulate notes which it shall be felony to counterfeit, to receive goods on loans, to purchase lands, to sell also or alienate them, and to deal in bills of exchange; when these powers are no other than have been trusted for many years with the bank of England, although in truth but a private bank?
272. Qu. Whether the objection from monopolies and an overgrowth of power, which are made against private banks, can possibly hold against a national one?
273. Qu. Whether banks raised by private subscription would be as advantageous to the public as to the subscribers? and whether risks and frauds might not be more justly apprehended from them?
274. Qu. Whether the evil effects which of late years have attended paper-money and credit in Europe did not spring from subscriptions, shares, dividends, and stock-jobbing?
275. Qu. Whether the great evils attending paper-money in the British Plantations of America have not sprung from the overrating their lands, and issuing paper without discretion, and from the legislators breaking their own rules in favour of themselves, thus sacrificing the public to their private benefit? And whether a little sense and honesty might not easily prevent all such inconveniences?
276. Qu. Whether an argument from the abuse of things, against the use of them, be

conclusive?

277. Qu. Whether he who is bred to a part be fitted to judge of the whole?

278. Qu. Whether interest be not apt to bias judgment? and whether traders only are to be consulted about trade, or bankers about money?

279. Qu. Whether the subject of Freethinking in religion be not exhausted? And whether it be not high time for our freethinkers to turn their thoughts to the improvement of their country?

280. Qu. Whether any man hath a right to judge, that will not be at the pains to distinguish?

281. Qu. Whether there be not a wide difference between the profits going to augment the national stock, and being divided among private sharers? And whether, in the former case, there can possibly be any gaming or stock-jobbing?

282. Qu. Whether it must not be ruinous for a nation to sit down to game, be it with silver or with paper?

283. Qu. Whether, therefore, the circulating paper, in the late ruinous schemes of France and England, was the true evil, and not rather the circulating thereof without industry? And whether the bank of Amsterdam, where industry had been for so many years subsisted and circulated by transfers on paper, doth not clearly decide this point?

284. Qu. Whether there are not to be seen in America fair towns, wherein the people are well lodged, fed, and clothed, without a beggar in their streets, although there be not one grain of gold or silver current among them?

285. Qu. Whether these people do not exercise all arts and trades, build ships and navigate them to all parts of the world, purchase lands, till and reap the fruits of them, buy and sell, educate and provide for their children? Whether they do not even indulge themselves in foreign vanities?

286. Qu. Whether, whatever inconveniences those people may have incurred from not observing either rules or bounds in their paper money, yet it be not certain that they are in a more flourishing condition, have larger and better built towns, more plenty, more industry, more arts and civility, and a more extensive commerce, than when they had gold and silver current among them?

287. Qu. Whether a view of the ruinous effects of absurd schemes and credit mismanaged, so as to produce gaming and madness instead of industry, can be any just objection against a national bank calculated purely to promote industry?

288. Qu. Whether a scheme for the welfare of this nation should not take in the whole inhabitants? And whether it be not a vain attempt, to project the flourishing of our Protestant gentry, exclusive of the bulk of the natives?

289. Qu. Whether, therefore, it doth not greatly concern the State, that our Irish natives should be converted, and the whole nation united in the same religion, the same allegiance, and the same interest? and how this may most probably be effected?

290. Qu. Whether an oath, testifying allegiance to the king, and disclaiming the pope's authority in temporals, may not be justly required of the Roman Catholics? And whether, in common prudence or policy, any priest should be tolerated who refuseth to take it?

291. Qu. Whether there have not been Popish recusants? and, if so, whether it would be right to object against the foregoing oath, that all would take it, and none think themselves bound by it?

292. Qu. Whether those of the Church of Rome, in converting the Moors of Spain or the Protestants of France, have not set us an example which might justify a similar treatment of themselves, if the laws of Christianity allowed thereof?

293. Qu. Whether compelling men to a profession of faith is not the worst thing in Popery, and, consequently, whether to copy after the Church of Rome therein, were not to become Papists ourselves in the worst sense?

294. Qu. Whether, nevertheless, we may not imitate the Church of Rome, in certain places, where Jews are tolerated, by obliging our Irish Papists, at stated times, to hear Protestant sermons? and whether this would not make missionaries in the Irish tongue useful?

295. Qu. Whether the mere act of hearing, without making any profession of faith, or joining in any part of worship, be a religious act; and, consequently, whether their being obliged to hear, may not consist with the toleration of Roman Catholics?

296. Qu. Whether, if penal laws should be thought oppressive, we may not at least be allowed to give premiums? And whether it would be wrong, if the public encouraged Popish families to become hearers, by paying their hearth-money for them?

297. Qu. Whether in granting toleration, we ought not to distinguish between doctrines purely religious, and such as affect the State?

298. Qu. Whether the case be not very different in regard to a man who only eats fish on Fridays, says his prayers in Latin, or believes transubstantiation, and one who professeth in temporals a subjection to foreign powers, who holdeth himself absolved from all obedience to his natural prince and the laws of his country? who is even persuaded, it may be meritorious to destroy the powers that are?

299. Qu. Whether, therefore, a distinction should not be made between mere Papists and recusants? And whether the latter can expect the same protection from the Government as the former?

300. Qu. Whether our Papists in this kingdom can complain, if they are allowed to be as much Papists as the subjects of France or of the Empire?

301. Qu. Whether there is any such thing as a body of inhabitants, in any Roman Catholic country under the sun, that profess an absolute submission to the pope's orders in matters of an indifferent nature, or that in such points do not think it their duty to obey the civil government?

302. Qu. Whether since the peace of Utrecht, mass was not celebrated and the sacraments administered in divers dioceses of Sicily, notwithstanding the Pope's interdict?

303. Qu. Whether every plea of conscience is to be regarded? Whether, for instance, the German Anabaptists, Levellers, or Fifth Monarchy men would be tolerated on that pretence?

304. Qu. Whether Popish children bred in charity schools, when bound out in apprenticeship to Protestant masters, do generally continue Protestants?

305. Qu. Whether a Sum, which would go but a little way towards erecting hospitals for maintaining and educating the children of the native Irish, might not go far in binding them out apprentices to Protestant masters, for husbandry, useful trades, and the service of families?

306. Qu. Whether if the parents are overlooked, there can be any great hopes of success in converting the children?

307. Qu. Whether there be any instance, of a people's being converted in a Christian sense, otherwise than by preaching to them and instructing them in their own language?

308. Qu. Whether catechists in the Irish tongue may not easily be procured and subsisted? And whether this would not be the most practicable means for converting the natives?

309. Qu. Whether it be not of great advantage to the Church of Rome, that she hath clergy suited to all ranks of men, in gradual subordination from cardinals down to mendicants?

310. Qu. Whether her numerous poor clergy are not very useful in missions, and of much influence with the people?

311. Qu. Whether, in defect of able missionaries, persons conversant in low life, and speaking the Irish tongue, if well instructed in the first principles of religion, and in the popish controversy, though for the rest on a level with the parish clerks, or the school-masters of charity-schools, may not be fit to mix with and bring over our poor illiterate natives to the Established Church? Whether it is not to be wished that some parts of our liturgy and homilies were publicly read in the Irish language? And whether, in these views, it may not be right to breed up some of the better sort of children in the charity-schools, and qualify them for missionaries, catechists, and readers?

312. Qu. Whether there be any nation of men governed by reason? And yet, if there was not, whether this would be a good argument against the use of reason in pubic affairs?

313. Qu. Whether, as others have supposed an Atlantis or Utopia, we also may not suppose an

Hyperborean island inhabited by reasonable creatures?

314. Qu. Whether an indifferent person, who looks into all hands, may not be a better judge of the game than a party who sees only his own?

315. Qu. Whether one, whose end is to make his countrymen think, may not gain his end, even though they should not think as he doth?

316. Qu. Whether he, who only asks, asserts? and whether any man can fairly confute the querist?

317. Qu. Whether the interest of a part will not always be preferred to that of the whole?

Part II

Query 1.
Whether there be any country in Christendom more capable of improvement than Ireland?
2. Qu. Whether we are not as far before other nations with respect to natural advantages, as we are behind them with respect to arts and industry?
3. Qu. Whether we do not live in a most fertile soil and temperate climate, and yet whether our people in general do not feel great want and misery?
4. Qu. Whether my countrymen are not readier at finding excuses than remedies?
5. Qu. Whether it can be reasonably hoped, that our state will mend, so long as property is insecure among us?
6. Qu. Whether in that case the wisest government, or the best laws can avail. us?
7. Qu. Whether a few mishaps to particular persons may not throw this nation into the utmost confusion?
8. Qu. Whether the public is not even on the brink of being undone by private accidents?
9. Qu. Whether the wealth and prosperity of our country do not hang by a hair, the probity of one banker, the caution of another, and the lives of all?
10. Qu. Whether we have not been sufficiently admonished of this by some late events?
11. Qu. Whether therefore it be not high time to open our eyes?
12. Qu. Whether a national bank would not at once secure our properties, put an end to usury, facilitate commerce, supply the want of coin, and produce ready payments in all parts of the kingdom?
13. Qu. Whether the use or nature of money, which all men so eagerly pursue, be yet sufficiently understood or considered by all?
14. Qu. Whether mankind are not governed by Citation rather than by reason?
15. Qu. Whether there be not a measure or limit, within which gold and silver are useful, and beyond which they may be hurtful?
16. Qu. Whether that measure be not the circulating of industry?
17. Qu. Whether a discovery of the richest gold mine that ever was, in the heart of this kingdom, would be a real advantage to us?
18. Qu. Whether it would not tempt foreigners to prey upon us?
19. Qu. Whether it would not render us a lazy, proud, and dastardly people?
20. Qu. Whether every man who had money enough would not be a gentleman? And whether a nation of gentlemen would not be a wretched nation?
21. Qu. Whether all things would not bear a high price? And whether men would not increase their fortunes without being the better for it?
22. Qu. Whether the same evils would be apprehended from paper-money under an honest and thrifty regulation?
23. Qu. Whether, therefore, a national bank would not be more beneficial than even a mine of gold?
24. Qu. Whether private ends are not prosecuted with more attention and vigour than the public? And yet, whether all private ends are not included in the pubic?
25. Qu. Whether banking be not absolutely necessary to the pubic weal?
26. Qu. Whether even our private banks, though attended with such hazards as we all know them to be, are not of singular use in defect of a national bank?
27. Qu. Whether without them what little business and industry there is would not stagnate? But whether it be not a mighty privilege for a private person to be able to create a hundred pounds with a dash of his pen?
28. Qu. Whether the mystery of banking did not derive its original from the Italians? Whether this acute people were not, upon a time, bankers over all Europe? Whether that business was not practised by some of their noblest families who made immense profits by it, and whether

to that the house of Medici did not originally owe its greatness?
29. Qu. Whether the wise state of Venice was not the first that conceived the advantage of a national bank?
30. Qu. Whether at Venice all payments of bills of exchange and merchants' contracts are not made in the national or pubic bank, the greatest affairs being transacted only by writing the names of the parties, one as debtor the other as creditor in the bank-book?
31. Qu. Whether nevertheless it was not found expedient to provide a chest of ready cash for answering all demands that should happen to be made on account of payments in detail?
32. Qu. Whether this offer of ready cash, instead of transfers in the bank, hath not been found to augment rather than diminish the stock thereof?
33. Qu. Whether at Venice, the difference in the value of bank money above other money be not fixed at twenty per cent?
34. Qu. Whether the bank of Venice be not shut up four times in the year twenty days each time?
35. Qu. Whether by means of this bank the public be not mistress of a million and a half sterling?
36. Qu. Whether the great exactness and integrity with which this bank is managed be not the chief support of that republic?
37. Qu. Whether we may not hope for as much skill and honesty in a Protestant Irish Parliament as in a Popish Senate of Venice?
38. Qu. Whether the bank of Amsterdam was not begun about one hundred and thirty years ago, and whether at this day its stock be not conceived to amount to three thousand tons of gold, or thirty millions sterling?
39. Qu. Whether besides coined money, there be not also great quantities of ingots or bars of gold and silver lodged in this bank?
40. Qu. Whether all payments of contracts for goods in gross, and letters of exchange, must not be made by transfers in the bank-books, provided the sum exceed three hundred florins?
41. Qu. Whether it be not true, that the bank of Amsterdam never makes payments in cash?
42. Qu. Whether, nevertheless, it be not also true, that no man who hath credit in the bank can want money from particular persons, who are willing to become creditors in his stead?
43. Qu. Whether any man thinks himself the poorer, because his money is in the bank?
44. Qu. Whether the creditors of the bank of Amsterdam are not at liberty to withdraw their money when they please, and whether this liberty doth not make them less desirous to use it?
45. Qu. Whether this bank be not shut up twice in the year for ten or fifteen days, during which time the accounts are balanced?
46. Qu. Whether it be not owing to this bank that the city of Amsterdam, without the least confusion, hazard, or trouble, maintains and every day promotes so general and quick a circulation of industry?
47. Qu. Whether it be not the greatest help and spur to commerce that property can be so readily conveyed and so well secured by a compte en banc, that is, by only writing one man's name for another's in the bank-book?
48. Qu. Whether, at the beginning of the last century, those who had lent money to the public during the war with Spain were not satisfied by the sole expedient of placing their names in a compte en banc, with liberty to transfer their claims?
49. Qu. Whether the example of those easy transfers in the compte en banc, thus casually erected, did not tempt other men to become creditors to the public, in order to profit by the same secure and expeditious method of keeping and transferring their wealth?
50. Qu. Whether this compte en banc hath not proved better than a mine of gold to Amsterdam?
51. Qu. Whether that city may not be said to owe her greatness to the unpromising accident of her having been in debt more than she was able to Pay?
52. Qu. Whether it be known that any State from such small beginnings, in so short a time,

ever grew to so great wealth and power as the province of Holland hath done; and whether the bank of Amsterdam hath not been the real cause of such extraordinary growth?

53. Qu. Whether we are by nature a more stupid people than the Dutch? And yet whether these things are sufficiently considered by our patriots?

54. Qu. Whether anything less than the utter subversion of those Republics can break the banks of Venice and Amsterdam?

55. Qu. Whether at Hamburgh the citizens have not the management of the bank, without the meddling or inspection of the Senate?

56. Qu. Whether the directors be not four principal burghers chosen by plurality of voices, whose business is to see the rules observed, and furnish the cashiers with money?

57. Qu. Whether the book-keepers are not obliged to balance their accounts every week, and exhibit them to the controllers or directors?

58. Qu. Whether any besides the citizens are admitted to have compte en banc at Hamburgh?

59. Qu. Whether there be not a certain limit, under which no sum can be entered into the bank?

60. Qu. Whether each particular person doth not pay a fee in order to be admitted to a compte en banc at Hamburgh and Amsterdam?

61. Qu. Whether the effects lodged in the bank of Hamburgh are liable to be seized for debt or forfeiture?

62. Qu. Whether this bank doth not lend money upon pawns at low interest and only for half a year, after which term, in default of payment, the pawns are punctually sold by auction?

63. Qu. Whether the book-keepers of the bank of Hamburgh are not obliged upon oath never to reveal what sums of money are paid in or out of the bank, or what effects any particular person has therein?

64. Qu. Whether, therefore, it be possible to know the state or stock of this bank; and yet whether it be not of the greatest reputation and most established credit throughout the North?

65. Qu. Whether the success of those public banks in Venice, Amsterdam and Hamburg would not naturally produce in other States an inclination to the same methods?

66. Qu. Whether an absolute monarchy be so apt to gain credit, and whether the vivacity of some humours could so well suit with the slow steps and discreet management which a bank requires?

67. Qu. Whether the bank called the general bank of France, contrived by Mr Law, and established by letters patent in May, 1716, was not in truth a particular and not a national bank, being in the hands of a particular company privileged and protected by the Government?

68. Qu. Whether the Government did not order that the notes of this bank should pass on a par with ready money in all payments of the revenue?

69. Qu. Whether this bank was not obliged to issue only such notes as were payable at sight?

70. Qu. Whether it was not made a capital crime to forge the notes of this bank?

71. Qu. Whether this bank was not restrained from trading either by sea or land, and from taking up money upon interest?

72. Qu. Whether the original stock thereof was not six millions of livres, divided into actions of a thousand crowns each?

73. Qu. Whether the proprietors were not to hold general assemblies twice in the year, for the regulating of their affairs?

74. Qu. Whether the accompts of this bank were not balanced twice every year?

75. Qu. Whether there were not two chests belonging to this bank, the one called the general chest containing their specie, their bills and their copper plates for the printing of those bills, under the custody of three locks, whereof the keys were kept by the director, the inspector and treasurer. also another called, the ordinary chest, containing part of the stock not exceeding two hundred thousand crowns, under the key of the treasurer?

76. Qu. Whether out of this last mentioned sum, each particular cashier was not to be intrusted with a share not exceeding the value of twenty thousand crowns at a time, and that under good security?

77. Qu. Whether the Regent did not reserve to himself the power of calling this bank to account, so often as he should think good, and of appointing the inspector?

78. Qu. Whether in the beginning of the year 1719 the French King did not convert the general bank of France into a Banque Royale, having himself purchased the stock of the company and taken it into his own hands, and appointed the Duke of Orleans chief manager thereof?

79. Qu. Whether from that time, all matters relating to the bank were not transacted in the name, and by the sole authority, of the king?

80. Qu. Whether his Majesty did not undertake to receive and keep the cash of all particular persons, subjects, or foreigners, in his said Royale Banque, without being paid for that trouble? And whether it was not declared, that such cash should not be liable to seizure on any pretext, not even on the king's own account?

81. Qu. Whether the treasurer alone did not sign all the bills, receive all the stock paid into the bank, and keep account of all the ingoings and out-goings?

82. Qu. Whether there were not three registers for the enregistering of the bills kept in the Banque Royale, one by the inspector, another by the controller, and a third by the treasurer?

83. Qu. Whether there was not also a fourth register, containing the profits of the bank, which was visited, at least once a week, by the inspector and controller?

84. Qu. Whether, beside the general bureau or compter in the city of Paris, there were not also appointed five more in the towns of Lyons, Tours, Rochelle, Orleans, and Amiens, each whereof was provided with two chests, one of specie for discharging bills at sight, and another of bank bills to be issued as there should be demand?

85. Qu. Whether, in the above mentioned towns, it was not prohibited to make payments in silver, exceeding the sum of six hundred livres?

86. Qu. Whether all creditors were not empowered to demand payment in bank bills instead of specie?

87. Qu. Whether, in a short compass of time, this bank did not undergo many new changes and regulations by several successive acts of council?

88. Qu. Whether the untimely, repeated, and boundless fabrication of bills did not precipitate the ruin of this bank?

89. Qu. Whether it be not true, that before the end of July, 1719, they had fabricated four hundred millions of livres in bank-notes, to which they added the sum of one hundred and twenty millions more on the twelfth of September following, also the same sum of one hundred and twenty millions on the twenty-fourth of 3 October, and again on the twenty-ninth of December, in the same year, the farther sum of three hundred and sixty millions, making the whole, from an original stock of six millions, mount, within the compass of one year, to a thousand millions of livres?

90. Qu. Whether on the twenty-eighth of February, 1720, the king did not make an union of the bank with the united company of the East and West Indies, which from that time had the administration and profits of the Banque Royale?

91. Qu. Whether the king did not still profess himself responsible for the value of the bank bills, and whether the company were not responsible to his Majesty for their management?

92. Qu. Whether sixteen hundred millions of livres, lent to his majesty by the company, was not a sufficient pledge to indemnify the king?

93. Qu. Whether the new directors were not prohibited to make any more bills without an act of council?

94. Qu. Whether the chests and books of the Banque were not subjected to the joint inspection of a Counsellor of State, and the Prevot des Marchands, assisted by two Echevins, a judge, and a consul, who had power to visit when they would and without warning?

95. Qu. Whether in less than two years the actions or shares of the Indian Company (first established for Mississippi, and afterwards increased by the addition of other compares and further? and whether this privileges) did not rise to near 2000 per cent must be ascribed to real advantages of trade, or to mere frenzy?

96. Qu. Whether, from first to last, there were not fabricated bank bills, of one kind or other, to the value of more than two thousand and six hundred millions of livres, or one hundred and thirty millions sterling?

97. Qu. Whether the credit of the bank did not decline from its union with the Indian Company?

98. Qu. Whether, notwithstanding all the above-mentioned extraordinary measures, the bank bills did not still pass at par with gold and silver to May, 1720, when the French king thought fit, by a new act of council, to make a reduction of their value, which proved a fatal blow, the effects whereof, though soon retracted, no subsequent skill or management could ever repair?

99. Qu. Whether, what no reason, reflexion, or foresight could do, this simple matter of fact (the most powerful argument with the multitude) did not do at once, to wit, open the eyes of the people?

100. Qu. Whether the dealers in that sort of ware had ever troubled their heads with the nature of credit, or the true use and end of banks, but only considered their bills and actions as things, to which the general demand gave a price?

101. Qu. Whether the Government was not in great perplexity to contrive expedients for the getting rid of those bank bills, which had been lately multiplied with such an unlimited passion?

102. Qu. Whether notes to the value of about ninety millions were not sunk by being paid off in specie, with the cash of the Compagnie des Indes, with that of the bank, and that of the Hotels des Monnoyes? Whether five hundred and thirty millions were not converted into annuities at the royal treasury? Whether several hundred millions more in bank bills were not extinguished and replaced by annuities on the City of Paris, on taxes throughout the provinces, &c., &c?

103. Qu. Whether, after all other shifts, the last and grand resource for exhausting that ocean, was not the erecting of a compte en banc in several towns of France?

104. Qu. Whether, when the imagination of a people is thoroughly wrought upon and heated by their own example, and the arts of designing men, this doth not produce a sort of enthusiasm which takes place of reason, and is the most dangerous distemper in a State?

105. Qu. Whether this epidemical madness should not be always before the eyes of a legislature, in the framing of a national bank?

106. Qu. Whether, therefore, it may not be fatal to engraft trade on a national bank, or to propose dividends on the stock thereof?

107. Qu. Whether it be possible for a national bank to subsist and maintain its credit under a French government?

108. Qu. Whether it may not be as useful a lesson to consider the bad management of some as the good management of others?

109. Qu. Whether the rapid and surprising success of the schemes of those who directed the French bank did not turn their brains?

110. Qu. Whether the best institutions may not be made subservient to bad ends?

111. Qu. Whether, as the aim of industry is power, and the aim of a bank is to circulate and secure this power to each individual, it doth not follow that absolute power in one hand is inconsistent with a lasting and a flourishing bank?

112. Qu. Whether our natural appetites, as well as powers, are not limited to their respective ends and uses? But whether artificial appetites may not be infinite?

113. Qu. Whether the simple getting of money, or passing it from hand to hand without industry, be an object worthy of a wise government?

114. Qu. Whether, if money be considered as an end, the appetite thereof be not infinite? But whether the ends of money itself be not bounded?

115. Qu. Whether the mistaking of the means for the end was not a fundamental error in the French councils?

116. Qu. Whether the total sum of all other powers, be it of enjoyment or action, which belong

to man, or to all mankind together, is not in truth a very narrow and limited quantity? But whether fancy is not boundless?

117. Qu. Whether this capricious tyrant, which usurps the place of reason, doth not most cruelly torment and delude those poor men, the usurers, stockjobbers, and projectors, of content to themselves from heaping up riches, that is, from gathering counters, from multiplying figures, from enlarging denominations, without knowing what they would be at, and without having a proper regard to the use or end or nature of things?

118. Qu. Whether the ignis fatuus of fancy doth not kindle immoderate desires, and lead men into endless pursuits and wild labyrinths?

119. Qu. Whether counters be not referred to other things, which, so long as they keep pace and proportion with the counters, it must be owned the counters are useful; but whether beyond that to value or covet counters be not direct folly?

120. Qu. Whether the public aim ought not to be, that men's industry should supply their present wants, and the overplus be converted into a stock of power?

121. Qu. Whether the better this power is secured, and the more easily it is transferred, industry be not so much the more encouraged?

122. Qu. Whether money, more than is expedient for those purposes, be not upon the whole hurtful rather than beneficial to a State?

123. Qu. Whether there should not be a constant care to keep the bills at par?

124. Qu. Whether, therefore, bank bills should at any time be multiplied but as trade and business were also multiplied?

125. Qu. Whether it was not madness in France to mint bills and actions, merely to humour the people and rob them of their cash?

126. Qu. Whether we may not profit by their mistakes, and as some things are to be avoided, whether there may not be others worthy of imitation in the conduct of our neighbours?

127. Qu. Whether the way be not clear and open and easy, and whether anything but the will is wanting to our legislature?

128. Qu. Whether jobs and tricks are not detested on all hands, but whether it be not the joint interest of prince and people to promote industry?

129. Qu. Whether, all things considered, a national bank be not the most practicable, sure, and speedy method to mend our affairs, and cause industry to flourish among us?

130. Qu. Whether a compte en banc or current bank bills would best answer our occasions?

131. Qu. Whether a public compte en banc, where effects are received, and accounts kept with particular persons, be not an excellent expedient for a great city?

132. Qu. What effect a general compte en banc would have in the metropolis of this kingdom with one in each province subordinate thereunto?

133. Qu. Whether it may not be proper for a great kingdom to unite both expedients, to wit, bank notes and a compte en banc?

134. Qu. Whether, nevertheless, it would be advisable to begin with both at once, or rather to proceed first with the bills, and afterwards, as business multiplied, and money or effects flowed in, to open the compte en banc?

135. Qu. Whether, for greater security, double books of compte en banc should not be kept in different places and hands?

136. Qu. Whether it would not be right to build the compters and public treasuries, where books and bank notes are kept, without wood, all arched and floored with brick or stone, having chests also and cabinets of iron?

137. Qu. Whether divers registers of the bank notes should not be kept in different hands?

138. Qu. Whether there should not be great discretion in the uttering of bank notes, and whether the attempting to do things per saltum be not often the way to undo them?

139. Qu. Whether the main art be not by slow degrees and cautious measures to reconcile the bank to the public, to wind it insensibly into the affections of men, and interweave it with the constitution?

140. Qu. Whether the promoting of industry should not be always in view, as the true and sole end, the rule and measure, of a national bank? And whether all deviations from that object should not be carefully avoided?
141. Qu. Whether a national bank may not prevent the drawing of specie out of the country (where it circulates in small payments), to be shut up in the chests of particular persons?
142. Qu. Whether it may not be useful, for supplying manufactures and trade with stock, for regulating exchange, for quickening commerce, for putting spirit into the people?
143. Qu. Whether tenants or debtors could have cause to complain of our monies being reduced to the English value if it were withal multiplied in the same, or in a greater proportion? and whether this would not be the consequence of a national bank?
144. Qu. If there be an open sure way to thrive, without hazard to ourselves or prejudice to our neighbours, what should hinder us from putting it in practice?
145. Qu. Whether in so numerous a Senate, as that of this kingdom, it may not be easie to find men of pure hands and clear heads fit to contrive and model a public bank?
146. Qu. Whether a view of the precipice be not sufficient, or whether we must tumble headlong before we are roused?
147. Qu. Whether in this drooping and dispirited country, men are quite awake?
148. Qu. Whether we are sufficiently sensible of the peculiar security there is in having a bank that consists of land and paper, one of which cannot be exported, and the other is in no danger of being exported?
149. Qu. Whether it be not delightful to complain? And whether there be not many who had rather utter their complaints than redress their evils?
150. Qu. Whether, if 'the crown of the wise be their riches' (Prov., xiv.24), we are not the foolishest people in Christendom?
151. Qu. Whether we have not all the while great civil as well as natural advantages?
152. Qu. Whether there be any people who have more leisure to cultivate the arts of peace, and study the public weal?
153. Qu. Whether other nations who enjoy any share of freedom, and have great objects in view, be not unavoidably embarrassed and distracted by factions? But whether we do not divide upon trifles, and whether our parties are not a burlesque upon politics?

154. Qu. Whether it be not an advantage that we are not embroiled in foreign affairs, that we hold not the balance of Europe, that we are protected by other fleets and armies, that it is the true interest of a powerful people, from whom we are descended, to guard us on all sides?
155. Qu. Whether England doth not really love us and wish well to us, as bone of her bone, and flesh of her flesh? And whether it be not our part to cultivate this love and affection all manner of ways?
156. Qu. Whether, if we do not reap the benefits that may be made of our country and government, want of will in the lower people, or want of wit in the upper, be most in fault?
157. Qu. What sea-ports or foreign trade have the Swisses; and yet how warm are those people, and how well provided?
158. Qu. Whether there may not be found a people who so contrive as to be impoverished by their trade? And whether we are not that people?
159. Qu. Whether it would not be better for this island, if all our fine folk of both sexes were shipped off, to remain in foreign countries, rather than that they should spend their estates at home in foreign luxury, and spread the contagion thereof through their native land?
160. Qu. Whether our gentry understand or have a notion of magnificence, and whether for want thereof they do not affect very wretched distinctions?
161. Qu. Whether there be not an art or skill in governing human pride, so as to render it subservient to the pubic aim?
162. Qu. Whether the great and general aim of the public should not be to employ the people?
163. Qu. What right an eldest son hath to the worst education?

164. Qu. Whether men's counsels are not the result of their knowledge and their principles?
165. Qu. Whether an assembly of freethinkers, petit maitres, and smart Fellows would not make an admirable Senate?
166. Qu. Whether there be not labour of the brains as well as of the hands, and whether the former is beneath a gentleman?
167. Qu. Whether the public be more interested to protect the property acquired by mere birth than that which is the Mediate fruit of learning and vertue?
168. Qu. Whether it would not be a poor and ill-judged project to attempt to promote the good of the community, by invading the rights of one part thereof, or of one particular order of men?
169. Qu. Whether the public happiness be not proposed by the legislature, and whether such happiness doth not contain that of the individuals?
170. Qu. Whether, therefore, a legislator should be content with a vulgar share of knowledge? Whether he should not be a person of reflexion and thought, who hath made it his study to understand the true nature and interest of mankind, how to guide men's humours and passions, how to incite their active powers, how to make their several talents co-operate to the mutual benefit of each other, and the general good of the whole?
171. Qu. Whether it doth not follow that above all things a gentleman's care should be to keep his own faculties sound and entire?
172. Qu. Whether the natural phlegm of this island needs any additional stupefier?
173. Qu. Whether all spirituous liquors are not in truth opiates?
174. Qu. Whether our men of business are not generally very grave by fifty?
175. Qu. Whether there be really among us any parents so silly, as to encourage drinking in their children?
176. Qu. Whence it is, that our ladies are more alive, and bear age so much better than our gentlemen?
177. Qu. Whether all men have not faculties of mind or body which may be employed for the public benefit?
178. Qu. Whether the main point be not to multiply and employ our people?
179. Qu. Whether hearty food and warm clothing would not enable and encourage the lower sort to labour?
180. Qu. Whether, in such a soil as ours, if there was industry, there could be want?
181. Qu. Whether the way to make men industrious be not to let them taste the fruits of their industry? And whether the labouring ox should be muzzled?
182. Qu. Whether our landlords are to be told that industry and numbers would raise the value of their lands, or that one acre about the Tholsel is worth ten thousand acres in Connaught?
183. Qu. Whether our old native Irish are not the most indolent and supine people in Christendom?
184. Qu. Whether they are yet civilized, and whether their habitations and furniture are not more sordid than those of the savage Americans?
185. Qu. Whether this be altogether their own fault?
186. Qu. Whether it be not a sad circumstance to live among lazy beggars? And whether, on the other hand, it would not be delightful to live in a country swarming, like China, with busy people?
187. Qu. Whether we should not cast about, by all manner of means, to excite industry, and to remove whatever hinders it? And whether every one should not lend a helping hand?
188. Qu. Whether vanity itself should not be engaged in this good work? And whether it is not to be wished that the finding of employment for themselves and others were a fashionable distinction among the ladies?
189. Qu. Whether idleness be the mother or the daughter of spleen?
190. Qu. Whether it may not be worth while to publish the conversation of Ischomachus and his wife in Xenophon, for the use of our ladies?

191. Qu. Whether it is true that there have been, upon a time, one hundred millions of people employed in China, without the woollen trade, or any foreign commerce?

192. Qu. Whether the natural inducements to sloth are not greater in the Mogul's country than in Ireland, and yet whether, in that suffocating and dispiriting climate, the Banyans are not all, men, women, and children, constantly employed?

193. Qu. Whether it be not true that the great Mogul's subjects might undersell us even in our own markets, and clothe our people with their stuffs and calicoes, if they were imported duty free?

194. Qu. Whether there can be a greater reproach on the leading men and the patriots of a country, than that the people should want employment? And whether methods may not be found to employ even the lame and the blind, the dumb, the deaf, and the maimed, in some or other branch of our manufactures?

195. Qu. Whether much may not be expected from a biennial consultation of so many wise men about the public good?

196. Qu. Whether a tax upon dirt would not be one way of encouraging industry?

197. Qu. Whether it may not be right to appoint censors in every parish to observe and make returns of the idle hands?

198. Qu. Whether a register or history of the idleness and industry of a people would be an useless thing?

199. Qu. Whether we are apprized, of all the uses that may be made of political arithmetic?

200. Qu. Whether it would be a great hardship if every parish were obliged to find work for their poor?

201. Qu. Whether children especially should not be inured to labour betimes?

202. Qu. Whether there should not be erected, in each province, an hospital for orphans and foundlings, at the expense of old bachelors?

203. Qu. Whether it be true that in the Dutch workhouses things are so managed that a child four years old may earn its own livelihood?

204. Qu. What a folly is it to build fine houses, or establish lucrative posts and large incomes, under the notion of providing for the poor?

205. Qu. Whether the poor, grown up and in health, need any other provision but their own industry, under public inspection?

206. Qu. Whether the poor-tax in England hath lessened or increased the number of the poor?

207. Qu. Why the workhouse in Dublin, with so good an endowment, should yet be of so little use? and whether this may not be owing to that very endowment?

208. Qu. Whether that income might not, by this time, have gone through the whole kingdom, and erected a dozen workhouses in every county?

209. Qu. Whether workhouses should not be made at the least expense, with clay floors, and walls of rough stone, without plastering, ceiling, or glazing?

210. Qu. Whether the tax on chairs or hackney coaches be not paid, rather by the country gentlemen, than the citizens of Dublin?

211. Qu. Whether it be an impossible attempt to set our people at work, or whether industry be a habit which, like other habits, may by time and skill be introduced among any people?

212. Qu. Whether all manner of means should not be employed to possess the nation in general with an aversion and contempt for idleness and all idle folk?

213. Qu. Whether it would be a hardship on people destitute of all things, if the public furnished them with necessaries which they should be obliged to earn by their labour?

214. Qu. Whether other nations have not found great benefit from the use of slaves in repairing high roads, making rivers navigable, draining bogs, erecting public buildings, bridges, and manufactures?

215. Qu. Whether temporary servitude would not be the best cure for idleness and beggary?

216. Qu. Whether the public hath not a right to employ those who cannot or who will not find employment for themselves?

217. Qu. Whether all sturdy beggars should not be seized and made slaves to the public for a certain term of years?
218. Qu. Whether he who is chained in a jail or dungeon hath not, for the time, lost his liberty? And if so, whether temporary slavery be not already admitted among us?
219. Qu. Whether a state of servitude, wherein he should be well worked, fed, and clothed, would not be a preferment to such a fellow?
220. Qu. Whether criminals in the freest country may not forfeit their liberty, and repair the damage they have done the public by hard labour?
221. Qu. What the word 'servant' signifies in the New Testament?
222. Qu. Whether the view of criminals chained in pairs and kept at hard labour would not be very edifying to the multitude?
223. Qu. Whether the want of such an institution be not plainly seen in England, where the disbelief of a future state hardeneth rogues against the fear of death, and where, through the great growth of robbers and housebreakers, it becomes every day more necessary?
224. Qu. Whether it be not easier to prevent than to remedy, and whether we should not profit by the example of others?
225. Qu. Whether felons are not often spared, and therefore encouraged, by the compassion of those who should prosecute. them?
226. Qu. Whether many that would not take away the life of a thief may not nevertheless be willing to bring him to a more adequate punishment?
227. Qu. Whether there should not be a difference between the treatment of criminals and that of other slaves?
228. Qu. Whether the most indolent would be fond of idleness, if they regarded it as the sure road to hard labour?
229. Qu. Whether the industry of the lower part of our people doth not much depend on the expense of the upper?
230. Qu. What would be the consequence if our gentry affected to distinguish themselves by fine houses rather than fine clothes?
231. Qu. Whether any people in Europe are so meanly provided with houses and furniture, in proportion to their incomes, as the men of estates in Ireland?
232. Qu. Whether building would not peculiarly encourage all other arts in this kingdom?
233. Qu. Whether smiths, masons, bricklayers, plasterers, carpenters, joiners, tilers, plumbers, and glaziers would not all find employment if the humour of building prevailed?
234. Qu. Whether the ornaments and furniture of a good house do not employ a number of all sorts of artificers, in iron, wood, marble, brass, pewter, copper, wool, flax, and divers other materials?
235. Qu. Whether in buildings and gardens a great number of day-labourers do not find employment?
236. Qu. Whether by these means much of that sustenance and wealth of this nation which now goes to foreigners would not be kept at home, and nourish and circulate among our own people?
237. Qu. Whether, as industry produced good living, the number of hands and mouths would not be increased; and in proportion thereunto, whether there would not be every day more occasion for agriculture? And whether this article alone would not employ a world of people?
238. Qu. Whether such management would not equally provide for the magnificence of the rich, and the necessities of the poor?
239. Qu. Whether an expense in building and improvements doth not remain at home, pass to the heir, and adorn the public? And whether any of those things can be said of claret?
240. Qu. Whether fools do not make fashions, and wise men follow them?
241. Qu. Whether, for one who hurts his fortune by improvements, twenty do not ruin themselves by foreign luxury?
242. Qu. Whether in proportion as Ireland was improved and beautified by fine seats, the

number of absentees would not decrease?

243. Qu. Whether he who employs men in buildings and manufactures doth not put life in the country, and whether the neighbourhood round him be not observed to thrive?

244. Qu. Whether money circulated on the landlord's own lands, and among his own tenants, doth not return into his own pocket?

245. Qu. Whether every squire that made his domain swarm with busy hands, like a bee-hive or ant-hill, would not serve his own interest, as well as that of his country?

246. Qu. Whether a gentleman who hath seen a little of the world, and observed how men live elsewhere, can contentedly sit down in a cold, damp, sordid habitation, in the midst of a bleak country, inhabited by thieves and beggars?

247. Qu. Whether, on the other hand, a handsome seat amidst well-improved lands, fair villages, and a thriving neighbourhood may not invite a man to dwell on his own estate, and quit the life of an insignificant saunterer about town for that of a useful country-gentleman?

248. Qu. Whether it would not be of use and ornament if the towns throughout this kingdom were provided with decent churches, townhouses, workhouses, market-places, and paved streets, with some order taken for cleanliness?

249. Qu. Whether, if each of these towns were addicted to some peculiar manufacture, we should not find that the employing many hands together on the same work was the way to perfect our workmen? And whether all these things might not soon be provided by a domestic industry, if money were not wanting?

250. Qu. Whether money could ever be wanting to the demands of industry, if we had a national bank?

251. Qu. Whether when a motion was made once upon a time to establish a private bank in this kingdom by public authority, divers gentlemen did not shew themselves forward to embark in that design?

252. Qu. Whether it may not now be hoped, that our patriots will be as forward to examine and consider the proposal of a public bank calculated only for the public good?

253. Qu. Whether any people upon earth shew a more early zeal for the service of their country, greater eagerness to bear a part in the legislature, or a more general parturiency with respect to politics and public counsels?

254. Qu. Whether, nevertheless, a light and ludicrous vein be not the reigning humour; but whether there was ever greater cause to be serious?

Part III

Query 1.
Whether the fable of Hercules and the carter ever suited any nation like this nation of Ireland?
2. Qu. Whether it be not a new spectacle under the sun, to behold, in such a climate and such a soil, and under such a gentle government, so many roads untrodden, fields untilled, houses desolate, and hands unemployed?
3. Qu. Whether there is any country in Christendom, either kingdom or republic, depending or independent, free or enslaved, which may not afford us a useful lesson?
4. Qu. Whether the frugal Swisses have any other commodities but their butter and cheese and a few cattle, for exportation; whether, nevertheless, the single canton of Berne hath not in her public treasury two millions sterling?
5. Qu. Whether that small town of Berne, with its scanty barren territory, in a mountainous corner, without sea-ports, without manufactures, without mines, be not rich by mere dint of frugality?
6. Qu. Whether the Swisses in general have not sumptuary laws, prohibiting the use of gold, jewels, silver, silk, and lace in their apparel, and indulging the women only to wear silk on festivals, weddings, and public solemnities?
7. Qu. Whether there be not two ways of growing rich, sparing and getting? But whether the lazy spendthrift must not be doubly poor?
8. Qu. Whether money circulating be not the life of industry; and whether the want thereof doth not render a State gouty and inactive?
9. Qu. But whether, if we had a national bank, and our present cash (small as it is) were put into the most convenient shape, men should hear any public complaints for want of money?
10. Qu. Whether all circulation be not alike a circulation of credit, whatsoever medium (metal or paper) is employed, and whether gold be any more than credit for so much power?
11. Qu. Whether the wealth of the richest nations in Christendom doth not consist in paper vastly more than in gold and silver?
12. Qu. Whether Lord Clarendon doth not aver of his own knowledge, that the Prince of Orange, with the best credit, and the assistance of the richest men in Amsterdam, was above ten days endeavouring to raise L20,000 in specie, without being able to raise half the sum in all that time? (See Clarendon's History, BK. XII)
13. Qu. Whether the whole city of Amsterdam would not have been troubled to have brought together twenty thousand pounds in one room?
14. Qu. Whether it be not absolutely necessary that there must be a bank and must be a trust? And, if so, whether it be not the most safe and prudent course to have a national bank and trust the legislature?
15. Qu. Whether objections against trust in general avail, when it is allowed there must be a trust, and the only question is where to place this trust, whether in the legislature or in private hands?
16. Qu. Whether it can be expected that private persons should have more regard to the public than the public itself?
17. Qu. Whether, if there be hazards from mismanagement, those may not be provided against in the framing of a pubic bank; but whether any provision can be made against the mismanagement of private banks that are under no check, control, or inspection?
18. Qu. Whatever may be said for the sake of objecting, yet, whether it be not false in fact, that men would prefer a private security to a public security?
19. Qu. Whether a national bank ought to be considered as a new experiment; and whether it be not a motive to try this scheme that it hath been already tried with success in other countries?
20. Qu. If power followeth money, whether this can be anywhere more properly and securely

placed, than in the same hands wherein the supreme power is already placed?
21. Qu. Whether there be more danger of abuse in a private than in a public management?
22. Qu. Whether the proper usual remedy for abuses of private banks be not to bring them before Parliament, and subject them to the inspection of a committee; and whether it be not more prudent to prevent than to redress an evil?
23. Qu. Supposing there had been hitherto no such thing as a bank, and the question were now first proposed, whether it would be safer to circulate unlimited bills in a private credit, or bills to a limited value on the public credit of the community, what would men think?
24. Qu. Whether experience and example be not the plainest proof; and whether any instance can be assigned where a national bank hath not been attended with great advantage to the public?
25. Qu. Whether the evils apprehended from a national bank are not much more to be apprehended from private banks; but whether men by custom are not familiarized and reconciled to common dangers, which are therefore thought less than they really are?
26. Qu. Whether it would not be very hard to suppose all sense, honesty, and public spirit were in the keeping of only a few private men, and the public was not fit to be trusted?
27. Qu. Whether it be not ridiculous to suppose a legislature should be afraid to trust itself?
28. Qu. But, whether a private interest be not generally supported and pursued with more zeal than a public?
29. Qu. Whether the maxim, 'What is everybody's business is nobody's,' prevails in any country under the sun more than in Ireland?
30. Qu. Whether, nevertheless, the community of danger, which lulls private men asleep, ought not to awaken the public?
31. Qu. Whether there be not less security where there are more temptations and fewer checks?
32. Qu. If a man is to risk his fortune, whether it be more prudent to risk it on the credit of private men, or in that of the great assembly of the nation?
33. Qu. Where is it most reasonable to expect wise and punctual dealing, whether in a secret impenetrable recess, where credit depends on secrecy, or in a public management regulated and inspected by Parliament?
34. Qu. Whether a supine security be not catching, and whether numbers running the same risk, as they lessen the caution, may not increase the danger?
35. Qu. What real objection lies against a national bank erected by the legislature, and in the management of public deputies, appointed and inspected by the legislature?
36. Qu. What have we to fear from such a bank, which may not be as well feared without it?
37. Qu. How, why, by what means, or for what end, should it become an instrument of oppression?
38. Qu. Whether we can possibly be on a more precarious foot than we are already? Whether it be not in the power of any particular person at once to disappear and convey himself into foreign parts? or whether there can be any security in an estate of land when the demands upon it are unknown?
39. Qu. Whether the establishing of a national bank, if we suppose a concurrence of the government, be not very practicable?
40. Qu. But, whether though a scheme be never so evidently practicable and useful to the pubic, yet, if conceived to interfere with a private interest, it be not forthwith in danger of appearing doubtful, difficult, and impracticable?
41. Qu. Whether the legislative body hath not already sufficient power to hurt, if they may be supposed capable of it, and whether a bank would give them any new power?
42. Qu. What should tempt the pubic to defraud itself?
43. Qu. Whether, if the legislature destroyed the public, it would not be felo de se; and whether it be reasonable to suppose it bent on its own destruction?
44. Qu. Whether the objection to a pubic national bank, from want of secrecy, be not in truth

an argument for it?
45. Qu. Whether the secrecy of private banks be not the very thing that renders them so hazardous? and whether, without that, there could have been of late so many sufferers?
46. Qu. Whether when all objections are answered it be still incumbent to answer surmises?
47. Qu. Whether it were just to insinuate that gentlemen would be against any proposal they could not turn into a job?
48. Qu. Suppose the legislature passed their word for any private banker, and regularly visited his books, would not money lodged in his bank be therefore reckoned more secure?
49. Qu. In a country where the legislative body is not fit to be trusted, what security can there be for trusting any one else?
50. Qu. If it be not ridiculous to question whether the pubic can find cash to circulate bills of a limited value when private bankers are supposed to find enough to circulate them to an unlimited value?
51. Qu. Whether the united stock of a nation be not the best security? And whether anything but the ruin of the State can produce a national bankruptcy?
52. Qu. Whether the total sum of the public treasure, power, and wisdom, all co-operating, be not most likely to establish a bank of credit, sufficient to answer the ends, relieve the wants, and satisfy the scruples of all people?
53. Qu. Whether those hazards that in a greater degree attend private banks can be admitted as objections against a public one?
54. Qu. Whether that which is an objection to everything be an objection to anything; and whether the possibility of an abuse be not of that kind?
55. Qu. Whether, in fact, all things are not more or less abused, and yet notwithstanding such abuse, whether many things are not upon the whole expedient and useful?
56. Qu. Whether those things that are subject to the most general inspection are not the least subject to abuse?
57. Qu. Whether, for private ends, it may not be sometimes expedient to object novelty to things that have been often tried, difficulty to the plainest things, and hazard to the safest?
58. Qu. Whether some men will not be apt to argue as if the question was between money and credit, and not (as in fact it is) which ought to be preferred, private credit or public credit?
59. Qu. Whether they will not prudently overlook the evils felt, or to be feared, on one side?
60. Qu. Whether, therefore, those that would make an impartial judgment ought not to be on their guard, keeping both prospects always in view, balancing the inconveniencies on each side and considering neither absolutely?
61. Qu. Whether wilful mistakes, examples without a likeness, and general addresses to the passions are not often more successful than arguments?
62. Qu. Whether there be not an art to puzzle plain cases as well as to explain obscure ones?
63. Qu. Whether private men are not often an over-match for the public; want of weight being made up for by activity?
64. Qu. If we suppose neither sense nor honesty in our leaders or representatives, whether we are not already undone, and so have nothing further to fear?
65. Qu. Suppose a power in the government to hurt the pubic by means of a national bank, yet what should give them the will to do this? Or supposing a will to do mischief, yet how could a national bank, modelled and administered by Parliament, put it in their power?
66. Qu. Whether even a wicked will entrusted with power can be supposed to abuse it for no end?
67. Qu. Whether it be not much more probable that those who maketh such objections do not believe them?
68. Qu. Whether it be not vain to object that our fellow-subjects of Great Britain would malign or obstruct our industry when it is exerted in a way which cannot interfere with their own?
66. Qu. Whether it is to be supposed they should take delight in the dirt and nakedness and famine of our people, or envy them shoes for their feet and beef for their belies?

70. Qu. What possible handle or inclination could our having a national bank give other people to distress us?
71. Qu. Whether it be not ridiculous to conceive that a project for cloathing and feeding our natives should give any umbrage to England?
72. Qu. Whether such unworthy surmises are not the pure effect of spleen?
73. Qu. Whether London is not to be considered as the metropolis of Ireland? And whether our wealth (such as it is) doth not circulate through London and throughout all England, as freely as that of any part of his Majesty's dominions?
74. Qu. Whether therefore it be not evidently the interest of the people of England to encourage rather than to oppose a national bank in this kingdom, as well as every other means for advancing our wealth which shall not impair their own?
75. Qu. Whether it is not our interest to be useful to them rather than rival them; and whether in that case we may not be sure of their good offices?
76. Qu. Whether we can propose to thrive so long as we entertain a wrongheaded distrust of England?
77. Qu. Whether, as a national bank would increase our industry, and that our wealth, England may not be a proportionable gainer; and whether we should not consider the gains of our mother-country as some accession to our own?
78. Qu. Whether the Protestant colony in this kingdom can ever forget what they owe to England?
79. Qu. Whether there ever was in any part of the world a country in such wretched circumstances, and which, at the same time, could be so easily remedied, and nevertheless the remedy not applied?
80. Qu. What must become of a people that can neither see the plainest things nor do the easiest?
81. Qu. Be the money lodged in the bank what it will, yet whether an Act to make good deficiencies would not remove all scruples?
82. Qu. If it be objected that a national bank must lower interest, and therefore hurt the monied man, whether the same objection would not hold as strong against multiplying our gold and silver?
83. Qu. But whether a bank that utters bills, with the sole view of promoting the public weal, may not so proportion their quantity as to avoid several inconveniencies which might attend private banks?
84. Qu. Whether there be any difficulty in comprehending that the whole wealth of the nation is in truth the stock of a national bank? And whether any more than the right comprehension of this be necessary to make all men easy with regard to its credit?
85. Qu. Whether any Thing be more reasonable than that the pubic, which makes the whole profit of the bank, should engage to make good its credit?
86. Qu. Whether the prejudices about gold and silver are not strong, but whether they are not still prejudices?
87. Qu. Whether paper doth not by its stamp and signature acquire a local value, and become as precious and as scarce as gold? And whether it be not much fitter to circulate large sums, and therefore preferable to gold?
88. Qu. Whether, in order to make men see and feel, it be not often necessary to inculcate the same thing, and place it in different lights?
89. Qu. Whether it doth not much import to have a right conception of money? And whether its true and just idea be not that of a ticket, entitling to power, and fitted to record and transfer such power?
90. Qu. Whether the managers and officers of a national bank ought to be considered otherwise than as the cashiers and clerks of private banks? Whether they are not in effect as little trusted, have as little power, are as much limited by rules, and as liable to inspection?
91. Qu. Whether the mistaking this point may not create some prejudice against a national

bank, as if it depended on the credit, or wisdom, or honesty, of private men, rather than on the pubic, which is really the sole proprietor and director thereof, and as such obliged to support it?

92. Qu. Though the bank of Amsterdam doth very rarely, if at all, pay out money, yet whether every man possess'd of specie be not ready to convert it into paper, and act as cashier to the bank? And whether, from the same motive, every monied man throughout this kingdom would not be cashier to our national bank?

93. Qu. Whether a national bank would not be the great means and motive for employing our poor in manufactures?

94. Qu. Whether money, though lent out only to the rich, would not soon circulate among the poor? And whether any man borrows but with an intent to circulate?

95. Qu. Whether both government and people would not in the event be gainers by a national bank? And whether anything but wrong conceptions of its nature can make those that wish well to either averse from it?

96. Qu. Whether it may not be right to think, and to have it thought, that England and Ireland, prince and people, have one and the same interest?

97. Qu. Whether, if we had more means to set on foot such manufactures and such commerce as consists with the interest of England, there would not of course be less sheep-walk, and less wool exported to foreign countries? And whether a national bank would not supply such means?

98. Qu. Whether we may not obtain that as friends which it is in vain to hope for as rivals?

99. Qu. Whether in every instance by which we prejudice England, we do not in a greater degree prejudice ourselves? See Part II. qu. 153 and 154.

100. Qu. Whether in the rude original of society the first step was not the exchanging of commodities; the next a substituting of metals by weight as the common medium of circulation; after this the making use of coin; lastly, a further refinement by the use of paper with proper marks and signatures? And whether this, as it is the last, so it be not the greatest improvement?

101. Qu. Whether we are not in fact the only people who may be said to starve in the midst of plenty?

102. Qu. Whether business in general doth not languish among us? Whether our land is not untilled? Whether its inhabitants are not upon the wing?

103. Qu. Whether there can be a worse sign than that people should quit their country for a livelihood? Though men often leave their country for health, or pleasure, or riches, yet to leave it merely for a livelihood, whether this be not exceeding bad, and sheweth some peculiar mismanagement?

104. Qu. Whether our circumstances do not call aloud for some present remedy? And whether that remedy be not in our power?

105. Qu. Whether, in order to redress our evils, artificial helps are not most wanted in a land where industry is most against the natural grain of the people?

106. Qu. Whether, of all the helps to industry that ever were invented, there be any more secure, more easy, and more effectual than a national bank?

107. Qu. Whether medicines do not recommend themselves by experience, even though their reasons be obscure? But whether reason and fact are not equally clear in favour of this political medicine?

108. Qu. Whether, although the prepossessions about gold and silver have taken deep root, yet the example of our Colonies in America doth not make it as plain as day-light that they are not so necessary to the wealth of a nation as the vulgar of all ranks imagine?

109. Qu. Whether it be not evident that we may maintain a much greater inward and outward commerce, and be five times richer than we are, nay, and our bills abroad be of far greater credit, though we had not one ounce of gold or silver in the whole island?

110. Qu. Whether wrongheaded maxims, customs, and fashions are not sufficient to destroy

any people which hath so few resources as the inhabitants of Ireland.

111. Qu. Whether it would not be a horrible thing to see our matrons make dress and play their chief concern?

112. Qu. Whether our ladies might not as well endow monasteries as wear Flanders lace? And whether it be not true that Popish nuns are maintained by Protestant contributions?

113. Qu. Whether England, which hath a free trade, whatever she remits for foreign luxury with one hand, doth not with the other receive much more from abroad? Whether, nevertheless, this nation would not be a gainer, if our women would content themselves with the same moderation in point of expense as the English ladies?

114. Qu. But whether it be not a notorious truth that our Irish ladies are on a foot, as to dress, with those of five times their fortune in England?

115. Qu. Whether it be not even certain that the matrons of this forlorn country send out a greater proportion of its wealth, for fine apparel, than any other females on the whole surface of this terraqueous globe?

116. Qu. Whether the expense, great as it is, be the greatest evil; but whether this folly may not produce many other follies, an entire derangement of domestic life, absurd manners, neglect of duties, bad mothers, a general corruption in both sexes?

117. Qu. Whether therefore a tax on all gold and silver in apparel, on all foreign laces and silks, may not raise a fund for the bank, and at the same time have other salutary effects on the public?

118. Qu. But, if gentlemen had rather tax themselves in another way, whether an additional tax of ten shillings the hogshead on wines may not supply a sufficient fund for the national bank, all defects to be made good by Parliament?

119. Qu. Whether upon the whole it may not be right to appoint a national bank?

120. Qu. Whether the stock and security of such bank would not be, in truth, the national stock, or the total sum of the wealth of this kingdom?

121. Qu. Whether, nevertheless, there should not be a particular fund for present use in answering bills and circulating credit?

122. Qu. Whether for this end any fund may not suffice, provided an Act be passed for making good deficiencies?

123. Qu. Whether the sole proprietor of such bank should not be the public, and the sole director the legislature?

124. Qu. Whether the managers, officers, and cashiers should not be servants of the pubic, acting by orders and limited by rules of the legislature?

125. Qu. Whether there should not be a standing number of inspectors, one-third men in great office, the rest members of both houses, half whereof to go out, and half to come in every session?

126. Qu. Whether those inspectors should not, all in a body, visit twice a year, and three as often as they pleased?

127. Qu. Whether the general bank should not be in Dubin, and subordinate banks or compters one in each province of Munster, Ulster, and Connaught?

128. Qu. Whether there should not be such provisions of stamps, signatures, checks, strong boxes, and all other measures for securing the bank notes and cash, as are usual in other banks?

129. Qu. Whether these ten or a dozen last queries may not easily be converted into heads of a bill?

130. Qu. Whether any one concerns himself about the security or funds of the banks of Venice or Amsterdam? And whether in a little time the case would not be the same as to our bank?

131. Qu. Whether the first beginning of expedients do not always meet with prejudices? And whether even the prejudices of a people ought not to be respected?

132. Qu. Whether a national bank be not the true philosopher's stone in a State?

133. Qu. Whether it be not the most obvious remedy for all the inconveniencies we labour

under with regard to our coin?

134. Qu. Whether it be not agreed on all hands that our coin is on very bad foot, and calls for some present remedy?

135. Qu. Whether the want of silver hath not introduced a sort of traffic for change, which is purchased at no inconsiderable discount to the great obstruction of our domestic commerce?

136. Qu. Whether, though it be evident silver is wanted, it be yet so evident which is the best way of providing for this want? Whether by lowering the gold, or raising the silver, or partly one, partly the other?

137. Qu. Whether a partial raising of one species be not, in truth, wanting a premium to our bankers for importing such species? And what that species is which deserves most to be encouraged?

138. Qu. Whether it be not just, that all gold should be alike rated according to its weight and fineness?

139. Qu. Whether this may be best done, by lowering some certain species of gold, or by raising others, or by joining both methods together?

140. Qu. Whether all regulations of coin should not be made with a view to encourage industry, and a circulation of commerce, throughout the kingdom?

141. Qu. Whether the North and the South have not, in truth, one and the same interest in this matter?

142. Qu. Whether to oil the wheels of commerce be not a common benefit? And whether this be not done by avoiding fractions and multiplying small silver?

143. Qu. But, whether a pubic benefit ought to be obtained by unjust methods, and therefore, whether any reduction of coin should be thought of which may hurt the properties of private men?

144. Qu. Whether those parts of the kingdom where commerce doth most abound would not be the greatest gainers by having our coin placed on a right foot?

145. Qu. Whether, in case a reduction of coin be thought expedient, the uttering of bank bills at the same time may not prevent the inconveniencies of such a reduction?

146. Qu. But, whether any pubic expediency could countervail a real pressure on those who are least able to bear it, tenants and debtors?

147. Qu. Whether, nevertheless, the political body, as well as the natural, must not sometimes be worse in order to be better?

148. Qu. Whether, all things considered, a general raising the value of gold and silver be not so far from bringing greater quantities thereof into the kingdom that it would produce a direct contrary effect, inasmuch as less, in that case, would serve, and therefore less be wanted? And whether men do not import a commodity in proportion to the demand or want of it?

149. Qu. Whether the lowering of our gold would not create a fever in the State? And whether a fever be not sometimes a cure, but whether it be not the last cure a man would choose?

150. Qu. What if our other gold were raised to a par with Portugal gold, and the value of silver in general raised with regard to that of gold?

151. Qu. Whether the pubic ends may or may not be better answered by such augmentation, than by a reduction of our coin?

152. Qu. Provided silver is multiplied, be it by raising or diminishing the value of our coin, whether the great end is not answered?

153. Qu. Whether raising the value of a particular species will not tend to multiply such species, and to lessen others in proportion thereunto? And whether a much less quantity of cash in silver would not, in reality, enrich the nation more than a much greater in gold?

154. Qu. Whether, if a reduction be thought necessary, the obvious means to prevent all hardships and injustice be not a national bank?

155. Qu. Upon supposition that the cash of this kingdom was five hundred thousand pounds, and by lowering the various species each one-fifth of its value the whole sum was reduced to four hundred thousand pounds, whether the difficulty of getting money, and consequently of

paying rents, would not be increased in the proportion of five to four?

156. Qu. Whether such difficulty would not be a great and unmerited distress on all the tenants in the nation? But if at the same time with the aforesaid reduction there were uttered one hundred thousand pounds additional to the former current stock, whether such difficulty or inconvenience would then be felt?

157. Qu. Whether, ceteris paribus, it be not true that the prices of things increase as the quantity of money increaseth, and are diminished as that is diminished? And whether, by the quantity of money is not to be understood the amount of the denominations, all contracts being nominal for pounds, shillings, and pence, and not for weights of gold or silver?

158. Qu. Whether in any foreign market, twopence advance in a kilderkin of corn could greatly affect our trade?

159. Qu. Whether in regard of the far greater changes and fluctuations of prices from the difference of seasons and other accidents, that small rise should seem considerable?

160. Qu. Whether our exports do not consist of such necessaries as other countries cannot well be without?

161. Qu. Whether upon the circulation of a national bank more land would not be tilled, more hands employed, and consequently more commodities exported?

162. Qu. Whether, setting aside the assistance of a national bank, it will be easy to reduce or lower our coin without some hardship (at least for the present) on a great number of particular persons?

163. Qu. Whether, nevertheless, the scheme of a national bank doth not entirely stand clear of this question; and whether such bank may not completely subsist and answer its ends, although there should be no alteration at all made in the value of our coin?

164. Qu. Whether, if the ill state of our coin be not redressed, that scheme would not be still more necessary, inasmuch as a national bank, by putting new life and vigour into our commerce, may prevent our feeling the ill effects of the want of such redress?

165. Qu. Whether men united by interest are not often divided by opinion; and whether such difference in opinion be not an effect of misapprehension?

166. Qu. Whether two things are not manifest, first, that some alteration in the value of our coin is highly expedient, secondly, that whatever alteration is made, the tenderest care should be had of the properties of the people, and even a regard paid to their prejudices?

167. Qu. Whether our taking the coin of another nation for more than it is worth be not, in reality and in event, a cheat upon ourselves?

168. Qu. Whether a particular coin over-rated will not be sure to flow in upon us from other countries beside that where it is coined?

169. Qu. Whether, in case the wisdom of the nation shall think fit to alter our coin, without erecting a national bank, the rule for lessening or avoiding present inconvenience should not be so to order matters, by raising the silver and depressing the gold, as that the total sum of coined cash within the kingdom shall, in denomination, remain the same, or amount to the same nominal value, after the change that it did before?

170. Qu. Whether all inconvenience ought not to be lessened as much as may be; but after, whether it would be prudent, for the sake of a small inconvenience, to obstruct a much greater good? And whether it may not sometimes happen that an inconvenience which in fancy and general discourse seems great shall, when accurately inspected and cast up, appear inconsiderable?

171. Qu. Whether in public councils the sum of things, here and there, present and future, ought not to be regarded?

172. Qu. Whether silver and small money be not that which circulates the quickest, and passeth through all hands, on the road, in the market, at the shop?

173. Qu. Whether, all things considered, it would not be better for a kingdom that its cash consisted of half a million in small silver, than of five times that sum in gold?

174. Qu. Whether there be not every day five hundred lesser payments made for one that

requires gold?

175. Qu. Whether Spain, where gold bears the highest value, be not the laziest, and China, where it bears the lowest, be not the most industrious country in the known world?

176. Qu. Money being a ticket which entitles to power and records the title, whether such power avails otherwise than as it is exerted into act?

177. Qu. Whether it be not evidently the interest of every State, that its money should rather circulate than stagnate?

178. Qu. Whether the principal use of cash be not its ready passing from hand to hand, to answer common occasions of the common people, and whether common occasions of all sorts of people are not small ones?

179. Qu. Whether business at fairs and markets is not often at a stand and often hindered, even though the seller hath his commodities at hand and the purchaser his gold, yet for want of change?

180. Qu. Whether beside that value of money which is rated by weight, there be not also another value consisting in its aptness to circulate?

181. Qu. As wealth is really power, and coin a ticket conveying power, whether those tickets which are the fittest for that use ought not to be preferred?

182. Qu. Whether those tickets which singly transfer small shares of power, and, being multiplied, large shares, are not fitter for common use than those which singly transfer large shares?

183. Qu. Whether the public is not more benefited by a shilling that circulates than a pound that lies dead?

184. Qu. Whether sixpence twice paid be not as good as a shilling once paid?

185. Qu. Whether the same shilling circulating in a village may not supply one man with bread, another with stockings, a third with a knife, a fourth with paper, a fifth with nails, and so answer many wants which must otherwise have remained unsatisfied?

186. Qu. Whether facilitating and quickening the circulation of power to supply wants be not the promoting of wealth and industry among the lower people? And whether upon this the wealth of the great doth not depend?

187. Qu. Whether, without the proper means of circulation, it be not vain to hope for thriving manufacturers and a busy people?

188. Qu. Whether four pounds in small cash may not circulate and enliven an Irish market, which many four-pound pieces would permit to stagnate?

189. Qu. Whether a man that could move nothing less than a hundred-pound weight would not be much at a loss to supply his wants; and whether it would not be better for him to be less strong and more active?

190. Qu. Whether the natural body can be in a state of health and vigour without a due circulation of the extremities, even? And whether the political body, any in the fingers and toes more than the natural, can thrive without a proportionable circulation through the minutest and most inconsiderable parts thereof?

191. Qu. If we had a mint for coining only shillings, sixpences, and copper-money, whether the nation would not soon feel the good effects thereof?

192. Qu. Whether the greater waste by wearing of small coins would not be abundantly overbalanced by their usefulness?

193. Qu. Whether it be not the industry of common people that feeds the State, and whether it be possible to keep this industry alive without small money?

194. Qu. Whether the want of this be not a great bar to our employing the people in these manufactures which are open to us, and do not interfere with Great Britain?

195. Qu. Whether therefore such want doth not drive men into the lazy way of employing land under sheep-walk?

196. Qu. Whether the running of wool from Ireland can so effectually be prevented as by encouraging other business and manufactures among our people?

197. Qu. Whatever commodities Great Britain importeth which we might supply, whether it be not her real interest to import them from us rather than from any other people?

198. Qu. Whether the apprehension of many among us (who for that very reason stick to their wool), that England may hereafter prohibit, limit, or discourage our linen trade, when it hath been once, with great pains and expense, thoroughly introduced and settled in this land, be not altogether groundless and unjust?

199. Qu. Whether it is possible for this country, which hath neither mines of gold nor a free trade, to support for any time the sending out of specie?

200. Qu. Whether in fact our payments are not made by bills? And whether our foreign credit doth not depend on our domestic industry, and our bills on that credit?

201. Qu. Whether, in order to mend it, we ought not first to know the peculiar wretchedness of our state? And whether there be any knowing of this but by comparison?

202. Qu. Whether there are not single market towns in England that turn more money in buying and selling than whole counties (perhaps provinces) with us?

203. Qu. Whether the small town of Birmingham alone doth not, upon an average, circulate every week, one way or other, to the value of fifty thousand pounds? But whether the same crown may not be often paid?

204. Qu. Whether there be any woollen manufacture in Birmingham?

205. Qu. Whether bad management may not be worse than slavery? And whether any part of Christendom be in a more languishing condition than this kingdom?

206. Qu. Whether any kingdom in Europe be so good a customer at Bordeaux as Ireland?

207. Qu. Whether the police and economy of France be not governed by wise councils? And whether any one from this country, who sees their towns, and manufactures, and commerce, will not wonder what our senators have been doing?

208. Qu. What variety and number of excellent manufactures are to be met with throughout the whole kingdom of France?

209. Qu. Whether there are not everywhere some or other mills for many uses, forges and furnaces for iron-work, looms for tapestry, glass-houses, and so forth?

210. Qu. What quantities of paper, stockings, hats; what manufactures of wool, silk, linen, hemp, leather, wax, earthenware, brass, lead, tin, &c?

211. Qu. Whether the manufactures and commerce of the single town of Lyons do not amount to a greater value than all the manufactures and all the trade of this kingdom taken together?

212. Qu. Whether it be not true, that within the compass of one year there flowed from the South Sea, when that commerce was open, into the single town of St. Malo's, a sum in gold and silver equal to four times the whole specie of this kingdom? And whether that same part of France doth not at present draw from Cadiz, upwards of two hundred thousand pounds per annum?

213. Qu. Whether, in the anniversary fair at the small town of Beaucaire upon the Rhone, there be not as much money laid out as the current cash of this kingdom amounts to?

214. Qu. Whether it be true that the Dutch make ten millions of livres, every return of the flota and galleons, by their sales at the Indies and at Cadiz?

215. Qu. Whether it be true that England makes at least one hundred thousand pounds per annum by the single article of hats sold in Spain?

216. Qu. Whether the very shreds shorn from woollen cloth, which are thrown away in Ireland, do not make a beautiful tapestry in France?

217. Qu. Whether the toys of Thiers do not employ five thousand families?

218. Qu. Whether there be not a small town Or two in France which supply all Spain with cards?

219. Qu. Whether there be not French towns subsisted merely by making pins?

220. Qu. Whether the coarse fingers of those very women, those same peasants who one part of the year till the ground and dress the vineyards, are not another employed in making the finest French point?

221. Qu. Whether there is not a great number of idle fingers among the wives and daughters of our peasants?
222. Qu. Whether, about twenty-five years ago, they did not first attempt to make porcelain in France; and whether, in a few years, they did not make it so well, as to rival that which comes from China?
223. Qu. Whether the French do not raise a trade from saffron, dyeing drugs, and the like products, which may do with us as well as with them?
224. Qu. Whether we may not have materials of our own growth to supply all manufactures, as well as France, except silk, and whether the bulk of what silk even France manufactures be not imported?
225. Qu. Whether it be possible for this country to grow rich, so long as what is made by domestic industry is spent in foreign luxury?
226. Qu. Whether part of the profits of the bank should not be employed in erecting manufactures of several kinds, which are not likely to be set on foot and carried on to perfection without great stock, public encouragement, general regulations, and the concurrence of many hands?
227. Qu. Whether our natural Irish are not partly Spaniards and partly Tartars, and whether they do not bear signatures of their descent from both these nations, which is also confirmed by all their histories?
228. Qu. Whether the Tartar progeny is not numerous in this land? And whether there is an idler occupation under the sun than to attend flocks and herds of cattle?
229. Qu. Whether the wisdom of the State should not wrestle with this hereditary disposition of our Tartars, and with a high hand introduce agriculture?
230. Qu. Whether it were not to be wished that our people shewed their descent from Spain, rather by their honour and honesty than their pride, and if so, whether they might not easily insinuate themselves into a larger share of the Spanish trade?
231. Qu. Whether once upon a time France did not, by her linen alone, draw yearly from Spain about eight millions of livres?
232. Qu. Whether the French have not suffered in their linen trade with Spain, by not making their cloth of due breadth; and whether any other people have suffered, and are still likely to suffer, through the same prevarication?
233. Qu. Whether the Spaniards are not rich and lazy, and whether they have not a particular inclination and favour for the inhabitants of this island? But whether a punctual people do not love punctual dealers?
234. Qu. Whether about fourteen years ago we had not come into a considerable share of the linen trade with Spain, and what put a stop to this?
235. Qu. Whether we may not, with common industry and common honesty, undersell any nation in Europe?
236. Qu. Whether, if the linen manufacture were carried on in the other provinces as well as in the North, the merchants of Cork, Limerick, and Galway would not soon find the way to Spain?
237. Qu. Whether the woollen manufacture of England is not divided into several parts or branches, appropriated to particular places, where they are only or principally manufactured; fine cloths in Somersetshire, coarse in Yorkshire, long ells at Exeter, saies at Sudbury, crapes at Norwich, linseys at Kendal, blankets at Witney, and so forth?
238. Qu. Whether the united skill, industry, and emulation of many together on the same work be not the way to advance it? And whether it had been otherwise possible for England to have carried on her woollen manufacture to so great perfection?
239. Qu. Whether it would not on many accounts be right if we observed the same course with respect to our linen manufacture; and that diapers were made in one town or district, damasks in another, sheeting in a third, fine wearing linen in a fourth, coarse in a fifth, in another cambrics, in another thread and stockings, in others stamped linen, or striped linen, or tickings,

or dyed linen, of which last kinds there is so great a consumption among the seafaring men of all nations?

240. Qu. Whether it may not be worth while to inform ourselves of the different sorts of linen which are in request among different people?

241. Qu. Whether we do not yearly consume of French wines about a thousand tuns more than either Sweden or Denmark, and yet whether those nations pay ready money as we do?

242. Qu. Whether they are not the Swiss that make hay and gather in the harvest throughout Alsatia?

243. Qu. Whether it be not a custom for some thousands of Frenchmen to go about the beginning of March into Spain, and having tilled the lands and gathered the harvest of Spain, to return home with money in their pockets about the end of November?

244. Qu. Whether of late years our Irish labourers do not carry on the same business in England to the great discontent of many there? But whether we have not much more reason than the people of England to be displeased at this commerce?

245. Qu. Whether, notwithstanding the cash supposed to be brought into it, any nation is, in truth, a gainer by such traffic?

246. Qu. Whether the industry of our people employed in foreign lands, while our own are left uncultivated, be not a great loss to the country?

247. Qu. Whether it would not be much better for us, if, instead of sending our men abroad, we could draw men from the neighbouring countries to cultivate our own?

248. Qu. Whether, nevertheless, we are not apt to think the money imported by our labourers to be so much clear gains to this country, but whether a little reflexion and a little political arithmetic may not shew us our mistake?

249. Qu. Whether our prejudices about gold and silver are not very apt to infect or misguide our judgments and reasonings about the public weal?

250. Qu. Whether it be not a good rule whereby to judge of the trade of any city, and its usefulness, to observe whether there is a circulation through the extremities, and whether the people round about are busy and warm?

251. Qu. Whether we had not, some years since, a manufacture of hats at Athlone, and of earthenware at Arklow, and what became of those manufactures?

252. Qu. Why we do not make tiles of our own, for flooring and roofing, rather than bring them from Holland?

253. Qu. What manufactures are there in France and Venice of gilt-leather, how cheap and how splendid a furniture?

254. Qu. Whether we may not, for the same use, manufacture divers things at home of more beauty and variety than wainscot, which is imported at such expense from Norway?

255. Qu. Whether the use and the fashion will not soon make a manufacture?

256. Qu. Whether, if our gentry used to drink mead and cider, we should not soon have those liquors in the utmost perfection and plenty?

257. Qu. Whether it be not wonderful that with such pastures, and so many black cattle, we do not find ourselves in cheese?

258. Qu. Whether great profits may not be made by fisheries; but whether those of our Irish who live by that business do not contrive to be drunk and unemployed one half of the year?

259. Qu. Whether it be not folly to think an inward commerce cannot enrich a State, because it doth not increase its quantity of gold and silver? And whether it is possible a country should not thrive, while wants are supplied, and business goes on?

260. Qu. Whether plenty of all the necessaries and comforts of life be not real wealth?

261. Qu. Whether Lyons, by the advantage of her midland situation and the rivers Rhone and Saone, be not a great magazine or mart for inward commerce? And whether she doth not maintain a constant trade with most parts of France; with Provence for oils and dried fruits, for wines and cloth with Languedoc, for stuffs with Champagne, for linen with Picardy, Normandy, and Brittany, for corn with Burgundy?

262. Qu. Whether she doth not receive and utter all those commodities, and raise a profit from the distribution thereof, as well as of her own manufactures, throughout the kingdom of France?

263. Qu. Whether the charge of making good roads and navigable rivers across the country would not be really repaid by an inward commerce?

264. Qu. Whether, as our trade and manufactures increased, magazines should not be established in proper places, fitted by their situation, near great roads and navigable rivers, lakes, or canals, for the ready reception and distribution of all sorts of commodities from and to the several parts of the kingdom; and whether the town of Athlone, for instance, may not be fitly situated for such a magazine, or centre of domestic commerce?

265. Qu. Whether an inward trade would not cause industry to flourish, and multiply the circulation of our coin, and whether this may not do as well as multiplying the coin itself?

266. Qu. Whether the benefits of a domestic commerce are sufficiently understood and attended to; and whether the cause thereof be not the prejudiced and narrow way of thinking about gold and silver?

267. Qu. Whether there be any other more easy and unenvied method of increasing the wealth of a people?

268. Qu. Whether we of this island are not from our peculiar circumstances determined to this very commerce above any other, from the number of necessaries and good things that we possess within ourselves, from the extent and variety of our soil, from the navigable rivers and good roads which we have or may have, at a less expense than any people in Europe, from our great plenty of materials for manufactures, and particularly from the restraints we lie under with regard to our foreign trade?

269. Qu. Whether commissioners of trade or other proper persons should not be appointed to draw up plans of our commerce both foreign and domestic, and lay them at the beginning of every session before the Parliament?

270. Qu. Whether registers of industry should not be kept, and the pubic from time to time acquainted what new manufactures are introduced, what increase or decrease of old ones?

271. Qu. Whether annual inventories should not be published of the fairs throughout the kingdom, in order to judge of the growth of its commerce?

272. Qu. Whether there be not every year more cash circulated at the card tables of Dublin than at all the fairs of Ireland?

273. Qu. Whether the wealth of a country will not bear proportion to the skill and industry of its inhabitants?

274. Qu. Whether foreign imports that tend to promote industry should not be encouraged, and such as have a tendency to promote luxury should not be discouraged?

275. Qu. Whether the annual balance of trade between Italy and Lyons be not about four millions in favour of the former, and yet, whether Lyons be not a gainer by this trade?

276. Qu. Whether the general rule, of determining the profit of a commerce by its balance, doth not, like other general rules, admit of exceptions?

277. Qu. Whether it would not be a monstrous folly to import nothing but gold and silver, supposing we might do it, from every foreign part to which we trade? And yet, whether some men may not think this foolish circumstance a very happy one?

278. Qu. But whether we do not all see the ridicule of the Mogul's subjects, who take from us nothing but our silver, and bury it under ground, in order to make sure thereof against the resurrection?

279. Qu. Whether he must not be a wrongheaded patriot or politician, whose ultimate view was drawing money into a country, and keeping it there?

280. Qu. Whether it be not evident that not gold but industry causeth a country to flourish?

281. Qu. Whether it would not be a silly project in any nation to hope to grow rich by prohibiting the exportation of gold and silver?

282. Qu. Whether there can be a greater mistake in politics than to measure the wealth of the

nation by its gold and silver?

283. Qu. Whether gold and silver be not a drug, where they do not promote industry? Whether they be not even the bane and undoing of an idle people?

284. Qu. Whether gold will not cause either industry or vice to flourish? And whether a country, where it flowed in without labour, must not be wretched and dissolute like an island inhabited by buccaneers?

285. Qu. Whether arts and vertue are not likely to thrive, where money is made a means to industry? But whether money without this would be a blessing to any people?

286. Qu. Whether therefore Mississippi, South Sea, and such like schemes were not calculated for pubic ruin?

287. Qu. Whether keeping cash at home, or sending it abroad, just as it most serves to promote industry, be not the real interest of every nation?

288. Qu. Whether commodities of all kinds do not naturally flow where there is the greatest demand? Whether the greatest demand for a thing be not where it is of most use? Whether money, like other things, hath not its proper use? Whether this use be not to circulate? Whether therefore there must not of course be money where there is a circulation of industry?

289. Qu. Whether all such princes and statesmen are not greatly deceived who imagine that gold and silver, any way got, will enrich a country?

290. Qu. Whether it is not a great point to know what we would be at? And whether whole States, as well as private persons, do not often fluctuate for want of this knowledge?

291. Qu. Whether gold may not be compared to Sejanus's horse, if we consider its passage through the world, and the fate of those nations which have been successively possess'd thereof?

292. Qu. Whether the effect is not to be considered more than the kind or quantity of money?

293. Qu. Whether means are not so far useful as they answer the end? And whether, in different circumstances, the same ends are not obtained by different means?

294. Qu. If we are a poor nation, abounding with very poor people, will it not follow that a far greater proportion of our stock should be in the smallest and lowest species than would suit with England?

295. Qu. Whether, therefore, it would not be highly expedient if our money were coined of peculiar values, best fitted to the circumstances and uses of our own country; and whether any other people could take umbrage at our consulting our own convenience, in an affair entirely domestic, and that lies within ourselves?

296. Qu. Whether every man doth not know, and hath not long known, that the want of a mint causeth many other wants in this kingdom?

297. Qu. What harm did England sustain about three centuries ago, when silver was coined in this kingdom?

298. Qu. What harm was it to Spain that her provinces of Naples and Sicily had all along mints of their own?

299. Qu. Whether those who have the interests of this kingdom at heart, and are concerned in the councils thereof, ought not to make the most humble and earnest representations to his Majesty, that he may vouchsafe to grant us that favour, the want of which is ruinous to our domestic industry, and the having of which would interfere with no interest of our fellow-subjects?

300. Qu. Whether it may not be presumed that our not having a privilege which every other kingdom in the world enjoys, be not owing to our want of diligence and unanimity in soliciting for it?

301. Qu. Whether his most gracious Majesty hath ever been addressed on this head in a proper manner, and had the case fairly stated for his royal consideration, and if not, whether we may not blame ourselves?

302. Qu. If his Majesty would be pleased to grant us a mint, whether the consequences thereof may not prove a valuable consideration to the crown?

303. Qu. Whether it be not the interest of England that we should cultivate a domestic commerce among ourselves? And whether it could give them any possible jealousy, if our small sum of cash was contrived to go a little further, if there was a little more life in our markets, a little more buying and selling in our shops, a little better provision for the backs and bellies of so many forlorn wretches throughout the towns and villages of this island?
304. Qu. Whether Great Britain ought not to promote the prosperity of her Colonies, by all methods consistent with her own? And whether the Colonies themselves ought to wish or aim at it by others?
305. Qu. Whether the remotest parts from the metropolis, and the lowest of the people, are not to be regarded as the extremities and capillaries of the political body?
306. Qu. Whether, although the capillary vessels are small, yet obstructions in them do not produce great chronical diseases?
307. Qu. Whether faculties are not enlarged and improved by exercise?
308. Qu. Whether the sum of the faculties put into act, or, in other words, the united action of a whole people, doth not constitute the momentum of a State?
309. Qu. Whether such momentum be not the real stock or wealth of a State; and whether its credit be not proportional thereunto?
310. Qu. Whether in every wise State the faculties of the mind are not most considered?
311. Qu. Whether every kind of employment or business, as it implies more skill and exercise of the higher powers, be not more valued?
312. Qu. Whether the momentum of a State doth not imply the whole exertion of its faculties, intellectual and corporeal; and whether the latter without the former could act in concert?
313. Qu. Whether the divided force of men, acting singly, would not be a rope of sand?
314. Qu. Whether the particular motions of the members of a State, in opposite directions, will not destroy each other, and lessen the momentum of the whole; but whether they must not conspire to produce a great effect?
315. Qu. Whether the ready means to put spirit into this State, to fortify and increase its momentum, would not be a national bank, and plenty of small cash?
316. Qu. Whether private endeavours without assistance from the public are likely to advance our manufactures and commerce to any great degree? But whether, as bills uttered from a national bank upon private mortgages would facilitate the purchases and projects of private men, even so the same bills uttered on the public security alone may not answer pubic ends in promoting new works and manufactures throughout the kingdom?
317. Qu. Whether that which employs and exerts the force of a community deserves not to be well considered and well understood?
318. Qu. Whether the immediate mover, the blood and spirits, be not money, paper, or metal; and whether the soul or will of the community, which is the prime mover that governs and directs the whole, be not the legislature?
319. Qu. Supposing the inhabitants of a country quite sunk in sloth, or even fast asleep, whether, upon the gradual awakening and exertion, first of the sensitive and locomotive faculties, next of reason and reflexion, then of justice and piety, the momentum of such country or State would not, in proportion thereunto, become still more and more considerable?
320. Qu. Whether that which in the growth is last attained, and is the finishing perfection of a people, be not the first thing lost in their declension?
321. Qu. Whether force be not of consequence, as it is exerted; and whether great force without great wisdom may not be a nuisance?
322. Qu. Whether the force of a child, applied with art, may not produce greater effects than that of a giant? And whether a small stock in the hands of a wise State may not go further, and produce more considerable effects, than immense sums in the hands of a foolish one?
323. Qu. Whether as many as wish well to their country ought not to aim at increasing its momentum?
324. Qu. Whose fault is it if poor Ireland still continues poor?

A Defence of Free-Thinking in Mathematics

In answer
To a Pamphlet of Philalethes Cantabrigiensis, intituled, Geometry no Friend to Infidelity, or a Defence of Sir ISAAC NEWTON, and the BRITISH Mathematicians.
Also an Appendix concerning Mr. WALTON's Vindication of the Principles of Fluxions contained in the ANALYST

A Defence of Free-Thinking in Mathematics

I. When I read your Defence of the British Mathematicians, I could not Sir, but admire your Courage in asserting with such undoubting Assurance things so easily disproved. This to me seemed unaccountable, till I reflected on what you say (P. 32.) when upon my having appealed to every thinking Reader, whether it be possible to frame any clear Conception of Fluxions, you express your self in the following manner, "Pray sir who are those thinking Readers you appeal to? Are they Geometricians or Persons wholly ignorant of Geometry? If the former I leave it to them: if the latter, I ask how well are they qualified to judge of the Method of Fluxions?" It must be acknowledged you seem by this Dilemma secure in the favour of one Part of your Readers, and the ignorance of the other. I am nevertheless persuaded there are fair and candid Men among the Mathematicians. And for those who are not Mathematicians, I shall endeavour so to unveil this Mystery, and put the Controversy between us in such a Light, as that every Reader of ordinary Sense and Reflection may be a competent Judge thereof.

II. You express an extreme Surprize and Concern, "that I should take so much Pains to depreciate one of the noblest Sciences, to disparage and traduce a Set of learned Men whose Labours so greatly conduce to the Honour of this Island (P. 5), to lessen the Reputation and Authority of Sir Isaac Newton and his Followers, by shewing that they are not such Masters of Reason as they are generally presumed to be; and to depreciate the Science they profess, by demonstrating to the World, that it is not of that Clearness and certainty as is commonly imagined." All which, you insist, "appears very strange to you and the rest of that famous University, who plainly see of how great Use Mathematical Learning is to Mankind." Hence you take occasion to declaim on the usefulness of Mathematics in the several Branches, and then to redouble your Surprize and Amazement (P. 19 and 20). To all which Declamation I reply that it is quite beside the Purpose. For I allow, and always have allowed, its full claim of Merit to whatever is useful and true in the Mathematics: But that which is not so, the less it employs Men's time and thoughts, the better. And after all you have said or can say, I believe the unprejudiced Reader will think with me, that things obscure are not therefore sacred; and that it is no more a Crime, to canvass and detect unsound Principles or false Reasonings in Mathematics, than in any other Part of Learning.

III. You are, it seems, much at a loss to understand the Usefulness or Tendency or Prudence of my Attempt. I thought I had sufficiently explained this in the Analyst. But for your further Satisfaction shall here tell you, it is very well known, that several Persons who deride Faith and Mysteries in Religion, admit the Doctrine of Fluxions for true and certain. Now if it be shewn that Fluxions are really most incomprehensible Mysteries, and that those, who believe them to be clear and scientific, do entertain an implicite Faith in the Author of that Method; will not this furnish a fair Argumentum ad Hominem against Men, who reject that very thing in Religion which they admit in humane Learning? And is it not a proper Way to abate the Pride, and discredit the Pretensions of those, who insist upon clear Ideas in Points of Faith, if it be shewn that they do without them even in Science?

IV. As to my timing this Charge; why now and not before, since I had published Hints thereof many Years ago? Surely I am obliged to give no Account of this: If what hath been said in the

Analyst be not sufficient; suppose that I had not Leisure, or that I did not think it expedient, or that I had no Mind to it. When a Man thinks fit to publish any Thing, either in Mathematics, or in any other Part of Learning; what avails it, or indeed what Right hath any one to ask, why at this or that Time; in this or that Manner; upon this or that Motive? Let the Reader judge, if it suffice not, that what I publish is true, and that I have a Right to publish such Truths, when and how I please in a free Country.

V. I do not say, that Mathematicians, as such, are Infidels; or that Geometry is a Friend to Infidelity, which you untruly insinuate, as you do many other Things; whence you raise Topics for invective: But I say there are certain Mathematicians, who are known to be so; and that there are others, who are not Mathematicians, who are influenced by a Regard for their Authority. Some perhaps, who live in the University, may not be apprised of this; but the intelligent and observing Reader, who lives in the World, and is acquainted with the Humour of the Times, and the Characters of Men, is well aware, there are too many that deride Mysteries, and yet admire Fluxions; who yield that Faith to a mere Mortal, which they deny to Jesus Christ, whose Religion they make it their Study and Business to discredit. The owning this is not to own, that Men who reason well, are Enemies to Religion, as you would represent it: On the contrary, I endeavour to shew, that such men are defective in Point of Reason and Judgement, and that they do the very Thing they would seem to despise.

VI. There are, I make no doubt, among the Mathematicians many sincere Believers in Jesus Christ; I know several such my self; but I addressed my Analyst to an Infidel; and on very good Grounds, I supposed that besides him, there were other Deriders of Faith, who had nevertheless a profound Veneration for Fluxions; and I was willing to set forth the Inconsistence of such Men. If there be no such Thing as Infidels, who pretend to Knowledge in the modern Analysis, I own my self misinformed, and shall gladly be found in a Mistake; but even in that Case, my Remarks upon Fluxions are not the less true; nor will it follow, that I have no Right to examine them on the Foot of Humane Science, even though Religion were quite unconcerned, and though I had no End to serve but Truth. But you are very angry (P. 13 and 14.) that I should enter the Lists with reasoning Infidels, and attack them upon their Pretensions to Science: And hence you take Occasion to shew your Spleen against the Clergy. I will not take upon me to say, that I know you to be a Minute Philosopher your self: But I know, the Minute Philosophers make just such Compliments as you do to our Church, and are just as angry as you can be at any, who undertake to defend Religion by Reason. If we resolve all into Faith, they laugh at us and our Faith: And if we attempt to Reason, they are angry at us: They pretend we go out of our Province, and they recommend to us a blind implicite Faith. Such is the Inconsistence of our Adversaries. But it is to be hoped, there will never be wanting Men to deal with them at their own Weapons; and to shew, they are by no Means those Masters of Reason; which they would fain pass for.

VII. I do not say, as you would represent me, that we have no better Reason for our Religion, than you have for Fluxions: but I say, that an Infidel, who believes the Doctrine of Fluxions, acts a very inconsistent Part, in pretending to reject the Christian Religion, because he cannot believe what he doth not comprehend; or because he cannot assent without Evidence; or because he cannot submit his Faith to Authority. Whether there are such Infidels, I submit to the Judgement of the Reader. For my own Part I make no Doubt of it, having seen some shrewd Signs thereof my self, and having been very credibly informed thereof by others. Nor doth this Charge seem the less credible, for your being so sensibly touched, and denying it with so much Passion. You, indeed, do not stick to affirm, that the persons who informed me are a pack of base profligate and impudent liars (P. 27). How far the Reader will think fit to adopt your passions I cannot say; but I can truly say, the late celebrated Mr. Addison is one of the persons, whom you are pleased to characterize in those modest and mannerly terms. He assured me that the Infidelity of a certain noted Mathematician, still living, was one principal reason assigned by a witty man of those times for his being an Infidel. Not, that I imagine Geometry disposeth men to Infidelity; but that from other causes, such as Presumption,

Ignorance, or Vanity, like other Men Geometricians also become Infidels, and that the supposed light and evidence of their science gains credit to their Infidelity.

VIII. You reproach me with "Calumny, detraction, and artifice" (P. 15). You recommend such means as are "innocent and just, rather than the criminal method of lessening or detracting from my opponents" (ibid.). You accuse me of the "odium Theologicum, the intemperate Zeal of Divines," that I do "stare super vias antiquas," (P. 13.) with much more to the same effect. For all which charge I depend on the reader's candour, that he will not take your word, but read and judge for himself. In which case he will be able to discern (though he should be no Mathematician) how passionate and unjust your reproaches are, and how possible it is, for a man to cry out against Calumny and practise it in the same breath. Considering how impatient all mankind are when their prejudices are looked into, I do not wonder to see you rail and rage at the rate you do. But if your own Imagination be strongly shocked and moved, you cannot therefore conclude, that a sincere endeavour to free a science, so useful and ornamental to Humane Life, from those subtilties, obscurities, and paradoxes which render it inaccessible to most men, will be thought a criminal undertaking by such as are in their right mind. Much less can you hope that an illustrious Seminary of Learned men, which hath produced so many free-spirited inquirers after Truth, will at once enter into your passions and degenerate into a nest of Bigots.

IX. I observe upon the Inconsistency of certain Infidel Analysts. I remark some defects in the principles of the modern Analysis. I take the liberty decently to dissent from Sir Isaac Newton. I propose some helps to abridge the trouble of Mathematical studies and render them more useful. What is there in all this that should make you declaim on the usefulness of practical Mathematics? that should move you to cry out Spain, Inquisition, Odium Theologicum? By what figure of Speech, do you extend, what is said of the modern Analysis, to Mathematics in general, or what is said of Mathematical Infidels to all Mathematicians, or the confuting an errour in Science to burning or hanging the Authors? But it is nothing new or strange, that men should choose to indulge their passions, rather than quit their opinions how absurd soever. Hence the frightful visions and tragical uproars of Bigoted men, be the Subject of their Bigotry what it will. A very remarkable instance of this you give (P. 27) where, upon my having said that a deference to certain Mathematical Infidels, as I was credibly informed, had been one motive to Infidelity, you ask with no small emotion, "For God's sake are we in England or in Spain? Is this the language of a Familiar who is whispering an Inquisitor, &c?" And the page before you exclaim in the following Words. "Let us burn or hang up all the Mathematicians in Great Britain, or halloo the mob upon them to tear them to pieces every Mother's son of them, Tros Rutulusve fuat, Laymen or Clergymen, &c. Let us dig up the bodies of Dr. Barrow and Sir Isaac Newton, and burn them under the Gallows," &c.

X. The Reader need not be a Mathematician, to see how vain all this tragedy of yours is. And if he be as thoroughly satisfied as I am, that the cause of Fluxions cannot be defended by reason, he will be as little surprised as I am, to see you betake your self to the arts of all bigoted men, raising terrour and calling in the passions to your assistance. Whether those Rhetorical flourishes about the Inquisition and the Gallies are not quite ridiculous, I leave to be determined by the Reader. Who will also judge (though he should not be skilled in Geometry) whether I have given the least grounds, for this and a World of such like declamation? and whether I have not constantly treated those celebrated Writers, with all proper respect, though I take the liberty in certain points to differ from them?

XI. As I heartily abhor an Inquisition in Faith, so I think you have no right to erect one in Science. At the time of writing your defence you seem to have been overcome with Passion: But now you may be supposed cool, I desire you to reflect whether it be not wrote in the true spirit of an Inquisitor. Whether this becomes a Person so exceeding delicate himself upon that Point? And whether your Brethren the Analysts will think themselves honoured or obliged by you, for having defended their Doctrine, in the same manner as any declaiming Bigot would defend Transubstantiation? The same false colours, the same intemperate Sallies, and the same

Indignation against common Sense!

XII. In a matter of mere Science, where authority hath nothing to do, you constantly endeavour to overbear me with authorities, and load me with envy. If I see a Sophism in the writings of a great Author, and, in compliment to his understanding, suspect he could hardly be quite satisfyed with his own demonstration: This sets you on declaiming for several pages. It is pompously set forth, as a criminal method of detracting from great men, as a concerted project to lessen their reputation, as making them pass for imposters. If I publish my free thoughts, which I have as much right to publish as any other man, it is imputed to rashness and vanity and the love of opposition. Though perhaps my late publication, of what had been hinted twenty five years ago, may acquit me of this charge in the eyes of an impartial Reader. But when I consider the perplexities that beset a man, who undertakes to defend the doctrine of Fluxions, I can easily forgive your anger.

XIII. Two sorts of learned men there are: one, who candidly seek Truth by rational means. These are never averse to have their principles looked into, and examined by the test of Reason. Another sort there is who learn by route a set of principles and a way of thinking which happen to be in vogue. These betray themselves by their anger and surprise, whenever their principles are freely canvassed. But you must not expect, that your Reader will make himself a party to your passions or your prejudices. I freely own that Sir Isaac Newton hath shew'd himself an extraordinary Mathematician, a profound Naturalist, a Person of the greatest Abilities and Erudition. Thus far I can readily go, but I cannot go the lengths that you do. I shall never say of him as you do, Vestigia pronus adoro (P. 70). This same adoration that you pay to him, I will pay only to Truth.

XIV. You may, indeed, your self be an Idolater of whom you please: But then you have no right to insult and exclaim at other men, because they do not adore your Idol. Great as Sir Isaac Newton was, I think he hath, on more occasions than one, shew'd himself not to be infallible. Particularly, his demonstration of the Doctrine of Fluxions I take to be defective, and I cannot help thinking that he was not quite pleased with it himself. And yet this doth not hinder but the method may be useful, considered as an art of Invention. You, who are a Mathematician, must acknowledge, there have been divers such methods admitted in Mathematics, which are not demonstrative. Such, for instance, are the Inductions of Doctor Wallis in his Arithmetic of Infinites, and such, what Harriot and, after him, Descartes have wrote concerning the roots of affected Æquations. It will not, nevertheless, thence follow that those methods are useless; but only, that they are not to be allowed of as Premises in a strict Demonstration.

XV. No great Name upon earth shall ever make me accept things obscure for clear, or Sophisms for Demonstrations. Nor may you ever hope to deter me from freely speaking what I freely think, by those arguments ad invidia which at every turn you employ against me. You represent your self (P. 52) as a man, "whose highest ambition is in the lowest degree to imitate Sir Isaac Newton." It might, perhaps, have suited better with your appellation of Philalethes, and been altogether as laudable, if your highest ambition had been to discover Truth. Very consistently with the character you give of your self, you speak of it as a sort of crime (P. 70) to think it possible, you should ever "see further, or go beyond Sir Isaac Newton." And I am persuaded you speak the Sentiments of many more besides your self. But there are others who are not afraid to sift the Principles of human Science, who think it no honour to imitate the greatest man in his Defects, who even think it no crime to desire to know, not only beyond Sir Isaac Newton, but beyond all mankind. And whoever thinks otherwise, I appeal to the Reader, whether he can properly be called a Philosopher.

XVI. Because I am not guilty of your mean Idolatry, you inveigh against me as a person conceited of my own Abilities; not considering that a person of less Abilities may know more on a certain point than one of greater; not considering that a purblind eye, in a close and narrow view, may discern more of a thing, than a much better eye in a more extensive prospect; not considering that this is to fix a ne plus ultra, to put a stop to all future inquiries;

Lastly, not considering that this is in fact, so much as in you lies, converting the Republick of Letters into an absolute monarchy, that it is even introducing a kind of Philosophic Popery among a free People.

XVII. I have said (and I venture still to say) that a Fluxion is incomprehensible: That second, third and fourth Fluxions are yet more incomprehensible: That it is not possible to conceive a simple Infinitesimal: That it is yet less possible to conceive an Infinitesimal of an Infinitesimal, and so onward. [NOTE: Analyst, Sect. 4, 5, 6, &c.] What have you to say in answer to this? Do you attempt to clear up the notion of a Fluxion or a Difference? Nothing like it; you only "assure me (upon your bare word) from your own experience, and that of several others whom you could name, that the Doctrine of Fluxions may be clearly conceived and distinctly comprehended; and that if I am puzzled about it and do not understand it, yet others do." But can you think, Sir, I shall take your word when I refuse to take your Master's?

XVIII. Upon this point every Reader of common sense may judge as well as the most profound Mathematician. The simple apprehension of a thing defined is not made more perfect by any subsequent progress in Mathematics. What any man evidently knows, he knows as well as you or Sir Isaac Newton. And every one can know whether the object of this method be (as you would have us think) clearly conceivable. To judge of this, no depth of Science is requisite, but only a bare attention to what passes in his own mind. And the same is to be understood of all definitions in all Sciences whatsoever. In none of which can it be supposed, that a man of Sense and Spirit will take any definition or principle on trust, without sifting it to the bottom, and trying how far he can or he cannot conceive it. This is the course I have taken and shall take, however you and your Brethren may declaim against it, and place it in the most invidious Light.

XIX. It is usual with you to admonish me to look over a second time, to consult, examine, weigh the words of Sir Isaac. In answer to which I will venture to say, that I have taken as much pains as (I sincerely believe) any man living, to understand that great Author and to make sense of his principles. No industry nor caution nor attention, I assure you, have been wanting on my part. So that, if I do not understand him, it is not my fault but my misfortune. Upon other subjects you are pleased to compliment me with depth of thought and uncommon abilities, (P. 5 and 84.) But I freely own, I have no pretence to those things. The only advantage I pretend to, is that I have always thought and judged for my self. And, as I never had a master in Mathematics, so I fairly followed the dictates of my own mind in examining, and censuring the authors I read upon that subject, with the same freedom that I used upon any other; taking nothing on trust, and believing that no writer was infallible. And a man of moderate parts, who takes this painful course in studying the principles of any Science, may be supposed to walk more surely than those of greater abilities, who set out with more speed and less care.

XX. What I insist on is, that the idea of a Fluxion simply considered is not at all improved or amended by any progress, though ever so great, in the Analysis: neither are the demonstrations of the general rules of that method at all cleared up by applying them. The reason of which is, because in operating or calculating, men do not return to contemplate the original principles of the method, which they constantly presuppose, but are employed in working, by notes and symbols, denoting the Fluxions supposed to have been at first explained, and according to rules supposed to have been at first demonstrated. This I say to encourage those, who are not far gone in these Studies, to use intrepidly their own judgement, without a blind or a mean deference to the best of Mathematicians, who are no more qualified than they are, to judge of the simple apprehension, or the evidence of what is delivered in the first elements of the method; men by further and frequent use or exercise becoming only more accustomed to the symbols and rules, which doth not make either the foregoing notions more clear, or the foregoing proofs more perfect. Every Reader of common sense, that will but use his faculties, knows as well as the most profound Analyst what idea he frames or can frame of Velocity without motion, or of motion without extension, of magnitude which is neither finite nor infinite, or of a quantity having no magnitude which is yet divisible, of a figure where there is no space, of proportion between nothings, or of a real product from nothing multiplied by something. He need not be far gone in Geometry to know, that obscure principles are not to be admitted in Demonstration: That if a man destroys his own Hypothesis, he at the same time destroys what was built upon it: That errour in the premises, not rectified, must produce errour in the conclusion.

XXI. In my opinion the greatest men have their Prejudices. Men learn the elements of Science from others: And every learner hath a deference more or less to authority, especially the young learners, few of that kind caring to dwell long upon Principles, but inclining rather to take them upon trust: And things early admitted by repetition become familiar: And this familiarity at length passeth for Evidence. Now to me it seems, there are certain points tacitly admitted by Mathematicians, which are neither evident nor true. And such points or principles ever mixing with their reasonings do lead them into paradoxes and perplexities. If the great author of the fluxionary method were early imbued with such notions, it would only shew he was a man. And if by vertue of some latent errour in his principles a man be drawn into fallacious reasonings, it is nothing strange that he should take them for true: And, nevertheless, if, when urged by perplexities and uncouth consequences, and driven to arts and shifts, he should entertain some doubt thereof, it is no more than one may naturally suppose, might befall a great genius grappling with an insuperable difficulty: Which is the light in which I have placed Sir Isaac Newton. [NOTE: Analyst, Sect. 18.] Hereupon you are pleased to remark, that I represent the great author not only as a weak but an ill man, as a Deceiver and an Impostor. The Reader will judge how justly.

XXII. As to the rest of your colourings and glosses, your reproaches and insults and outcries, I shall pass them over, only desiring the Reader not to take your word, but read what I have written, and he will want no other answer. It hath been often observed that the worst cause produceth the greatest clamour, and indeed you are so clamorous throughout your defence that the Reader, although he should be no Mathematician, provided he understands common sense and hath observed the ways of men, will be apt to suspect that you are in the wrong. It should seem, therefore, that your Brethren the Analysts are but little obliged to you, for this new method of declaiming in Mathematics. Whether they are more obliged by your Reasoning I shall now examine.

XXIII. You ask me (P. 32) where I find Sir Isaac Newton using such expressions as the Velocities of Velocities, the second, third, and fourth Velocities, &c. This you set forth as a pious fraud and unfair representation. I answer, that if according to Sir Isaac Newton a Fluxion be the velocity of an increment, then according to him I may call the Fluxion of a Fluxion the Velocity of a Velocity. But for the truth of the antecedent see his introduction to the Quadrature of Curves, where his own words are, motuum vel incrementorum velocitates nominando Fluxiones. See also the second Lemma of the second Book of his mathematical principles of natural Philosophy where he expresseth himself in the following manner, velocitates incrementorum ac decrementorum quas etiam, motus, mutationes & fluxiones quantitatum nominare licet. And that he admits Fluxions of Fluxions, or second, third, fourth Fluxions, &c. see his Treatise of the Quadrature of Curves. I ask now, Is it not plain, that if a Fluxion be a Velocity, then the Fluxion of a Fluxion may agreeably thereunto be called the Velocity of a Velocity? In like manner if by a Fluxion is meant a nascent augment, will it not then follow, that the Fluxion of a Fluxion or second Fluxion is the nascent augment of a nascent augment? Can anything be plainer? Let the Reader now judge who is unfair.

XXIV. I had observed, that the Great Author had proceeded illegitimately, in obtaining the Fluxion or moment of the Rectangle of two flowing quantities; and that he did not fairly get rid of the Rectangle of the moments. In answer to this you alledge, that the errour arising from the omission of such rectangle (allowing it to be an errour) is so small that it is insignificant. This you dwell upon and exemplify to no other purpose, but to amuse your Reader and mislead him from the Question; which in truth is not concerning the accuracy of computing or measuring in practice, but concerning the accuracy of the reasoning in science. That this was really the case, and that the smallness of the practical errour no wise concerns it, must be so plain to any one who reads the Analyst, that I wonder how you could be ignorant of it.

XXV. You would fain persuade your Reader, that I make an absurd quarrel against errours of no significancy in practice, and represent Mathematicians as proceeding blindfold in their approximations, in all which I cannot help thinking there is on your part either great ignorance or great disingenuity. If you mean to defend the reasonableness and use of approximations or of the method of Indivisibles, I have nothing to say. But then you must remember this is not the Doctrine of Fluxions: it is none of that Analysis with which I am concerned. That I am far from quarrelling at approximations in Geometry is manifest from the thirty third and fifty third Queries in the Analyst. And that the method of Fluxions pretends to somewhat more than the method of indivisibles is plain; because Sir Isaac disclaims this method as not Geometrical. [NOTE: See the Scholium at the end of the first section. Lib. i., Phil. Nat. Prin. Math.] And that the method of Fluxions is supposed accurate in Geometrical rigour is manifest, to whoever considers what the Great Author writes about it; especially in his Introduction to the Quadrature of Curves where he saith In rebus mathematicis errores quam minimi non sunt contemnendi. Which expression you have seen quoted in the Analyst, and yet you seem ignorant thereof, and indeed, of the very end and Design of the Great Author in this his invention of Fluxions.

XXVI. As oft as you talk of finite quantities inconsiderable in practice Sir Isaac disowns your apology. Cave, saith he, intellexeris finitas. And, although Quantities less than sensible may be of no account in practice, yet none of your masters, nor will even you your self venture to say, they are of no account in Theory and in Reasoning. The application in gross practice is not the point questioned, but the rigour and justness of the reasoning. And it is evident that, be the subject ever so little, or ever so inconsiderable, this doth not hinder but that a person treating thereof may commit very great errours in Logic, which Logical errours are in no wise to be measured by the sensible or practical inconveniences thence arising, which, perchance may be none at all. It must be owned, that after you have misled and amused your less qualified Reader (as you call him) you return to the real point in controversy, and set your self to justifie Sir Isaac's method of getting rid of the abovementioned Rectangle. And here I must intreat the Reader to observe how fairly you proceed.

XXVII. First then you affirm (P. 44), "that, neither in the Demonstration of the Rule for finding the fluxion of the rectangle of two flowing quantities, nor in anything preceding or following it, is any mention so much as once made of the increment of the rectangle of such flowing quantities." Now I affirm the direct contrary. For in the very passage by you quoted in this same page, from the first case of the second lemma of the second Book of Sir Isaac's principles, beginning with Rectangulum quodvis motu perpetuo auctum, and ending with igitur laterum incrementis totis a and b generatur rectanguli incrementum aB + bA. Q.E.D. In this very passage I say is express mention made of the increment of such Rectangle. As this is matter of fact, I refer it to the Reader's own eyes. Of what rectangle have we here the Increment? is it not plainly of that whose sides have a and b for their incrementa tota, that is, of AB. Let any Reader judge whether it be not plain from the words, the sense, and the context, that the Great Author in the end of his demonstration understands his incrementum as belonging to the Rectangulum quodvis at the beginning. Is not the same also evident from the very lemma it self prefixed to the Demonstration? The sense whereof is (as the author there explains it) that if the moments of the flowing quantities A and B are called a and b, then the momentum vel mutatio geniti rectanguli AB will be aB + bA. Either therefore the conclusion of the demonstration is not the thing which was to be demonstrated, or the Rectanguli incrementum aB + bA belongs to the rectangle AB.

XXVIII. All this is so plain that nothing can be more so; and yet you would fain perplex this plain case by distinguishing between an increment and a moment. But it is evident to every one, who has any notion of Demonstration, that the incrementum in the conclusion must be the momentum in the Lemma; and to suppose it otherwise is no credit to the Author. It is in effect supposing him to be one who did not know what he would demonstrate. But let us hear Sir Isaac's own words: Earum (quantitatum scilicet fluentium) incrementa vel decrementa momentanea sub nomine momentorum intelligo. And you observe your self that he useth the word moment to signify either an increment or decrement. Hence with an intention to puzzle me you propose the increment and decrement of AB, and ask which of these I would call the moment? The case you say is difficult. My answer is very plain and easy, to wit, Either of them. You, indeed, make a different answer, and from the Author's saying that, by a moment he understands either the momentaneous increment or decrement of the flowing quantities, you would have us conclude, by a very wonderful inference, that his moment is neither the increment nor decrement thereof. Would it not be as good an inference, Because a number is either odd or even, to conclude it is neither? Can any one make sense of this? Or can even your self hope that this will go down with the Reader, how little soever qualified? It must be owned, you endeavour to obtrude this inference on him, rather by mirth and humour than by reasoning. Your are merry, I say, and (P. 46) represent the two mathematical quantities as pleading their rights, as tossing up cross and pile, as disputing amicably. You talk of their claiming preference, their agreeing, their boyishness and their gravity. And after this ingenious digression you address me in the following words —-Believe me there is no remedy, you must acquiesce. But my answer is that I will neither believe you nor acquiesce; there is a plain remedy in common sense; and to prevent surprise I desire the Reader always to keep the controverted point in view, to examine your reasons, and be cautious how he takes your word, but most of all when you are positive or eloquent or merry.

XXIX. A page or two after, you very candidly represent your case to be that of an ass between two bottles of hay: it is your own expression. The cause of your perplexity is that you know not, whether the velocity of AB increasing or of AB decreasing is to be esteemed the Fluxion, or proportional to the moment of the rectangle. My opinion, agreeably to what hath been premised, is that either may be deemed the Fluxion. But you tell us (P. 49) "that you think, the venerable ghost of Sir Isaac Newton whispers you, the Velocity you seek for is neither the one nor the other of these, but is the velocity which the flowing rectangle hath, not while it is greater or less than AB, but at that very instant of time that it is AB." For my part, in the rectangle AB considered simply in it self, without either increasing or diminishing, I can conceive no velocity at all. And if the Reader is of my mind, he will not take either your word, or even the word of a Ghost how venerable soever, for velocity without motion. You proceed and tell us that, in like manner, the moment of the rectangle is neither it's increment or decrement. This you would have us believe on the authority of his Ghost, in direct opposition to what Sir Isaac himself asserted when alive. Incrementa (saith he) vel decrementa momentanea sub nomine momentorum intelligo: ita ut incrementa pro momentis additititis seu affirmativis, ac decrementa pro subductitiis seu negativis habeantur. [NOTE: Princip. Phil. Nat. Lib. II, Lem. II.] I will not in your style bid the Reader believe me, but Believe his eyes.

XXX. To me it verily seems, that you have undertaken the defence of what you do not understand. To mend the matter, you say, "you do not consider AB as lying at either extremity of the moment, but as extended to the middle of it; as having acquired the one half of the moment, and as being about to acquire the other; or, as having lost one half of it, and being about to lose the other." Now, in the name of Truth, I entreat you to tell what this moment is, to the middle whereof the rectangle is extended? This moment, I say, which is acquired, which is lost, which is cut in two, or distinguished into halfs? Is it a finite quantity, or an infinitesimal, or a mere limit, or nothing at all? Take it in what sense you will, I cannot make your defence either consistent or intelligible. For if you take it in either of the two former senses, you contradict Sir Isaac Newton. And if you take it in either of the latter, you contradict common sense; it being plain, that what hath no magnitude, or is no quantity, cannot be divided. And here I must entreat the reader to preserve his full freedom of mind intire, and not weakly suffer his judgment to be overborn by your imagination and your prejudices, by great names and authorities, by Ghosts and Visions, and above all by that extreme satisfaction and complacency with which you utter your strange conceits; if words without a meaning may be called so. After having given this unintelligible account, you ask with your accustomed air, "What say you Sir? Is this a just and legitimate reason for Sir Isaac's proceeding as he did? I think you must acknowledge it to be so." But alas! I acknowledge no such thing. I find no sense or reason in what you say. Let the Reader find it if he can.

XXXI. In the next Place (P. 50) you charge me with want of caution. "Inasmuch (say you) as that quantity which Sir Isaac Newton through his whole Lemma, and all the several Cases of it, constantly calls a Moment, without confining it to be either an increment or decrement, is by you inconsiderately and arbitrarily, and without any Shadow of Reason given, supposed and determined to be an increment." To which Charge I reply that it is as untrue as it is peremptory. For that, in the foregoing citation from the first case of Sir Isaac's Lemma, he expressly determines it to be an Increment. And as this particular Instance or Passage was that which I objected to, it was reasonable and proper for me to consider the Moment in that same Light. But take it increment or decrement as you will, the Objections still lie and the Difficulties are equally insuperable. You then proceed to extoll the great Author of the fluxionary Method, and to bestow some Brusqueries upon those who unadvisedly dare to differ from him. To all which I shall give no answer.

XXXII. Afterwards to remove (as you say) all Scruple and Difficulty about this affair, you observe that the Moment of the Rectangle determined by Sir Isaac Newton, and the Increment of the Rectangle determined by me are perfectly and exactly equal, supposing a and b to be diminished ad infinitum: and for proof of this, you refer to the first Lemma of the first Section of the first Book of Sir Isaac's Principles. I answer, that if a and b are real quantities, then ab is something, and consequently makes a real difference: but if they are nothing, then the Rectangles whereof they are coefficients become nothing likewise: and consequently the momentum or incrementum, whether Sir Isaac's or mine, are in that Case nothing at all. As for the abovementioned Lemma, which you refer to, and which you wish I had consulted sooner, both for my own sake and for yours; I tell you I had long since consulted and considered it. But I very much doubt whether you have sufficiently considered that Lemma, it's Demonstration and it's Consequences. For, however that way of reasoning may do in the Method of exhaustions, where quantities less than assignable are regarded as nothing; yet for a Fluxionist writing about momentums, to argue that quantities must be equal because they have no assignable difference, seems the most injudicious Step that could be taken: it is directly demolishing the very Doctrine you would defend. For it will thence follow, that all homogeneous momentums are equal, and consequently the velocities, mutations, or fluxions proportional thereto, are all likewise equal. There is, therefore, only one proportion of equality throughout, which at once overthrows the whole System you undertake to defend. Your moments (I say) not being themselves assignable quantities, their differences cannot be assignable: and if this be true, by that way of reasoning it will follow, they are all equal, upon which Supposition you cannot make one Step in the Method of Fluxions. It appears from hence, how unjustly you blame me (P. 32) for omitting to give any Account of that first Section of the first Book of the Principia, wherein (you say) the Foundation of the Method of Fluxions is geometrically demonstrated and largely explained, and difficulties and objections against it are clearly solved. All which is so far from being true, that the very first and fundamental Lemma of that Section is incompatible with, and subversive of the doctrine of Fluxions. And, indeed, who sees not that a Demonstration ad absurdum more veterum proceeding on a Supposition, that every difference must be some given quantity, cannot be admitted in, or consist with, a method, wherein Quantities, less than any given, are supposed really to exist, and be capable of division?

XXXIII. The next point you undertake to defend is that method for obtaining a rule to find the Fluxion of any Power of a flowing Quantity, which is delivered in the introduction to the

Quadratures, and considered in the Analyst [NOTE: Sect. 13, 14, &c.]. And here the question between us is, whether I have rightly represented the sense of those words, evanescant jam augmenta illa, in rendering them, let the increments vanish i.e. let the increments be nothing, or let there be no increments? This you deny, but, as your manner is, instead of giving a reason you declaim. I, on the contrary affirm, the increments must be understood to be quite gone and absolutely nothing at all. My reason is, because without that supposition you can never bring the quantity or expression

down to nx^{n-1}, the very thing aimed at by supposing the evanescence. Say whether this be not the truth of the case? Whether the former expression is not to be reduced to the latter? And whether this can possibly be done so long as o is supposed a real Quantity? I cannot indeed say you are scrupulous about your affirmations, and yet I believe that even you will not affirm this; it being most evident, that the product of two real quantities is something real; and that nothing real can be rejected either according to the ἀκρίβεια of Geometry, or according to Sir Isaac's own Principles; for the truth of which I appeal to all who know any thing of these matters. Further by evanescant must either be meant let them (the increments) vanish and become nothing, in the obvious sense, or let them become infinitely small. But that this latter is not Sir Isaac's sense is evident from his own words in the very same page, that is, in the last of the Introduction to the Quadratures, where he expressly saith volui ostendere quod in methodo fluxionum non opus sit figuras infinite parvas in geometriam introducere. Upon the whole, you seem to have considered this affair so very superficially, as greatly to confirm me in the opinion, you are so angry with, to wit, that Sir Isaac's followers are much more eager in applying his method, than accurate in examining his principles. You raise a dust about evanescent augments which may perhaps amuse and amaze your Reader, but I am much mistaken if it ever instructs or enlightens him. For, to come to the point, those evanescent augments either are real quantities, or they are not. If you say they are; I desire to know, how you get rid of the rejectaneous quantity? If you say they are not; you indeed get rid of those quantities in the composition whereof they are coefficients; but then you are of the same opinion with me, which opinion you are pleased to call (P. 58) "a most palpable, inexcusable, and unpardonable blunder," although it be a Truth most palpably evident.

XXXIV. Nothing I say can be plainer to any impartial Reader, than that by the Evanescence of augments, in the above-cited passage, Sir Isaac means their being actually reduced to nothing. But to put it out of all doubt, that this is the truth, and to convince even you, who shew so little disposition to be convinced, I desire you to look into his Analysis per æquationes infinitas (P. 20) where, in his preparation for demonstrating the first rule for the squaring of simple Curves, you will find that on a parallel occasion, speaking of an augment which is supposed to vanish, he interprets the word evanescere by esse nihil. Nothing can be plainer than this, which at once destroys your defence. And yet, plain as it is, I despair of making you acknowledge it; though I am sure you feel it, and the Reader if he useth his eyes must see it. The words Evanescere sive esse nihil do (to use your own expression) stare us in the face. Lo! This is what you call (P. 56) "so great, so unaccountable, so horrid, so truly Boeotian a blunder" that, according to you, it was not possible Sir Isaac Newton could be guilty of it. For the future, I advise you to be more sparing of hard words: Since, as you incautiously deal them about, they may chance to light on your friends as well as your adversaries. As for my part, I shall not retaliate. It is sufficient to say you are mistaken. But I can easily pardon your mistakes. Though, indeed, you tell me on this very occasion, that I must expect no quarter from Sir Isaac's followers. And I tell you that I neither expect nor desire any. My aim is truth. My reasons I have given. Confute them, if you can. But think not to overbear me either with authorities or harsh words. The latter will recoil upon your selves: The former in a matter of science are of no weight with indifferent Readers; and as for Bigots, I am not concerned about what they say or think.

XXXV. In the next place you proceed to declaim upon the following passage taken from the seventeenth section of the Analyst. "Considering the various arts and devices used by the great author of the fluxionary method: in how many lights he placeth his Fluxions: and in what different ways he attempts to demonstrate the same point: One would be inclined to think, he was himself suspicious of the justness of his own demonstrations." This passage you complain of as very hard usage of Sir Isaac Newton. You declaim copiously, and endeavour to show that placing the same point in various lights is of great use to explain it; which you illustrate with much Rhetoric. But the fault of that passage is not the hard usage it contains: But on the contrary, that it is too modest, and not so full and expressive of my sense, as perhaps it should have been. Would you like it better if I should say, the various inconsistent accounts, which this great author gives of his momentums and his fluxions, may convince every intelligent Reader that he had no clear and steady notions of them, without which there can be no demonstration? I own frankly that I see no clearness or consistence in them. You tell me indeed, in Miltonic verse that the fault is in my own eyes,

So thick a drop serene has quench'd their orbs
Or dim suffusion veil'd.

at the same time you acknowledge your self obliged for those various lights, which have enabled you to understand his Doctrine. But as for me who do not understand it, you insult me saying: "For God's sake what is it you are offended at, who do not still understand him?" May not I answer, that I am offended for this very reason; because I cannot understand him or make sense of what he says? You say to me, that I am all in the dark. I acknowledge it, and intreat you who see so clearly to help me out.

XXXVI. You Sir with the bright eyes, be pleased to tell me, whether Sir Isaac's momentum be a finite quantity, or an infinitesimal, or a mere limit? If you say a finite quantity: Be pleased to reconcile this with what he saith in the Scholium of the second Lemma of the first Section of the first book of his Principles: Cave intelligas quantitates magnitudine determinatas, sed cogita semper diminuendas sine limite. If you say, an infinitesimal: reconcile this with what is said in the Introduction to the Quadratures: Volui ostendere quod in methodo Fluxionum non opus sit figuras infinite parvas in Geometriam introducere. If you should say, it is a mere limit, be pleased to reconcile this with what we find in the first case of the second Lemma in the second book of his Principles: Ubi de lateribus A et B deerant momentorum dimidia, &c. where the moments are supposed to be divided. I should be very glad, a person of such a luminous intellect would be so good as to explain, whether by Fluxions we are to understand the nascent or evanescent quantities themselves, or their motions, or their Velocities, or simply their proportions: and having interpreted them in what sense you will, that you would then condescend to explain the Doctrine of second, third, and fourth Fluxions, and shew it to be consistent with common sense if you can. You seem to be very sanguine when you express your self in the following terms: "I do assure you, Sir, from my own Experience, and that of many others whom I could name that the Doctrine may be clearly conceived and distinctly comprehended" (P. 31). And it may be uncivil not to believe what you so solemnly affirm, from your own experience. But I must needs own, I should be better satisfied of this, if, instead of entertaining us with your Rhetoric, you would vouchsafe to reconcile those difficulties, and explain those obscure points abovementioned. If either you, or any one of those many whom you could name, will but explain to others what you so clearly conceive your selves, I give you my word that several will be obliged to you who, I may venture to say, understand those matters no more than my self. But, if I am not mistaken, you and your friends will modestly decline this task.

XXXVII. I have long ago done what you so often exhort me to do, diligently read and considered the several accounts of this Doctrine given by the great Author in different parts of his writings: any upon the whole I could never make it out to be consistent and intelligible. I was even led to say, that "one would be inclined to think, He was himself suspicious of the justness of his own demonstrations: and that he was not enough pleased with any one notion steadily to adhere to it." After which I added, "Thus much is plain that he owned himself satisfied concerning certain points, which nevertheless he could not undertake to demonstrate to others." See the seventeenth section of the Analyst. It is one thing when a Doctrine is placed in various lights: and another, when the principles and notions are shifted. When new devices are introduced and substituted for others, a Doctrine instead of being illustrated may be explained away. Whether there be not something of this in the present case I appeal to the writings of the Great Author. His methodus rationum primarum et ultimarum, His second Lemma in the second book of his Principles, his Introduction and Treatise of the Quadrature of Curves. In all which it appears to me, there is not one uniform doctrine explained and carried throughout the whole, but rather sundry inconsistent accounts of this new method, which still grows more dark and confused the more it is handled: I could not help thinking, the greatest genius might lye under the influence of false principles; and where the object and notions were exceeding obscure, he might possibly distrust even his own demonstrations. "At least thus much seemed plain, that Sir Isaac had sometime owned himself satisfied, where he could not demonstrate to others." In proof whereof I mentioned his letter to Mr. Collins; Hereupon you tell me: "there is a great deal of difference between saying, I cannot undertake to prove a thing, and I will not undertake it." But in answer to this, I desire you will be pleased to consider, that I was not making a precise extract out of that letter, in which the very words of Sir Isaac should alone be inserted. But I made my own remark and inference, from what I remembered to have read in that letter; where, speaking of a certain mathematical matter, Sir Isaac expresseth himself, in the following terms: "It is plain to me by the fountain I draw it from; though I will not undertake to prove it to others." Now whether my inference may not be fairly drawn from those words of Sir Isaac Newton; and whether the difference as to the sense be so great between will and can in that particular case, I leave to be determined by the Reader.

XXXVIII. In the next paragraph you talk big but prove nothing. You speak of driving out of intrenchments, of sallying and attacking and carrying by assault; of slight and untenable works, of a new-raised and undisciplined militia, and of veteran regular troops. Need the Reader be a Mathematician to see the vanity of this paragraph? After this you employ (P. 65) your usual colouring, and represent the great Author of the Method of Fluxions "as a Good old Gentleman fast asleep, and snoring in his easy chair; while dame Fortune is bringing him her apron full of beautiful theorems and problems, which he never knows or thinks of." This you would have pass for a consequence of my notions. But I appeal to all those who are ever so little knowing in such matters, whether there are not divers fountains of Experiment, Induction, and Analogy, whence a man may derive and satisfy himself concerning the truth of many points in Mathematics and Mechanical Philosophy, although the proofs thereof afforded by the modern Analysis should not amount to demonstration? I further appeal to the conscience of all the most profound Mathematicians, whether they can, with perfect acquiescence of mind free from all scruple, apply any proposition merely upon the strength of a Demonstration involving second or third Fluxions, without the aid of any such experiment or analogy or collateral proof whatsoever? Lastly, I appeal to the Reader's own heart, whether he cannot clearly conceive a medium between being fast asleep and demonstrating? But you will have it, that I represent Sir Isaac's Conclusions as coming out right, because one errour is compensated by another contrary and equal errour, which perhaps he never knew himself nor thought of: that by a twofold mistake he arrives though not at science yet at Truth: that he proceeds blindfold, &c. All which is untruly said by you, who have misapplied to Sir Isaac what was intended for the Marquis de l'Hospital and his followers, for no other end (as I can see) but that you may have an opportunity, to draw that ingenious portraiture of Sir Isaac Newton and Dame Fortune, as will be manifest to whoever reads the Analyst.

XXXIX. You tell me (P. 70), if I think fit to persist in asserting, "that this affair of a double errour is entirely a new discovery of my own, which Sir Isaac and his followers never knew or thought of, that you have unquestionable evidence to convince me to the contrary, and that all his followers are already apprised, that this very objection of mine was long since foreseen, and clearly and fully removed by Sir Isaac Newton in the first section of the first book of his

Principia." All which I do as strongly deny as you affirm. And I do aver, that this is an unquestionable proof of the matchless contempt which you, Philalethes, have for Truth. And I do here publickly call upon you, to produce that evidence which you pretend to have, and to make good that fact which you so confidently affirm. And, at the same time, I do assure the Reader that you never will, nor can.

XL. If you defend Sir Isaac's notions as delivered in his Principia, it must be on the rigorous foot of rejecting nothing, neither admitting nor casting away infinitely small quantities. If you defend the Marquis, whom you also style your Master, it must be on the foot of admitting that there are infinitesimals, that they may be rejected, that they are nevertheless real quantities, and themselves infinitely subdivisible. But you seem to have grown giddy with passion, and in the heat of controversy to have mistaken and forgot your part. I beseech you, Sir, to consider, that the Marquis (whom alone, and not Sir Isaac this double errour in finding the subtangent doth concern) rejects indeed infinitesimals, but not on the foot that you do, to wit, their being inconsiderable in practical Geometry or mixed Mathematics. But he rejects them in the accuracy of Speculative Knowledge: in which respect there may be great Logical errours, although there should be no sensible mistake in practice: which, it seems, is what you cannot comprehend. He rejects them likewise in vertue of a Postulatum, which I venture to call rejecting them without ceremony. And though he inferreth a conclusion accurately true, yet he doth it, contrary to the rules of Logic, from inaccurate and false premises. And how this comes about, I have at large explained in the Analyst, and shewed in that particular case of Tangents, that the Rejectaneous Quantity might have been a finite quantity of any given magnitude, and yet the conclusion have come out exactly the same way; and consequently, that the truth of this method doth not depend on the reason assigned by the Marquis, to wit, the postulatum for throwing away Infinitesimals, and therefore that he and his follows acted blindfold, as not knowing the true reason for the conclusions coming out accurately right, which I shew to have been the effect of a double errour.

XLI. This is the truth of the matter, which you shamefully misrepresent and declaim upon, to no sort of purpose but to amuse and mislead your Reader. For which conduct of yours throughout your remarks, you will pardon me if I cannot otherwise account, than from a secret hope that the Reader of your defence would never read the Analyst. If he doth, He cannot but see what an admirable Method you take to defend your cause: How instead of justifying the Reasoning, the Logic or the Theory of the case specified, which is the real point, you discourse of sensible and practical errours: And how all this is a manifest imposition upon the Reader. He must needs see that I have expressly said, "I have no controversy except only about your Logic and method: that I consider how you demonstrate; what objects you are conversant about; and whether you conceive them clearly?" That I have often expressed my self to the same effect desiring the Reader to remember, "that I am only concerned about the way of coming at your theorems, whether it be legitimate or illegitimate, clear or obscure, scientific or tentative: That I have on this very occasion, to prevent all possibility of mistake, repeated and insisted that I consider the Geometrical Analyst as a Logician i.e. so far forth as he reasons and argues; and his mathematical conclusions not in themselves but in their premises; not as true or false, useful or insignificant, but as derived from such principles, and by such inferences." [NOTE: 'Analyst,' Sect. 20.] You affirm (and indeed what can you not affirm?) that the difference between the true subtangent and that found without any compensation is absolutely nothing at all. I profess my self of a contrary opinion. My reason is because nothing cannot be divided into parts. But this difference is capable of being divided into any, or into more than any given number of parts; For the truth of which consult the Marquis de l'Hospital. And, be the errour in fact or in practice ever so small, it will not thence follow that the errour in Reasoning, which is what I am alone concerned about, is one whit the less, it being evident that a man may reason most absurdly about the minutest things.

XLII. Pray answer me fairly, once for all, whether it be your opinion that whatsoever is little and inconsiderable enough to be rejected without inconvenience in practice, the same may in like manner be safely rejected and overlooked in Theory and Demonstration. if you say no, it will then follow, that all you have been saying here and elsewhere, about yards and inches and decimal fractions, setting forth and insisting on the extreme smallness of the rejectaneous quantity, is quite foreign to the argument, and only a piece of skill to impose upon your Reader. If you say yes, it follows that you then give up at once all the orders of Fluxions and Infinitesimal Differences; and so most imprudently turn all your sallies and attacks and Veterans to your own overthrow. If the Reader is of my mind, he will despair of ever seeing you get clear of this dilemma. The points in controversy have been so often and so distinctly noted in the Analyst, that I very much wonder how you could mistake if you had no mind to mistake. It is very plain, if you are in earnest, that you neither understand me nor your Masters. And what shall we think of other ordinary Analysts, when it shall be found that even you, who, like a Champion step forth to defend their principles, have not considered them?

XLIII. The impartial reader is entreated to remark throughout your whole performance how confident you are in asserting and withall how modest in proving or explaining: How frequent it is with you to employ Figures and Tropes instead of Reasons: How many difficulties proposed in the Analyst are discreetly overlooked by you, and what strange work you make with the rest: How grossly you mistake and misrepresent, and how little you practise the advice which you so liberally bestow. Believe me Sir, I had long and maturely considered the principles of the modern Analysis, before I ventured to publish my thoughts thereupon in the Analyst. And since the publication thereof, I have my self freely conversed with Mathematicians of all ranks, and some of the ablest Professors, as well as made it my business to be informed of the Opinions of others, being very desirous to hear what could be said towards clearing my difficulties or answering my objections. But though you are not afraid or ashamed, to represent the Analysts as very clear and uniform in their Conception of these matters, yet I do solemnly affirm (and several of themselves know it to be true) that I found no harmony or agreement among them, but the reverse thereof, the greatest dissonance and even contrariety of Opinions, employed to explain what after all seemed inexplicable.

XLIV. Some fly to proportions between nothings. Some reject quantities because infinitesimal. Others allow only finite quantities, and reject them because inconsiderable. Others place the method of Fluxions on a foot with that of exhaustions, and admit nothing new therein. Some maintain the clear conception of Fluxions. Others hold they can demonstrate about things incomprehensible. Some would prove the Algorism of Fluxions by reductio ad absurdum; others a priori. Some hold the evanescent increments to be real quantities, some to be nothings, some to be limits. As many Men, so many minds: each differing one from another, and all from Sir Isaac Newton. Some plead inaccurate expressions in the great Author, whereby they would draw him to speak their sense, not considering that if he meant as they do, he could not want words to express his meaning. Others are magisterial and positive, say they are satisfied, and that is all, not considering that we, who deny Sir Isaac Newton's Authority, shall not submit to that of his Disciples. Some insist, that the Conclusions are true, and therefore the principles, not considering what hath been largely said in the Analyst [NOTE: Sect. 19, 20. &c.] on that head. Lastly several (and those none of the meanest) frankly owned the objections to be unanswerable. All which I mention by way of Antidote to your false Colours: and that the unprejudiced Inquirer after Truth may see, it is not without foundation, that I call on the celebrated Mathematicians of the present Age to clear up these obscure Analytics, and concur in giving to the publick some consistent and intelligible account of the principles of their great Master: for if they do not, I believe the World will take it for granted that they cannot.

XLV. Having gone through your defence of the British Mathematicians, I find in the next place, that you attack me on a point of Metaphysics, with what success the Reader will determine. I had upon another occasion many years ago wrote against Abstract general Ideas. [NOTE: Introduction to a Treatise concerning the Principles of Human Knowledge printed in the Year MDCCX.] In opposition to which, you declare your self to adhere to the vulgar opinion, that neither Geometry nor any other general Science can subsist without general Ideas (P. 74). This implies that I hold there are no general Ideas. But I hold the direct contrary, that there are indeed general Ideas, but not formed by abstraction in the manner set forth by Mr. Locke. To me it is plain, there is no consistent Idea, the likeness whereof may not really exist. Whatsoever therefore is said to be somewhat which cannot exist, the Idea thereof must be inconsistent. Mr Locke acknowledgeth it doth require Pains and Skill to form his general Idea of a triangle. He farther expressly saith, it must be neither oblique nor rectangular, neither equilateral, equicrural, nor scalenum; but all and none of these of these at once. He also saith, it is an idea wherein some parts of several different and inconsistent Ideas are put together. [NOTE: Essay on Humane Understanding, b. iv, c. vii, § ix.] All this looks very like a Contradiction. But to put the matter past dispute, it must be noted, that he affirms it to be somewhat imperfect that cannot exist; consequently the Idea thereof is impossible or inconsistent.

XLVI. I desire to know, whether it is not possible for any thing to exist, which doth not include a contradiction: And if it is, whether we may not infer, that what may not possibly exist, the same doth include a contradiction: I further desire to know, whether the reader can frame a distinct idea of anything that includes a contradiction? For my part, I cannot, nor consequently of the abovementioned triangle; Though you (you it seems know better than my self what I can do) are pleased to assure me of the contrary. Again, I ask whether that, which it is above the power of man to form a compleat idea of, may not be called incomprehensible? And whether the Reader can frame a compleat idea of this imperfect impossible triangle? And if not, whether it doth not follow that it is incomprehensible? It should seem, that a distinct aggregate of a few consistent parts was nothing so difficult to conceive or impossible to exist; and that, therefore, your Comment must be wide of the Author's meaning. You give me to understand (P. 82) that this account of a general triangle was a trap which Mr. Locke set to catch fools. Who is caught therein let the Reader judge.

XLVII. It is Mr. Locke's opinion, that every general name stands for a general abstract idea, which prescinds from the species or individuals comprehended under it. Thus, for example, according to him, the general name Colour stands for an idea, which is neither Blue, Red, Green, nor any particular colour, but somewhat distinct and abstracted from them all. To me it seems the word Colour is only a more general name applicable to all and each of the particular colours; while the other specific names, as Blue, Red, Green, and the like are each restrained to a more limited signification. The same can be said of the word Triangle. Let the Reader judge whether this be not the case; and whether he can distinctly frame such an idea of colour as shall prescind from all the species thereof, or of a triangle which shall answer Mr. Locke's account, prescinding and abstracting from all the particular sorts of triangles, in the manner aforesaid.

XLVIII. I entreat my Reader to think. For if he doth not, he may be under some influence from your confident and positive way of talking. But any one who thinks may, if I mistake not, plainly perceive that you are deluded, as it often happens, by mistaking the terms for ideas. Nothing is easier, than to define in terms or words that which is incomprehensible in idea, forasmuch as any words can be either separated or joined as you please, but ideas always cannot. It is as easy to say a round square as an oblong square, though the former be inconceivable. If the Reader will but take a little care to distinguish between the Definition and the Idea, between words or expressions and the conceptions of the mind, he will judge of the truth of what I now advance, and clearly perceive how far you are mistaken, in attempting to illustrate Mr. Locke's Doctrine, and where your mistake lies. Or, if the Reader is minded to make short work, he needs only at once to try, whether laying aside the words he can frame in his mind the idea of an impossible triangle; upon which trial the issue of this dispute may be fairly put. This doctrine of abstract general ideas seemed to me a capital errour, productive of numberless difficulties and disputes, that runs not only throughout Mr. Locke's book but through most parts of Learning. Consequently, my animadversions thereupon were not an effect of being inclined to carp or cavil at a single passage, as you would wrongfully insinuate, but proceeded from a love of Truth, and a desire to banish, so far as in me lay, false principles and wrong ways of thinking, without respect of persons. And indeed, though you and other Party-men are violently attached to your respective Masters, yet I, who profess my self only attached to Truth, see no reason why I may not as freely animadvert on Mr. Locke or Sir Isaac Newton, as they would on Aristotle or Descartes. Certainly the more extensive the influence of any Errour, and the greater the authority which supports it, the more it deserves to be considered and detected by sincere Inquirers after Knowledge.

XLIX. In the close of your performance, you let me understand, that your Zeal for Truth and the reputation of your Masters have occasioned your reprehending me with the utmost freedom. And it must be owned you have shewn a singular talent therein. But I am comforted under the severity of your reprehensions, when I consider the weakness of your arguments, which, were they as strong as your reproofs, could leave no doubt in the mind of the Reader concerning the matters in dispute between us. As it is, I leave him to reflect and examine by your light, how clearly he is enabled to conceive a fluxion, or a fluxion of a fluxion, a part infinitely small subdivided into an infinity of parts, a nascent or evanescent increment, that which is neither something nor nothing, a triangle formed in a point, velocity without motion, and the rest of those arcana of the modern Analysis. To conclude, I had some thoughts of advising you how to conduct your self for the future, in return for the advice you have so freely imparted to me: but, as you think it becomes me rather to inform my self than instruct others, I shall, for my farther information, take leave to propose a few Queries to those learned Gentlemen of Cambridge, whom you associate with your self, and represent as being equally surprised at the tendency of my Analyst.

L. I desire to know, whether those who can neither demonstrate nor conceive the principles of the modern Analysis, and yet give in to it, may not be justly said to have Faith, and be styled believers of mysteries? Whether it is impossible to find among the Physicians, mechanical Philosophers, Mathematicians, and Philomathematicians of the present age, some such Believers, who yet deride Christians for their belief of Mysteries? Whether with such men it is not a fair, reasonable, and legitimate method to use the Argumentum ad Hominem? And being so, whether it ought to surprise either Christians or Scholars? Whether in an age wherein so many pretenders to science attack the Christian Religion, we may not be allowed to make reprisals, in order to shew that the Irreligion of those men is not to be presumed an effect of deep and just thinking? Whether an attempt to detect false reasonings, and remedy defects in Mathematics, ought to be ill received by Mathematicians? Whether the introducing more easy methods and more intelligible principles in any science should be discountenanced? Whether there may not be fair objections as well as cavils? And whether to inquire diligently into the meaning of terms and the proof of propositions, not excepting against anything without assigning a reason, nor affecting to mistake the signification of words, or stick at an expression where the sense was clear, but considering the subject in all lights, sincerely endeavouring to find out any sense or meaning whatsoever, candidly setting forth what seems obscure and what fallacious, and calling upon those, who profess the knowledge of such matters, to explain them, whether I say such a proceeding can be justly called cavilling? Whether there be an ipse dixit erected? And if so, when, where, by whom, and upon what Authority? Whether even where Authority was to take place, one might not hope the Mathematics, at least, would be excepted? Whether the chief end, in making Mathematics so considerable a part of Academical Education, be not to form in the minds of young Students habits of just and exact Reasoning? And whether the study of abstruse and subtile matters can conduce to this end, unless they are well understood, examined, and sifted to the bottom? Whether, therefore, the bringing Geometrical demonstrations to the severest test of Reason should be reckoned a discouragement to the studies of any learned Society? Whether to separate the clear parts of things from the obscure, to distinguish the real Principles whereon Truths rest, and whence they are derived, and to proportion the just measures of assent according to the various degrees of evidence, be a useless or unworthy undertaking? Whether the making more of an argument than it will bear, and placing it in an undue rank of evidence, be not the likely way to disparage it? Whether it may not be of some use, to provoke and stir up the learned professors to explain a part of Mathematical Learning, which is acknowledged to be most profound, difficult, and obscure, and at the same time set forth by Philalethes and many others, as the greatest instance that has ever been given of the extent of humane abilities? Whether for the sake of a Great man's discoveries, we must adopt his errours? Lastly, whether in an age wherein all other principles are canvassed with the utmost freedom, the principles of Fluxions are to be alone excepted?

An Appendix Concerning Mr. Walton's Vindication Of Sir Isaac Newton's Principles of Fluxions

I. I had no sooner considered the performance of Philalethes, but Mr. Walton's Vindication of Fluxions was put into my hands. As this Dublin professor gleans after the Cantabrigian, only endeavouring to translate a few passages from Sir Isaac Newton's Principia, and enlarge on a hint or two of Philalethes, he deserves no particular notice. It may suffice to advertise the Reader, that the foregoing defence, contains a full and explicit answer to Mr. Walton, as he will find, if he thinks it worth his pains to read what this Gentleman hath written, and compare it therewith: Particularly with Sect. 18, 20, 30, 32, 33, 34, 35, 36, 43. It is not, I am sure, worth mine to repeat the same things, or confute the same notions twice over, in mere regard to a writer who hath copied even the manners of Philalethes, and whom in answering the other I have, if I am not much mistaken, sufficiently answered.

II. Mr. Walton touches on the same points that the other had touched upon before him. He pursues a hint which the other had given, [NOTE: Philalethes, p. 32.] about Sir Isaac's first Section concerning the Rationes primae et ultimae. He discreetly avoids, like the other, to say one syllable of second, third, or fourth Fluxions, and of divers other points mentioned in the Analyst, about all which I observe in him a most prudent and profound silence. And yet he very modestly gives his Reader to understand, that he is able to clear up all difficulties and objections, that have ever been made (P. 5). Mr. Walton in the beginning, like Philalethes, from a particular case makes a general inference, supposing that Infidelity to be imputed to Mathematicians in general, which I suppose only in the person to whom the Analyst was addressed, and certain other persons of the same mind with him. Whether this extraordinary way of reasoning be the cause or effect of his passion, I know not: But before I had got to the end of his Vindication, I ceased to be surprized at his Logic and his temper in the beginning. The double errour, which in the Analyst was plainly meant to belong to others, he with Philalethes (whose very oversight he adopts) supposeth to have been ascribed to Sir Isaac Newton (P. 36). And this writer also, as well as the Cantabrigian, must needs take upon him to explain the motive of my writing against Fluxions: which he gives out, with great assurance, to have been, because Sir Isaac Newton had presumed to interpose in Prophecies and Revelations, and to decide in religious affairs (P. 4) which is so far from being true, that, on the contrary, I have a high value for those learned remains of that Great Man, whose original and free Genius is an eternal reproach to that tribe of followers, who are always imitating, but never resemble him. This specimen of Mr. Walton's truth will be a warning to the Reader to use his own eyes, and in obscure points never to trust the Gentleman's Candour, who dares to misrepresent the plainest.

III. I was thinking to have said no more concerning this Author's performance, but lest he should imagine himself too much neglected, I entreat the Reader to have the patience to peruse it; and if he finds any one point of the doctrine of Fluxions cleared up, or any one objection in the Analyst answered, or so much as fairly stated, let him then make his compliments to the Author. But, if he can no more make sense of what this Gentleman has written than I can, he will need no answer to it. Nothing is easier, than for a man to translate or copy, or compose a plausible discourse of some pages in technical terms, whereby he shall make a shew of saying somewhat, although neither the Reader nor himself understand one Tittle of it. Whether this be the case of Mr. Walton, and whether he understands either Sir Isaac Newton, or me, or himself, (whatever I may think) I shall not take it upon me to say. But one thing I know, that many an unmeaning Speech passeth for significant by the mere assurance of the Speaker, till he cometh to be catechised upon it; and then the truth sheweth it self. This Vindicator, indeed, by his dissembling nine parts in ten of the difficulties proposed in the Analyst, sheweth no inclination to be catechised by me. But his Scholars have a right to be informed. I therefore, recommend it to them, not to be imposed on by hard words and magisterial assertions, but carefully to pry into his sense, and sift his meaning, and particularly to insist on a distinct answer to the following Questions.

IV. Let them ask him, whether he can conceive velocity without motion, or motion without extension, or extension without magnitude? If he answers that he can, let him teach them to do the same. If he cannot, let him be asked, how he reconciles the idea of a Fluxion which he gives (P. 13,) with common sense? Again, let him be asked, whether nothing be not the product of nothing multiplied by something? And if so, when the difference between the Gnomon and the sum of the rectangles [NOTE: See Vindication, p. 17.] vanisheth, whether the rectangles themselves do not also vanish? i.e. when ab is nothing, whether Ab + Ba be not also nothing? i.e. whether the momentum of AB be not nothing? Let him then be asked, what his momentums are good for, when they are thus brought to nothing? Again, I wish he were asked to explain the difference, between a magnitude infinitely small and a magnitude infinitely diminished. If he saith there is no difference: Then let him be farther asked, how he dares to explain the method of Fluxions, by the Ratio of magnitudes infinitely diminished (P. 9), when Sir Isaac Newton hath expressly excluded all consideration of quantities infinitely small? [NOTE: See his Introduction to the Quadratures.] If this able vindicator should say that quantities infinitely diminished are nothing at all, and consequently that, according to him, the first and last Ratio's are proportions between nothings, let him be desired to make sense of this, or explain what he means by proportion between nothings. If he should say the ultimate proportions are the Ratio's of mere limits, then let him be asked how the limits of lines can be proportioned or divided? After all, who knows but this Gentleman, who hath already complained of me for an uncommon way of treating Mathematics and Mathematicians (P. 5), may (as well as the Cantabrigian) cry out Spain and the Inquisition, when he finds himself thus closely pursued and beset with Interrogatories? That we may not, therefore seem too hard on an innocent man, who probably meant nothing, but was betray'd by following another into difficulties and straits that he was not aware of, I shall propose one single expedient, by which his Disciples (whom it most concerns) may soon satisfy themselves, whether this Vindicator really understands what he takes upon him to vindicate. It is in short, that they would ask him to explain the second, third or fourth Fluxions upon his Principles. Be this the Touchstone of his vindication. If he can do it, I shall own my self much mistaken: If he cannot, it will be evident that he was much mistaken in himself, when he presumed to defend Fluxions without so much as knowing what they are. So having put the merits of the cause on this issue, I leave him to be tried by his Scholars.

Printed in Great Britain
by Amazon